Interactions for Development and Learning
Birth Through Eight Years

Second Edition

D0869797

Kathleen S. Ralph
Whittier College

E. Anne Eddowes
University of Alabama at Birmingham, retired

Merrill
Prentice Hall

Upper Saddle River, New Jersey
Columbus, Ohio

Library of Congress Cataloging-in-Publication Data

Ralph, Kathleen S.

Interactions for development and learning : birth through eight years /
Kathleen S. Ralph, E. Anne Eddowes.

p. cm.

Originally published as: Interactions for development and learning / E. Anne Eddowes,
Kathleen S. Ralph.

Includes bibliographical references and index.

ISBN 0-13-094134-4

1. Social interatction in children. 2. Child development. I. Eddowes, E. Anne.
Interactions for development and learning. II. Title.

HQ784.S56 R35 2002

305.231—dc21

2001036760

Vice President and Publisher: Jeffery W. Johnston
Executive Editor: Ann Castel Davis
Associate Editor: Christina Kalisch
Editorial Assistant: Keli Gemrich
Production Coordination: Holly Henjum, Clarinda Publication Services
Production Editor: Sheryl Glicker Langner
Design Coordinator: Diane C. Lorenzo
Cover Designer: Rod Harris
Cover Photo: Image Bank
Production Manager: Laura Messerly
Director of Marketing: Kevin Flanagan
Marketing Manager: Amy June
Marketing Coordinator: Barbara Koontz

This book was set in Palatino by The Clarinda Company. It was printed and bound by R.R. Donnelley & Sons Company. The cover was printed by Phoenix Color Corp.

Photo Credits: Janelle N. Ralph, pp. 2, 6, 20, 31, 35, 42, 48, 50, 52, 56, 60, 73, 75, 79, 99, 108, 113, 119, 125, 132, 134, 139, 173, 194, 198, 200, 203, 228, 230, 233, 252, 256, 257, 260; E. Anne Eddowes, pp. 13, 164; Kara N. Ralph, pp. 27, 83, 87, 98, 128, 138, 142, 169, 170, 173, 206, 223, 226, 258.

Pearson Education Ltd., *London*
Pearson Education Australia Pty. Limited, *Sydney*
Pearson Education Singapore Pte. Ltd.
Pearson Education North Asia Ltd., *Hong Kong*
Pearson Education Canada, Ltd., *Toronto*
Pearson Educación de Mexico, S.A. de C.V.
Pearson Education—Japan, *Tokyo*
Pearson Education Malaysia Pte. Ltd.
Pearson Education, *Upper Saddle River, New Jersey*

10 9 8 7 6 5 4 3 2 1
ISBN: 0-13-094134-4

Preface

Interactions for Development and Learning: Birth Through Eight Years is about positive interactions and the important role that they play in development and learning. As the 21st century begins, the technological revolution is bringing many changes to the home, school, and workplace. Information is shared and communicated in new ways. This new emphasis on technology may make some individuals feel isolated. At best, it provides a less personal form of interaction than when one person responds to another face to face. Because of this aspect of technology in the lives of individuals, personal interaction skills are becoming ever more complex than they are today. It is even more important to emphasize the humaneness in daily exchanges. It is particularly important for young children to have quality interactions with the adults whose lives they share.

Interactions occur continually during the early childhood years in different settings. These exchanges take place between adults and children, between peers, between children of different ages, and between children and objects in a variety of activities. In addition, the physical surroundings may play a role.

We believe that high-quality interactions will never be replaced by technology. Furthermore, adults must understand appropriate forms of interaction, their context, and how to use them with young children. We provide information concerning the role that positive interactions can play in all areas of development and learning throughout the early years. It is written for parents, caregivers, and teachers who wish to enhance the quality of their interactions with children from birth through eight years of age.

CHANGES IN THE SECOND EDITION

As is reflected in the title, *Interactions for Development and Learning,* the emphasis in this edition is on using reciprocal interactions as a basis for curricular development. New materials include additional theoretical support for a child-centered interactive curriculum (from Bruner, Dewey, Montessori and Reggio Emilia); a new chapter on "Developing an Understanding of Young Children," with a focus on working with children and families in culturally diverse communities; specific suggestions for planning, using a developmental area framework; and ties to other methods of curriculum planning being used in early childhood education. New material is included and previous material has been reorganized to make it more reader-friendly. The developmentally focused activities are arranged by strands of development and age levels near the end of each of the last five chapters. In addition, the activities are coded to indicate the type of interaction they support: adult-child, child-child, or child-object.

The interactive curriculum is a unique lens to curriculum development for programs serving young children from birth through age eight. It has a dual focus. The first focus is on promoting reciprocal interactions between adults and children, among children, and between children and objects. The second focus is on developmental areas, including personal-social, physical, cognitive, communication, and creative. With a dual focus, an interactive curriculum is a comprehensive approach to planning for children throughout early childhood. The planning process shifts from thinking about what adults do to children to considering ways of creating a learning environment that fosters reciprocal interactions. For example, interactions initiated by either children or adults feature the scaffolding or co-constructing role of teaching.

Secondly, the use of developmental areas for planning is more balanced than a traditional approach to curriculum planning based on subject matter areas. In the primary grades in particular, a developmental focus is often overlooked. Elementary schools tend to center on the cognitive and communication areas, viewing physical and creative development as supplementary to the core curriculum. Personal-social development is even less likely to be a focus of curriculum planning in the elementary school.

❧ WHY HAVE A BOOK FOCUSING ON INTERACTION?

Most books concerning child development and early childhood education make little mention of the value of appropriate interactions with young children. The emphasis has been on the adult as a facilitator of children's learning through the provision of materials and activities in the environment. There have been few suggestions in the literature concerning ways in which interactions can support and extend the learning of young children. Although there are times when adult-child interaction is inappropriate, in many instances the development and learning of individual children can be enhanced by supportive reciprocal interaction.

Interactions take place all of the time, whether or not the participants give them any thought. Although young children can learn much on their own, thoughtful positive reciprocal interactions support and extend their development and learning (Piaget, 1948/1973; Vygotsky, 1978). The early childhood years are a time when growth and development proceed rapidly. Learning takes place continually. Adults must know the kinds of interactions that are most supportive of development and learning.

Positive adult-child interactions *must* take place in some areas of development, if change is to occur at all. For example, without appropriate interactions between the caregiver and infant in the first year of life, trust does not develop. Another critical area is communication. The development of spoken language depends on the interaction of adults and children. Adult-child interaction can also assist children in learning skills and concepts. For example, most children could use the assistance of adults to learn to tie shoes or to understand how a map works. In the area of creativity, adults can provide materials and support their use in new ways.

Positive interactions can enhance development and learning throughout the early childhood years. We focus on the types of interactions that are most beneficial throughout the young child's development. Examples of appropriate activities are provided in each area of development for young children. Specific interaction activities are described for each of the following age groups: (1) birth to one, (2) one to two, (3) two, (4) three and four, (5) five and six, and (6) seven and eight years.

❧ WHO WILL FIND THE BOOK USEFUL?

The book is written for all adults who interact with children at one time or another. Caregivers in child-care programs will find information concerning those settings and many appropriate activities to use in the daily program. We use the term *caregiver* to refer to any staff member of a child-care program who works directly with children. Whether they are family child-care providers caring for children in their own home or workers in part-day programs or in full-day child-care centers, they can use a variety of interaction activities with children. Child-care programs in community colleges and technical schools will find it a useful text, first for introductory child development or preschool education courses, and then for continued use throughout the practicum courses. The content is related to the Child Development Associate (CDA) competencies and functional areas (Council for Early Childhood Professional Recognition, 1992). The book could be used in connection with CDA training, in-service child-care staff training, or other types of child development education.

Teachers in kindergartens and primary grades will also find information related to their classroom environments and activities for children in their classes. We use the term *teacher* for the person in a classroom who has primary responsibility for instruction. Teachers are usually certified by the state in which they work. The book can be used in preservice programs in colleges and universities. It is an appropriate text for introductory early childhood courses, practicum courses, and student teaching. The book could also be a resource for beginning teachers and school in-service activities. In addition, there is information concerning school-age child-care programs for caregivers in schools, child-care centers, and community agencies.

Parents will find information and activities that are helpful in the home. Since many parental caregivers fill this role, we use the term *parent* to refer to such people as a child's guardian, stepparent, foster parent, or adult relative. The book is an appropriate text for parent education, parent-child interaction classes, and home visitor programs.

❧ ORGANIZATION OF THE BOOK

The book is arranged in three parts. Part 1 includes chapters 1 through 4, which provide a theoretical background and the foundation for interaction, information on planning, and ideas for creating a physical environment, all of which enhance reciprocal interactions. In Part 2, chapters 5 through 10 include a description of types of interactions and examples of activities in each area of development for children up to eight years old. A variety of resources for interaction are found in the five appendixes in Part 3.

❧ ACKNOWLEDGMENTS

Much of our experience as parents, caregivers, and teachers is found in this book. Our thanks go to the children and adults with whom we have worked and whom we have observed over the years throughout different regions of the United States. Many co-workers and friends in the field of early childhood education have offered encouragement. We particularly acknowledge the assistance of Dr. Jerry Aldridge at the University of Alabama at Birmingham, and Dr. Tom Jambor, formerly at the University of Alabama at Birmingham, for their thoughtful comments on the first edition. Our editor, Ann Davis, has given us excellent assistance and advice, and our associate editor, Christina Kalisch, has patiently responded to our frequent requests. We greatly appreciate your assistance.

The photos, taken by Janelle and Kara Ralph, depict a variety of interactions. They add an important dimension by illustrating visually many of the ideas described in the book. We would like to thank Claudia and David Wiedeman, Gina and Rick Cisneros, and Angela Chavez, colleagues at Whittier College, for allowing the photographers into their homes to capture their children on film. We also express our gratitude to the children, teachers, and staff at Broadoaks, Whittier College's demonstration school, for permitting us to photograph the numerous daily interactions that promote development and learning. A special note of appreciation goes to Janelle Ralph for her invaluable assistance in completing the manuscript for the second edition.

Comments from the following reviewers have made this a better book: Beverly B. Dupré, Southern University at New Orleans; Barbara Foulks-Boyd, Radford University; Patricia Hofbauer, Northwest Community College; Peg A. Ketron-Marose, United States Air Force; and Edythe H. Schwartz, California State University, Sacramento.

Last, we thank our families, colleagues, and friends for their assurance that the task could be completed.

Kathleen S. Ralph
E. Anne Eddowes

Discover the Companion Website Accompanying This Book

THE PRENTICE HALL COMPANION WEBSITE: A VIRTUAL LEARNING ENVIRONMENT

Technology is a constantly growing and changing aspect of our field that is creating a need for content and resources. To address this emerging need, Prentice Hall has developed an online learning environment for students and professors alike—Companion Websites—to support our textbooks.

In creating a Companion Website, our goal is to build on and enhance what the textbook already offers. For this reason, the content for each user-friendly website is organized by topic and provides the professor and student with a variety of meaningful resources. Common features of a Companion Website include:

FOR THE PROFESSOR—

Every Companion Website integrates **Syllabus Manager**™, an online syllabus creation and management utility.

- **Syllabus Manager**™ provides you, the instructor, with an easy, step-by-step process to create and revise syllabi, with direct links into Companion Website and other online content without having to learn HTML.
- Students may log on to your syllabus during any study session. All they need to know is the web address for the Companion Website and the password you've assigned to your syllabus.
- After you have created a syllabus using **Syllabus Manager**™, students may enter the syllabus for their course section from any point in the Companion Website.
- Clicking on a date, the student is shown the list of activities for the assignment. The activities for each assignment are linked directly to actual content, saving time for students.
- Adding assignments consists of clicking on the desired due date, then filling in the details of the assignment—name of the assignment, instructions, and whether or not it is a one-time or repeating assignment.
- In addition, links to other activities can be created easily. If the activity is online, a URL can be entered in the space provided, and it will be linked automatically in the final syllabus.
- Your completed syllabus is hosted on our servers, allowing convenient updates from any computer on the Internet. Changes you make to your syllabus are immediately available to your students at their next logon.

✒ FOR THE STUDENT—

Topic Overviews—outline key concepts in topic areas

Web Links—general websites related to topic areas as well as associations and professional organizations

Read About It—timely articles that enable you to become more aware of important issues in early childhood education

Learn by Doing—put concepts into action, participate in activities, complete lesson plans, examine strategies, and more

For Teachers—access information that you will need to know as an in-service teacher, including information on materials, activities, lessons, curriculum, and state standards

Visit a School—visit a school's website to see concepts, theories, and strategies in action

Electronic Bluebook—send homework or essays directly to your instructor's email with this paperless form

Message Board—serves as a virtual bulletin board to post—or respond to—questions or comments to/from a national audience

Chat—real-time chat with anyone who is using the text anywhere in the country—ideal for discussion and study groups, class projects, etc.

To take advantage of these and other resources, please visit the *Interactions for Development and Learning: Birth Through Eight Years,* Second Edition, Companion Website at **www.prenhall.com/ralph**

CONTENTS

Foundations of an Interactive Curriculum

The four chapters in part 1 present the basis for using reciprocal interactions to support development and learning in the early childhood years. Chapter 1 furnishes the rationale for an interactive curriculum and the underlying theory of interaction in relation to specific areas of child development. Chapter 2 includes information about the role of play in learning and strategies for understanding children by gathering information about their families and communities and observing them and for guiding young children individually and in groups. In chapters 3 and 4, the supportive role of the physical environment and planning for an interactive curriculum are explored.

Chapter One

Theoretical Perspective for an Interactive Curriculum

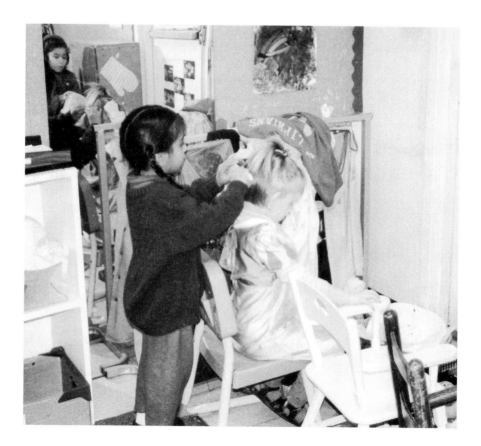

o b j e c t i v e s

After reviewing this chapter, you will be able to

- List major theorists who are supportive of interactive curricula.
- Identify five areas of development and learning in which reciprocal interaction could occur.
- Discuss *strands* within each area of development and learning in which reciprocal interaction is important in the early years.
- Define the *zone of proximal development.*
- Give examples of the three major temperament constellations.

*T*here are many ways of providing early childhood programming. A variety of curriculum approaches and models have evolved over many years. They are discussed and compared in detail elsewhere (Evans, 1975; Goffin, 1994; Roopnarine & Johnson, 2000). However, in each approach the goal for the program is to provide experiences that assist young children with their development and learning. Philosophies of how children learn vary among the models and approaches. The adults who implement the programs play an important role (Morrison, 2000).

In some approaches, the adult is considered the primary decision maker concerning the content of the program activities, which focus on subject matter. The child engages in the activities but contributes little toward their formulation. In a quite different approach, the content of the activities is based almost entirely on the interests of the children. Children make suggestions for activities in which they would choose to engage, and there is little or no agenda related to specific curriculum content. However, the adult carefully observes individual children and is responsive to their learning potentials.

In contrast to these approaches is one in which both the adult and child (or children) initiate activities. The adult introduces content, but the interests and developmental levels of the individual children are considered in planning daily activities. Children assist with the planning and have some choice in the activities in which they engage. Both teacher and children are facilitators of the learning (Goffin, 1994; Roopnarine & Johnson, 2000).

✥ THE INTERACTIVE CURRICULUM

The interactive curriculum has evolved from the experience of the authors. Whether used in a home, child-care program or school, the interactive curriculum is based on knowledge of child development and learning. The strengths of each child are considered, along with background information on the social and cultural contexts in which the child lives. The method is based on a belief that there are certain things that children should learn. However, there must be a "match" among the learner, the necessary skill, and the content. The levels, interests, and input from the children must be considered when planning activities and experiences.

An interactive curriculum is a particular educational plan or program that is enhanced through incorporation of a variety of reciprocal actions. There is a conscious effort to include various two-way interactions during each day. These interactions can take place between two or among more children or adults or between a person and an object. The interaction may be related to an activity or to some element of the environment or context. The interactions usually concern some aspect of the curriculum, but they may also be random. Any interaction may be positive or negative for the participants. In either case, interactions contribute to development and learning. In the interactive curriculum, the emphasis is on positive reciprocal interaction.

✥ PLAY IN THE INTERACTIVE CURRICULUM

Play can be defined in different ways depending on the context in which it takes place, the perspective from which the play is interpreted, and the meaning attributed to it by the player (Fromberg & Bergen, 2000). Many theorists have considered play to be important for development and learning. Each theorist mentioned in this chapter includes some aspect of play in their theory.

For children, play is usually a spontaneous activity. All children engage in some form of play no matter where they reside in the world. Play, development, and learning are closely linked (Bodrova & Leong, 1999; Van Hoorn, Nourot, Scales & Alward, 1999). Play is a medium that supports self-esteem and social skills, physical skills, concept formation and problem solving, language and literacy skills, and creativity. For many years, early childhood educators have valued play in the curriculum. The importance of play in the interactive curriculum is emphasized throughout this book.

✑ OVERVIEW OF THEORIES

Many theorists, researchers, and writers have made contributions to the study of child development and its relationship to learning and curriculum theory. Some are referred to in this book. These writers were selected as major contributors because they are interested in some of the concepts reflected in the interactive curriculum. Their contributions to the aspects of child development and interactive curriculum theory are divided into three groups: child development, curriculum, and interaction.

✑ CHILD DEVELOPMENT THEORY

These theorists are major contributors to child development theory.

Erik H. Erikson

Erikson's (1963) major contribution to growth and learning theory has been in the area of psychosocial development. He thought that a school curriculum should include a balance of work and play, a mix of games and study (Erikson, 1980). He believed that play is the child's attempt to synchronize bodily and social processes with the self. Play satisfies the need to master the areas of a child's life. It is serious, and useful, and necessary for growing and learning (Erikson, 1963; 1972; 1977).

Erikson has made a substantial contribution to the construct of reciprocal interaction. His work stresses the need for mutual functioning between mother and child. Infants depend on their mothers and the other adults in their world for all things connected with life. For example, food, shelter, and nurturing love are significant factors in developing basic *trust*. The need for adult-child interaction continues throughout early childhood. As children develop *autonomy*, outer control must be firmly reassuring, and adults must provide gradual experiences of independence and choice. As children develop *initiative*, they need an environment that allows them to try out different materials and activities. Responsibility begins to develop as practice allows for greater competence and independence. This leads to a sense of *industry*, and mastery, which begins at the end of the early childhood years (Erikson, 1963). Table 1.1 depicts the first four stages of Erikson's theory.

Howard Gardner

Gardner (1983) is a relatively new theorist with novel ideas concerning multiple intelligences: He believes that all humans have core abilities in each of these intelligences. Until the age of eight or nine years, children engage in free exploration, fantasy, and experimentation with boundaries and focus on development of broad concepts. Careful observation and assessment of deficiencies, however, can suggest alternative routes to an educational goal (Gardner, 1993). Gardner has identified seven types of intelligence that cover the spectrum of development.

Linguistic intelligence includes the ability to use words effectively, in speaking, through gesture, and in writing. Although there are similarities between language and music, Gardner (1983) thinks they have different purposes. The ability to produce and appreciate musical forms is the foundation for *musical* intelligence.

Table 1.1   Erikson's theory of psychosocial development: Four stages covering the early childhood years.

Stage	Approximate Age (Years)
1. Trust vs. mistrust	0–1
2. Autonomy vs. shame, doubt	2–3
3. Initiative vs. guilt	4–5
4. Industry vs. inferiority	6–11

Note: Adapted from *Childhood and Society* (2nd ed.) by E. H. Erikson, 1963, New York: W. W. Norton. Copyright 1963 by W. W. Norton.

The basis for *logical-mathematical* ability is found in the young child's manipulation of objects (Gardner, 1983). However, after this initial experience, the intelligence becomes more and more abstract and encompasses an understanding of relationships between objects and numeric patterns and the concurrent development of reasoning. Although some aspects of *spatial* intelligence may seem to be related to logical-mathematical intelligence, Gardner considers it a separate intelligence. It includes the capacity both to understand space and to use the information in the manipulation of objects and movement in space. *Bodily kinesthetic* intelligence also relates to space and consists of the ability to control body movements in space and manipulate, arrange, and transform objects easily.

Gardner (1983,1993) has identified two personal intelligences, which he calls *interpersonal* and *intrapersonal*. The basis for *interpersonal* intelligence is the ability to understand and respond to the moods, temperaments, motivations, and intentions of others. In contrast, *intrapersonal* intelligence relates to understanding of self, including a personal identity, emotions, strengths, and weaknesses.

Gardner has recently added an eighth form of intelligence, called *naturalist*. It involves the ability to recognize important differences among living and nonliving things in the natural world. He believes that this ability is not part of the seven other intelligences (Gardner, 1998). However, no matter how many types of intelligence there are, the appropriate form of adult-child interaction must be found to assist children in learning to their potential in any of the types of intelligence identified by Gardner (1993).

Jean Piaget

Piaget is best known for his work in the development of knowledge, learning, and thinking in children. He identified three ways in which children learn (Piaget, 1970). The first is *social knowledge* gained through interaction with other people, which is determined by society. For example, the word *red* describes a particular color; and the Independence Day holiday is celebrated on July 4th. Next is an understanding of the *physical knowledge* of objects through observation, for example, the color and size of an object. The last, *logico-mathematical knowledge*,[1] is an understanding of relationships such as numeration, seriation, classification, time, spatial relationships, and conservation. For example, the concept of "two" is a relationship between two objects. The "twoness" cannot be observed in either object alone.

Although Piaget does not address educational practice and curriculum in his work, he

---

[1]A note on terminology: Jean Piaget (1969/1970) used the term *logico-mathematical*. Howard Gardner (1983) uses the term *logical-mathematical* for one of the intelligences in his theory. Both terms are used in this book in discussions of these theories.

believed that play is a powerful force in the learning process of young children. Play helps the child in developing perceptions, intelligence, the impulse to experiment, and social instincts. Much of Piaget's work in cognitive development is based on processes that children use in constructing their own knowledge, in which adults may play a role. Although Piaget did not believe that the teacher (or another adult who assumes the teaching role) should use a direct teaching method (Piaget 1969/1970; 1972), he thought that the adult should organize the environment to create situations that present useful problems for the child to solve. In addition, he believed that the adult should provide counterexamples that, on reflection, could extend the child's thinking (Piaget, 1948/1973).

L. S. Vygotsky

The work of Vygotsky (1978) has made a substantial contribution to the role of the adult (or more capable peer) in the child's development and learning. He believes that learning plays an important part in a child's development. A Vygotskian curriculum is activity centered. The adult designs an educative environment and collaborates with children to assist them in planning, guiding, and monitoring their own behavior. There is a dialogue between adult and child in solving problems that fosters autonomous learning, interest, and creative thinking (Berk & Winsler, 1995). Vygotsky (1978) believed that imaginative play becomes important to a child's development by helping to separate thought from actions and objects and by allowing development of self-regulating activity.

Vygotsky (1978) believed that a child has an actual developmental level when trying to solve some problem independently. He suggested that there is a difference between the child's actual level and the level the child attains when given assistance to solve the prob-

Older sister interacts by assisting her younger sister with her raincoat.

lem. He called this the **zone of proximal development.** It is the distance between the actual developmental level, determined by independent problem solving, and the level of potential development, determined through problem solving under adult guidance or in collaboration with more capable peers (Vygotsky, 1978, p. 86). Using the concept of the zone of proximal development, a supportive adult can assist the child in many areas of development and learning.

Vygotsky emphasized that the larger cultural context has an effect on the development of social, cognitive, communication, and creative skills. For example, higher mental function first develops through external interaction and collaboration with others. Only then can the process become internalized (Berk & Winsler, 1995).

✨ CHILD-CENTERED CURRICULUM

These theorists were major contributors to curriculum theory.

Jerome S. Bruner

Bruner (1960, 1966) studied the thought processes of perception, memory, strategic thinking, and classification. He believed that a curriculum should involve the mastery of skills and the development of concepts and that facts should not be learned in isolation. Instead, experiences should be provided so that a fact may be meaningfully connected to others. One premise of his theory is that there is an appropriate version or level of any skill or knowledge that may be imparted at whatever age teaching begins. For example, a level of knowledge for young children in learning about the topic of light might be observation of and experimentation with shadows.

Bruner viewed children as active learners. Learning experiences are planned to stimulate children's curiosity through inquiries, experiments, and discovery learning in the areas of math, science, social studies, and language (Bruner, 1966, 1990). He believed that the teacher's role is to ask questions that encourage problem solving and to provide activities that promote decision making and an exchange of ideas. A variety of equipment and materials and time to explore them should be available. Although Bruner was particularly interested in the development of thought processes, he believed that play activity helped children realize their potential in many other areas of development (Bruner, 1983).

Bruner viewed schools as communities of learning, but they are only one context in which learning takes place. He came to realize that human action cannot be fully understood from the inside out but must be continuous within a cultural world in interaction with others. There must be shared modes of discourse in which meanings are formed and concepts develop (Bruner, 1990).

John Dewey

Dewey's (1916, 1938) primary interest was in the preparation of citizens for a democratic society. He believed that education should prepare children for the realities of the present through a child-centered curriculum. This curriculum is activity oriented, not focused on subject matter, and includes physical activity, use of objects, intellectual pursuits, and social interaction.

The teacher's role is to capitalize on opportunities to integrate traditional subject matter into the classroom experience. The teacher is the link between the children's personal interests and the objective, ordered world of fields of study. Children begin with active occupations that have a social origin and proceed to scientific insight by assimilating into their direct experience the ideas and facts communicated by others who have greater experience (Dewey, 1916).

Observation of and obtaining background information about the children is necessary so that the teachers can draw on their past experience and select relevant new activities. Materials are available to construct things and for gardening, woodworking, weaving, cooking, printing, and other similar experiences. The teacher asks questions, provides **extensions,** and helps to integrate understandings across several subject areas. In this curriculum, it is acceptable to make mistakes because learning takes place through them. Both constructive and make-believe play are important in Dewey's theory, as are reciprocal interactions of all kinds (Dewey, 1916).

J. McVickar Hunt

In the implementation of a curriculum, it is helpful to use Hunt's (1961) notion of the "problem of the match." The trick is to find the activity or experience that is neither too familiar so as to be boring nor too much outside the child's experience so that it has no relevance. Experimentation through play can provide a method by which a child can make a "match" (Hunt, 1964). When the child's ability is matched with the activity, optimum learning occurs. The adult may include activities in the environment that are self-selected by the children and assist children in making choices. When activities match the interests and needs of each child, they are said to be developmentally appropriate (Bredekamp, 1987).

Maria Montessori

Montessori (1912/1964) began her work with 4- to 7-year-old children from lower-income families in 1907 at her school, Casa dei Bambini, located in Rome, Italy. In her "Montessori Method," the curriculum covers the areas of practical life, muscular education, nature, art/music, senses, language, mathematics, and geography/science. She believed that young children have "absorbent" minds and that learning can occur internally without external motivation. Children are usually in mixed-age groups (i.e., 4- to 7-year-olds) and work independently or in small groups. They choose their activities with guidance from the teacher, and there is little whole-group instruction. The environment is well organized, with equipment on shelves in specific places. Much of this didactic equipment, designed by Montessori, is self-correcting.

Teachers in Montessori schools are careful observers who provide the learners with appropriate, responsive materials and consistent structure. Encouragement is a key role for the teacher. He or she prepares the environment, and the children participate in the experiences.

Montessori believed that play is a child's work and that children absorb knowledge through an active involvement with materials in a prepared environment (Montessori, 1949/1967). Little emphasis is placed on free creative expression with materials, experimentation with equipment, or interpersonal relationships. Interactions are largely between teacher and child or between the child and objects (Hunt, 1964).

Reggio Emilia

Reggio Emilia is a city in northern Italy in which a progressive educational program for young children has evolved. The approach, developed by Loris Malaguzzi, provides a unique environment that encourages and supports learning. There are programs for two age groups. The first was founded in 1963 and is for children ages three to six. The other is for children ages three months to three years and began in 1971 (Reggio Emilia, 1996).

In Malaguzzi's approach, there are close links among the children, parents, teachers, and community. Children are viewed as individuals with many strengths. Teachers develop an understanding of the potential of each child and use it to develop both the environment and activities. Parents, who have a crucial role in the program, are expected to participate in a variety of ways. They are viewed as active partners in their child's learning and development (Reggio Emilia, 1997; Ceppi & Zini, 1998).

The physical environment is an essential element of the program. It is designed to encourage communication, interaction, choice, and problem solving. The schools are beautiful sensory places and incorporate selected use of light, texture, color, sound, and smell to enhance the space. In addition, furniture, materials, plants, and displays of children's work are carefully arranged to provide a pleasing setting for learning (Ceppi & Zini, 1998).

The curriculum is continually evolving. Teachers have general goals for activities and projects based on the interests of the children. However, as they observe the children engaging in the activities, they make changes when necessary. Many of the activities involve some aspect of constructive, dramatic, or imaginative play. Projects, an integral part of the program, incorporate the skills of cooperation, motor and cognitive development, communication, and creativity. Reciprocal interactions are encouraged among adults, children, peers, and objects and through working on projects.

✍ INTERACTION THEORY

These authors are major contributors to interaction theory.

T. Berry Brazelton

Brazelton's work is concerned with the development of the youngest children, from birth through age three. He believes that development and learning are closely aligned. Motor, social, and cognitive development should be considered in combination, with no emphasis on any one area when planning activities. Activities should be age-appropriate. Play is his choice in supporting a young child's way of mastering his or her world. He does not believe in teaching concepts per se to these very young children but allows them to find their own way of learning in each area of development. He believes that as play becomes more complex, a child's imagination develops, and new learning is assimilated through fantasy play (Brazelton, 1987, 1992).

Brazelton has emphasized positive reciprocal interaction between parent (or other caregiver) and the child. He describes it as a process, with cycles of engagement and disengagement that are related to various areas of personal-social development. For example, a young infant begins to coo and her mother imitates her sounds. After they have interacted in this experience several times, the mother pauses so that the infant can stop the activity if she wishes. In this way, each participant has a role in the child's continuing pursuit of independence in social action. Parents or caregivers sometimes may not realize the importance of the child's need to regulate an interaction to avoid overstimulation. When this happens, the interaction may become negative instead of positive (Brazelton, 1992; Brazelton & Cramer, 1990).

Urie Bronfenbrenner

The theory of Bronfenbrenner (1979) centers on the interaction of persons in different contexts. Although he does not focus on curriculum in his work, Bronfenbrenner believes that educational activities are relevant for development and learning. He would include the cognitive and social domains, with emphasis on non-fantasy and fantasy play, games, responsibilities of work, and social activities. When effectively used, these methods promote initiative, independence, and equalitarianism.

Bronfenbrenner believes that the child is a dynamic entity who interacts with the environment and can restructure it. However, the environment also has an influence and can cause change. In his theory of human ecosystems, he describes an ecological environment consisting of nested structures. The first level of interaction is called a **microsystem.** It is the innermost structure and the immediate setting in which the child is found, including activities, interpersonal relations, and roles. The child may have an influence on the people and objects in the setting, just as they may have an influence on the child. The next structure is the **mesosystem.** It comprises the interrelations among settings in which the child is an active participant, such as the home, child-care center, school, and neighborhood peer group. A mesosystem is a combination of microsystems. The third stucture, the **exosystem,** includes one or more settings that do not involve the child as an active participant but can affect the child. These might include parents' workplaces, the park commission, and community agencies. The last interaction system mentioned in the theory is the **macrosystem,** which refers to consistencies in the other three systems that could have cultural implications for society as a whole. All interactions within and among the various levels of systems can be reciprocal; change may be influenced by any of them.

Bronfenbrenner's work concerning the reciprocal relationship between adult and child includes the ecological context and the culture of the child. A family's culture is transmitted through interactions between family members, the extended family, and people and experiences in the greater community. The reciprocal interaction between children and their surroundings is continuous.

Richard M. Lerner

The developmental contextualism of Lerner (Ford & Lerner, 1992; Lerner, 1978, 1982, 1984) includes the key idea, *dynamic interactionism.* It focuses on the interaction of environment and the person. The biological inheritance of the person (we replace, Lerner's word "person" with "child") is considered in interaction with several levels of contextual organization at a particular moment. Varied interactions among the contextual levels can produce developmental change. One event within a pattern of interactions can change things in all related contexts. All interactions are reciprocal and can cause change in both the child and in the child's context. Lerner terms this the *child-in-context.*

The biological characteristics of the child, such as the genes, bone structure, and skin color, dynamically interact with contextual levels of organization, such as a specific diet, type of parental care, or social customs. A child with Down syndrome serves as an example to show how the gene-environment dynamic interaction might work.

Down syndrome is caused by a specific extra chromosome, and children with Down syndrome may be recognized by certain physical characteristics. The interaction of heredity and environment in these children's lives can create vastly different levels of capability. Before 1975, these children were usually put in institutions, a practice that severely limited their possibilities. Federal legislation in 1975 and 1986 provided the families of the children with a variety of support opportunities that allow the children to live at home. Education and training can assist many children with Down syndrome in becoming self-reliant. Many of these children are now participating in **inclusive settings**. A change in the environment has made a change in the child and, since the child is now in a different context, the child has changed the environment.

In many other instances, the genetic makeup of the child may interact with a social or educational context to change the outcome for the child. It can also change the adults working with the child, and the settings in which the interactions occur.

✺ AREAS OF DEVELOPMENT AND LEARNING

Although all areas of development overlap within the child, child development, as it relates to learning and interaction, is divided here into five areas, which we briefly summarize for ease of study. In each area of develop-

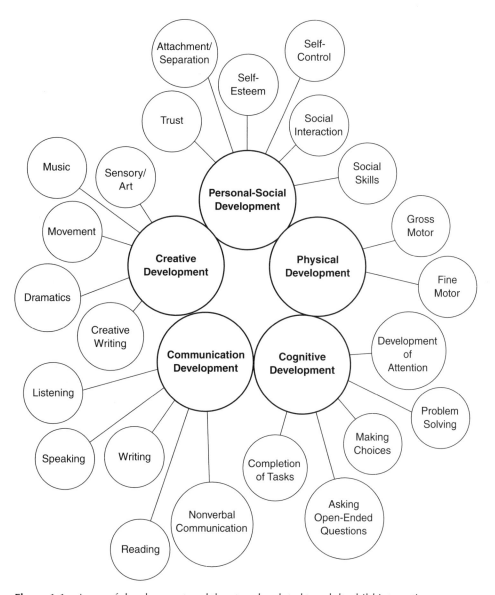

Figure 1.1   Areas of development and the strands related to adult–child interaction.

ment, representative **strands** have been selected in which reciprocal interaction is required for the development and learning of young children.

The detailed description of each strand in relation to interactive curricula includes exam-

ples of selected activities. The areas of development and the strands may be seen in Figure 1.1. Individual differences among children are identified in relationship to each strand. The role of culture in learning and development is included, when appropriate.

ᘂ PERSONAL–SOCIAL DEVELOPMENT

Personal-social development includes emotional well-being, self-worth, self-control, interaction with others, and cultural convention. Positive interactions with parents and other adults are essential to this area of development. Strands that are discussed in this section are trust, attachment/separation, self-esteem, self-control, social interaction, and social skills.

Trust

Throughout infancy and the early years, children depend on adults in their environment for basic survival—food, clothing, and shelter—as well as loving interactions and **consistency of care.**

The first stage of Erik H. Erikson's (1963) "eight ages of man" is basic trust versus basic mistrust. When children experience comfort as infants, trust in people and the environment begins to develop. Children learn that their needs will be met and that there is predictability to life. Consistency, continuity, and similarity in care help children build confidence that the world is a good place to be.

Parents and other adults must be available to assist in building this trust. When there is an absence of trust, there may be a withdrawal from interaction, which can have lasting results on development. The interaction in building trust goes two ways: the child accepts the care and gives positive feedback to the adult, who then continues to give the care. For example, a baby (three months old) wakes from a nap and begins to cry. Her mother knows from experience that she is probably wet. After checking, the mother talks and plays with her baby as she changes the diaper. The infant smiles and reacts positively because she has come to expect this kind of interaction and it is predictable for her. This is an example of a positive two-way interaction.

The child in the example is an **"easy baby,"** as defined by Thomas and Chess (1980), who identified three temperamental constellations. The first group, of babies, termed "easy," has regular, positive responses to new situations and is highly adaptable to change. These children develop regular sleep and feeding schedules, try new things easily, and have a positive mood.

The second group of babies has characteristics that are opposite to those of the first group. This group, termed **"difficult,"** is irregular in biological function, has intense moods, and is usually not readily adaptable in new situations. The infants have trouble adjusting to new routines, are easily frustrated, and have a negative attitude toward most people and things. The accompanying vignette gives an example of a "difficult" child.

----------- -----------

It is time for lunch at a child-care center. Sarah (age one year) is playing with a toy on the rug. The caregiver says, "Sarah, it's time for lunch." She picks the child up to help her sit at a feeding table. Sarah screams and stiffens her legs, which makes it difficult to seat her. When the caregiver tries to wash Sarah's hands, she pulls them away and continues to yell. Even though Sarah has been enrolled at the child-care center for seven months, there are many days when she has difficulty cooperating in center routines.

----------- -----------

A child with this characteristic temperament has a more difficult time developing trust. Because the child often provides negative feedback to the adult, the adult must consciously remain positive to provide the security that the child needs.

The third group of the temperament constellation describes the **"slow-to-warm-up" child.** These children have negative responses of mild intensity and adapt slowly to new situations. "Slow-to-warm-up" children are less likely than "difficult" children to have irregularity in biological functions. They are unlikely to want to try new things, but after some experience, they become interested. An example of a child with these temperament characteristics follows.

A two-year-old child is going to a restaurant with her family. Her older brother is very excited about going, but she is apprehensive. When they arrive at the restaurant, her mother orders a sandwich for her that is similar to those she has eaten at home. However, she does not want to try it: no amount of talking will help. She leaves without eating anything.

Children who are "slow to warm up" take some time to watch, listen, experiment, and think about things before they try them. Although they are not like "easy" children, they can learn to be adaptable and provide positive feedback to the adults who care for them. It just takes a little more time.

The temperamental constellations each represent variations within normal limits. Some children have a combination of the different temperament characteristics. When this happens, the adult must be sensitive to the child's cues in a positive way. To form a reciprocal trusting relationship, the adult must remember several things. Care must be unconditional, no matter what the temperament of the child. When children experience difficulty in adapting to experiences in their environment, the adult must believe that a positive attitude can make a difference.

Attachment/Separation

From the time a child is born, a mutual **attachment** between parents and child develops. Both the mother and father integrate their own experiences of childhood with their ac-

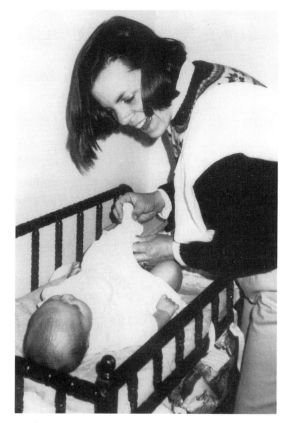

Mother interacts playfully while changing her infant's diapers.

ceptance of the new infant. They look for responses to their affection in the newborn. The baby's behavior is sensitive to the wishes of the parents, and the connection is established (Brazelton & Cramer, 1990).

Interactions between primary caregivers and infant continue, and the infant builds a mental image of them. As this representation of the caregiver develops, the child comes to realize that the person is separate from the child. That is when a "**separation** reaction" can appear (Stern, 1977). Mentally, the child must learn that what disappears can reappear before the child can become comfortable with a separation from that person. The following is an example of a helpful activity.

------------------------------ ------------------------------

Jason (age seven months) has begun to fuss when he is left with a baby-sitter. When Jason's mother is at home with him, she plays a peek-a-boo game with him. She covers her face with a small towel and asks, "Where's Mommy?" Jason pulls the towel from her face, and she says, "Peek-a-boo!" Then they both laugh.

------------------------------ ------------------------------

Cycles of engagement and disengagement continue throughout the early years. The **goal** of parents and other primary caregivers should be a gradual development of independence so that the child learns to function as a separate individual.

Sometimes the reciprocal relations between adult and child can be impaired. When the infant's ability to respond to the adult is disturbed (or perceived as such by the adult), the adult may respond negatively. This can be the beginning of the adult's withdrawal and may contribute to a negative feedback loop (Erikson, 1963). The "difficult" child, as described in the previous section, can trigger this type of adult reaction.

Adults in the child's world must understand the significance of attachment and separation in the child's development. Only through consistent adult-child interactions can these attachments develop appropriately.

Self-Esteem

To understand **self-esteem**, it must be contrasted with other terms that are also used to define self. Self-image is the way we perceive ourselves; **self-concept** is how we think about ourselves. In contrast, self-esteem relates to a person's feelings about self (Aldridge, 1993). Hopefully, self esteem is positive. A lack of self esteem shows negative feeling about self. Feelings about a person's self come in part from the people in the environment. The quality of interaction that children experience helps them to develop confidence that they have value. It is one of the most worthwhile possessions that a person can have (Storr, 1988).

In infancy, children gradually begin to recognize feelings and to discriminate among them. Certain feelings are linked with particular individuals and events. External social and emotional experiences provide information that helps children to understand their worth in relation to others (Gardner, 1983). Positive reciprocal interactions are crucial to the development of self-esteem. For example, a three-year-old child attends a child-care center while her parents work. The caregiver is teaching the children to pick up their toys after they are finished playing with them. Martha has been playing with the dishes in the home living center. She remembers to put the dishes away on the shelf when she is finished. As she finishes, the caregiver says, "Martha, you remembered to put the dishes away." Martha has the feeling that she is a good person.

Temperament can also be a factor in the development of self-esteem. A child with an "easy" temperament usually enjoys many positive interactions. Through their words and actions, adults tend to give these children the impression that they have value. The children with "slow to warm up" or "difficult" temperaments may have a great many negative interactions in their everyday life. This can have an effect on the way they interpret their own feelings of self-worth (Aldridge, 1993). An example shows a positive interaction with a "slow-to-warm-up" child.

------------------------------ ------------------------------

Steve (age five years) watches any new activity for a long time before he decides to participate. Today, the kindergarten children are fixing their own snack, which consists of spreading peanut butter on crackers and decorating them with raisins. Steve stands for 15 minutes watching other children completing the activity. The teacher knows that Steve will participate when he is ready. She does not rush Steve or make any negative comments about his nonparticipation. When Steve decides to try, he has a positive experience.

Adults must be sensitive to a child's background, including temperament style. A child who has already experienced a great deal of negative interaction needs consistent positive experiences to overcome any feelings of negative worth.

Self-Control

The control of one's feelings and actions begins in Erikson's (1963) second stage, autonomy versus shame and doubt. Children learn early that they can manipulate interactions. As early as five months, a baby can both initiate an interaction and turn away from it (Brazelton & Cramer, 1990). As the child becomes more mobile and language begins, he or she strives for independence. Adults must be flexible in their expectations of children aged fifteen to thirty months. At that age, children are inclined to want to control situations, even when the end result is not necessarily what they desire. An example of such a situation follows.

Tenisha (age twenty-two months) is sitting on the floor. She picks up a book and tries to open the cover. Her father tells her to bring the book over to him and that he will look at it with her. She says, "No!" He tries to get her to change her mind. But she repeats, "No!" Even though she would really like to look at the book with her Dad, she wants to assert control.

Children of this age need to begin making choices. Perhaps Tenisha's father would have had more success at the beginning of the ex-

change if he had asked her to *choose* a book that she wanted to look at with him. In that way she would have thought she had control over the choice of book. This may have allowed her to proceed with the activity in a more positive way.

Self-control is forming during the early years. Autonomy, the ability to govern oneself, is an important skill for children to learn. Self-control must develop without a loss of self-esteem. Permitting children to do as much as they can is essential (even though it takes more time or the result is not perfect). After his nap at the child-care center, Jeremy (four years) is trying to put on his polo shirt. He doesn't want any help. He works at it, and he finally gets it on backward. Even though it is on backward, the caregiver compliments him and says nothing about the fact that it isn't quite right. Jeremy is pleased with the job. The caregiver quietly explains the situation to Jeremy's mother when she comes to get him at the end of the day.

Adults must be sensitive to differences in children's abilities. Some children of four years can successfully put on their own clothes. Others need practice. Adults should be supportive of appropriate emotions, actions, and behaviors. It takes time and many opportunities for children to learn self-control.

Social Interaction

Social interaction begins with the interplay between parent and infant. Adults talk with babies about what is happening in their world. Infants learn differences in feelings, expressions, and moods through their interactions, first with adults and then with other children or peers (Gardner, 1983). This adult role continues as children move through the early years. Adults interact verbally, facilitating both communication and interaction skills. They provide a foundation for the development of mutual respect (Piaget, 1981).

Young children begin learning child-to-child relationship skills at an early age. Whether in formal child-care programs or in the less formal home or neighborhood settings, children must learn to play together. They must learn to share toys and materials, and to communicate their thoughts and wishes in an appropriate manner. As children have interactive experiences, they must learn how to use their developing self-control, because cooperation sometimes depends on compromise.

Adults can assist children in understanding their feelings. The adult can sometimes provide the words necessary for children to ask (or sometimes tell) other children their desires or feelings. Here is an example of this type of assistance.

Roberto (age five years) decides he wants to play with a red car. He doesn't notice one on the shelf in his child-care room. He walks over and takes one from another child. The child starts to scream. A caregiver intervenes and asks Roberto to tell her what happened. He turns his head from her. She says quietly, "Ginny had that red car first. If you want to play with that one, you must ask her first. Maybe you can find another red car on the shelf. Why don't you look and see if there is one over there."

To assist children in their interactions, as in this example, adults should give children words to use, as well as alternative plans that are acceptable. Young children need to learn to understand another point of view (Dewey, 1916). This takes many experiences. A child's temperament may also be a help or hindrance concerning social interaction. Although the "slow-to-warm-up" child may take a little longer than the "easy" child to interact in a group situation, the "difficult" child presents the greatest challenge. That child must learn to be someone with whom another child would like to interact.

Social Skills

Along with learning social interaction skills, young children must also learn the social skills required by the society in which they are participating. These skills may need to change, depending on the setting. For example, the skills required in the home may vary somewhat from those needed in school or at a restaurant. However, some basic social skills are required in any setting. Children learn these skills only from others.

Social customs may become the basis for the rules of a society, serving a social regulatory function (Ford & Lerner, 1992). Manners are a less formal function of social customs. Both rules and manners are learned in context. It is necessary for young children to have many experiences in different settings for them to learn the expected behaviors, as illustrated in the following scenario.

Jane (age seven years) is eating dinner with her family. She thinks of something that happened in school that day. She begins to speak with her mouth full of food. Her mother reminds her that she must chew and swallow her food before continuing with her story.

For young children to begin to internalize the customs of their society, they must assist in developing rules for their own communities, at home, child-care center, or school. Adults can guide young children to discuss the reasons for rules (Kamii, 1982).

Experience in developing rules is also a part of children's moral development. Group games can be valuable in giving experience with rule structures to both preschool and primary school children (DeVries & Kohlberg, 1987; Kamii & DeVries, 1980), because a context is provided in which children can learn to use rules.

Group games need not have winners or losers. Children may play against themselves or teams can work together to meet the objectives of the game. Players choose to submit to a system of rules, they practice cooperation in following and enforcing the rules, and they have experience in role taking and looking at ideas from another perspective. These are essential skills, both while playing the game and in the rest of life (DeVries & Kohlberg, 1987). Games help children learn the values, attitudes, and beliefs of their society (Freitag, 2000).

PHYSICAL DEVELOPMENT

The area of physical development includes both **gross and fine motor skills.** Within each of those domains, there are abilities that are dependent on adult-child interaction and support to develop. Specific characteristics within each of the two strands are identified with examples that describe types of adult-child interaction.

Gross Motor

Gross motor skills are used in large-muscle and whole-body movement. The operation of a motor system is complex, requiring the coordination of a number of neural and muscular components to be successful. Many of the gross motor skills have a genetic link (Gardner, 1983), and the infant begins developing these skills early. Between two and three months, babies can hold up their heads. By six months, infants can roll over, and by fifteen months, they walk well (Frankenburg & Dodds, 1990). Most children can learn these skills with adult support and a little coaching. Other gross motor skills may develop more

easily if an adult demonstrates the skill or interacts with the child in practice. For example, rolling, kicking, or throwing a ball can be aided by adult participation.

―――――――― ――――――――

Elizabeth (age three years) can roll a ball to her mother on the floor. However, she cannot throw it overhand. She wants to do it, but she just lets the ball drop from her hand to the floor. Her mother demonstrates how to hold the ball and how to pitch it out from her body. Elizabeth tries to do it the same way. After some practice, she is able to do much better. She continues to practice on her own.

―――――――― ――――――――

Gross motor development depends on both **maturation** and experience. However, the experience must match the interest and skill level of the child (Hunt, 1961). Children must have the opportunity to repeat skills to integrate learning. Adults should not direct the child to practice a skill, rather the practice should be initiated and directed by the child (Bredekamp, 1987). If the child requests assistance, the adult can provide appropriate support.

Fine Motor

Fine motor skills are related to small muscle development and eye-hand coordination. Fine motor skills require that an even greater variety of neural and muscular movements be differentiated and integrated into the child's repertoire (Gardner, 1983). Gross motor skills begin to develop before fine motor skills. However, the infant of four months can grasp a rattle and, at six months, can reach for an object (see chapter 7, activity 7.2). By eleven months, the thumb-finger grasp is well developed, and a child can make a tower of at least four cubes by two years of age (Frankenburg & Dodds, 1990). Generally, fine motor development proceeds from hand to fingers and from feet to toes.

Fine motor skills are developed as the child matures through experience. The adult can plan activities for children to do on their own. However, some fine motor skills require demonstration and, sometimes, substantial assistance from an adult or a more accomplished peer before a child becomes competent.

A child has an actual developmental level when trying to solve a problem independently. Vygotsky (1978) has suggested that there is a difference, called the *zone of proximal development*, between the child's actual problem-solving level and the level that is attainable when the child is given assistance in solving the problem.

For example, when learning to scribble, a child must know how to hold the crayon and color on the paper. Similarly, buttoning, lacing, tying, and zipping usually take some assistance before voluntary repetitive practice begins. A little coaching may be necessary when a child begins to cut with scissors. Some children may have difficulty working with plastic interlocking builders until they have learned exactly how to fit them together. Here is an example of a dressing skill.

Brad (five years) is trying to put on his jacket before the kindergarten class goes home for the day. The teacher suggests that he watch another child. He watches as the child goes through several motions to put her jacket on. She lays her jacket on the floor in front of her. The inside lining of the jacket is facing upward. The collar is pointed toward her feet. The child puts her arms through the sleeves and flips the jacket over her head. The teacher says, "Brad, you try it." He does and is successful.

Children are like adults in their desire for success. Sometimes just a little help at the beginning of an activity can give a child the support necessary to enable successful comple-tion of the task. The child will want to attempt the task again, which is as true in the area of physical development as in other developmental areas.

COGNITIVE DEVELOPMENT

The area of cognitive development includes knowing and seeking information, solving problems, making decisions, and attending to a task long enough to complete it. Although children must explore, experiment, and construct their own knowledge, the adult provides materials and experiences from which the child can choose. There are also times when adult-child interaction can enhance the child's ability to learn. Strands discussed in this section are development of attention, problem-solving skills, making choices, divergent thinking through asking open-ended questions, and completion of tasks.

Development of Attention

Attention has a critical function in a person's life; it helps to organize behavior. Attending behavior may be observed in earliest childhood. Infants can focus on both internal and external stimuli. For example, young infants may focus momentarily on the sensation of gas in their stomach or the rustle of leaves outside the window. This type of attention is involuntary and, as soon as the stimulus is gone, the attending behavior disappears. Voluntary **sustained attention,** sometimes termed "cultural attention" (Golod & Knox, 1993), must be artificially induced.

Cultural, or voluntary, attention begins to develop with language (Vygotsky, 1978). Young infants begin to look in the same direction as the caregiver does. As adults notice this, they may comment to children about what they see. When caregivers point to an object and name it, the object stands out from its surroundings. This captures the child's attention. In this way, children can be encouraged to attend. However, children themselves must be able to create stimuli on which they can focus their attention. Adults can assist children in focusing their attention by labeling, offering cues, and supporting children in staying with an activity. Here is an example of an adult helping a child remain on task.

*Pablo (age four years) is putting a wooden puzzle together in a **family child-care home**. He has put in two pieces and begins to work on a third one but cannot figure out where it goes. Another child, who is playing with plastic builders, distracts him. He starts to stand. The caregiver moves over to him and asks, "Would you like a little help?" Pablo sits down and looks again at the puzzle. The caregiver says, "Try turning that piece around and see if it will work." He tries it and it fits. He continues to work on the puzzle.*

The development of sustained attention can be a difficult task for children. It includes (1) coming to attention, (2) focusing attention on the task at hand, (3) maintaining attention, and (4) resisting distractors (Eddowes & Aldridge, 1990). Voluntary attention develops first between people and then inside the child (Ford & Lerner, 1992; Vygotsky, 1978). Temperament plays a part in the development of attention. Some children are more distractible than others. Parents and other adults must remain positive and assist those children in keeping focused on a task (Thomas & Chess, 1977).

Problem Solving

The successful problem solver is able to work with many variables and possible solutions at one time. Problem solving requires logical thought (Gardner, 1983). In learning to solve problems, young children need to have physi-cal experience working with real objects. They can see that a block is red or blue and that it is a square or a rectangle, and they can compare similarities and differences among blocks. These are physical properties that are external and can be compared by observation.

As children move from concrete experience with objects to more abstract thinking, they begin to construct logico-mathematical knowledge. They develop an internal understanding of relationships. For example, three beads can be seen as beads. They may all be red and round, or they may be different. However, the "threeness" doesn't exist in any one of them. A child cannot look at one of the beads and determine that it is a part of a group of three. The "threeness" is an abstract concept that is found in the relationship among members of the group (Kamii, 1982; Kamii & DeVries, 1978).

Young children can learn a lot through their exploration and experimentation with raw materials and equipment. However, a parent or teacher can sometimes facilitate the thinking process or reasoning activity of the child (Bruner, 1966; Piaget, 1978) by being an organizer who creates situations that present useful problems for children to solve. The adult can also provide alternate examples that may make a child reconsider a solution or try a new one. The role of the adult is not one of transmitting solutions but rather that of **mentor** (Piaget, 1948/1973). Here is an example of an adult extending a child's thinking.

Carrie (age seven years) is counting pumpkin seeds that were in a class jack-o'-lantern. There are so many, she keeps getting mixed up. The teacher says, "Why not sort them into groups of ten? Then you can count by tens to find out how many are there." Carrie says, "Good idea." She begins to count with the new plan.

Children need lots of practice in solving problems. They gain this practice by solving all kinds of practical dilemmas. **Toddlers** want to find out how things work. Three- and four-year-old children want to make things out of blocks, play dough, and art media. Kindergarten children like to predict what may happen next. **Primary-aged children** like to work together to solve problems.

Adults should provide interesting materials in the environment for children to explore and be available to extend children's thinking or pose new problems. Remember that the zone of proximal development is the range between the child's actual independent problem-solving level and the level of potential development when problem solving under adult guidance or with more capable peers (Vygotsky, 1978).

Making Choices

When children are allowed to make choices, they are better able to make wise decisions. For some theorists, decision making is a part of all problem solving (Ford & Lerner, 1992). However, before young children can make decisions, they must have the experience of making simple choices. Even infants can choose between two toys. Young children can pick which of two shirts to wear. As children gain experience in making choices, they can contribute to decision making in family and classroom settings.

In the child-care center or school, adults should provide opportunities for children to choose from many different materials, types of equipment, and activities (Bredekamp, 1987). When a child has difficulty in making a selection, the adult can narrow the choice by asking which of two activities the child prefers. An example of this type of situation is given here.

———————— ————————

Jakarius (age five years) is wandering around the kindergarten classroom and cannot seem to find an

activity that interests him. The teacher says, "Jakarius, you seem to be having trouble deciding what you would like to do. Would you rather work in the art center and make a string painting or build something at the sand table?" With the choice narrowed, he picks the sand table and moves over to it.

———————— ————————

The adult must know the children well enough to help them make selections they would enjoy. Children who have had little

Preschool children choose outdoor area during free play time.

experience in making choices need more assistance than others as they begin to learn the skill.

Young children can make group decisions about circumstances in their classroom, but the process takes the time, patience, and persistence of the teacher. However, the benefits to the children are substantial. They begin to feel a responsibility toward classmates. The teacher has less authority because some of it is transferred back to the children. Helping to make classroom rules assists children in the development of self-control, a first step in building a moral community (DeVries & Kohlberg, 1987).

Asking Open-Ended Questions

Open-ended questions are those that have more than one answer. A question is usually (but not always) asked of another person. When adults ask children open-ended questions, they give the children the opportunity to do some divergent thinking, so that they are not just parroting a correct response. The adult can show children the value of asking these kinds of questions and set up situations in which children have an opportunity to ask similar kinds of questions.

Children ask a variety of questions in their early childhood years (Dewey, 1916). Piaget (1955) analyzed the questions of a seven-year-old child. There were six categories of questions: (1) causal explanation, (2) reality and history, (3) actions and intentions, (4) rules, (5) classification, and (6) calculation. Piaget concluded that the function of a question is to induce mental activity in a certain direction. A child's own questions and answers to the questions of others provide valuable information concerning the child's level of thinking (Bredekamp, 1987).

Although questioning is not the only strategy that can be used to stimulate thinking, it is valuable as long as the questions are asked in the context of an ongoing activity or child's interest (DeVries & Kohlberg, 1987). Here is an example.

A second-grade class of seven-year-old children has just finished a recycling project. The teacher asks the group, "What would it be like to live in a world where almost everything is recycled? How would it be different from our world? Why would you like it? Why not?" The children use the information learned in the project to figure out answers to the questions.

Critical thinking skills can be developed through questioning strategies. Six categories of cognitive functioning have been identified (Bloom, Engelhart, Frost, Hill, & Krathwohl, 1956): (1) knowledge (recalling information), (2) comprehension (understanding meaning), (3) application (using learning in new situations), (4) analysis (seeing parts and their relationships), (5) synthesis (using information to create a new original), and (6) evaluation (making judgments based on selected criteria). Adults should ask children questions related to these categories, and children should be encouraged to ask similar kinds of questions (Bredekamp & Copple, 1997). Unfortunately, many adults ask questions at the child's "knowledge" level, seeking only right answers. This limits children's chances for learning to ask open-ended questions and their development of critical thinking skills.

Completion of Tasks

Toddlers engage in play with objects as a process. They have little interest in completing anything. However, as children move into Erikson's (1963) third stage, initiative versus guilt, they begin to see a task differently. There is a shift to more responsible participation and accomplishment in manipulating objects and participating cooperatively in activities.

During this stage, adults can give support and guidance and encourage children to achieve the success that comes from completing a task (Montessori, 1912/1964). This kind of activity can give children the opportunity to try something yet more challenging. Here is an example.

Gil (age five years) is sorting 50 plastic disks by color and then making a graph to show how many there are of each. The teacher says, "You are almost finished." As Gil completes the task, the teacher says, "I bet you are pleased with your work. If you do it again sometime, what other ways could you sort the disks?" Gil thinks and says, "By shape."

Young children have a natural desire to make sense of their world. There is an internal motivation at work. By following children's interests when planning activities, adults can build on this motivation (Bredekamp, 1987). Some children have difficulty in completing tasks because of a low skill level or their lack of sustained attention. When a child is having problems, the adult must be sure that the available activities match the interests of the child and be able to assist the child in acquiring the skills necessary to successfully complete the task.

COMMUNICATION DEVELOPMENT

The area of communication development includes both the receptive and expressive domains. Listening and reading are receptive skills. Speaking and writing are expressive skills, and nonverbal communication conveys meaning without the use of words. No communication skill can develop without reciprocal interaction between children and adults, and parents play a crucial role. Furthermore, a child's culture is transmitted through language. Because all of the strands in the area of communication development are important, each is covered in this section.

Listening

Infants can hear before they are born and begin to learn to **listen** to sounds in the environment soon after birth. Parents and other adults talk with infants, describing routines and empathizing with the feelings they exhibit. Infants learn to discriminate between sounds. As children begin to make sounds, the adults listen and interact with the children. Adults should continue in their role as listeners to children's utterances, whether understandable or not. This interaction between child and adult provides both with practice in listening.

Similarly, parents should read to the young child early and often. In addition to giving the child the opportunity to listen to interesting information, reading also fosters a sense of security within the caring interaction between the child and an adult. As children get older, they interact with peers during play and have discussions in group child-care or school programs. These activities provide a means for children to practice listening skills. An example of a listening activity follows.

Noah (age three years) has a favorite book about ducks. His mother reads to him each evening before he goes to bed. It is a ritual that takes place almost every night, and Noah looks forward to it. He brings his book to the chair where they read. His mother says, "Would you like to hear that book again? You really like it don't you?" Noah smiles and climbs up next to her. She reads the book, and then she talks with him about it.

Sometimes children have temporary problems that keep them from hearing, for example, enlarged tonsils or adenoids, fluid in the middle ear, or a buildup of wax in the ears. Whenever there is a hearing loss, a loss of learning occurs. Parents and other adults in the child's world should be sure that the child can hear. If there is a problem, it should be corrected quickly.

Speaking

Infants begin by babbling all of the sounds in any language in the world. As they interact with the language of their own culture, they begin to assign meanings and internalize the sounds (Donoghue, 1990). Speech assists children in organizing, unifying, and integrating many aspects of their behavior (Vygotsky, 1978). This is a powerful tool for young children because they are now able to communicate with others through language.

The development of oral language depends on reciprocal interaction with adults. There must be many opportunities for **speaking** in different contexts. In addition, oral language is the foundation for writing (Vygotsky, 1978). Young children must be able to talk about their ideas and feelings before they are able to write about them.

Adults can extend children's language during oral communication. Whether an adult is speaking to an individual child or having an oral discussion in a group, information is being shared. Children also enhance their communication skills when playing or working with other children. Child-care centers and early childhood classrooms in schools should be environments rich in oral language, including both adult-child and child-child interaction (Donoghue, 1990). Next is an example of adult-child interaction in oral communication.

Children in a first-grade class (six-year-olds) are seated in a large group in the front of the classroom.

The teacher is conducting a class discussion related to a field trip to a farm that the children will be taking tomorrow. After the oral discussion, the teacher asks the children to list the most important things that they want to learn on the field trip. The teacher writes down the things that the group thinks are most important on chart paper.

Young children also need an abundance of oral language experiences in the home, community, and any group programs in which they participate. Parents and other adults should provide a variety of oral language activities for them.

Writing

The foundation for **writing** is oral language and drawing (Bredekamp, 1987). The use of crayons, pencils, and markers gives young children experience in manipulating these tools on paper. They learn to control both the tool and their own actions. Babies can begin to scribble (with supervision) as soon as they are no longer using their mouths for exploration. As children gain experience, they reach a stage in their development when they can write alphabetic letters, usually between the ages of four and six years.

If children are to write, they need to see writing modeled by parents and teachers in their environment. They need experience in watching the letters of their language being formed. An example of a class writing activity follows.

Children in a first-grade class (six-year-olds) are grouped around the teacher. They are discussing things that have happened at home and at school since yesterday (Daily News chart). After a discussion, they decide which things to include in the

news. The teacher writes them on a piece of chart paper in manuscript printing. The chart is hung in the classroom for all to read.

For children to have experience in writing on their own, they first must have in mind the images about which they wish to write (Vygotsky, 1962). Then they begin to put their thoughts on paper. When they have finished the first draft, it is time to revise and edit. In working through the editing process, they begin to be concerned with spelling and grammar. They may work in small groups within a classroom to accomplish this. After they are finished, they share the writing with others. This is called *process writing* (Andreason, Cadenhead, Havens, Riley, & Tyra, 1980). A more detailed description of the writing process is found in chapter 9.

Adults can be helpful and supportive throughout the early years as children begin the cultural process of writing. They supply materials, model writing, and are supportive as children attempt the editing of their own work.

Reading

Children are introduced to **reading** when adults read to them. They learn that they can gain pleasure, as well as information, from hearing books read. Children absorb meaning from the illustrations as the book is read. As they come in contact with words in other contexts, such as advertising logos, they learn that different symbols have meanings (Aldridge, Kirkland, & Kuby, 1996; Kirkland, Aldridge, & Kuby, 1991). This is the beginning of reading on their own, sometimes called "emergent literacy" (Strickland & Morrow, 1989).

Although children may begin to associate print in their environment with meaning as early as two years, they usually do not begin reading books until they are closer to age five

or six. They need many experiences with print in context to be able to read it with comprehension (Bredekamp, 1987). Here is an example of a classroom reading activity.

In a kindergarten classroom, a group of four children (five-year-olds) develop a group book. Since each has a pet cat, they decide to write the book about cats. The teacher first discusses the attributes and habits of cats with the children orally. Each child contributes some information from first-hand experience. The children then decide what they would like to include in the book. The teacher writes down the ideas on different pieces of paper in manuscript printing. Children take turns reading the pages. The teacher puts the pages together with a cover. The children each illustrate a page or two. Each child is able to read the book.

When children contribute phrases and sentences to projects such as this, they have ownership of those words. They understand the oral meaning, and that facilitates their ability to understand the verbal symbol. Only through interaction with adults or more capable peers can this process occur.

Young children of school age are entering Erikson's (1963) fourth stage, industry versus inferiority. They become interested in mastering skills and tasks. In all cultures, children in this stage receive some systematic instruction, which is helpful in acquiring the skills of both reading and writing. However, there is a wide range of individual differences among children who are learning those skills.

Nonverbal Communication

Nonverbal communication begins at birth. Babies make their needs known through facial expressions, body language, gestures, and nonverbal utterances. This kind of communication precedes oral and written language (Vygotsky, 1978). Adults learn these signs and respond to them. Young children understand body language before they can understand words or respond verbally (Bredekamp, 1987).

There are many other ways that young children can communicate nonverbally, including through the visual arts, music, dance, and mime. Deaf children may use sign language. Adults must understand the need for nonverbal communication, be supportive, and provide opportunities for children to have relevant experiences. Here is an example of nonverbal interaction.

Kara (age seven years) is listening to music on a tape. She is picking up the rhythm, and she begins to dance to the music. Kara's father is watching from the doorway. He claps along with the rhythm. Kara smiles and continues to dance.

Adults, both in the home and in group programs for children, should provide a variety of experiences in which children can engage in nonverbal behaviors.

CREATIVE DEVELOPMENT

Creative development includes many areas of experience and is part of almost any activities in which young children engage. Many of these activities include some aspect of play (Bruce, 1993), such as the aesthetic experiences of art, music, movement, woodworking, drama, and dance. Play can also be found in creative approaches to building with blocks, role-playing, problem solving, and writing. Adults can facilitate creativity in young children by providing materials and activities that allow them to experience the process of creative endeavor. Strands discussed in this sec-

tion are sensory/art, music, movement, dramatics, and creative writing.

Sensory/Art

Babies learn through their senses (sight, hearing, taste, smell, and touch). They need safe places and the freedom to explore. As the senses develop, art activities can be a means of enhancing sensory learning for young children. The use of artistic media requires spatial intelligence, which is the ability to form a mental model of something in space and to be able to use or maneuver it (Gardner, 1983). Young children learn best when they can be actively involved with materials and media. They are usually able to figure out ways of experimenting and doing projects on their own (Gardner, 1993).

Daily experiences in art media should be integrated into the curriculum in preschool and primary school programs (Bredekamp, 1987). The activities may include finger painting, painting with tempera, drawing with crayons and markers, modeling with dough and clay, using papier-mâché, making a collage, and sewing. Adults can provide activities and can be supportive in their appreciation of the work of the individual children in the group. An example of an art interaction experience follows.

Marcus (age three years) is enrolled in a child-care center. He has several creative activities to choose from each day. Marcus particularly likes to paint at the easel. The caregiver helps him put on a smock. She lets him "do his own thing" as long as he keeps the paint on the paper. When he is finished, she asks him to tell her about his painting experience. He enjoys talking with her about his painting.

Young children can be introduced to the artwork of others through rotating classroom displays of reproductions of visual art from well-known artists. Similarly, as children move into kindergarten and the primary grades, they become familiar with the variety of illustrations available in their picture books.

Music

Music is found in the rhythms and sounds of the environment. It is something that almost everyone enjoys in one form or another. Infants should hear music sung and played at an early age. By the middle of the second year of life, young children make sounds in various intervals and engage in spontaneous sound play (Gardner, 1983). Toddlers enjoy singing along with others. There is a wide range of musical ability in young children but, with experience, most can reproduce a tune by the age of five or six.

Adult-child musical interaction begins when the parent sings "Rock-a-Bye Baby" to the baby. Later, the adult must sing with the child so that the child can learn the words. Adults can also assist children in the use of rhythm patterns and rhythm instruments. They can play recordings and introduce singing games, such as "The Farmer in the Dell." A variety of music should be available daily. Here is an example of a parent-child music activity.

Lucia (age two years) is going to the store with her mother. While driving the car, her mother begins singing "Old MacDonald Had a Farm." As they drive, Lucia joins her mother in singing part of the song, particularly "E-I, E-I, O." With this kind of practice, soon Lucia is able to sing the song by herself.

Music activities must be integrated into the curriculum. Some child-care programs and schools may have music specialists to assist in teaching music. If the music specialist can work with the classroom teacher, the music content is more likely to be related to other classroom experiences.

Movement

Creative movement, usually a gross motor action, is related to rhythms in sounds, words, or music. Voluntary motor activity, which features the subtle interaction between perceptual and motor systems, is a part of Gardner's (1983) bodily kinesthetic intelligence. Motor development can be translated creatively into dance, which is part of many world cultures and can provide an opportunity for exploring them.

Young children develop their gross motor movements in many ways. Creative movement can provide enjoyment and improve motor coordination. Various activities can be used in the program. Adults can set the scene for the movement or dance: a poem may be read, or music may be played. Young children use their imaginations in creative movement activities, as this example of a movement activity in a classroom shows.

Jemal (age four years) is in a classroom in a child-care center. Most of the class is participating in a movement activity. The caregiver asks each child to select an animal to portray in the activity. Jemal picks a lion. The caregiver reads a poem that describes the actions of different animals; when he gets to the lion's part, Jemal acts the way he thinks a lion would act.

Cultures have dances that are unique to them. For example, many Native American tribes still do ancient traditional dances. Children watch the dances and like to imitate them. When appropriate music is available in group care programs or schools, children enjoy dancing.

Kindergarten children use props in imaginative play.

Dramatics

In dramatic play, young children use activities or materials to represent the real world. Recasting experiences through play is a way of consolidating, extending, and creating knowledge (Franklin, 2000). Toddlers can pretend to drink from a cup or talk on a toy telephone. Some children prefer working with objects instead of interacting with people; for example, as early as age four, some may prefer to experiment and build blocks in patterns. These children are less likely to be interested in reenacting familiar transportation scenes and sequences in the block center (Storr, 1988). Children who are interested in objects have a stronger intrapersonal intelligence, and those who like to practice contrasts in mood, temperament, and intention in their role play are more interested in interpersonal relations (Gardner, 1983, 1993).

Adults provide children with the materials and a time to play various roles. Adults can move in and out of children's role play, showing interest, asking questions, and being supportive (Bredekamp, 1987; Reggio Emilia,

1997). Dramatization activities may take place in different ways. In a dramatic play center, the props should be changed frequently to stimulate imagination. Props can also be coordinated with other curriculum projects. Some suggestions beyond the commonly used housekeeping theme are restaurant, space shuttle, or shoe store settings. The block center can also have various props related to transportation and community themes. Another method of enhancing role play and imagination is the use of puppets, flannel board pieces, and plays. Here is an example of a child who enjoys using her imagination.

Kiley (age five years) is in a kindergarten class. She likes to play with the hand puppets and puppet stage and to act out various stories that the class has heard read or experiences that she has had. She always looks for one or two children to play with her and gets along well with others. This kind of activity increases her peer interaction skills.

Children in child-care centers and schools come from varied home backgrounds. They sometimes play out incidents that they encounter in the home that they find distressing or do not understand. The caregiver or teacher can gain information from these role-playing situations to assist in understanding the child. However, any information of this sort should be handled confidentially, because the adult observer may not fully understand it.

Creative Writing   Writing can be looked at from two points of view: (1) the technical, or handwriting, function and (2) the thought process that goes into the writing. When children are expected to excel in both areas at the same time, they can become frustrated; the thought processes of writing get lost.

The thought that goes into writing evolves out of oral language and drawing. Young children express their thoughts in drawings before they write about them. Adults can write the children's thoughts down for them on a picture. This process, called "dictation," helps children to see the print that reflects their thoughts.

When children begin to write, the emphasis should be on getting the thoughts on paper. The technical side, which includes legibility, spelling, and grammar, should be secondary, so that children can focus on the creative thoughts. After the thoughts are on paper, the editing process can be used (see chapter 9) to improve the technical aspects of the writing. Children begin writing earlier and more when this method is used. Here is an example of this type of activity.

Wang (age eight years) is in a third-grade class. He has a good idea for a science fiction story. He tells the teacher a little about the potential plot. The teacher suggests he write it in a book. Wang begins to write down his story on paper. When he finishes, he reads it to his editing group. They give him some sugges-

tions for revision and discuss editing the spelling and grammar. Wang makes the changes, and then he puts his story in a book form with illustrations.

When a classroom teacher thinks the children need handwriting practice, a handwriting center can be provided. Children can copy poems and short prose passages that are on cards in the center in either manuscript or cursive writing, depending on the age of the children. This gives them practice in handwriting, but they do not have to be creative at the same time.

✍ SUMMARY

Young children experience several different areas of development in the course of their learning. In each area, there must be a balance between independent activities and those that can be enhanced through reciprocal interaction with an adult or more competent peer. This is the basis of the interactive curriculum. The ideas of major theorists who support this type of curriculum are summarized in relation to child development, curriculum, and interaction.

Strands that are representative of the different areas of development and learning are described and examples that would be found in an interactive curriculum were given. Personal-social development follows the strands of trust, attachment and separation, self-esteem, self-control, social interaction, and social skills. Gross and fine motor skills are part of physical development. In cognitive development, the strands are development of attention, problem solving, making choices, asking open-ended questions, and completion of tasks. The adult's role in providing communication activities in support of listening, speaking, reading, writing, and nonverbal communication is crucial for that area of development. Creative development follows the strands of sensory/art, music, movement, dramatics, and creative writing.

Young children should have many opportunities for interaction with adults, children, and objects. These interactions begin at birth and continue through the first eight years of life, and beyond.

QUESTIONS AND PROJECTS FOR THE READER

1. List the major theorists discussed in the first part of this chapter by their interests in the following categories: child development, curriculum, and interaction.
2. Develop a chart that shows the five areas of development. Include the strands in each area that are enhanced by the use of reciprocal interaction.
3. Observe in a preschool or primary classroom. Note the use of interaction by adults in the setting. Were interactions positive or negative? What was the result for the child? Relate the interactions to the areas of development and strands described in the chapter.
4. Think of children you have known. Select one child in each of the three major temperament constellations. Write a paragraph telling why you classified each child as you did.
5. Select an area of development. Then write an example of a negative adult-child interaction. How could you have made that interaction more positive?
6. In each of the five developmental areas, discuss one example of a positive interaction.

FOR FURTHER READING

Bredekamp, S., & Copple, C. (Eds.). (1997). *Developmentally appropriate practice in early childhood programs*. (Rev. ed.) Washington, DC: National Association for the Education of Young Children (NAEYC). An overview of practices with young children that are positive and supportive of development and learning. Specific examples are described.

Bruner, J. S. (1966). Patterns of growth. In *Toward a theory of instruction* (Chapter 1). Cambridge, MA: Harvard University Press. How children learn and how they can best be helped to learn are the themes of this book. In this chapter, growth is related to instruction. This is one of several books that the author has written on the topic of education.

DeVries, R., & Kohlberg, L. (1987). Education for development. In *Constructivist early education: Overview and comparison with other programs* (Chapter 1). Washington, DC: NAEYC. This chapter describes the teacher's role in a constructivist classroom: organizing materials and activities that combine a mixture of interaction and independence.

Dewey, J. (1916). Play and work in the curriculum. In *Democracy and education* (Chapter 15). New York: Macmillan. This short chapter shows the importance the author places on integrating play and work in the curriculum. He advocates bringing the real world into the classroom.

Erikson, E. H. (1963). Eight ages of man. In *Childhood and society* (Chapter 7, 2nd ed). New York: W. W. Norton. This chapter provides a description of Erikson's eight stages of psychosocial development. The first four stages cover birth through adolescence.

Gardner, H. (1983). *Frames of mind*. New York: Basic Books. An overview of the theory of multiple intelligences, including information on each intelligence with examples and cross-cultural information.

Montessori, M. (1912/1964). History of methods. In *The Montessori method* (Chapter 2). New York: Schocken. This chapter is an overview of the background that contributed to the author's development of her "method" of working with children.

Staley, L. (1998). Beginning to implement the Reggio philosophy. *Young Children, 53* (5), 20–25. The article gives some background concerning Reggio Emilio schools, including examples of projects.

Thomas, T., & Chess, S. (1980). The structure of behavior: abilities, motivations, styles. In *The dynamics of psychological development* (Chapter 6). New York: Brunner/Mazel. This chapter describes the different temperament constellations, is based on a longitudinal research study conducted by the authors.

Vygotsky, L. S. (1978). Interactions between learning and development. In *Mind and society: the development of higher psychological processes* (Chapter 6). Cambridge, MA: Harvard University Press. Examines the relationship between learning and development and explains the zone of proximal development.

Chapter Two

Developing an Understanding of Young Children

Objectives

After reviewing this chapter, you will be able to

- Generate examples of children's individual differences based on their membership in various subcultures.
- Identify ways of obtaining background information concerning children and their families.
- List and define five methods of observation.
- Suggest age-appropriate strategies for guiding children in an interactive curriculum.

Although young children of similar age may have many of the same characteristics, each is unique. To work effectively with them, it is important to have an overall knowledge of typical expectations for the different areas of development (i.e., personal-social, physical, cognitive, communication, creative). However, for optimum understanding, as much information as possible should be sought concerning each child's personal traits and family background.

INDIVIDUAL DIFFERENCES

A child's personal characteristics may include factors that range from unique temperament styles to conditions related to physical or intellectual abilities. Although some individual traits have biological components, others may be more influenced by environmental conditions. However, most of an individual's characteristics are influenced by both genetic and environmental factors. The early childhood years are a critical period for identifying conditions that hinder normal development and providing the necessary developmentally appropriate interventions.

Family background includes multiple factors that influence the social-cultural context of a child's development (Banks & Banks, 2001; Gollnick & Chinn, 1998). Understanding the child requires that the caregiver take into account how specific ethnic, religious, linguistic, and socioeconomic class factors play a role in the child's environment. Likewise, in an age of great geographic mobility, the teacher or caregiver profits from an awareness of regional differences; the differences in urban, suburban, and rural settings; and variations in immigrant experiences.

Gollnick and Chinn (1998) provide a useful framework for examining the microcultures of families in the United States, which, in turn, assists teachers and caregivers in understanding children. A child's cultural identity is comprised of the interaction of numerous subcultures. The relative influence of one subculture in regard to another subculture varies among individuals. For example, a third-generation, middle-class Mexican American girl growing up in an urban Los Angeles neighborhood at the turn of the 21st century is likely to be much different from her first-generation Mexican-American classmate from a working-class family.

The following section describes seven of the subcultures, or microcultures, in more detail. The subcultures include: **ethnicity, religion, language, socioeconomic class, gender, age,** and **ability.** Each subculture description is followed by a brief example from a home, center, or classroom setting.

Ethnic diversity is a hallmark of American society. The Harvard Encyclopedia of American Ethnic Groups (Thernstrom, 1980) identifies at least 276 different ethnic groups in the United States, including 170 different Native American groups. Members of **ethnic** groups often share common behavioral and linguistic bonds and cultural rituals. However, the strength of the membership in an ethnic group varies greatly among groups, particularly among members who share a national origin but not a recent historical tie to the group (Banks, 2001). The manifestations of ethnic culture are shared patterns, such as those of family structure, child-raising, and food preparation. Effective teachers or caregivers do not make assumptions or act on stereotypes about children or their families.

Mr. Ramirez, a second-grade teacher, is reading aloud a picture book, Seven Candles for Kwanzaa *by Andrea Davis Pinkney, to his ethnically diverse class. One of the children makes a comment that implies that she assumes all African-American*

families in the class celebrate Kwanzaa. Mr. Ramirez capitalizes on the comment by leading a discussion on different traditional types of family holiday celebrations.

Likewise, the strength of the influence of **religious** differences on a child's individuality varies tremendously from family to family. Parents' child-raising beliefs may be heavily influenced by their religious culture, and their expectations for their child's interaction with adults, peers, and even the curriculum may conflict with those of the program planners. For example, a child who is prohibited from participating in mainstream-culture holiday celebrations may experience peer interactions that invite the child to question family beliefs. Religious differences may have a profound influence on gender-related participation in activities and interactions between people.

Ms. Gilbert overhears one of her kindergarten children, Beth, bragging about the Valentine's Day cards that her mother bought her over the weekend. Ms. Gilbert jots down a reminder to talk to the mother of one of her other students, Sarah, about preferences concerning the upcoming Valentine's Day holiday. Sarah's family are members of Jehovah's Witnesses, a religious group that prohibits members from participating in many holiday activities. Although the school has chosen to emphasize the historical and cultural aspects of holidays rather than the commercial aspects, Mrs. Gilbert is sensitive to Sarah's feelings and respectful of family beliefs.

A third subculture is **language.** Linguistic diversity in early childhood, although commonly viewed as differences in the first and second languages of children, has many cul-

tural implications. Children may vary in their use of nonverbal communication systems. An act that is viewed as appropriate in one culture, such as looking at an adult speaker, may in fact be considered rude in another culture. Bilingualism, dialect differences, and the use of nonstandard English may be perceived as indicators of social class rather than merely differences in language use (Erickson, 2001; Ovando, 2001). Since language development is critical for children, teachers and caregivers must recognize individual differences in cultural aspects of language (Nieto, 2000).

During snack time, three-year-old Jerome points to a new food on the raw vegetable tray and asks, "What's that?" (deleting the final "t" of "what" as he speaks). Instead of responding to his question, the newly hired aide insists that he repeat the question, clearly articulating the final "t" sound by responding, "It's what's that" Jerome looks confused and the aide again repeats, "Say, what's that?" Jerome ignores her request and turns away from the table.

Socioeconomic class has a significant effect on individual differences among children and families. As a subculture, people who share similar occupations, educational attainment, and income levels often have common values, beliefs, and behaviors (Banks & Banks, 2001; Gollnick and Chinn, 1998). The availability of educational resources in homes and communities varies among families in different socioeconomic groups. Although people tend to participate socially and occupationally within a socioeconomic class structure, teachers and caregivers interact with children from a variety of socioeconomic groups. There is considerable evidence that teachers lower their expectations and alter the curriculum for children from lower-level socioeconomic groups, which perpetuates differences (Gollnick and Chinn, 1998). Becoming aware of stereotypes and teaching practices that limit development helps teachers and caregivers plan for interactions that enhance rather than impede development.

Buddy lives with his five-member migrant family in a local motel room. During journal writing, Buddy raises his hand for help in spelling a word. His first-grade teacher discovers Buddy's keen interest in uncommon words after he watches her look up the spelling of "rhinoceros" in a picture dictionary. He comments, "My mom has a bigger dictionary than that but not as many pictures." Mrs. Lee reflects on her assumption that Buddy's family's possessions wouldn't include a dictionary.

Another category of subculture is **gender** identity. As previously noted, gender identity may be influenced by religious, ethnic, and even socioeconomic class subcultures. In the last 30 years, numerous studies have focused on individual and group differences between the sexes that can be credited more to culture than biology (Sadker & Sadker, 2001; Sadker, Sadker, & Klein, 1991). In a review of studies related to children in early childhood programs, Sadker, Sadker, and Klein (1991) found that teachers have a greater number of interactions with boys; they ask preschool girls more personal-social questions than boys; and girls were less likely to participate in block play, climbing, sand play, and construction play. A component of understanding young children is recognizing the significant role that cultural expectations play in gender development. Since actions with and reactions to children make a difference in this area, proponents of a nonsexist curriculum must be conscious of gender-biased interactions in all of a child's environments.

Mr. Washington, a Head Start teacher of four-year-olds, overhears a boy teasing another for choosing to play in the dramatic play corner of the classroom. "Why do you want to play with the girls? You must be a sissy." Mr. Washington walks over to the play kitchen and asks, "What would you like for lunch? It's my turn to cook." The children in the interest center rush to the table to wait to be served lunch by Mr. Washington.

Gollnick and Chinn (1998) classify **age** as a microculture that influences cultural identity because members of a particular age cohort, similar to other subcultures, have shared cultural traits, values, and behaviors. In most respects, young children are less likely to be influenced by their peers than they are to be influenced by their parents, teachers, and caregivers. Each generation or age cohort tends to have similar life experiences, which in part influences their individual differences. Young children in today's society grow up in a global-oriented, highly technological world, allowing them to communicate instantaneously with others in ways that their grandparents could only imagine. Similarly, their parents grew up with computers in schools, if not in homes, sharing a common social, cultural, and political history of their generation. Children reared by grandparents are likely to have life experiences that are different from those of children raised by parents, which may lead to unique individual traits.

Mrs. Ramirez, director of a home visitor program is leading a discussion during a monthly inservice training session for home visitors. The topic is parenting behaviors and attitudes towards appropriate infant clothing. One home visitor remarks on the difficulty she is having convincing an older woman to allow her infant granddaughter to practice

Center director greets parent volunteer as she signs in for the day.

crawling in bare feet on warm days. Another home visitor adds that this belief may be as much ethnic as it is related to certain age groups.

A seventh subculture identified by Gollnick and Chinn (1998) is **ability,** or exceptionality. Exceptional individuals include those with disabilities as well as giftedness. Due to their special personal and social needs and interests, many exceptional individuals participate in a common subculture with other individuals with similar exceptionalities. As a result of legal mandates or personal choice, programs and schools for young children mainstream exceptional children into their regular programs. A thorough knowledge of an exceptional individual's abilities, needs, and interests is critical for those who plan for positive interactions in schools and children's programs.

Miss Vivero, a first-year teacher, notices that many of the children in her second-grade classroom want to baby Briana, a petite, limited-mobility student who is mainstreamed in the class. Although Briana is fully capable of using her walker to move around

the room, there are several girls in particular who try to pick her up and carry her or beg to go get supplies for her. Miss Vivero seeks the advice of the school's Resource Specialist for strategies to build Briana's independence without discouraging the genuine expressions of kindness.

A child's individual differences related to cultural diversity are an essential component of background information, which enhances an adult's understanding of the child and serves as a foundation for planning an interactive curriculum. Background information can be obtained through various means, such as questionnaires, interviews, and home visits. In addition, different methods of observation can provide firsthand information concerning a child's behavior in specific settings.

BACKGROUND INFORMATION

When adults are involved in some aspect of a children's program, it is helpful to collect information about the children as they are enrolled. Many programs have questionnaires that the parents can complete before the child arrives on the first day. A typical child information

CHILD INFORMATION FORM

Child's Name _____ Nickname _____

Address _____ Phone _____

Date of Birth: Year _____   Month _____   Day _____

Father's Name _____

Father's Position _____ Phone _____

Mother's Name _____

Mother's Position _____ Phone _____

Emergency Number _____ (This should be someone other than the parent(s) or guardian.)

Children or other persons living in the household:

Name _____ Age _____ Relationship _____

Name _____ Age _____ Relationship _____

Name _____ Age _____ Relationship _____

Name _____ Age _____ Relationship _____

Language(s) spoken in home _____

Is the child accustomed to being in the care of a sitter?

        Often _____   Occasionally _____   Never _____

What age playmates does your child usually have? _____

Does your child prefer to play alone? _____ With children? _____

Weight at birth _____   Premature? _____   Age first walked _____

Age first begain to talk _____   age child accepted toilet training _____

Does child have temper tantrums? _____   Does child dress alone? _____

Describe any known disabling conditions _____

_____

List any fears (i.e., rain, animals, dark) _____

_____

Has the child had previous group experience? _____

Where? _____   How did your child get along? _____

Has the family a pet? _____   What? _____   Name _____

Does the child go to sleep easily? _____

Does the child enjoy mealtime? _____

Child's interests _____

Favorite toy _____

What disciplinary measures are used in the home? _____

_____

What kind of adjustment do you expect your child to make in the first days at the child care center?

_____

Add any information or comments that may be of help in getting to know your child:

Figure 2.1   Sample of a child information form.

form includes pertinent demographic information, such as name, address, home telephone number, parental work telephone numbers; physical characteristics, including any special needs or problems; and personal preferences. Records of allergies and immunizations and other information related to health should be completed by a physician. Figure 2.1 shows an example of a child information form that can be modified to fit individual program needs. In some programs, translating the forms into other languages or having translators available to interview parents who cannot complete the forms in English may be necessary. Figure 2.2 shows an example of a child medical report; information required on this type of report may vary from state to state.

Most states require emergency telephone numbers, for use when a parent cannot be reached, or a sickness and injury treatment permission card, for use when a serious illness or accident occurs while the child is involved in program activities. However, legal requirements vary, so the state law should be followed. Figure 2.3 shows an example of such a card, which can be modified to meet local standards.

Another type of questionnaire might be used to survey the parents about their occupations, interests, and hobbies. Some parents may be able to supplement program content. For example, Sue's mother is a cook in a restaurant specializing in Mexican food: She may be able to visit during the study of "Breads from Many Cultures" and assist the four-year-old

---

CHILD'S MEDICAL REPORT

Child's Name _____ Date of Birth _____

Parent's or Guardian's Name _____

Address _____ Phone _____

Immunizations   Date(s)

DPT or DT (diphtheria, tetanus toxoids, and pertussis)   _____

Polio (OPV, oral polio virus)   _____

MMR (measles, mumps, rubella)   _____

HbPV (hemophilus b polysaccharide vaccine)   _____

Other   _____

Immunizations are up-to-date for age of child: Yes _____ No _____

Laboratory and other tests (if indicated):   Yes _____ No _____

History of allergies: _____

_____

I examined this child on (date) _____ I find him or her to be in good physical condition, free of contagious and infectious diseases, and capable of participating in day-care activities, except as noted below: _____

_____

_____

_____   _____
       Date   Physician's Signature

Figure 2.2   Sample of a child's medical report.

EMERGENCY RELEASE

Name _____ Birth Date _____

Address _____ Home Phone _____

Father's Name _____ Business Phone _____

Mother's Name _____ Business Phone _____

Emergency Phone _____

Family Doctor's Name _____

Office Phone _____   Home Phone _____

Known Drug Allergies _____

Parents will assume financial responsibility of services used.

I understand that in case of injury to my child, the Director or Child-Care Center representative will carry out the following procedures:

1. Emergency first aid

2. Phone parents for directions

3. Phone family doctor for directions

4. Call police or ambulance to transport child to nearest hospital emergency room.

In an emergency, I authorize the person in charge of the activity to use his or her discretion regarding the above procedures.

Signed _____ (mother)

Signed _____ (father)

Witness _____ Date _____

Figure 2.3   Sample of an emergency release form.

children in making tortillas. Bill's father is an auto mechanic: He might arrange to spend an hour discussing bicycle maintenance with seven-year-olds. Connie's grandmother is Japanese, and she has just returned from a trip to Japan: She may enjoy sharing information about her trip and showing pictures and souvenirs to the kindergarten children in Connie's class. An example of a parent information form is shown in Figure 2.4.

Probably one of the best ways to gain information concerning a child is by making a home visit. Some programs require this, but most do not. During a visit to a child's home, the adult visitor can learn about the neighborhood, the type of housing, family members, pets, and in-

terests of the child and family. A home visit made before the child first attends the program can serve as an informal introduction of the caregiver or teacher to the child. Both the children and the families usually enjoy this type of visit. Home visits are also helpful at other times during the year. The following procedures may be helpful in making a home visit:

1. Build rapport with family members by showing a friendly interest in their lives.
2. Provide information concerning the child's progress and the program.
3. Discuss any questions or concerns of the parents.
4. Invite parents to visit the program site.

PARENT INFORMATION FORM

Child's Name _____

Parent's Name _____ Phone _____

Would you be willing to volunteer as a room parent in planning a holiday party or other event
for the class?   Yes _____ No _____

Would you be able to attend field trips with the class?   Yes _____ No _____

Would you be interested in attending small group discussions?

    Afternoons?   Yes _____ No _____

    Evenings?   Yes _____ No _____

    Please list topics in which you are most interested:

    _____   _____

    _____   _____

    Please list any hobbies, special interests, or talents either parent has that could be shared with the children:

    _____   _____

    _____   _____

Do you know anyone who might be interested in sharing their talents or professions with the children? (for example:
firefighter, musician, puppeteer, artist, traveler)   Yes _____ No _____

    Name _____ Phone _____

    Name _____ Phone _____

Figure 2.4 Sample of a parent information form.

Although the primary purpose of these visits is not parent education, they can provide a forum for sharing information about a child's development. Generally, programs have policies concerning safety on home visits. It may be advisable for two adults to go together when making home visits in urban areas.

Another useful strategy for gaining valuable information about children and their families is to complete a physical survey of the attendance area of a school or the area a program serves. A drive through the area allows informal assessment of the community resources available to children and their families. Surveys may ask questions such as:

1. Are parks and other recreational facilities within walking distance or easily accessible to children?

2. What types of housing are available and how does that contribute to the availability of age-appropriate playmates?

3. What transportation systems do families use? Is there access to public transportation?

4. What do churches, store signs, and businesses indicate about the cultural or linguistic characteristics of the community?

5. Are public or private community resources, such as libraries, museums, historical sites, community centers, and social service agencies, readily accessible to families?

Teachers and caregivers can use the information obtained from community surveys to better understand children and their families and to plan activities and environments that build on home and community experiences in ways that reflect the cultural backgrounds of the children. In addition, community surveys assist teachers and caregivers in making referrals when needed.

OBSERVATION

Adults should be good observers of young children, no matter what the setting. Through careful observation, they can learn helpful information about the children in their care. Parents gain knowledge about their children's development that can assist them in providing appropriate toys and experiences. Caregivers and teachers can learn about characteristics of individual children and the ways in which they respond in the program environment, which may assist them in planning both individual and group activities that meet the needs of these children.

Adults become better observers by first having a knowledge of the range of development typical of a child's age group. They need to know the kinds of things for which to look. This information may be found in various standardized assessment instruments, such as the *Denver II* (Frankenburg & Dodds, 1990), which is the revision and restandardization of the Denver Development Screening Test (DDST), or the *Brigance® Diagnostic Inventory of Early Development* (Brigance, 1991). Child skills checklists can be found in books concerning child development (Beaty, 1998, pp. 37–43) or can be developed by adults who teach or care for young children.

For example, caregivers or teachers may need to know the types of interaction a child has with other adults or children in a particular setting. When a child's dominant language is different from that of others in a group, the adult can use observation skills in connection with the teaching of the primary language to enhance development in the nondominant

language. If a child has a handicapping condition that is a cause for concern, the adult can use observation to gain information to assist the child. Skill in observation techniques is an acquired ability. Only through practice do observation skills become part of the process of planning experiences.

Role of the Adult

Observation of children takes time. Adults must arrange for it by planning times when children are engaged in activities and the adults can stand back and observe them. Observations can be related to typical development for the age, as in the following example.

---------------- ----------------

Eddie (age thirteen months) still crawls most of the time. He pulls himself up and walks while holding on to furniture and drops to the floor and crawls across open spaces. The caregiver has observed this and is concerned that he is not walking more. However, the caregiver knows that the typical age that a majority (75% to 90%) of children are able to walk well is from fourteen to sixteen months (Frankenburg & Dodds, 1990).

---------------- ----------------

Caregivers who are aware of the typical age for walking are less concerned about a child's walking ability at age thirteen months. Weekly observation of the child's progress toward walking well over the next few months will assist the caregiver in determining if Eddie is improving in his walking ability. If progress is not seen by his sixteenth month, then some form of intervention may be necessary. Encouragement can help the child in developing the ability. However, he must develop the skill on his own.

At certain times, adult observation of interaction between children becomes necessary. Some children choose to interact with others much of the time, and other children prefer to work alone with objects and materials. Research related to interaction in play can assist adults when they make these observations.

Parten (1932) identified six types of social participation, which have been used in the observation of young children's play. Although the ages of the subjects in the social participation study were not well defined, the six types were thought to proceed developmentally and were described as follows:

1. *Unoccupied behavior.* The children are not playing but watch anything of momentary interest.
2. *Onlooker.* The children spend most of the time watching other children play.
3. *Solitary play.* The children play alone and center their interest on their own play.
4. *Parallel play.* The children play independently, but they play with toys that are like those that children around them are using.
5. *Associative play.* The children play in a group that has a common activity, interests, and personal associations. Interactions take place, but there is little cooperation in the play.
6. *Cooperative play.* The children play in a group that is organized for attaining some goal.

For many years, the preceding categories were used in observing children's social interactions. Solitary play was considered the first stage in a social play hierarchy and was thought to be an immature behavior. There was little expectation that older preschool children would benefit from solitary play.

Smilansky (1968) identified four categories, which were based on Piaget's (1951) work. These categories were more closely related to children's cognitive development than those of Parten. They have also been used in the observation of children's interaction in play. The levels in the model were thought to

develop in a relatively fixed sequence, with functional play being the least mature:

1. *Functional play.* The child makes simple repetitive movements, with or without the use of objects.
2. *Constructive play.* The child uses objects to build or create something.
3. *Dramatic play.* The child uses imagination to act out roles.
4. *Games with rules.* The child accepts prearranged rules and adjusts to these rules.

In the Smilansky hierarchy, dramatic play was considered social but the other categories of play were thought to be more object- or materials-oriented.

Sara Smilansky continued her research in play, identifying critical components of sociodramatic play in preschool-aged children (Smilansky & Shefatya, 1990). The critical elements include role-playing; make-believe with actions, objects, and situations; social interaction; verbalization; and persistence. Smilansky advocates that adults use informal play interactions to enhance children's abilities to employ these specific play elements (Smilansky, 1968; Smilansky & Shefatya, 1990).

Rubin (1977) reported two studies that combined the play categories of Parten and Smilansky. For example, Parten's solitary play category was linked with Smilansky's functional, constructive, and dramatic play categories. These then became *solitary-functional,* *solitary-constructive,* and *solitary-dramatic* play categories. Figure 2.6 shows a complete listing with a rating scale. Rubin examined forms of social and cognitive play as well as age differences in play behaviors. Results indicated that solitary play did not disappear with age but became more cognitively mature. In other words, solitary play in young children continues to become more complex and should be considered separately from social play.

Using the combined categories (Coplan & Rubin, 1998; Rubin, 1977), adults can watch to see how children use equipment when playing alone. For example, with unit blocks, children in the solitary-functional stage may line up the blocks or stack them and knock them down. In the solitary-constructive stage, children build something with the blocks. When they have progressed to the solitary-dramatic stage, they begin to use the structure they have built in imaginary play with toy vehicles, animals, or people.

Age, genetic factors, temperament, physiology, and parenting behaviors have been found to influence social play, sociability, and competence (Coplan & Rubin, 1998). In observing children's play and interactive behavior, balance must be sought between social interaction and solitary activities. The adult should determine the level at which the child is functioning in each. Children need interaction with peers to improve their social competence. However, solitary play can assist them in the development of attention, physical skills, pretend play, and problem solving. An example of a child who manages a balance of solitary and social play follows.

Shana (age four years) is playing alone with a dollhouse and props in the corner of the classroom. Two friends ask her to come and join them at the water table. She talks to them for a few minutes and says that she will play with them another time, but then she continues with her solitary-dramatic play with the dollhouse.

The observer should note how much time a child engages in both solitary and social play. The child in this example was able to make a choice between pursuing a solitary play activity and joining the others in a group activity.

An extreme in solitary activity or social interaction, which makes intervention neces-

sary, may result in part from the degree to which children tend to be introverted or extroverted. Children who tend to be introverted are likely to turn their energies inward, and those who are more extroverted look outside of themselves for stimulation in interaction (Eysenck, 1969; Schaefer, 1971). At one end of the continuum is the child who plays alone and rarely or never plays with others. For this child, social interaction skills are difficult and should be encouraged. Another child may rarely play alone and always looks for other children with whom to interact. The social interaction skills of this child will probably be good, but the child may have difficulty in

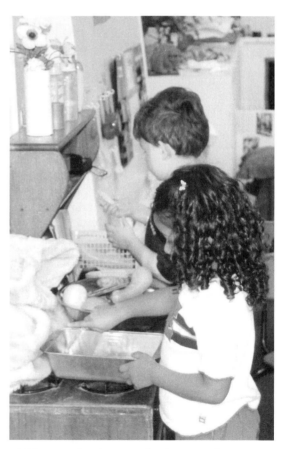

Children use family center for dramatic play.

interaction with objects, task persistence, and development of inner resources. An effort should be made to assist young children in achieving some balance between solitary and peer play in self-selected activities.

Communication is another area in which observation skills may be helpful. Through observation, adults can learn about the language skills and problems of children in their care. A child may have a language delay or another problem demonstrating a deviation from the language considered typical for the child's age. These kinds of problems may reflect neurological, emotional, learning, or interpretive differences (Safford, 1989). One or more children may have a different dialect or dominant language than the one used in the classroom. Observation of children with language differences can assist in understanding the children's needs and feelings knowing whether intervention is necessary and, if so, the best way to proceed. In the following example, the teacher's observation made a difference for a child.

Jerold (age five years) is in a kindergarten classroom. He does not speak clearly and rarely includes the endings of words when he speaks. The teacher has observed him speaking in different situations. She knows that he has a history of colds and allergies. She suspects that he may have a hearing loss, and she refers him for an examination, which shows that Jerold has fluid in his inner ears caused by enlarged tonsils and adenoids. Surgery and ear tubes correct the hearing loss; Speech therapy is used to solve the speech problem.

The teacher's observation of Jerold helped in finding a solution to his problem. Much of the time, handicapping problems cannot be so easily solved. However, observation can provide substantial assistance to the caregiver or

teacher in planning appropriate activities for individual children in the group.

Observations of many different kinds of behaviors can be helpful in planning for individual children and for the program as a whole. There are different ways to make and record observations. The next section gives suggestions that can be used in a variety of settings.

Observation Techniques

Several different methods can be used when observing and recording the behavior of young children. Each method has advantages and disadvantages. The reason for the observation must be determined to know which method is best.

In a *running behavior record,* as much detail as possible is recorded related to both the setting and the behavior of a child (Beaty, 1998; Nicolson & Shipstead, 1998). This kind of observation provides comprehensive information concerning the overall development and the behavior of an individual child in a particular context. It is an open-ended, objective recording that includes as much accuracy as possible. Theoretically, this kind of observation record would be continuous. However, because it is very tiring and time-consuming, it is usually done in one-hour segments. The observations can occur at selected times over a period of days or weeks. This type of observation record provides as complete an account as possible during the selected periods. However, it takes time, skill, and energy to do well. It is not efficient when specific samples of a child's behavior are needed.

Figure 2.5 is an example of the beginning of a running behavior record.

If information is needed concerning specific incidents of behavior, a method called *time sampling* can be useful (Bentzen, 1985; Nicolson & Shipstead, 1998). In this method, a coding sheet is provided for each child observed

Child's name ___Jerry Sample___   Date __4-22-01__   Time __7:00 a.m.__

Jerry's mother brought him into the room. He started to cry as they entered. His mother could not stay. She hugged him and held him out to me. She said, "Goodbye," and left the room. He continued to cry, but I was able to talk with him, remove his coat, and interest him in a truck. I rolled the truck to him, and he rolled it . .

Figure 2.5   Part of a running behavior record.

and the kind of information sought is decided in advance. Types of behavior to be observed are noted, as are the length, spacing, and number of intervals of the observation period; for example, observation of a child's play interactions in a group of children. Using a combination of Parten's and Smilansky's play categories (Rubin, 1977) the coding sheet might look like the one shown in Figure 2.6. Observers record the frequency of play behaviors on various dates to assess a child's preferred mode of play interactions.

When using a coding sheet similar to Figure 2.6, the observer decides which children to observe and the length of time, spacing, and number of intervals to use. One child, several children, or a whole class might be observed using this method. For example, all 15 three-year-olds in a class might be observed. During free-choice playtime, the first is observed for 3 minutes with the observer checking the behavior(s) observed. Then the next child and the next are each observed for 3 minutes until all children in the class have been observed. The next day they are each observed again. In using this method, it is a good idea to rotate the order in which the children are being observed daily, so that the first child is not always observed first. All children should be observed at different times during the free-choice playtime

throughout the observation days. Results of the observation can indicate at what level each child is interacting in both solitary and interactive play.

The advantages of this method are that many different kinds of behaviors can be studied. The information obtained is representative and reliable. However, the method may take too much time if all children are observed, and it provides no details of the context of the play behavior or materials used by individual children. Because of the limited time each child is being observed each day, behaviors could be missed.

Another method can be used that alleviates some of the problems of time sampling; it is called *event sampling* and is similar to time sampling, except the time is not limited. (Beaty, 1998; Bentzen, 1985; Nicolson & Shipstead, 1998). A predetermined event is observed of one or two children, depending on the type of event to be observed. The observer records the entire event when it occurs, including what happens before and after the event. For example, one child has taken a toy away from another child during several recent play periods. The child who has taken the toy is the one who has been reprimanded. However, the teacher is interested in knowing exactly what has been happening, so she stations

PLAY INTERACTION CODING SHEET

Child's Name _____

Play Category   *Frequency of Behavior*

Date							Total
Solitary-functional							
Solitary-constructive							
Solitary-dramatic							
Parallel-functional							
Parallel-constructive							
Parallel-dramatic							
Associative-functional							
Associative-constructive							
Associative-dramatic							
Cooperative-functional							
Cooperative-constructive							
Cooperative-dramatic							
Cooperative-games with rules							

Figure 2.6   Sample play interaction coding sheet.

herself near the area where the two children are playing. Although not appearing to watch them, she listens carefully to their conversation. One child has a frog puppet. He begins to tease the other child by saying, "I have the frog [puppet], and you can't have it." He says this several times. All at once, the other child takes the puppet. The first child starts to cry, waiting for the teacher to come and reprimand the other child. This time, however, because of the observation, the teacher has a better understanding of the situation and will change her reaction, perhaps by asking the children to discuss the incident.

Event sampling has the advantage of yielding detailed descriptions of children's behavior in context and of being less time-consuming than a running behavior record and less limiting than a time sample. However,

the specific behaviors exhibited by a child may occur infrequently enough to make observation of an entire event difficult. An observer may not have the time to wait for another similar event to occur. The same type of form (Figure 2.6) is suitable for event sampling.

A method for regularly recording behavior of children within a group is called the *anecdotal record* (Bentzen, 1985). It can be helpful in better understanding a child's personality or the varied aspects of the child's behavior or development, and can provide information to use in planning activities for an individual child. An anecdotal record is an objective report of a specific event as it occurs, written without interpretation and including the date, time, context, and description of the event.

The records can be written on blank index cards, which can be kept in convenient locations within the setting. They could then be placed in the child's individual folder for use during parent conferences or in making plans for activities.

Figure 2.7 shows an example of an anecdotal record card for a five-year-old child. The event described in Figure 2.7 was important because it described a change in Jason's behavior. He had been uncooperative within the group from the beginning of the school year. However, the teacher had been talking with him to help him understand his behavior. He was finally becoming less aggressive and was beginning to understand the value of friendship. The teacher put the card into his file for future reference.

Another strategy for managing anecdotal records is to keep clipboards of individual adhesive labels in various areas of the center or classroom. Anecdotal notes are recorded on the labels and later transferred to a child's page in a notebook or portfolio, which can be organized by developmental areas and used for assessment and parent conferences. Anecdotal records are especially valuable when they are maintained regularly. Some programs identify two to four children, depending on the number of adults who are available, as focus children of the day. By rotating the schedule, all children can be targeted several times a month.

Records such as these can be kept relatively easily, and they give a running account that helps in understanding children's behavior in particular settings and circumstances. The disadvantage is that they must be **objective,** without interpretation, and are difficult to write. Because they are usually written quickly, they are sometimes not complete enough to give an accurate account of the event.

The last observation method to be described is the *checklist* (Beaty, 1998). A simple-to-use checklist can be developed for any observable behavior. It can help to determine whether or not a child exhibits a specific behavior or ability. Usually, a check is placed by an item if a child exhibits the behavior. The checklist may provide a place to mark the level of attainment, such as "not yet," "working toward," and "doing well," or may have a place to give evidence of the behavior or ability; the date should also be noted. An example of a checklist based on the strands of development discussed in this book is shown in Figure 2.8.

Although checklists are easy to use, they do not provide detailed information—only a rough estimate of a child's ability at a particular time. However, they can be useful along with other methods in giving overall information concerning an individual child. The observer must know what to look for, when and where to look, and what to do with the information (Eddowes, 1974).

Specific information gained through various observation techniques can be useful in planning appropriate activities for an individual child or a group. Skills and abilities should be identified for each child in relation to program objectives. A child's level of progress in each area should be noted. Information concerning areas in which a child needs more

---

February 6, 2001   2:30 p.m.

Jason bumped into Maxie near the art center, causing her to drop her box of crayons on the floor. Instead of moving on, he stopped and helped her pick them up. She thanked him for helping her.

Figure 2.7   Sample of an anecdotal record card.

CHILD INVENTORY

Name _____ Group _____ Birth Date _____

Post the date observed in the appropriate column.

Development Areas	Not yet	Working toward	Doing well
Personal-social			
Trusts others			
Separates from parent			
Has positive self-esteem			
Exhibits autonomy			
Solitary and peer play			
Practices social skills			
Physical			
Gross motor skills			
Walks well			
Catches ball			
Fine motor skills			
Uses pincer grasp			
Controls crayon			
Cognitive			
Is able to attend			
Large group			
Small group			
Individually			
Can solve problems			
Makes choices easily			
Asks open-ended questions			
Completes tasks			
Communication			
Listens in varied contexts			
Speaks often and fluently			
Writes easily			
Reads independently			
Exhibits nonverbal skills			
Creative			
Art activities			
Painting			
Playdough/clay			
Drawing			
Collage			

Figure 2.8 Sample of a child developmental inventory checklist.

Development Areas	Not yet	Working toward	Doing well
Music activities			
Singing			
Rhythm			
Composing			
Is creative in movement			
Engages in dramatic play			
Role playing			
Puppets			
Is creative in writing			

Figure 2.8   *(continued)*

experience should be used to plan specific activities. Some activities may be planned for an individual child, and others may be appropriate for the whole group. For example, if a child is having difficulty with rhythm in the music strand of creative development, an activity could be planned for the individual child or a group creative rhythm activity could be planned that the whole class will enjoy.

✎ GUIDANCE TECHNIQUES

An understanding of young children as individuals and in groups is essential for implementing a curriculum based on reciprocal interactions. In group-based programs, both the shared needs and interests of the group and the unique needs and interests of the individual need to be taken into account in planning and organizing the curriculum. In home-based programs, the individual needs and interests of the child must reflect the larger social context. Three of the strands of Personal-Social Development described in more detail in chapter 6, Self-Control, Social Interactions, and Social Skills, focus on strategies and activities for children from birth through age eight to develop and learn within a social-cultural framework.

Successfully guiding children as they explore activities and their environment requires that teachers and caregivers consider how positive interactions between adults and children,

Teen-age volunteer socializes with young infant.

among children, and between children and objects are fostered. A positive learning environment supports activities and experiences in a physically and socially safe setting. Charney (1992) details plans for creating communities of learners, built on mutual respect, strong interpersonal skills, and a quest for independent and group learning. She outlines a step-by-step process for building group cohesiveness and individual responsibility for learning. Ultimately, the immediate goal is for the child to be a socially responsible, yet autonomous, learner. Charney's (1992) long-term goal is transferring a child's social skills and self-motivation for learning to the greater society.

Charney (1992) encourages teachers and caregivers to help children in developing a sense of ownership by directly involving them in creating classroom rules. The "golden rule," or treating others the way one wishes to be treated, permeates rules for social interactions. Other rules are founded on safety and personal preferences. Charney models positive social interactions and uses real-life classroom dilemmas to teach children to problem solve.

Setting expectations and limits for young children is another guidance technique that encompasses both home and group settings. A child develops a sense of security and trust when parents, caregivers, and teachers establish reasonable and age-appropriate boundaries for behavior. A positive daily routine assists the child in learning what to expect within a time frame. In some children, the unknown increases feelings of anxiety, causing them to withdraw; other children react to uncertainty by continually testing limits and the patience of the adults in their lives. Being firm and consistent goes a long way in establishing an environment that promotes positive interactions.

Parents, caregivers, and teachers often find that individualizing guidance strategies is particularly effective in relation to temperament styles of children. A child's temperament style, a basic pattern of behavior that can be characterized by a person's activity level, irritability

level, and degree of inhibition, is thought to have a strong genetic component. Gentle reminders and developmentally appropriate choices may assist the easy-going child in learning socially acceptable behavior. On the other hand, anticipating potentially difficult transitions and planning for gradual adjustments to new situations may help the slow-to-warm-up infant and child to achieve long-range success. In contrast, the difficult child often needs a combination of clear expectations and emotional support to grow socially.

Guidance strategies can also be tied to language development. The frustration of toddlers may in part be caused by their inability to communicate effectively with adults and other children. Adults can help toddlers learn to express their needs and wants both orally and nonverbally. Preschool and young school-aged children can be encouraged to use language rather than physical actions to mediate social interactions. Modeling and creating opportunities to learn and practice interpersonal communication skills are essential teacher and caregiver behaviors.

A final guidance strategy based on development connects to both physical and cognitive development. Adults who spend time helping children learn to be independent may find that their efforts have a long-term payoff. A young child who has abundant successful interactions with materials and activities learns to be competent and self-confident. For example, most children can readily learn self-help skills related to dressing and feeding. Adult interaction time that has been devoted to personal caregiving activities can be devoted to planning and implementing other learning opportunities. Building a child's sense of independence has a similar payoff in promoting cognitive development. Children become more responsible for their own learning and seek new opportunities without needing to rely on adult assistance.

Implementing a curriculum based on interactions requires guidance techniques built

Preschool teacher helps girls
resolve their conflict.

on personal-social, physical, language, and
cognitive development. Adults can help children learn to interact with them, other children, and materials in positive ways. The next
chapter discusses physical environments that
support an interactive curriculum.

🙵 SUMMARY

Understanding children involves knowledge
of developmental milestones for particular
age groups and recognition of each individual
child's differences. Individual differences in
children, ranging from genetically influenced
traits and abilities to environmentally influenced patterns of behavior, can be identified
and used in planning and implementing early
childhood programs. A useful organizer for
exploring cultural differences is to learn about
a child's and family's membership in various
subcultures: ethnic, linguistic, socioeconomic,
religious, gender-related, age-related, and

exceptionality-related. Background information can be obtained through questionnaires
and interviews during conferences, home visits, and community surveys. Several observation methods may assist adults in gaining information about children's skills and abilities.
Guidance strategies establish children's positive interactions with adults, other children,
and objects. These strategies include setting
expectations and limits, helping children learn
self-control and interpersonal social skills,
building language skills to facilitate interactions, and encouraging independence.

QUESTIONS AND PROJECTS FOR THE READER

1. Reflect on your personal cultural background, by describing your subcultures in
relation to ethnicity, religion, language, socioeconomic class, gender identity, age co-

hort, and exceptionality. Use a pie chart to evaluate the relative influence of each subculture.

2. Conduct a community survey of the attendance area of a center or school. Refer to the questions posed in the background information section of this chapter. What conclusions might you draw as to the cultural context of a community and the availability of resources to its families?

3. This project may be completed in any setting. Choose a young child whom you can observe for 1 hour. Write a detailed running behavior record of the child.

4. Using either the time sampling or event sampling technique, observe children in a child-care center or school.

5. While observing children in a child-care center or school, write five anecdotal record cards.

6. Reread the section of this chapter on guidance techniques. Which strategies do you see demonstrated in centers or classrooms you have observed? Share your findings with a peer. What strategies are most and least frequently observed on a consistent basis?

FOR FURTHER READING

Beaty, J. J. (1998). *Observing development of the young child* (4th ed.). Upper Saddle River, New Jersey: Merrill/Prentice-Hall. This comprehensive book tells how to observe young children, what to look for while doing it, and provides many suggestions for observing and recording behavior in all areas of a child's development.

Charney, R. (1992). *Teaching children to care: Management in the responsive classroom.* Greenfield, MA: Northeast Foundation for Children. This is a highly readable framework for establishing a classroom management system that fosters both independent and community learning. It is based on Charney's own journey as a teacher learning to teach children to care about themselves and their classmates and teachers and, ultimately, about the community at-large. She includes numerous anecdotes to illustrate her philosophy of teaching, built on helping children live by the "golden rule," maintain self-control, and participate in a community of learners.

Gollnick, D. M., & Chinn, P. C. (1998). *Multicultural education in a pluralistic society* (5th edition). Upper Saddle River, New Jersey: Merrill/Prentice Hall. Although this textbook encompasses all levels of education, the issues discussed apply equally to early childhood educators. An understanding of cultural pluralism is relevant to teachers and caregivers in their work with both children and their families. It will help early childhood educators understand the complexity of cultural backgrounds and experiences and their impact on the developing child.

Brazelton, T. B., & Greenspan, S. I. (2000). *The irreducible needs of children: What every child must have to grow, learn, and flourish.* New York: Perseus. Brazelton and Greenspan identify what children really need from their parents and society, including the need for ongoing, nurturing relationships; physical protection, safety, and regulation; stable, supportive communities and cultural continuity; and protection of the future. The authors offer solutions to improve living and learning conditions for children now and in the future.

Chapter Three

Supporting an Interactive Curriculum with Physical Environments

O b j e c t i v e s

After reviewing this chapter, you will be able to

- List and define elements commonly found in supportive environments.
- Identify ways in which the home environment can support interaction.
- Describe a parent interaction program.
- Identify a variety of group-care programs.
- Describe the environment of a school program for the primary grades.
- Discuss similarities and differences between various types of children's environmental settings.
- List equipment that supports varied areas of development.

*A*child's environment includes the conditions surrounding and affecting development and learning. It comprises the external physical setting and any social, cultural and educational conditions that are related to it. The biological and physiological processes occurring within the child can also be considered a part of the environment. The specific situation in which an event occurs is sometimes referred to as the context of the experience. Generally, interactions occurring between the child and the various elements of the child's environment will be reciprocal (Brazelton & Cramer, 1990; Bronfenbrenner, 1979).

Young children are found in many different types of environments. The first setting in which they spend much of their time is usually the home, which is the base from which they move into the wider world of community and school. In the home, they may be cared for by parents, relatives, or **in-home caregivers.** At times, parents may be supported in the home by a parent educator or home visitor who comes periodically to assist them in understanding their child's development. Parents may also gain information concerning child development from parent education seminars available through schools or community programs.

Many young children also spend much of the day outside of the home in group-care environments, which include family child-care homes, **full-day child-care centers,** and part-day programs. Child-care workers provide the care in these settings. Later, around the age of five years, children usually begin to attend kindergarten in a **week-day school program.** They may also participate in a school-age child-care program on the school premises before the regular school program begins each day and/or after it ends. School-age child care may also take place in a full-day child-care center or community agency.

The quality of care can vary in the different settings. Some environments are generally positive and enhance the interactions that occur. In others, some elements do not support positive interactions. This could result in part from high adult-child ratios, little knowledge concerning child development, and/or a lack of program management skills. Both positive and negative interactions can occur in any early childhood setting. However, adults must provide as supportive a context as possible for the interactions that children experience while in their care.

Several areas should be considered when providing a positive environment for young children. Common to all settings are qualities concerning safety and health, comfort and well-being, routines, consistency of care, and a range of available experiences. Each child-care setting or program has unique characteristics concerning space, atmosphere, culture, materials, and equipment. Children with special problems, such as vision, hearing, or motor impairment, may require special arrangements for an environment to appropriately meet their needs. Some children need changes in the arrangement of the space; other children need special kinds of equipment. The location of the child within the classroom during the various activities may be a consideration.

ELEMENTS COMMONLY FOUND IN SUPPORTIVE ENVIRONMENTS

Similar elements are found in all supportive environments for young children; they are the same no matter what the setting and cover various aspects of the physical environment as it relates to the developing child.

Safety and Health

Young children need an abundance of space in which they can explore and experiment safely. Private homes vary in the amount of available space a child can use. However, in group-care programs, a minimum of 35 square feet of usable indoor playroom floor space and a minimum of 75 square feet of out-door play space per child are recommended. More space than the minimum is preferred (especially for infants and toddlers), but the arrangement of the space is an important fac-tor (National Association for the Education of Young Children [NAEYC], 1998). The space both inside and outside should be arranged to facilitate a variety of small group and individ-ual activities. Outside play areas should be fenced and should be checked daily for dan-gerous objects. Children must be supervised at all times both indoors and outside.

As babies become mobile, the adult should be sure that there are no small objects or dan-gerous substances that could be swallowed or other items that could cause accidents. Furni-ture must be sturdy and free from sharp edges, to provide stability for children who are pulling up to a standing position. The furni-ture is used by infants as a support for balance as they begin to walk, a motor skill known as **cruising.** Development should be supported by providing a safe place for exploration that can be supervised without stifling childrens' curiosity (Bredekamp & Copple, 1997).

As young children grow, they continue to need ample, safe space and equipment that al-lows both quiet and vigorous physical play. Gross motor experiences are the base from which fine motor skills are acquired and eye-hand coordination develops (Weiser, 1991). Young children need space both indoors and outdoors to practice new physical skills. This kind of activity, with appropriate adult inter-action, allows children to experience feelings of autonomy and success; an example follows.

--------------------- ---------------------

Interaction: Adult-Child

Setting: Head Start Center

Susan (age thirty-three months) is walking on a railroad tie. She balances as she takes small steps. She calls to a caregiver to watch her. The adult

turns to her and after observing the activity says, "You can balance without falling off." Susan smiles and keeps on walking on the tie.

--------------------- ---------------------

Although many group child-care pro-grams follow the criteria for safety and health described in the accreditation procedures of the NAEYC (1998), caregivers should become familiar with individual state guidelines as well. Each state has rules that may differ from those of the NAEYC.

Space not only must be safe but should support good health practices as well. The overall environment must be clean. Toys that are put into the mouth should be sanitized often with a bleach solution. Other equipment should be maintained in a safe working condi-tion and should be cleaned frequently. Tiled flooring is helpful in areas where water is used. In other areas, carpeting or rugs can pro-vide a soft, comfortable surface for floor play and also help to alleviate noise. All flooring materials should be cleaned regularly. Bath-rooms, sinks, and table surfaces must be sani-tized daily or more often, if necessary (NAEYC, 1998).

Children should be dressed appropriately, depending on the weather and the activities. Immunizations must be current, and adults should be aware of the symptoms of common illnesses. Adults working in the setting should be free of illness; a written policy should de-note limitations on attendance of sick children (NAEYC, 1998).

Nutritious meals and snacks support physical growth. They should meet children's daily nutritional requirements for the amount of time that the children are in the setting. Guidelines are available through state licens-ing manuals and are usually based on rec-ommendations of the U.S. Department of Agriculture.

Adults and children must wash their hands before and after eating, toileting, and after messy activities. Diaper changing areas should be easily sanitized after each change. Interactions within the environment between adults and children should be positive. When the basic needs of nutrition and health are not met, children may become lethargic and unable to participate fully in activities (Children's Defense Fund, 1999).

Adults working with young children need to maintain a safe, healthy environment. They should communicate with positive comments during hand washing and toileting procedures. Mealtimes should be pleasant, with adults sitting with children and conversing while eating. Adults should encourage developmentally appropriate independence in personal habits.

Comfort and Well-Being

All people need to feel a sense of comfort in the various environments where they live and work. When feelings of well-being are absent, the result is usually stress. Young children must have a secure and caring place in which to spend their time, a place with a sense of belonging. Whether at home, in a group-care program, or in school, children should believe that they fit in and can trust the people who are there (Brazelton, 1987; Erikson, 1963; Silin, 2000).

Through caring, positive relationships, the sense of trust continues to develop. The adult provides a secure base from which young mobile infants can explore and satisfy their curiosity. The following example illustrates this.

Interaction: Adult-Child

Setting: Family Child-Care Home

Roshan (age eighteen months) is playing on the floor near the family child caregiver. A large round plastic disk that he is using rolls out into the hall and disappears. He first looks at the adult and then *ventures out to look for the disk. The adult watches him. He finds the toy and returns to his play. The caregiver smiles at him on his return to the play area.*

This child has the confidence that he needs to venture outside the play area to look for the disk. He knows that the caregiver will be supportive and, if he needs help, will be there. The caregiver respects the child's need for independence, and this builds positive self-esteem (Bredekamp & Copple, 1997).

Children of school age continue to need a sense of stability and security in their lives. Even when they come from a secure home, they may have problems in the new school environment (Seefeldt & Barbour, 1998). When teachers in school are interested in the children and provide supportive interactions, the children feel safe in their environment. This feeling of well-being is helpful in the educational process because, when children are in a positive environment, they usually learn more effectively.

If young children do not have a supportive environment, they are likely to develop negative responses. They may exhibit regressive tendencies, such as thumb-sucking or having toileting accidents. If children experience continual feelings of failure in their interactions within any environment, they withdraw from the situation and may become depressed (Eddowes, 1992).

Adults can express respect and affection toward children by smiling, holding them, and speaking with them. Children who are experiencing difficulty should be provided with appropriate comfort and support.

Routines

Everyone needs some measure of regularity and predictability (Erikson, 1977; Montessori, 1912/1964). A chaotic environment leads to

Father reads a book to his infant son.

uncertainty and produces stress. For young children to experience feelings of security, they need predictable daily routines in any environment (Hamner & Turner, 1996).

In the home, it is helpful to have a daily schedule that is flexible, depending on the circumstances. This may mean arising and going to bed at similar times each day, eating meals at regular intervals with other family members, and setting times in the day for napping, playing, and studying. Parts of the schedule can be modified, but generally, a framework supportive of predictability should be present (Honig, 1996). An example of a predictable time sequence in the home is given here.

Interaction: Parent-Child

Setting: Child's Home

Atavia (age six years) is playing with cars on the floor of the living room. The routine established in Atavia's home requires that toys must be put away before dinner if they will not be used again after dinner. It is almost time for dinner. Tonight after dinner, the family will go shopping. Atavia's mother tells him that they will eat dinner in 10 minutes. He knows he must put away his toys and wash his hands before eating. Atavia rolls a car one more time and then puts the toys away. He washes his hands and is ready to eat on time.

This child knows that the toys must be put away because he will not play with them after dinner. He understands the routine that has been established over time in his household. Hand washing is also a part of the daily routine, and he is very familiar with it.

Routines are also important in child-care programs and schools (Seefeldt & Barbour, 1998). Both the adults and children should know the approximate order for the daily activities and the time periods for them. When there is a similar schedule from day to day, children are freed from always wondering what will come next (Gordon & Browne, 1989). They can spend their time on the activity of the moment, knowing that certain things will happen at predictable times. There are days when the sequence of events may change; when this happens, the adult must tell children about the change in advance.

The classroom is organized so that children and adults know where everything belongs. Children should be able to get materials and put them away independently. This promotes self-selection of activities for the children and frees the teacher to work with children individually or in small groups (Gartrell, 1994).

Some children are more dependent on predictable environments than others. The child with a "difficult" temperament (Thomas & Chess, 1980) may be more upset by schedule changes. However, any young child who experiences stress caused by unpredictability in the environment may have problems. Some children may become inattentive and ignore directions; others may become aggressive. De-

scriptive behaviors of aggressiveness include biting, hitting, destroying property, or other actions that give a feeling of control (Seefeldt & Barbour, 1998). Other children may exhibit behavior that is overly dependent. Because they do not understand what is going to take place, they cling to the parent or caregiver, which gives them a sense of security.

Adults can develop predictable daily routines; however, these should be flexible, allowing for changes according to the needs and interests of the children.

Consistency

Along with predictable routines, consistency should be provided in child care, which means that the daily care of and interactions with young children should be similar over time. When adults are observant and try to meet needs as they arise, children develop trust in the adults and the environment. For example, if food is available when needed, diapers are changed in a timely way, and empathy is expressed in ways that elicit reciprocal interaction. There is a positive atmosphere in the environment most of the time (Erikson, 1963).

Parents provide consistency of care when feeding and diapering routines are positive, and children enjoy those experiences. The parent talks to the child during the interaction, and there are positive feelings on both sides. As children grow, parents provide consistency in their expectations for behavior: certain practices in the environment are expected of everyone. Children learn the culture of the home by experiencing the same expectations on a regular basis and, when consequences for actions are consistently applied, they begin to internalize the rules and customs of the environment.

Group programs for children should have staffing patterns that allow for consistent interactions to take place daily. Small group sizes and low staff-child ratios have been found to be strong predictors of positive adult-child interactions. Suggested staff-child ratios within specified group sizes are available from the National Academy of Early Childhood Programs (NAEYC, 1998).

Caregivers in group programs for children must provide for consistency in interactions (Bredekamp & Copple, 1997; Seefeldt & Barbour, 1998). The same caregivers should be assigned to the same children daily; this is particularly true for infants and toddlers. When there is a change of shift, the caregivers' times should overlap so that they can communicate information about the children in their care. Also, procedures should allow for information concerning a child's day to be shared with the parents. This is sometimes done by completing a short form concerning the child's eating, toileting patterns, and other activities during the day. See Figure 3.1 for an example of such a form.

The behavior of the adults in child-care settings and schools must be predictable by the children. Adults who provide an extension of the interactions children have with their parents maintain consistency among the environments of young children. School-age children may be in several different environments during one day. They begin in the home, then go to school, and later may be enrolled in an after-school child-care program. Here is an example of consistency of care within a group program.

Interaction: Adult-Child

Setting: Second-Grade Class

Gisela (age seven years) has just arrived at school on the bus. She has been riding for 30 minutes. As she arrives at the classroom door, the teacher greets her by name. There is a place for Gisela to hang her coat. As she moves into the classroom, she knows that the first activity will be writing in her journal.

After that, there will be a short large-group time directed by the teacher. Gisela moves confidently in beginning her work.

In the preceding example, the teacher shows respect for the children by her consistent behaviors. She knows that children must feel welcome within the classroom environment. Having familiar routines and appropriate expectations for behavior provides consistency in the environment. When adults are inconsistent and erratic in their routines and expectations, they promote poor behavior and disrespect. Children have no way of knowing what they are supposed to be doing.

Caregivers have primary responsibility for an identified group of children and provide consistency between events that take place within that group. When more than one adult must have primary responsibility for the group during the day (because of shift changes), the shifts should be worked by the same adults from day to day (NAEYC, 1998).

Providing a Range of Experiences

Young children need to engage in a variety of meaningful experiences daily (Dewey, 1938). Some of the activities will be solitary, with little or no interaction with adults or children; others will include interactions with one or more people. There should be a balance of active and quiet and indoor and outdoor experiences (Bredekamp & Copple, 1997).

Whether in the home or a group program, the activities must match the developmental needs of the children involved, i.e., equipment and experiences must be appropriate for the specific age groups. Group programs usually have plans and materials for a range of activities to meet varied interests and developmental levels. In the home, parents must anticipate the need to have activities that provide a continual challenge.

Child's Name: _____ Date: _____

Information from Parents

Eating (When did your child last east, and what was eaten?):
_____

Sleeping (Did your child sleep the normal amount last night?):
_____

Toileting (Recent BM? Unusual stool condition?):
_____

Health or general concerns:
_____

Information to Parents

Eating Pattern	Time	Amount Eaten	Foods Eaten
Snack/bottle			
Snack/bottle			
Snack/bottle			
Meal/bottle			
Meal/bottle			

Sleeping	When?	How long?	
AM nap			
PM nap			

Bowel movements

Highlights of the day!

Figure 3.1   Daily communication form for infant/toddler care.

Infants and toddlers should have experiences that help them learn through their senses (i.e., seeing, hearing, touching, tasting, smelling) (Weiser, 1991). Infants who are not yet mobile should be carried and moved from place to place regularly so that they can gain fully from the environment. Children who are mobile need to be able to select activities in which they are interested. Adults should talk with the children throughout the day. Some adult-child interaction is necessary as children learn to use equipment and they may need assistance in mastering the steps necessary to complete some activities.

Preschool children need active experiences that include an abundance of language interaction with both adults and peers. They enjoy dramatic play, blocks, puzzles, creative art activities, cooking, and motor/movement activities. Children of this age can take short field trips that extend and change their environment. Here is an example of oral language interaction.

Dramatic play area encourages imaginative play among young preschool children.

----------------- -----------------

Interaction: Child-Child

Setting: Family Child-Care Home

Ben (age four years) is playing with another child in the backyard of the family child-care home. They have a big cardboard box and are playing house in it. The caregiver is observing their play. Ben says, "I'll drive (a tricycle) over to the tree, and I will call you on my cell phone." He gets out of the box and rides the tricycle to the tree. He holds his hand, pretending to use a phone and calls over to the child in the box, "I'm on my way home right now." The child in the box also pretends to use a phone and answers him by calling out, "Get some milk on your way home."

----------------- -----------------

When given the opportunity to improvise, young children are creative in their role playing. These experiences help them in language and also all other areas of development.

Primary-age children are able to engage in more complex activities than younger children. They are able to extend their reading, writing, and problem-solving skills. However, they still need an active environment with self-selected activities. They interact with both adults and peers. Children of this age can work independently both individually and in small groups to complete projects. They are beginning to take responsibility for their own learning.

Experiences should provide for children with special needs. For example, children with motor problems need special activities planned for them with the assistance of a physical therapist; the caregiver or teacher can help in implementing these activities. Multicultural materials and activities should be included for all age groups. Suggestions for these kinds of materials and activities are found in chapters 6 through 10.

Adults should be sure that the program provides activities in all developmental areas and that children are participating in a variety of appropriate activities. (Chapter 2 contains additional information concerning methods of observation.)

CONTEXTS FOR INTERACTION

Children spend time in many different environments each day. Each environment represents a context for reciprocal interaction. Sometimes the context is the home. It may be a group-care program or school. Activities in the community, such as church, the community center, library, or park, may also provide the context. It is important that the environment support positive interactions between adults and children (Reggio Emilio, 1997).

Home

The home is the first environment for most young children. Parents usually provide the child care in the home. Relatives and paid in-home caregivers may assist. Help could come from a home visitor, parent educator, or visiting nurse who comes into the home periodically and provides parents with information concerning child development and reasonable expectations for the roles they play as primary caregivers. Parents may also attend community-sponsored parent education programs.

A home can also provide a context for young children in family child care, in which a parent provides care on a regular basis for several young children of other families. It is the responsibility of family child-care providers to have a supportive environment for the children in their care.

Parents and Children Even the smallest homes usually have defined spaces for different activities, e.g., places to prepare food, eat, and sleep, and a communal living space for other kinds of activities. There may be space for washing clothes and a yard for outside activities. Children should have a place to put their things and space to be able to get away from the rest of the group if they desire (Eddowes, 1991).

The home reflects the culture of the family through things such as photographs, magazines, furnishings, cooking odors, and clothing. Children have certain places within the home in which to play, read, or study. This could be in a living room, family room, enclosed porch, hall, or bedroom. Toys and other playthings should be kept near the play area. Low shelves are a convenient and inexpensive way to store play materials and equipment. Activities should be available that support all areas of the child's development.

Relatives, such as grandparents or other family members, or paid full-time or part-time in-home caregivers may assist the family in caring for the children. When parents explain their routines and expectations for child care, substitute caregivers are able to maintain consistency in their interactions within the home.

Interactions between adults and children take place in any area of the home where two or more people are present. When the environment is organized, the atmosphere is pleasant, and there is enough space for everyone, interactions are likely to be positive. When there is crowding, positive interactions are more difficult (Heft, 1985).

Home Visitor Program Sometimes parents are supported in their child care by an experienced adult who comes into the home periodically to provide educational information. This may occur in conjunction with a school district, such as the Missouri Parent as Teacher Program (Parents as Teachers National Center & Missouri Department of Elementary and Secondary Education, 1993), or another educational or health program. Some home visitor programs are federally funded. Generally, in these kinds of programs, the supportive adult visits the home regularly, perhaps weekly or monthly. The role of the home visitor is to provide information concerning all areas of the child's development, child care, and appropriate interactions and activities. In planning, the home visitor considers the cultural background of the family.

The home visitor brings materials and ideas for activities to the home and works with one parent or guardian. Activities vary from visit to visit but over time will include all areas of the child's development. The visit usually takes place in one area of the home; a table and chairs with adjacent floor space are desirable. The home visitor plans the time period before arriving at the home.

The interchange begins with an update of family happenings since the last visit. Information is shared concerning activities that the parent has been doing with the target child (or children). Then information is shared that is relevant to the situation and the target child (e.g., teething, toileting, reading to the child). At that time, the target child engages in an activity during the adult discussion (e.g., a puzzle or a game). Informative material is left at the home for the parent. Then the visitor assists the parent in an interactive activity that the parent can do with the child. The parent introduces the activity while the visitor is present and also engages the child in that activity several times before the next home visit. The culture of the family is taken into consideration as the home visitor plans activities.

This type of supportive assistance can give parents the confidence they need to succeed in their parenting activities. Sometimes the children in this type of program also attend a two-hour socialization class bimonthly or monthly with children of the same age in a central location. The parent usually does not attend. The home visitor plans activities that may be done in the group. Sometimes these may be individual or small-group activities, such as blocks and sand play. At other times, these may be large-group activities, such as **listening** to a story, singing, or creative movement.

Family Child-Care Home   The home can become the site of a small business when adults provide care on a regular basis for young children in their home: Many states have licensing requirements for this type of care. Young children of different ages may be cared for at the same time. For example, a family may care for their own four-year-old child, in addition to two toddlers, two three-year-olds, and another four-year-old (Murphy, 1984).

For one person to care for a multiage group of young children can be challenging.

Some family child-care providers prefer that all of the children are of similar ages; however, this may not be realistic. Families may have children with different ages who need care. If there is a flexible policy as vacancies occur, it is easier to replace children who leave.

Children are usually cared for in this type of setting during the major part of the day, from early morning until dinner time. They eat some of their meals in the home and rest there. The caregiver plans activities for the children that cover all areas of child development (Eddowes & Ralph, 1987). Although the whole house may be used for the care, play activities usually take place in one specific space. There may be one room where toys and equipment are kept. However, at times there may be cooking activities in the kitchen. Children may nap in a bedroom. They also assist in setting the table and in cleanup activities. Outside activities usually take place in a fenced play area.

The family child-care environment must be inviting to the children. An advantage of this kind of care is that the environment is similar to the child's own home, which may be helpful to children in making the transition to a full-day child-care environment. Family child-care providers extend the interactions found in the home and provide personalized care. This makes the setting appropriate for infant and toddler care. The family child-care home usually has fewer children per adult caregiver than child-care centers do. In mixed-age groups, interactions between children are similar to those found in a big family (Katz, Evangelou, & Hartman, 1990). Older children can assist younger children in the completion of tasks.

Parent Interaction Program

Parents can be supported by a **parent interaction program,** which is similar to a home visitor program. In this educational program, parents bring their child to a central site for a series of classes. Other parents attend with similar-aged children. At the class, a facilitator has planned activities that a parent (or both parents) engage in with their child. For example, the parents of 12 children, aged sixteen months through twenty-four months, might all bring their children from 3:00 PM to 4:30 PM one afternoon a week for 10 weeks. (Early-evening sessions can be planned when parents work outside of the home during the day.) The total program usually includes seminars for parents, which they attend in the evening without the children. Printed materials concerning problems of child development are distributed at classes and seminars.

Parent interaction programs may be part of a nursery school or child-care program or may be sponsored by the Young Women's Christian Association (YWCA), a church, or family resource center. As a part of a college or university curriculum, these programs may be used to provide a practicum for students who wish to learn to become facilitators. The similarity of the programs is found in the emphasis on assisting parents to understand the importance of high-quality reciprocal interaction. In addition, parents learn about child development. They have the opportunity to observe children who are younger or older than their child and can make friends with parents of children similar in age to their own. Parents can learn how to make toys from free and inexpensive materials (Eddowes, 1993a; Linderman, 1979; Redleaf, 1987). Since the parent works with the child, children with disabilities are easily included in this kind of program.

Typically, the classroom environment has ample space, including learning areas based on different types of development. Figure 3.2 shows a diagram of a classroom for a parent interaction program. Personal-social activities are usually not assigned a separate area of the room; instead, they are part of the parent-child interactions related to trust, attachment, self-esteem, self-control, social interaction,

and social skills. However, there is an area for physical activities (both fine and gross motor). There may be an area for snacks. The cognitive area has activities that extend attention, provide for problem solving, and promote making choices. Parents are encouraged to ask open-ended questions. Children are encouraged to complete tasks. In the area of communication, activities are planned for listening, speaking, reading, writing, and nonverbal interactions. Sensory and art experiences, music, movement, dramatics, and creative writing may be a part of the creative area. Activities are planned for each developmental area, but not all types are covered in one evening. The facilitator selects a balance of activities that seem to meet the developmental levels of the children enrolled. The culture of the families is reflected in the activities. Although interactions focus on those taking place between adult and child, activities may also be planned for interactions between children. When an outside area is available and the weather is good, some activities may be scheduled there.

Group Child-Care Programs

Many kinds of programs provide care and education for young children in groups outside of the home. Sometimes full-day child care is needed for families of working parents. At other times, a part-day program provides activities and social interaction with other children. Children are taken to a central site for this kind of care. Centers usually accommodate a large number of children at one location. The children may be assigned to groups based on age, or they may be in multiage groups (Katz et al., 1990).

Caregivers in group care programs have the responsibility of providing quality interactions for the children in their care. Adult-child ratios must be low enough for this personalized care (NAEYC, 1998). The caregiver extends the interactions taking place in the home.

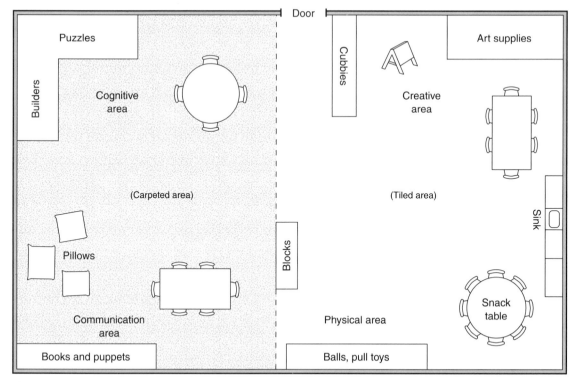

Figure 3.2   Classroom for parent interaction program (10 toddlers, 10 parents, 1 facilitator).

Interactions should follow the strands in each developmental area as outlined in chapters 1 and 5. In the area of personal-social development, adult-child interactions extend trust, assist children with separation problems, promote self-esteem, provide guidance supportive of self-control, provide social interaction, and teach social skills. Activities that support gross and fine motor skills assist children in the area of physical development. Adults can help children learn to focus their attention, solve problems, make choices, ask open-ended questions, and complete tasks, thus enhancing cognitive development. Without adult interaction, communication development would probably not occur. This covers the strands of listening, speaking, writing, reading, and nonverbal skills. Adults must plan experiences that include sensory/art, music, movement, and dramatic activities and creative writing to enhance creative development. The environment in which the children engage in the activities is critical to their total success.

Full-Day Child-Care Centers   Many parents require someone to care for their children while they work. Full-day child-care centers, which provide this kind of care, are usually open from 6:30 AM until 6:00 PM on weekdays. Some centers may be open longer, and some are open 24 hours a day. All of these centers must follow the licensing standards in their state.

Many states require standards for the care of children up to age thirty months (infants and toddlers) that differ from those for children over that age. The differences usually relate in part to the space necessary per child and the maximum number of children per adult. Generally, more space per child and fewer children per adult caregiver are desirable for the care of infants and toddlers. Young mobile children need plenty of room to move around. With fewer children per caregiver, each child is more likely to receive the individualized attention necessary in interactions with adults.

Infants and toddlers usually are separated from older preschool children, both indoors and on the playground. This is meant to prevent possible accidents involving the larger children. Infants and toddlers may also be separated within the group by developmental level. Nonmobile infants may be separated from mobile infants, crawlers separated from walkers. Three- to five-year-old children are usually separated by age in group-care programs; for example, all three-year-olds are placed in the same class. A few centers have begun to have multiage groups of children. In some settings, it is possible to find three- to five-year-olds in the same classroom. Studies have shown that mixed-age groups support both social and cognitive development (Katz et al., 1990). In each of the child-care sections, more than one adult is usually assigned to a group.

In arranging a room environment, a number of things should be considered. How much space is available? The amount of usable space can be increased by the use of a low loft. Activities can take place both on top and below the structure. Where are the windows and doors located? A place should be set aside near the entrance to the classroom where children can keep their personal belongings. If running water is available in the room, where is the sink? Art, sand, and cooking activities should be located near water. Where are the electrical outlets? Specific activities, such as

cooking, music, and science, must be located near an electrical outlet.

To facilitate adult-child, child-child, and child-object interaction, full-day child-care programs usually have interest centers in each classroom (Isbell, 1995; Kritchevsky, Prescott, & Walling, 1977; Sanoff, 1995; Van Hoorn, Nourot, Scales, & Alward, 1993). The personal-social area is represented in the positive interactions between caregiver and child and between child and child related to trust, attachment, self-esteem, self-control, social interaction, and social skills. The developmental areas are covered through large group activities and activities in the different interest centers.

Interest areas should be labeled with words and pictures; for example, the creative area in a toddler room might be labeled "Creative" and also have several pictures showing children engaged in the type of activities that take place in that area. **Objectives** should be developed for each interest center (Sanoff, 1995). What will the children learn from the activities taking place there? For example, the Block Center supports all areas of development (Hirsch, 1996). The list of objectives should be posted in each interest center. This reminds the adults working in the program, as well as parents, what children can learn through their experiences in that interest area. An example of objectives for the block center is shown in Figure 3.3.

Some activities encourage social interaction, and others are more likely to promote individual or parallel play. For example, gross motor, blocks, and dramatic play are usually the active, noisier areas. Some areas, such as those for sand, creative art, writing, and music may have a moderate level of noise. Listening and reading areas are usually quiet. The noise level depends on the specific activities in which the children are engaged in the area. A balance of types of activities is necessary in the classroom.

```
Block Center
This center will assist the children in development of:
        •  Self-esteem              •  Attention
        •  Self-control             •  Problem solving
        •  Social interaction       •  Completion of tasks
        •  Social skills            •  Listening
        •  Gross/fine motor skills  •  Speaking
                    •  Creative expression
```

Figure 3.3   Objectives for the block center.

Equipment and materials should be organized within interest areas so that children and adults can easily find them. Interest area boundaries must be marked, with clear pathways between them throughout the room. This helps children to focus on their play in a specific area and assists children in managing their own behavior (Van Hoorn et al., 1999). Because many young children are in group-care programs for a number of hours each day, they may have too much sensory stimulation and social interaction from the environment. Each classroom should have a place for children to retreat from the stimulation and distraction of the group (NAEYC, 1998; Eddowes, 1993b).

The room should have a pleasing atmosphere. Daylight and artificial light can be used together to produce contrasts in light and shadow. A neutral background using different textures in flooring, walls, and furniture can provide a backdrop for colorful pictures, photos of the children, equipment, and materials (Ceppi & Zini, 1998; Sanoff, 1995). Soft areas, such as a corner with pillows or a cushioned rocking chair, can help to make the room more comfortable and attractive. The environment should reflect a variety of cultures through books, pictures, dolls, and dramatic play props (Moyer, 1995; Vergeront, 1987).

Different types of bulletin boards can provide interest. They should be at the children's eye level. Display bulletin boards are usually created by the teacher and provide support for specific curriculum content. For example, pictures of community workers might be displayed for the children to look at and discuss. Children's bulletin boards display a variety of children's work, such as children's artwork, matted and hung (Gillespie, 2000). This personalizes the environment. Another type is the manipulative bulletin board, which extends the learning in an interest center by providing an activity for children to do there. For example, a child could match colors by putting a color card in an envelope of the same color on the board.

Suggestions for interest areas and equipment in group child care and kindergarten programs are listed here.

Infant Classroom Interest Areas

Physical: Gross motor (mats for crawling, balls)
          Fine motor (objects to reach for and pick up)
Cognitive: Problem solving (interactive toys, hidden objects)

Communication: Reading (board books, pictures, photographs)

Creative: Role play (objects familiar to child, such as cup, comb, stuffed animals)

Toddler Classroom Interest Areas

Physical: Gross motor (large lightweight blocks, small riding toys)
Fine motor (medium plastic builders, fill-and spill-containers, large beads)

Cognitive: Problem solving (simple puzzles, plastic builders, unit blocks)
Making choices (selecting activities from several choices)

Communication: Reading (board books, puppets)

Creative: Sensory/art (crayons and large paper)
Music (simple rhythm instruments)
Dramatic play (simple dress-ups, toy telephone, toy vehicles)

Preschool/Kindergarten Classroom Interest Centers

Physical: Indoor gross motor area (bean bag toss, riding toys, small climber) Note: Sometimes there is not enough space in the classroom for this center, but a multi-purpose area may be available indoors for this purpose.
Manipulative Center (small builders, beads, lacing frames)

Cognitive: Math Center (math card games, counters, puzzles, measuring equipment)
Science Center (plants, animals, rocks, shells, magnifying glasses, magnets, prism, tuning fork)
Cooking Center (kitchen utensils, pans, toaster oven, electric skillet, popcorn popper)
Block Center (unit blocks, hollow blocks, toy vehicles, miniature people)

Communication: Listening Center (audio-tapes and books)
Speaking Center (puppets, flannel board)

Library Center (books, magazines)
Writing Center (pencils, markers, paper, pictures)

Creative: Dream Center for solitary activity (books, magazines, mirror, small builders, crayons and paper, pictures)
Sand and Water Center (sand table, water table)
Creative Art Center (easel and paints, crayons, markers, variety of paper, scissors, glue, play dough, rolling pins)
Music Center (tapes of music, rhythm instruments, bells, pictures of authentic musical instruments)
Dramatic Play Center (play household equipment, dolls, dress-up, props to play career roles)
Woodworking Center (sturdy table, tools, scraps of wood and styrofoam, nails, screws) Note: This center may be found in the outdoor play area.

Figures 3.4 through 3.6 are diagrams of infant, toddler, and preschool indoor environments for both full-day child-care and part-day child-care programs. The lists of interest centers in the text present possibilities for additional equipment that is not shown on the figures.

Part-Day Programs A number of part-day child development programs generally are available for nonworking parents. Parents who work part-time or share jobs can also use this type of care. Some preschool or nursery school programs are located in churches, libraries, or community centers. Children may attend for several hours per day, or they can be enrolled for 1, 2, or 3 half-days per week. These centers may require state licensing. Space requirements and adult-child ratios are usually included when individual states require licensing for part-day programs.

Another type of program available in some states is the parent-participation or parent-cooperative preschool. Most of these centers

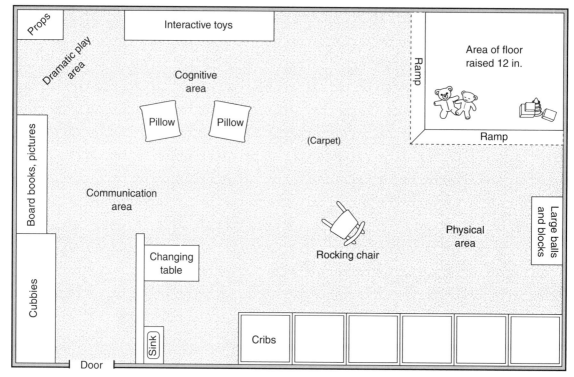

Figure 3.4 Classroom for infant child care (6 children, 2 adults).

are found in Arizona, California, Indiana, Maryland, Michigan, Ohio, Oregon, and Virginia. They are also prevalent in Canada and New Zealand (Parent Cooperative Preschools International, 2000). This kind of program provides education for the parents and supports positive interactions between adult and child. One parent is required to attend the program with the child at regular intervals. For example, in a weekly program of 5 half-days, one parent is required to attend at least 1 day each week.

Through this kind of parent participation program, parents have an opportunity to observe young children engaged in appropriate activities. They interact with their own child and others, thereby increasing their teaching skills. They can attend seminars and other programs to learn more about child development and early childhood education. A paid

director manages the educational program, but a parent board usually manages the entire center. In this way, parents learn about operating a small business.

Other types of part-day programs include the federally funded **Parent-Child Centers** for low-income parents of infants and toddlers, and the national **Head Start** program, also serving preschool children from low-income families. These are both comprehensive programs that include health, social, and educational services. Parents are required to participate in the Parent-Child Center programs. As a part of the program, they can attend high school and general equivalency diploma (GED) courses, but they also participate in the classrooms with the children and take parenting classes. The Head Start program also requires parent participation. Parents volunteer

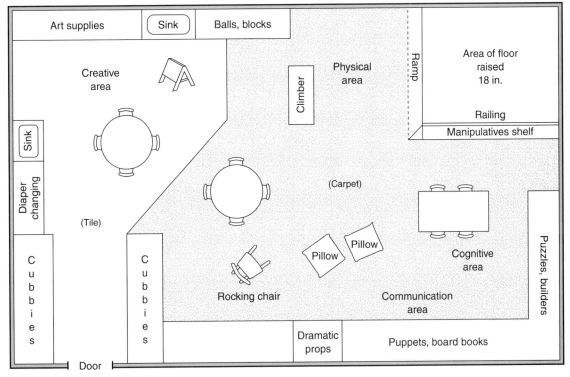

Figure 3.5   Toddler child-care room (8 children, 2 adults).

to help in classes, but they also help in other ways at the center. They may do repair work, make toys and equipment, or assist with field trips and other special activities.

The classroom environments and equipment for these part-day programs are much the same as for the full-day child-care centers. Figures 3.4 through 3.6 show how classrooms may be arranged. Interest areas and centers with equipment are the same as listed in the full-day child-care centers discussion, according to the ages of the children served.

School Programs

Schools traditionally provide a weekday program of education for the children enrolled. Because both parents work in an increasing number of families, some schools have added

before-school or after-school child-care programs. This service assists parents in providing a safe, stimulating place for children to stay when the regular school program is not in session. The program differs somewhat from the weekday program, although it may take place in the same location. The content of the weekday school program is primarily educational. The less structured school-age child-care program is less academically demanding and usually emphasizes recreational, creative, and play activities.

Children usually start kindergarten at the beginning of the school year that follows their fifth birthday. It may be either a half-day or full-day program, depending on the school district. The kindergarten classroom is usually in a building that also houses primary and upper elementary classes. Some children enter

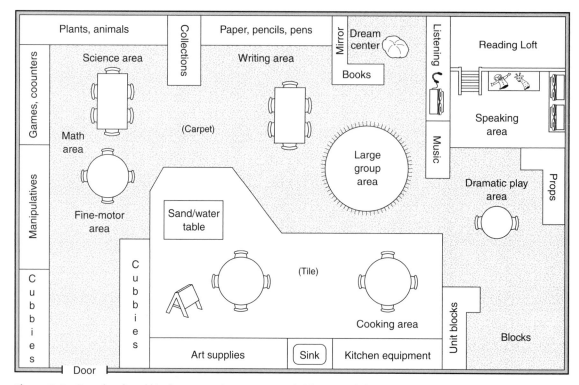

Figure 3.6 Preschool and kindergarten classroom (16 children, 2 adults).

kindergarten with little or no group-care experience. Others may have been attending a full-day child-care program in another location for up to 5 years.

In weekday public school programs, the state generally requires a basic curriculum that covers the subjects of language, math, science, social studies, art, music, physical education, and health (Alabama State Department of Education, no date). The teacher plans activities to further these curriculum goals. Although reciprocal teacher-child interaction is not usually mandated, wise teachers realize that their efforts in this regard enhance the overall development of the children.

As in group child-care programs, interactions in school programs should follow the strands in each developmental area, as outlined in chapters 1 and 5. In the area of per-

sonal-social development, teacher-child interactions extend trust, assist children in becoming independent learners, promote self-esteem, help children develop autonomy and self-control, and provide for social interaction with varied age groups. The social studies area helps further social skills and provides information about other cultures. The physical education program supports gross motor skills. Activities within the classroom enhance those in the fine motor area. The teacher should assist children in learning to focus their attention (Chapter 8). Teacher-child interactions in the math, science, social studies, and health areas facilitate problem solving, making choices, asking open-ended questions, and opportunities to complete tasks. Communication includes teacher-child interactions in the strands of listening, speaking, writing, reading, and nonverbal communication. Last, the curriculum areas of art and music provide some creative activities. Movement, dramatics, and creative writing activities promote creative development. The setting of the interactions and activities can make a great difference in the success of any individual child's ability to learn.

Weekday School Programs On weekdays, the school program provides a place for children to learn skills to function in the society as an adult. Teacher-child ratios may be governed by the state or local school district. The amount of space per child is usually not considered as important as it is for younger children. Sometimes there are two adults in a classroom, but in most places the teacher is the only adult. Resource teachers may assist with physical education, music, and/or art. Resource teachers may also be available for teaching English as a second language or working with children having other special learning needs.

Children are usually found in age-related grades, such as kindergarten for five- and six-year-olds, first grade for six- and seven-year-olds, and second grade for seven- and eight-year-olds. The age placement usually depends on the date of the child's birthday. In this system, a child who has just turned age five may be in the same classroom with a child who will soon turn age six. In other words, children in the same classroom could be almost an entire year apart in age. They will usually have quite different abilities, based on their past experience and developmental levels. In addition, with the advent of **inclusion** (including all similar-aged children with handicapping conditions in the regular classrooms), individualizing the program for each child becomes critically important

In some programs, the importance of an individualized program has been recognized, and the teachers are implementing it. Some schools provide classrooms with mixed-age groupings. In this system, children of varied ages are placed in the same classroom (e.g., kindergarten, first, and second grades together). This kind of program demands individualization and encourages the use of peer tutoring and cooperative learning (Katz et al., 1990).

Whether there is a multiage grouping or not, teachers must plan a range of activities that meet the developmental needs of each child. To provide interactions to enhance each child's success, teachers must be free to work with them on an individual basis throughout the day. The physical environment of the classroom is an important aspect supportive of total development and learning.

Adult-child and child-child interaction is best facilitated by using learning centers as an integral part of the kindergarten and primary education program. As in group care programs, the personal-social area is represented in the interactions between teacher and child related to trust, independence, self-esteem, self-control, social interaction, and social skills. The curriculum areas are covered through the learning centers. There should be a balance in the learning centers, similar to that found in group-care programs, that allows both active and quiet activities and places for individual children to retreat from group stimulation.

Centers for kindergarten classrooms are much the same as those for a preschool classroom. They are described in the section about group-care programs (Figure 3.6). Of course, activities within the center change with the age group. A few suggestions for learning centers and equipment (Moyer, 1995) for a primary classroom follow. Figure 3.7 shows a diagram of a primary classroom; equipment not shown on the diagram is listed here.

Primary Classroom Learning Centers

Physical: Manipulative Center (small
    builders, pick-up-sticks game, weaving)

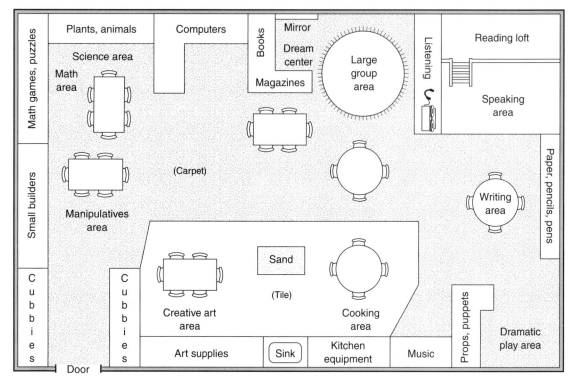

Figure 3.7 Primary classroom (25 children, 1 adult).

Cognitive: Math Center (math card games, board games, counters, abacus, puzzles, measuring equipment)
  Science Center (plants, animals, **collections,** simple experiments)
  Computer Center (math, science, and health programs)
Communication: Listening Center (audiotapes and books)
  Speaking Center (puppets, stage, flannel board)
  Library Center (reading books, reference books, magazines)
  Writing Center (pencils, markers, paper, pictures)
  Computer Center (writing and drawing program)

Creative: Dream Center (books, magazines, mirror, small builders, crayons and paper, pictures)
  Sand Center (sand table and props)
  Creative Art Center (paints, crayons, markers, chalk, variety of paper, scissors, glue, old magazines, clay)
  Music Center (tapes of music, real instruments)
  Dramatic Play Center (props from different cultures)

School-Aged Child-Care Parents of school-aged children quickly find out that the school day does not last as long as their working day. They have a dilemma as to how to manage the care of their children before and after the

Table arrangement facilitates collaborative learning in a second grade classroom.

weekday school hours. In many schools, this problem has been recognized, and programs are now being provided to care for the children before and after regular school hours.

Although the programs take place on the same site, they are usually managed quite differently. The children in the school-aged child-care program may be able to eat their breakfast at school. After that, there should be a place where children can read, finish any homework, or talk quietly with their friends until the time they can move into their classrooms. Adults should be available to interact with them in conversation or assist with questions concerning homework. Sometimes, children can work on a group project during that time. For example, at one school, volunteer participants made an enormous dinosaur out of chicken wire and papier-mâché in the foyer of the school; it took a while to complete but was the talk of the community.

Usually, school-aged child-care programs provide more time for a free choice of activi-

ties than is provided during the school day. In some programs, a snack is served right after school. This could include a cooking activity in which the children assist in preparing the snack. Next, a choice of activities can include sports, creative art, group projects, games, and time to complete any homework. An adult or high-school student may be in charge of each activity. It is the responsibility of those supervising to ensure a positive environment. Children in this situation must be comfortable in the setting where they are required to stay.

Some school-age childcare takes place in a regular classroom. At other times, it may occur in a multipurpose room in the school. See Figure 3.8 for a school multipurpose room used for school-age childcare.

Outdoor Play Spaces

Children have less access to outdoor play spaces than they have had in the past. Yards are smaller, neighborhoods are more crowded,

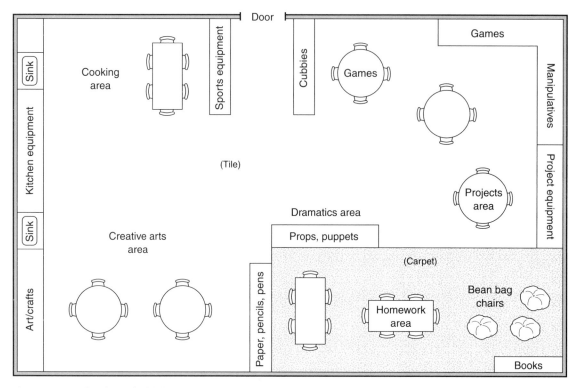

Figure 3.8   School-aged child-care program

and space for outdoor play is disappearing. However, group child-care and school programs can provide children with the necessary outdoor play space. Playgrounds in those settings can be interesting places for children to actively learn about the outdoor world. The spaces provide a place for interaction between people, equipment, and nature (Rivkin, 1995).

In some sections of the United States, the outside area may be used almost daily year-round, for play activities. Because of weather conditions in other geographic locations, the outside area is used less often. When there is abundant sunshine, outdoor play spaces should have shaded areas. Where wet weather is more likely and drainage is a problem, hard-surface areas should be considered.

Outdoor play areas are necessary for all young children, from infant through school age. If weather limits outdoor play, a multi-purpose room or other place indoors, in which activities similar to those experienced outdoors can take place, should be provided. When possible, it is helpful to have a covered, cemented area that provides a place for indoor and outdoor activities when the weather permits. Typical indoor activities, such as puzzles, games, blocks, books, writing, or painting, may then be done outdoors.

Although the gross motor strand in physical development is usually thought of first in connection with playing outdoors, strands in the other areas of development can be strongly supported as well. Social interaction in the personal-social area is enhanced by outdoor activity, as are the strands of speaking and listening in communication development. In the area of cognitive development, play interactions promote problem solving and making choices. Through involvement with sand, water, woodworking, and dramatic play, creative development is enhanced. When activities that are usually thought of as indoor activities are moved outside, all strands in each area of development are supported in the outdoor environment.

In designing an outdoor play space, several elements should be considered. If possible, the space should have different levels, with a low hill, and some structures of different heights. Different surfaces, such as grass, concrete or hard synthetic, organic mulch, sand, gravel, and artificial turf, accommodate different play needs. Water is necessary for drinking and as a play element for gardening, wading, mixing with sand, and other types of play.

Play structures, such as climbing frames, swings, tunnels, and balance beams, provide challenges. Young children must learn to choose the experiences with which they are comfortable. Some children take more risks than others on outdoor play equipment. However, when given the opportunity to try things in their own time, children usually take appropriate risks (Jambor, 1986). The role of the adult is to provide a safe environment. The U.S. Consumer Product Safety Commission handbook (1991) lists playground safety guidelines.

Also important are open spaces for games, game courts (e.g., hopscotch, ball), bike paths, and garden areas. Strategically located tables and seats and an outside storage space for equipment are necessary (Mason,

Playground equipment encourages interaction in a variety of developmental areas.

1982; Vergeront, 1988). Noise levels in the different playground areas should be considered when planning where to place the different activities. Quieter activities should be closer to the building and the noisier play farther away (Van Hoorn et al., 1999). Figure 3.9 shows a diagram of an outside play space.

Outdoor space should be differentiated according to the age of the user. Infants and toddlers should have an outdoor space that is separate from older children (Winter, 1995). Younger infants who are not mobile must be carried around outside so that they can see

what is going on. Mobile infants and toddlers can use low climbers and swings (with appropriate cushioning); low, wide slides; and cubes and tunnels to crawl through. Older toddlers can use sand and enjoy water play (Steele & Nauman, 1985; Winter, 1985, 1995).

Preschool-age children should be provided with spaces for running, equipment for climbing and jumping, wheel toys, and a playhouse. Construction using large hollow blocks with wooden planks is very popular with this age group, as are tricycle riding on pathways and activities that include pushing and

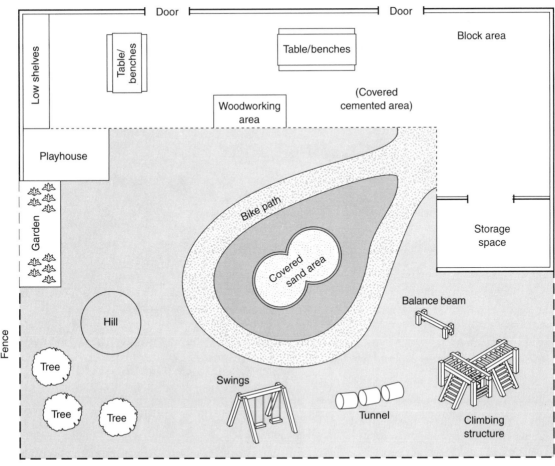

Figure 3.9   Outdoor play space for preschool/kindergarten children.

pulling, throwing, and catching (Seefeldt & Barbour, 1998). When possible, learning centers can be moved outdoors for sand and water play, easels for painting, small vehicles, and other dramatic props (Davidson, 1996).

While child-care programs usually have play spaces outdoors with an array of equipment, elementary school playgrounds can be austere. This may be a result of the potential for vandalism (Kritchevsky et al., 1977). However, if possible, a variety of outdoor activities should be available in elementary schools, both during regular weekday school hours and for school-aged child-care programs. There should be time and space for the children to organize and play games of their own choosing (Jarrett & Young, 1999). The playground should be designed to offer multilevel challenges to meet a variety of needs (Jambor, 1994; Rivkin, 1995), perhaps including a climbing area, swings, playhouse, and ball field. If possible, gardening, a particularly interesting activity for **kindergarten-age** and **primary-age** children, should be included. It is very satisfying to plant seeds, care for the garden, harvest the produce, and then prepare it to eat.

In conclusion, several further considerations must be made when planning an outdoor play space. One of the most important is maintenance. Grass must be mowed and weeds removed. Trees and plants should be tended, with branches trimmed. Play equipment must be consistently checked at frequent intervals for broken or damaged parts. Safety goes hand in hand with maintenance. The area should be fenced, and portable equipment stored at night. Use of the play area should be scheduled so that there is no overcrowding. Adult supervision should be continuous whenever children are present (Hudson & Thompson, 1999; Mason, 1982).

Surfaces where children could fall should be soft materials, such as sand or wood chips. The outdoor play area should be checked for poisonous plants. Depending on the location, snakes and poisonous insects may also pose a safety hazard. The U.S. Cooperative Extension Service can provide information and advice concerning potential hazards. With some foresight, outdoor play spaces can be safe and interesting extensions of the indoor environment (Rivkin, 1995).

❧ SUMMARY

Children have a close relationship with their environmental context. Several elements are common to all environments that are supportive of positive reciprocal interaction: They promote safety and health, comfort and well-being, and provide routines, consistency, and a range of experiences.

Children spend their waking hours in a number of contexts. The home is the first environment for most young children. In the home, parents, relatives, and paid in-home caregivers may play an interactive role. Home visitors may also assist the family. Homes can become supportive environments for other young children when they are used for family child-care programs. Parent interaction programs can also support parenting skills.

Group care can be full-day or part-day. A variety of types of programs are available, as are arrangements of the environment, activities, and equipment supportive of quality interaction.

Schools may have school-aged child care in addition to the weekday program. Floor plans for those environments and suggestions for activities in the various curriculum areas are provided.

The outdoor environment is supportive of development and learning. Information concerning considerations in planning for outside play spaces is included. When environments provide positive support for families and young children, the children thrive both developmentally and educationally.

QUESTIONS AND PROJECTS FOR THE READER

1. List the different environmental contexts in which young children are found, and discuss similarities and differences.
2. Select either a full-day child-care center or a weekday school program. Plan one interest area or center within that setting. Note the age of the children who will be using it. Draw the floor plan for the interest area or center, and list all equipment needed for that one area.
3. Design a floor plan for a classroom in an early childhood setting. Note the age or grade level of the children, whether they are all one age or a multiage group.
4. List the outdoor activities that children in kindergarten through third grade enjoy. Then draw a diagram of a playground for an elementary school setting in which children can engage in the activities that you have listed. State a rationale for each play component you include.
5. Describe potential environmental problems that should be addressed if a child in a wheelchair is to be included in a kindergarten group.

FOR FURTHER READING

Guddemi, M., Jambor, T., & Skrupskelis, A. (Eds). (1999). *Play in a changing society.* Little Rock, AR: Southern Early Childhood Association. This book gives information concerning environments both indoors and outdoors that support play activities.

Hirsch, E. S. (Ed.). (1996). *The block book* (3rd ed). Washington, DC: National Association for the Education of Young Children. This book contains information concerning all aspects of the use of blocks in the early childhood curriculum. It has activities for both preschool and elementary school classrooms.

Isbell, R. (1995). *The complete learning center book.* Beltsville, MD: Gryphon House. This recent publication has many ideas for planning learning centers. It has information concerning the traditional centers and new ideas for unique centers, including the kinds of equipment necessary for each center area and ideas for activities.

Moyer, J. (Ed.). (1995). *Selecting educational equipment and materials: For school and home.* Wheaton, MD: Association for Childhood Education International. This book assists the reader in creating the learning environment. It includes suggestions and equipment lists for those working with groups of infants/toddlers, preschool children, kindergartners, early elementary, later elementary, and middle-school students.

Murphy, K. (1984). *A house full of kids: Running a successful day care business in your home.* Boston: Beacon Press. This book provides a comprehensive description of family child care. It covers such areas as business matters, curriculum, child behaviors, equipment, and information for parents.

Rivkin, M. S. (1995). *The great outdoors: Restoring children's right to play outside.* Washington, DC: National Association for the Education of Young Children. Children have a right to play safely outdoors. This book covers many aspects of outside play including the design of playgrounds, activities, safety, and links with the community.

Sanoff, H. (1995). *Creating environments for young children.* Raleigh, NC: North Carolina State University. (This publication may be purchased from the author at the School of Design, North Carolina State University, Raleigh, NC 27695-7701.) This publication contains information concerning all aspects of the learning environment in an early childhood program. The workbook format assists the reader in planning the inside classroom environment, including a variety of learning centers. The book also includes information concerning the design of spaces for outdoor play.

Chapter Four

Planning for an Interactive Curriculum

O b j e c t i v e s

After reviewing this chapter, you will be able to

- Discuss considerations in planning a curriculum.
- Develop a lesson plan.
- Design a daily schedule for a specific program.
- Discuss ways of integrating the curriculum.
- Compare methods of formative and summative evaluation.

*W*hether a parent in the home setting, a child caregiver in a group program, or a primary teacher in a school, each adult needs to plan the routines, experiences, and activities in which children will participate. Parents will have less formal plans than adults working with children in group programs. However, no matter what the environment, planning provides a framework in which development and learning occur. The act of planning helps to organize thinking and to determine the sequence of the events that will take place.

Plans become the basis for the implementation and evaluation of single short-term experiences and of activities taking place during a day, a week, or a year. Although plans provide a course of action to follow, they should be flexible and easily changed if necessary. When used wisely, plans can assist adults both in enhancing children's development and in meeting educational goals.

The adults' philosophy concerning how children learn is important in planning. Some adults believe that particular information should be taught and transmitted to the child or children. If so, then the adults decide what the children will learn and determine the skills and concepts necessary to accomplish the task. Using this method, the adults plan for direct instruction, with specific content becoming the basis for the learning. This method is frequently used when teaching children with special needs.

In contrast, others may think that children learn much on their own. They are always learning, whether or not specific lessons have been planned. The underlying philosophy is that learning is continuous and cumulative. Each person constructs understanding in interacting with the environment. Using this method, the adults identify goals and plan the learning environment to enable considerable opportunities for child initiation and exploration. The specific content is not as important as the ability to know how to find information and use it.

Some adults use a combination of direct teaching and child initiation methods. A part of the content may be presented in a direct teaching mode, but time is also scheduled for children to experiment with materials and equipment. When using this method, the adults may have certain topics to address but are flexible in allowing children's interests to be voiced.

In using each of the methods, the adult must interact with individual children. As discussed in chapter 1, a number of strands in the various areas of development require reciprocal adult-child interaction for optimum growth and learning to occur. The adults are able to provide emotional support, assist with skills, expand cognitive functions, model language, and encourage the creative process.

Planning includes evaluating what children know and/or can do, designing activities that will promote their learning and development, implementing the plans, and assessing what has been learned from the experience. This circular process has been called the PIE Cycle (Figure 4.1), so named for the terms planning, implementation, and **evaluation.** Each term, or "slice" of the pie, is a part of the process, following the previous part in a circle that enables continuous success (Arizona Center for Educational Research and Development, 1973).

Before any planning begins, something must be known about the children for whom the planning is being done. A general knowledge of child development is necessary, as is information concerning the curriculum design and type of environment in which the plan will be used. The background of the children plays an important part in planning. This could include where they live, information concerning the family, ethnic and cultural considerations, and handicapping conditions. This information concerning each child must be incorporated when developing plans for a group of children.

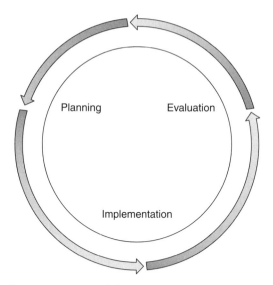

Figure 4.1 PIE model.
Note. Adapted from *P.I.E. Cycle,* Arizona Center for Educational Research and Development, 1973, Tucson: University of Arizona. Copyright 1973 by the University of Arizona.

Activities should be designed that are developmentally appropriate for children in the program. Bredekamp and Copple (1997) provide descriptions of three kinds of information or knowledge necessary in making planning decisions:

1. What is known about child development and learning, knowledge of age-related human characteristics that permits general predictions within an age range about what activities, materials, interactions or experiences will be safe, healthy, interesting, achievable, and also challenging to children;

2. What is known about the strengths, interests, and needs of each individual child in the group to be able to adapt for and be responsive to inevitable individual variation; and

3. Knowledge of the social and cultural contexts in which children live to ensure that learning experiences are meaningful, relevant, and respectful for the participating children and their families (Bredekamp & Copple, 1997, p. 9).

In addition to the child's developmental level, personal characteristics, and cultural background, knowledge of the setting is also essential. Is the setting the child's own home, a parent participation program, group-care facility, or a school? Characteristics of the setting are related to planning. How much space is available indoors and outside? What are the ages of the children? How many are there? How many adults will participate? Knowledge concerning the kinds of equipment and available materials is also necessary in planning.

In any setting with children, adults can learn more about them through observation of individual children and their interactions with people and objects. This information is necessary to plan activities that match the interests and abilities of each child (Hunt, 1961). Knowledge of the children, the setting, and curriculum considerations are all necessary to plan, implement, and evaluate an appropriate program for young children.

❧ UNDERSTANDING CHILDREN

Although young children of similar age can have many of the same characteristics, each is unique. To work effectively with them, an overall knowledge of typical expectations for the different areas of development (i.e., personal-social, physical, cognitive, communication, creative) is needed. For optimum understanding, as much information as possible should be discovered concerning each child's personal traits and family background. As outlined in chapter 2, this can be done through various means, such as questionnaires, interviews, and home visits. In addition, different methods of observation can give firsthand information concerning a child's behavior in specific settings.

✒ CURRICULUM CONTENT

The content of a curriculum in early childhood is related to the age of the children, the philosophy of how children learn, cultural considerations, and any requirements that a government agency may impose. To be successful, a program must have a connection between child development theory and curriculum content (Bredekamp & Rosegrant, 1992, 1995). The content must be age-appropriate and must match the child's developing abilities (Bredekamp & Copple, 1997).

The age of the children must be known because abilities develop through a combination of maturation and experience. Infants are not capable of doing the same kinds of things that three-year-old children can do. Three-year-olds are not as capable as six-year-olds. Therefore, although the area of development may have the same name, the activities will be different. For example, in the area of creative development that addresses sensory/art experience, an infant could enjoy splashing the water in a bath, a three-year-old could pour water from one container to another, and a six-year-old could create a different color of water in each of several containers with food coloring.

The philosophy of how children learn affects curriculum content. If curriculum content is thought to be transmitted to the children by the adult, then the adult decides what will be taught. However, if curriculum is thought of as a process for learning, then the program will place less emphasis on specific content and more on helping children to learn where and how to find information and then how to use it. The content-versus-process curriculum debate has gone on for years and will undoubtedly continue into the future. Since children need information to use in thinking, solving problems, and writing, a combination of content and process has been recognized as the most effective curriculum strategy for young children (Bredekamp & Rosegrant, 1992, 1995).

The cultural differences in race, ethnicity, gender, family background, and religion of young children can become an integral part of the curriculum content. Books, props, pictures, and other materials in a classroom setting should reflect not only the prevailing cultures of the children but other cultures as well. Materials about people with disabilities should also be included and integrated into the curriculum (Sapon-Shevin, 1992).

Table 4.1   Relationship of development to curriculum subjects and the multiple intelligences.

Area of Development	Subject	Multiple Intelligence
Personal-Social	Social Studies	Interpersonal Intrapersonal
Physical	Physical Education Health	Bodily-kinesthetic
Cognitive	Science Math	Logical-mathematical Spatial (also creative) Naturalistic
Communication	Language Arts	Linguistic
Creative	Art Music	Spatial (also cognitive) Musical

In looking at the range of ages between birth and eight years, the different areas of development (i.e., personal-social, physical, cognitive, communication, creative) can provide a framework with which to determine curriculum content. These areas of development can be broadened to include the more specific subject areas that are sometimes found in state curriculum guides (e.g., language arts, math, science, social studies, art, music, physical education, health) (Bredekamp & Rosegrant, 1995). The developmental framework can also be extended to fit Gardner's (1983, 1993) eight intelligences (i.e., linguistic, musical, logical-mathematical, spatial, bodily-kinesthetic, interpersonal, intrapersonal, naturalist) in a curriculum model (Armstrong, 1994; Chen, Krechusky & Viens with Isberg, 1998). The areas of development as related to subjects and the multiple intelligences are found in Table 4.1.

Depending on the age of the child or the group of children, strategies can be used to

First-grade teacher assists emergent reader during guided reading group time.

plan, implement, and evaluate both the content and the processes used in developing the curriculum. The first thing to consider is the planning necessary to implement the interactive curriculum.

✎ PLANNING

Planning is used for the purpose of ensuring that overall program aims are accomplished. Plans are completed in advance of their use and are usually written. They are based on type of setting, knowledge of child development, curriculum considerations, age of the children, and information concerning individual children's characteristics and abilities. Plans in a home, child-care, or school program can give direction when designing specific activities. They provide a framework that assists those working with young children in meeting family or program goals. Individual caregivers or teachers can make plans. They can also be made in collaboration with other adults in the program.

Considerations in Planning

Different levels of planning can be achieved. At the highest level is a somewhat general plan that indicates overall **purposes** of a program. This plan might include the areas of development or the particular subjects that the curriculum must include.

A middle-level plan lists broad program **goals** that are related to the age and nature of the children. Goals also reflect cultural and community values. These program goals are broadly stated and reflect purposes that include statements related to the different areas of development or subject matter included in the program. Behaviors described in these kinds of goals are not easily measured. Descriptions include words such as *understand, enjoy, develop,* and *build* (Seefeldt & Barbour, 1998). For example, in the area of personal-social development, a goal for four-year-old children might be: *Builds inner controls.* In the subject area of science, the following goal might be listed for six-year-olds: *Understands differences between plants and animals.*

The last level of planning includes the development of program **objectives,** which cover specific purposes that are more closely related to the design of specific daily activities. They define the behavior to be exhibited by a child or children, and they are measurable. Program goals provide the structure under which activities with specific objectives can be planned. Because objectives should be measurable, the terms used in writing them are more specific than those used for goals. For example, words such as *list, define, identify, compare, construct,* and *complete* can be used (Seefeldt & Barbour, 1998). An objective for five-year-olds in the area of communication development might be: *Puts story pictures in correct sequence.*

In addition to the objective(s) for an activity, think about the concepts that children will develop as they participate. A **concept** is an abstract thought, idea, or notion that is generalized from particular knowledge or experiences (Bruner, 1966). Children derive meaning in relationship to both context and their culture. Because of this, all children may not develop the same concepts from the same activity (Berk & Winsler, 1995). However, it is wise to consider the kinds of concepts children *might* form in relation to the learning potential of any activity.

Goals, then, are broad statements that relate to the potential benefits of a program over time. They are overall expectations in a developmental or content area. In the area of physical development, a goal might be: *Develops age-appropriate fine motor skills.* Three specific measurable objectives for different ages, which are related to that goal, are: *Turns pages of book one at a time* (age two and one-half years). *Cuts on line with scissors* (age four years). *Ties shoes* (age six years).

Concepts that children might develop related to these objectives are:

- By turning pages slowly, one at a time, a child realizes there are pictures that can be looked at on each page (age two and one-half years).
- By cutting on a line with scissors, a child realizes that this skill can be used to cut out other things (age four years).
- By learning to tie shoes, a child realizes that s/he can get completely dressed with no additional help (age six years).

Activities should be designed to be age-appropriate. They must also match the abilities of individual children in a group (Bredekamp & Copple, 1997). As much as possible should be known about each child: information can be obtained from parents and from observation of the children in the program setting.

There are considerations other than goals and objectives for daily activities. The following questions must be answered: Will the activity take place at home, in a child-care center or school, indoors or outside? Will the learning take place with the whole group, a small group, or on a one-to-one basis? If in a group program, will the activity take place in an interest center? Will the teacher participate in the interaction or will another child or children? What materials will be needed? What procedures will be used to complete the activity? How will the actions of the children be evaluated?

When information concerning the answers to these questions has been obtained, plans can be written. Within one child, all areas of development are working together. When activities are planned, some overlap between developmental areas will occur. The same is true for subject areas. For the best learning to occur, the subject areas should be integrated, with activities planned that incorporate several subjects at once around a theme or topic.

Developing Plans for Different Contexts

Some of the planning process will be similar for different contexts and programs. The overall aim of the program must be determined in order to provide a framework in which to develop program goals, objectives, and activities.

Many activities will include some kind of interaction. The type of interaction will vary depending on the activities. The interaction could be with objects or people; the people with whom a child interacts can be other children or adults. The children may be the same age, younger or older siblings, or a multiage group of children in a program or school. The adult with whom a child interacts may be a parent, a caregiver, or teacher.

In addition, materials and procedures should be identified. In particular, the method used to evaluate the children should be planned in advance. The evaluation method should provide some means of determining both the success of the activity and how well each child did, when the activity is completed. A plan form with a plan for a single activity is shown in Figure 4.2.

Planning processes will differ, depending on the setting and program. The planning a parent does in the home can be more general

---

LESSON PLAN

Level of children _____ *4-5 yrs.* _____   Area of development or subject _____ *Cognitive* _____

Developmental strand of topic _____ *Problem Solving* _____

Brief description of activity _____ *Match vehicles with the place where they are operated.* _____

Goal/Objective	Materials Needed	Prepreparation Needed
Goal: *To understand modes of travel.* Objective(s): *To match vehicles with the correct place of operation.* Organization/Interaction of Learners: *Small Group (1 - 4)*	*Pictures of different types of vehicles mounted on cardboard.* *Poster divided into sections for air, land, water.*	*Set out the pictures and poster in an interest area.*

Figure 4.2a   Lesson plan form for a single activity (two-sided form, front side).

Procedures	Method of Evaluation	Evaluation
1. Review the different types of transportation. 2. Explain the activity to the children. 3. Practice with several vehicles. 4. Suggest that the children take turns matching a vehicle with the correct section on the poster.	Teacher sits in interest center and asks individual children to match the pictures. She observes the number of correct matches each child makes.	Activity: The activity went well after the children had some practice. Children: All of the children could do the task.

Figure 4.2b Lesson plan form for a single activity, back side.

than that of a child-care center caregiver or a primary school teacher. For example, a parent may plan one daily activity for the child in each of the five developmental areas mentioned in this book (i.e., personal-social, physical, cognitive, communication, and creative). Implementation may be flexible. Individualization is relatively easy to accomplish, and all areas of development can be covered.

A visitor in a home visitor program may plan activities in each area of development to share with a parent in the home. The time spent each week in a visit is usually no more than an hour. Because of the time frame, the breadth of activities is completed over a period of weeks, because only one or two activi-ties are planned for each visit. One format (Parents as Teachers National Center & Missouri Department of Elementary & Secondary Education, 1993) for such a visit might be:

1. Rapport building
2. Observation
3. Discussion
4. Parent-child activity
5. Summary

A family child-care provider plans for several children in a multiage grouping during a whole day. Because this is an individualized program, activities should be planned that are at appropriate levels for each age represented (Eddowes & Ralph, 1987). For example, in a

Teachers meet on a regular basis for planning and professional growth.

cooking activity, two-year-olds can stir, three-year-olds can beat eggs with an egg beater, and four-year-olds can measure the ingredients.

Planning for multiage groups can be challenging. However, in a family child-care home, the caregiver should plan at least one activity in each developmental area each day. The focus is on choosing activities that are appropriate at different levels to match the abilities of the ages of children in the group.

In a parent interaction program, plans are usually made for a short time frame of 1 to 2 hours. However, parents interact in many of the activities on a one-to-one basis. The range between the children's ages is usually less than one year. In this kind of program, several activities can be planned in each developmental area, and the child and parent can select those that are appropriate and interesting.

A plan to use when incorporating activities that are based on developmental areas is shown in Figure 4.3. On the front of the plan, the strand, activity, objective, materials, prepreparation, and evaluation of children and activity are noted for each developmental area. On the back of the plan is a space for the type of interaction, time of day, and procedures for each activity. The teacher records the

type of interaction planned (e.g., adult-child, child-child). Activities that include more than one developmental area are noted, as are those that may take more than one day.

The matrix in appendix A (part 3) shows all of the activities found in chapters 6 through 10 in this book. There is a page for each age group, which includes the developmental area, the strands for the area, type of interaction, and the number of the activity, which shows where it is found in the designated chapter. Examples of two lesson plans using the matrix for age two (Fig. 4.4) and ages seven and eight (Fig. 4.6) are found in Figures 4.5 and 4.7. An activity has been selected for each developmental area for each day. Modifications for younger and older children may also be noted.

The plan form in Figure 4.3 can be used in a family child-care home. As shown in Figures 4.5 and 4.7, the plan can also be used in group child-care centers and with school-aged child care. However, in those programs, more children will be enrolled in one group, and the primary caregiver will be assisted by other adults. Depending on the age of the children in the group and the length of time they are participating during the day, it may be necessary to adapt the form to fit a particular situation.

LESSON PLAN

Date _____ Level of Children _____

	Developmental Area				
	Personal/Social	Physical	Cognitive	Communication	Creative
Strand					
Activity					
Objective					
Materials Needed					
Prepreparation					
Evaluation of Children					
Evaluation of Activity					

Figure 4.3a Lesson plan form for incorporating activities based on developmental areas, front.

Procedures and Interaction					
	Personal/Social	Physical	Cognitive	Communication	Creative
Activity					
Interaction					
Time					
			(See Figure 4.5 [back side] for use of this space)		

Figure 4.3b   Lesson plan form for procedures and type of interaction, back.

PERSONAL-SOCIAL DEVELOPMENT					
Trust	Attachment/ Separation	Self-Esteem	Self-Control	Social Interaction	Social Skills
Climbing Safety	Family Photos	Matching Faces	Helping Dress Myself	Playing with Peers	Simple Rules for Playing
Activity 6.3 Adult-child	Activity 6.9 Adult-child	Activity 6.14 Child-object	Activity 6.21 Child-object	Activity 6.27 Child-child	Activity 6.33 Adult-child

PHYSICAL DEVELOPMENT					
Gross Motor			Fine Motor		
Moving Arms to Music	Jumping off Stairs	Walking on a Line	Using Tongs	Towers of Cube Blocks	Beehive Fingerplay
Activity 7.7 Adult-child	Activity 7.8 Adult-child	Activity 7.9 Adult-child	Activity 7.25 Child-object	Activity 7.26 Child-object	Activity 7.27 Adult-child

COGNITIVE DEVELOPMENT				
Development of Attention	Problem Solving	Making Choices	Asking Open-Ended Questions	Completion of Tasks
Stringing Beads	Sink and Float	Mealtime Choices	Encourage Questioning	Build a Tower
Activity 8.3 Child-object	Activity 8.9 Child-object	Activity 8.15 Adult-child	Activity 8.21 Adult-child	Activity 8.27 Child-object

COMMUNICATION DEVELOPMENT				
Listening	Speaking	Writing	Reading	Nonverbal Communication
Listening to Music	Heads, Shoulders, Knees and Toes	Jotting a Note	Plastic Bag Books	Identifying Family Photos
Activity 9.3 Adult-child	Activity 9.9 Adult-child	Activity 9.15 Adult-child	Activity 9.21 Adult-child	Activity 9.27 Adult-child

CREATIVE DEVELOPMENT				
Sensory/Art	Music	Movement	Dramatics	Creative Writing
Play Dough	Kitchen Band	Popcorn	Animal Puppets	Story Starters
Activity 10.3 Child-object	Activity 10.9 Child-object	Activity 10.15 Adult-child	Activity 10.21 Adult-child	Activity 10.27 Adult-child

Figure 4.4 Matrix of activities for age two.

LESSON PLAN

Date ___11-2-02___ Level of Children ___Two___

	Developmental Area				
	Personal/Social	Physical*	Cognitive*	Communication	Creative
Strand	Social Interaction	Fine Motor	Open-ended Questions	Reading	Sensory/Art
Activity	Playing with peers 6.27	Beehive Fingerplay 7.27	Encourage Questioning 8.21	Plastic Bag Books 9.21	Play dough 10.3
Objective	Parallel play with sand	Able to copy motions	Ask about bees	Recognize pictures	Experiment with dough
Materials Needed	Sand box or sand table and containers	None	None	Books made from plastic bags	Homemade play dough, utensils, rolling pins
Prepreparation	None	Practice beehive fingerplay	Have information about bees	Make plastic bag books	Make playdough; Put in individual plastic bags marked with children's names
Evaluation of Children (observation during activity)	Did the children play in a group with the sand?	Could each child do the motions?	Which children asked questions?	Could the child recognize any pictures? Which ones?	How did the children use the dough?
Evaluation of Activity (completed after lesson is done)					

*Note: The two activities in these areas are on the same topic (bees). The activity numbers correspond to those in Figure 4.4.

Figure 4.5a Lesson plan form for incorporating activities based on developmental areas, front.

	Personal/Social	Physical	Cognitive	Communication	Creative
Procedures and Interaction					
Activity	Playing with peers	Beehive Fingerplay	Encourage Questioning	Plastic Bag Books	Play Dough
Interaction	Child-child (small group)	Adult-child (large group)	Adult-child (small group)	Adult-child (one-to-one)	Child-object (small groups)
Time	11:00-1:30	9:10-9:15	9:10-9:15	9:15-10:30	12:20-12:50
	All children in the group will not participate at the same time. If they choose they will play in the sand with plastic containers and shovels	Have a picture of a bee and a hive. Talk about bees. Demonstrate the fingerplay. Go through it with the children part by part. Practice once or twice.	Ask if anyone has a question about bees or wants to know more about them. Try to get the children to ask questions.	Sit in the book center with several plastic bag books. As children come up, invite them to look at the pictures. Ask each to identify items in the books. Elaborate on the children's comments.	Put homemade play dough bags on the table. Assist children in finding the bag with their name. Show how to roll dough but allow children to do it themselves.

Figure 4.5b Lesson plan form for procedures and types of interaction, back.

PERSONAL-SOCIAL DEVELOPMENT					
Trust	Attachment/ Separation	Self-Esteem	Self-Control	Social Interaction	Social Skills
Entering a New School	Sleepovers	Family Connections	Helping at Home	Games with Partners	Respecting the Property of Others
Activity 6.6 Adult-child	Activity 6.12 Adult-child	Activity 6.18 Adult-child	Activity 6.22 Child-object	Activity 6.30 Child-child	Activity 6.36 Child-child

PHYSICAL DEVELOPMENT					
Gross Motor			Fine Motor		
Jumping Rope	Dribbling a Soccer Ball	Parachutes	Ants on a Log	Origami	Stitchery
Activity 7.16 Adult-child	Activity 7.17 Child-object	Activity 7.18 Child-child	Activity 7.34 Adult-child	Activity 7.35 Child-object	Activity 7.36 Child-object

COGNITIVE DEVELOPMENT				
Development of Attention	Problem Solving	Making Choices	Asking Open-Ended Questions	Completion of Tasks
Collections	Conflict Resolution	Choosing a Project	Thinking of Open-Ended Questions	Completing a Weekly Contract
Activity 8.6 Adult-child	Activity 8.12 Child-child	Activity 8.18 Child-child	Activity 8.24 Child-child	Activity 8.30 Adult-child

COMMUNICATION DEVELOPMENT				
Listening	Speaking	Writing	Reading	Nonverbal Communication
Fact or Fiction?	On Stage	Author's Chair	Chapter Books	Mime
Activity 9.6 Adult-child	Activity 9.12 Child-child	Activity 9.18 Child-child	Activity 9.24 Adult-child	Activity 9.30 Child-child

CREATIVE DEVELOPMENT				
Sensory/Art	Music	Movement	Dramatics	Creative Writing
Foil Sculptures	Making Instruments	Building Bridges	Writing Plays	Stories of My Own
Activity 10.6 Child-object	Activity 10.12 Adult-Child	Activity 10.18 Child-child	Activity 10.24 Adult-child	Activity 10.30 Child-object

Figure 4-6 Matrix of activities for ages seven and eight.

LESSON PLAN

Date __1-18-02__   Level of Children __Ages 7 & 8, after-school program__

	Developmental Area				
	Personal/Social	Physical	Cognitive	Communication	Creative
Strand	Social Skills	Fine Motor*	Development of Attention	Speaking	Creative Writing*
Activity	Respecting Property 6.36	Origami 7.35	Collections 8.6	On Stage 9.12	Stories of My Own 10.30
Objective	Caring for Materials	Folding and cutting	Focus attention	Clear speaking	Writing a short story
Materials Needed	None	Paper for each student, scissors	Several items that could be collected (shells, bottlecaps)	Several simple plays that can be read or acted out	Pencils, markers crayons, and students' books
Prepreparation	None	Practice demonstrating how to make the book	None	Possible props for plays	None
Evaluation of Children (observation during activity)	Are students caring for their property and others'?	Could each student make a book? Any problems?	Did each student start a collection? Is each student working on it?	Did each student articulate clearly? Read fluently and with expression?	What kind of story did each student write?
Evaluation of Activity (completed after lesson is done)					

*Note: The two activities in these areas are used in sequence. First the origami book is made, and then the student writes a story for the blank book. The activity numbers correspond to those shown in Figure 4.6.

Figure 4.7 Lesson plan for incorporating activities based on developmental areas, front.

Procedures and Interaction					
	Personal/Social	Physical	Cognitive	Communication	Creative
Activity	Respecting Property 6.36	Origami 7.35	Collections 8.6	On Stage 9.12	Stories of My Own 10.30
Interaction	Child-child	Child-object	Adult-child	Child-child	Child-object
Time	3:45-4:00	4:00-5:15	4:00-4:15	5:15-5:45	4:00-5:15
	Discuss possible rules for taking care of property in the room. Ask students to give examples of ways to care for their own things and to respect property of the school and others.	Demonstrate how to make the book. Assist students as needed.	Introduce the idea of a collection in a small group. Ask if any student has a collection. Ask the students to give ideas for collections. Ask them to pick something to collect and work individually with each child.	Interested students select a simple play. This activity will take place at dramatics time each day for a week. Students will practice and then perform the play for the class at the end of the week.	During creative writing time, each student who has made an origami book will write a short story in it. It may be illustrated. This activity will take more than one day.

Figure 4.7b Lesson plan form for procedures and type of interaction, back.

In week-day school programs, the focus usually shifts from areas of development to subject-oriented curriculum content. Considerations in planning are similar to those mentioned previously. However, plans may include required subjects, such as language, math, science, social studies, art, music, physical education, and health (Bredekamp & Rosegrant, 1995). The form in Figure 4.3 probably will not be adequate for this type of program. A plan that has a place for the time and for each subject area can be individualized to meet the needs of the teacher and class.

The following section on implementation includes ways of developing schedules, methods of classroom management, and the integration of activities across the curriculum.

🐝 IMPLEMENTATION

Once plans are made, the program can be carried out. The plans form a structure in which the adult can function. However, plans should be flexible and adaptable for unforeseen situations. At some times, it may be necessary to discard plans altogether. Several elements must be considered when implementing a program. The first is the daily schedule. What will the children and adults be doing at different times of the day? Implementation also includes the arrangement of the environment, classroom organization and management, and ways of integrating the curriculum across developmental areas or subjects.

Schedule

A program's schedule is related to the kind of setting and the type of daily program, as well as the length. Some programs run for only an hour or so. Others may be in session during a half-day or a full day, and some centers are open 24 hours a day.

The schedule should include time for teacher-directed whole-group activities for children who are four years old and older. Children under three years of age should not be expected to sit in whole-group activities. Children of three years may have the opportunity to join a short whole-group activity but should be able to leave if they want to (Bredekamp, 1987). All whole-group activities for young children should be short. A rule to use when planning the schedule is to double the age of the children in years to help in deciding on the appropriate number of minutes for whole-group activities. For example, most four-year-olds can sit for 8 to 10 minutes and seven-year-olds, for about 15 minutes (Guddemi, 1988). Several short whole-group activity times during the day are better than including a number of activities in one sequence in a long time frame.

Blocks of time for child-initiated, self-selected small-group and individual activities should be longer than those planned for the whole group. An hour or more provides time for a child to engage in an activity in some depth. When teachers schedule too short a time for child-initiated learning periods, they create fragmentation: Children do not have time to start an activity before they are asked to stop it and go on to something else (Eddowes & Aldridge, 1990). However, children should be able to change from one interest area to another if they have completed an activity and there is space for them in another area.

In addition to providing appropriate times for small- and whole-group activities, there should be a balance of active and quiet activities. Experiences should be available both indoors and outdoors (weather permitting). Time must also be included for daily routines, such as meals and snacks, naps, hand washing, tooth brushing, and toileting. Some activities will be teacher-initiated, and others will be child-initiated.

The schedule includes times when the adults will move around the setting and interact with the children. Adults can offer suggestions and encouragement and work with children who have specific problems. At other times, an adult may schedule time to interact with a child for a specific purpose (i.e., a reading conference, contract conference). Children will also interact together both informally and, more formally, in groups that will solve problems or work on specific projects.

Infants and toddlers need personalized care, which is difficult to schedule. These kinds of schedules are related to the individual children for whom the care is being provided. They include large blocks of time for the routines of diapering, feeding, and play activities appropriate to the age of the children. No examples of infant and toddler child-care-center schedules are included here because of the need for individualization.

Examples of several schedules for older children in older group child-care and school programs follow. They are based on the amount of time the program is in operation.

Figure 4.8 shows a schedule for a parent-toddler interaction program that lasts for 90 minutes each week. Parents interact with their children on a one-to-one basis and in small groups in activities at interest centers. Since each toddler has a parent present, a short group snack and song time are planned, for participation by parents and children together.

An example of a schedule for a half-day morning program is found in Figure 4.9. Figure 4.10 shows the schedule for a full-day child-care program; Figure 4.11, a schedule for a week-day school program; and Figure 4.12, a schedule for a school-aged afternoon child-care program.

Schedules vary depending on the age of the children in the group and the length of the program. The schedules in Figures 4.8 through 4.12 can be adapted to fit most programs of the same type.

Classroom Management

The classroom climate is important when considering classroom management: It should be positive, accepting, and pleasant. The time schedule and the arrangement of the physical

3:00	Parents and toddlers arrive
3:00–4:00	Center time, indoors and outdoors
	Personal-social activities
	Physical activities
	Cognitive activities
	Communication activities
	Creative activities
4:00–4:10	Pickup, toileting, and hand washing
4:10–4:15	Movement activities
4:15–4:25	Parents and children enjoy a snack together
4:25–4:30	Parent and toddler do one-finger play together, and the group sings a song
4:30	Parents and toddlers leave

Figure 4.8 Parent-toddler interaction program: weekly afternoon schedule.

9:00–9:10	Opening, whole-group time
9:10–10:10	Self-selected small-group and individual activities
10:10–10:20	Clean up
10:20–10:30	Rest and listen to record
10:30–10:55	Outside activity time (weather permitting) or multipurpose room
10:55–11:05	Bathroom and hand washing
11:05–11:15	Snack
11:15–11:25	Story
11:25–11:30	Prepare to leave

Figure 4.9 Half-day children's schedule (five-year-olds).

6:30–8:30	Arrival of children and quiet activities, some outside activities (weather permitting)
8:30–8:40	Bathroom and wash hands
8:40–9:10	Breakfast snack
9:10–9:15	Whole group time
9:15–10:30	Self-selected small group and individual activities
10:30–10:40	Clean up
10:40–10:50	Music and games
10:50–11:30	Outdoor activities (weather permitting) or multipurpose room
11:30–11:40	Bathroom and wash hands
11:40–12:10	Lunch
12:10–12:20	Brush teeth
12:20–12:50	Self-selected small-group and individual activities
12:50–1:00	Prepare for rest
1:00–2:30	Rest or quiet time
2:30–2:40	Bathroom and hand washing
2:40–3:00	Afternoon snack
3:00–3:10	Story
3:10–6:00	Indoor and outdoor self-selected activities, children begin to leave

Figure 4.10 Full-day children's schedule (three-year-olds).

8:00–8:20	Journal writing
8:20–8:40	Opening, whole-group activity
8:40–10:00	Language arts centers and reading conferences
10:00–10:15	Clean up and get ready to leave classroom
10:15–10:45	Music or art (alternate days with resource teachers)
10:45–11:15	Physical education (with resource teacher)
11:15–11:25	Bathroom and hand washing
11:25–11:45	Story
11:45–12:15	Lunch
12:15–12:45	Independent reading
12:45–1:30	Math activities
1:30–2:30	Projects (small-group and independent work that incorporates social studies, science, health)
2:30–2:40	Clean up
2:40–2:55	Summary of the day, sharing
2:55–3:00	Prepare to leave

Figure 4.11 Daily school schedule (eight-year-olds).

space (chapter 3) are also essential components in classroom management. Those must be designed to meet the developmental and learning needs of the children.

When interest or learning centers are used, children need information concerning center rules. For example, the number of children who may use a center at any one time depends on the amount of space and the equipment and materials available. The maximum number of children permitted in an area at one time should be noted clearly in the center. This

Child is assisted in choosing learning center in kindergarten classroom.

3:15–3:45	Nutrition snack (children assist in preparation)
3:45–5:15	Choice of activities
	Sports (outdoors)
	Arts and crafts
	Games
	Projects
	Creative writing
	Dramatics
	Homework
5:15–5:45	Group meetings
	Story
	Dramatics
	Share projects
5:45–6:00	Prepare to leave

Figure 4.12   School-aged child-care schedule.

can be done with stick figures, colored clothespins in a can, necklaces the children wear when in the center, or some other method.

Children also need to know how long they will remain in a center and how they will know when to move to a different one. This depends on the management system used. Interest center use can be managed by several different means; a brief description of these is given here.

1. *Centers can be self-selected.* Each child selects a center. The choice depends only on the space available in the different centers. Children can change centers when they wish, and space is made available in the center chosen.

2. *An activity can be planned in each of five centers for the week.* These specific centers are not free-choice centers. Children are each assigned to one center each day. After completing the activity in the assigned center, children may select another center

that is designated a free-choice center. Children may move between those centers if space is available.

3. *Contracts can be used with children aged five years and older.* Activities are planned in various centers. Each child has a contract for the week. The teacher notes on each child's contract certain activities that must be completed by the end of the week (or other designated time). Other activities may be self-selected. It is the child's responsibility to complete the contract in the time allotted. The child moves to a center listed on this contract in which there is space. A copy of a contract form is found in Figure 4.13. An example of an activity using contracts is provided in chapter 8 (activity 8.30).

When an activity period is over, toys and materials must be put away. Children should assist with this task. Activity 8.28 in chapter 8 has some suggestions that may be helpful.

Facilities are planned to encourage children to clean up independently.

WEEKLY CONTRACT

Name _____ Date _____ Group/Class _____

1st Activity	2nd Activity	3rd Activity	4th Activity
5th Activity	6th Activity	7th Activity	8th Activity

Figure 4.13   A child's activity contract.

A goal of most parents and programs is to encourage children to take responsibility for their own learning; the methods suggested here do that. In addition, children should also learn to take responsibility for their own behavior. When at all possible, classroom and interest center rules should be developed by the children. This is usually possible by the time they are reasonably fluent in oral language (age three). A few simple rules should be stated in positive terms. These rules tell what children can do, rather than what they may not do. For example: "Walk in the building" or "Talk in quiet voices." An activity related to making rules is found in chapter 6, activity 6.24. When children have trouble following rules, the adult should try to talk through the problem with the children. In this kind of interaction, the reasons for the rules can be emphasized.

Integrating the Curriculum

The integrated curriculum is based on the belief that children's learning experiences should be presented as an integrated whole rather than as small pieces or fragments of content. Whenever possible, experiences should be real, not contrived (Dewey, 1916). As children develop and learn, adults help children connect skills and concepts. Activities that enhance development, as well as those related to subject matter concepts, should not be taught in isolation but should be integrated.

Several methods can help tie activities together in meaningful ways. The first is the book web. A child's book is selected, and age-appropriate activities that relate to different areas of the curriculum are developed around the book's content. Several available resources can assist in developing activities for book webs (Raines & Canady, 1989, 1991, 1992). A plan for using a book web is found in Figure 4.14.

Another method of integrating the curriculum is by using a theme or unit of study. An overall unit plan includes the topic, goals and objectives, content, materials and resources, initiation, learning experiences, summary, and evaluation (Seefeldt & Barbour, 1998). Activities for each area of the curriculum are developed around the topic selected. Possible topics include the study of dinosaurs,

Literature selection: _____

Author: _____ Publisher: _____

Date of publication _____ Age/grade level: _____ Genre: _____

Goals: _____

Reading	Writing	Listening	Speaking	Vocabulary Development
Mathematics	**Science**	**Social Studies**	**Cooking**	**Multicultural**
Art/Sensory	**Crafts**	**Music**	**Movement/Dance**	**Drama**

Multimedia resources: _____

Other books by this author: _____

Related books: _____

Figure 4.14   A plan for using a book web: Brainstorming matrix for planning.

plants, farms, sea animals, or the rain forest. The children's interests should be considered when choosing the topic. A unit can last for a few days or several weeks. It should include activities across the curriculum. A unit plan concerning insects—which includes activities from language arts, math, science, social studies, art, music, physical education, and health—is found in Figure 4.15.

The last method that will be discussed related to integrating the curriculum is the project approach. "A project is an in-depth study of a particular topic that one or more children undertake" (Katz & Chard, 1989, p. 2). It might consist of the study of the evolution of a neighborhood, how a road is built, or the life cycle of a butterfly. It grows out of the interests of the children.

Unit Title: Insects
Initiation Plan: The initiation of this unit will be done the first week through slowly introducing insects in various ways.

	Monday	Tuesday	Wednesday	Thursday	Friday
Week 1 Subtheme: Introduction to Insects	Insect Safari (social studies)	What it Feels Like (science)	Indoor Safari Insect Terrarium (social studies)	What Is Their Favorite Color (science)	Insect Match Worksheet (science) Animal Salad (cooking)
Week 2 Subtheme: Butterflies	Story "The Butterfly" (reading) Song "Grow Caterpillar" (music)	Life Cycle of the Butterfly (science)	Giant Butterfly (craft) Caterpillar Warm Up (movement)	All About Wings (science) Magic Moth (art)	Butterflies and Moths Moth or Butterfly? Compare and Contrast (science)
Week 3 Subtheme: Ants	Ants Are Busy (reading) Ants (science)	How Fast? (math)	Food Choices (science)	Room to Dig (science)	How to Make an Ant (craft)
Week 4 Subtheme: Beetles	Beetle Puzzles (science) Night and Day (reading)	Insect Drill Game (science)	Ladybug Magnets (craft) Ladybug Spots (math)	The Firefly Song (music) Beetle Tag (movement)	Lady Bird Beetle (craft)

Summary Plan: A mural will be created to summarize all of the subthemes and insects in general.

Figure 4.15   Unit plan.

In a Reggio Emilia school, a project is viewed as an adventure that includes research. It can evolve from a child's idea or a discussion with an adult. It might also emerge from an experience with an event, such as a rainstorm or a child's new pet. No matter how it begins, there must be enough time for the knowledge, thought processes, and actions of the children to develop (Edwards, Gandini, & Forman, 1993).

A project can be completed in a few days or may take several weeks. Many skills and much knowledge can be achieved through the use of projects. Adults can assist children in conducting web searches on the Internet and in doing research in libraries. Although school-age students are more able to do research that requires reading and writing, younger children can also participate in projects (Helm & Katz, 2001); for example, a group of four-year-olds are interested in the topic of shadows. With the help of an adult, they are able to learn where shadows come from, how they change during the day, why they disappear, and other relevant information. Through experimentation, they can collect data. They can use classroom equipment, such as block towers, to demonstrate how shadows change. Answers to the questions a project poses draw from a number of subject areas. A project allows children to apply the skills of information gathering, reading, and writing in a meaningful activity (Helm & Katz, 2001; Katz & Chard, 1989).

In a large project, smaller groups could each be working on one part of the task. For example, a project concerning the seasons could have four parts: spring, summer, fall, and winter. The class could be divided into four small groups, which would each find information on one season. All students in the class would be working on some aspect of the project. In addition, they would all work on a culminating activity, which would tie all of the parts of the project together. At other times, there might be several projects on different topics going on at the same time. For example, one group might be studying the habits of an animal, such as a turtle; another group might be finding out about rainbows.

Projects improve interaction skills for working with peers to solve problems and aid in developing concepts and extending learning on new topics. They are usually completed during a block of time scheduled on a daily basis (Figure 4.11). Both adults and children provide documentation for a project. Evaluation can be done for individual children and for the project as a whole.

✺ EVALUATION

After plans are implemented, adults need some way of assessing the success of each participating child and evaluating the implementation of the activity or activities as a whole. The purpose and method of the evaluation must be determined.

Purpose of Evaluation

The assessment of both children's progress and the program's success are important for several reasons. The two evaluations can work together to assist adults in planning activities that are of interest to young children. The planned experiences should also enhance children's development and learning. Activities provided for a group of children should be age-appropriate and match each child's ability (Bredekamp & Copple, 1997); this is not an easy task. If methods of evaluation have been included as plans are made, then assessing each child is easier. Determining the success of the activities as they fit into the total curriculum may be more difficult.

Both informal and formal assessments and tests can provide useful information concerning the abilities of children. The problem lies in the purpose of the assessments. If the information is used to plan specific activities to enhance the development of skills and abilities of a child or children in a group, the results of evaluation will be put to positive use. If the information is used solely to compare children, groups, schools, or school districts, it may be considered inappropriate (Kamii & Kamii, 1990).

Program evaluation can help the adult to look at the entire program and decide when curriculum content should be revised. Teachers get informal feedback concerning daily activities as they implement them. An adult usually knows how well an activity or plan went and the reaction of the children. When a problem occurs, the plan can sometimes be changed to correct it that day; at other times, some thought is necessary about how it could be revised if used again.

Program evaluation can also include a look at how a specific curriculum or program fits within the center or school as a whole. Sometimes a center or school program is compared to a set of standards that are determined by an outside agency. This can help to determine if adequate procedures are being used to meet the needs of all participants in the program.

Methods of Assessment

Two main kinds of assessment can be used. The first, called **formative evaluation,** is an ongoing assessment of children's growth and learning as they relate to the daily curricular experiences. It helps the adult to decide on goals and objectives for individual children and also those for the program. When doing formative evaluation, information is collected continuously concerning children's skills and abilities and the success or failure of various learning experiences. A guide for the use and selection of developmental screening instruments is available through the National Association for the Education of Young Children (Meisels with Atkins-Burnett, 1994).

Observation, discussed in chapter 2, is an important means of formative assessment. Many of the observation methods can provide ongoing information concerning the children's skills and abilities. Interviews with individual children and conferences are also helpful. A variety of types of information should be documented for use in planning activities and reporting children's progress to parents. Some of this information is supplied in record forms and documents and in samples of the children's work.

Assessment portfolios can be a helpful means of organizing the information. The portfolios are usually kept in collaboration with the children involved (Grace & Shores, 1991; MacDonald, 1996; Puckett & Black, 1994). As they are able to understand the concept of the portfolio, children should be encouraged to assist in selecting work to include. They may also help to decide when (or if) an item should be removed and something else substituted for it.

Portfolios may include children's artwork, conceptual and problem-solving activities, logs of books read, writing samples, documentation from projects. Teacher notes may be included; some of these are related to areas of development not easily captured in the children's products (e.g., motor, social, and emotional development). Information can also be included on children's progress through play (Van Hoorn, Nourat, Scales, & Alward, 1999). The portfolio is always evolving and is never finished; it is a continuing record of children's progress and a reflection of their learning.

Assessment information concerning individual children is usually conveyed in some way to the parents. It might be in the form of a report card, a letter outlining the child's strengths and areas for continued development, or a report at a parent conference.

Parent conferences can be valuable methods of communication. The conference should be a two-way interaction, in which both the parent and the caregiver or teacher can share information. Strengths of the child should be shared first. After that, any problems or concerns are discussed. A summary statement about the child's strengths should be last. The conference has been called an onion sandwich, with the bread on the top and bottom of the onion representing strengths and the onion representing problems and concerns. Portfolios can be positive, visual methods of transmitting information during parent conferences.

Caregivers and teachers working in early childhood programs must keep all information concerning children and families confidential. Such information should be used in developing appropriate learning experiences for a child. It should be shared only with the child's parents or personnel employed within the program.

The other major type of assessment is called **summative evaluation,** which takes place at the end of a learning period. It might be an assessment of a single lesson or a reading test covering lessons for an entire school year, and it is sometimes used for accountability purposes (Puckett & Black, 1994).

Teacher-made tests are a form of summative evaluation; the other major type is a standardized test. Both types are used to sum up performance at the end of a period of time. Standardized tests are so named because they are developed to tell how a child's score on a test compares with other children of the same age and grade (Seefeldt & Barbour, 1998). However, when given at the end of a school year, the teacher may not receive the results in time to be used for an individual child's benefit.

Summative evaluation can also be used in assessing programs. Information can be collected from parents and other community members. In addition, the National Association for the Education of Young Children has initiated the National Academy of Early Childhood Programs, which is a voluntary program of accreditation for child-care centers. The purpose is to improve the quality of all types of early childhood centers and schools, except family child-care home programs. Standards have been developed that accredited programs must meet (National Association for the Education of Young Children, 1998).

Another method of formal program evaluation for elementary schools is administered by the Association of Colleges and Schools. Standards for elementary school programs have been developed. Although this accreditation is also voluntary, many school districts participate in their regional association (e.g., Southern Association of Colleges and Schools).

✌ SUMMARY

In the interactive curriculum, planning provides a framework to use in developing appropriate activities and interactions for young children. For program planning to succeed, an understanding of the children involved in the program is necessary. The important connection between curriculum content and child development is discussed in the context of its relationship to planning.

The interrelations between planning, implementation, and evaluation are also considered: Each is dependent on the one that goes before. The area of planning includes written plans based on background and assessment information of the children. Implementation requires plans, a daily schedule, appropriate classroom management methods, and ways to integrate the curriculum across developmental areas and subjects. Evaluation and assessment measure the successful implementation of age-appropriate and individually appropriate activities for young children. Evaluation is the basis for continued planning and implementation.

QUESTIONS AND PROJECTS FOR THE READER

1. Write a goal and several objectives for one activity in each developmental area.
2. Using the lesson plan format in Figure 4.2, write a complete lesson plan for one activity.
3. Select an age group or grade level other than those in the schedules in the chapter. Plan the daily schedule for the group you select.
4. Using the plan found in Figure 4.14, select a children's book and complete a book web.
5. Develop a mock portfolio for a first-grade child; include anything that you think might be in such a portfolio.

FOR FURTHER READING

Helm, J. H., & Katz, L. (2001). *Young investigators: The project approach in the early years.* Jointly published by the Teachers College Press (New York) & the National Association for the Education of Young Children, (Washington, DC). This new resource gives information concerning the use of the project approach with children ages three through eight. It contains guidelines on how to get started and examples of projects in progress.

Kamii, C. (Ed.). (1990). *Achievement testing in the early grades: Games grown-ups play.* Washington, DC: National Association for the Education of Young Children. This book has chapters on different aspects of tests, testing, and alternate forms of assessment. Advantages and disadvantages of various kinds of assessment for young children are described.

MacDonald, S. (1996). *Portfolio and its use Book II: A road map for assessment.* Little Rock, AR: South-ern Early Childhood Association. Innovative suggestions for using the portfolio method are discussed. The book includes everything necessary to understand and use children's portfolios in the classroom.

Meisels, S. J. (with Atkins-Burnett, S.) (1994). *Developmental screening in early childhood: A guide* (4th ed.). Washington, DC: National Association for the Education of Young Children. The purpose of developmental screening and how to select a screening instrument is described in this book. It also includes information on ways to develop a screening program and the limitations of developmental screening.

Part 2

Activities for Interaction

*P*art 2 comprises Chapters 5 through 10. Chapter 5 presents theoretical support for reciprocal interactions and identifies possible types of interactions, including the kinds of interactions that are critical to each area of development. Each of the subsequent chapters covers one area of child development and focuses on the key strands in that area in which interaction is important for development and learning. In addition, the chapters include a section on curricular implications for planning. Connections are made to traditional subject matter areas and a suggestion for thematic planning is indicated.

Each chapter contains examples of interaction activities for children from birth through age eight years. Chapter 6, "Personal-Social Development," includes interactions supporting trust, attachment/separation, self-esteem, self-control, social interaction, and social skills. In chapter 7, "Physical Development," interactions related to gross and fine motor skills are described. Chapter 8, "Cognitive Development," includes interactions that support the development of attention, problem solving, making choices, asking open-ended questions, and completion of tasks. Chapter 9, "Communication Development," covers listening, speaking, writing, reading, and nonverbal interactions. The last chapter in this section, Chapter 10, "Creative Development," includes suggestions for interactions that support sensory/art, music, movement, dramatics, and creative writing.

Chapter Five

Types of Interaction

objectives

After reviewing this chapter, you will be able to

- Identify and compare three theories in which reciprocal interaction plays an integral part.
- Describe possible types of interaction.
- Discuss the meaning of the term *inappropriate interaction*.
- List the kinds of interactions that are important in each area of development.
- Give several examples of interactions in each area of development.

Quality interactions are a key aspect of an interactive curriculum. The adult, whether parent, caregiver or teacher, must understand how to design and implement a variety of interactions, in the daily program. This chapter is devoted to information concerning types of interactions, with examples of their function in different situations and settings.

Young children are changing, growing, and learning all of the time. Their development and pursuit of knowledge can be enhanced by the adults, peers, and older children with whom they have contact. Children also learn from their experiences with objects and activities. Their genetic heritage and the physical and social contexts in which they live are also contributing factors. From the time children are born (and perhaps before), they are building a continually expanding foundation for all of their further learning. The rules of the society and the cultural traditions of the family are transmitted to children by the accumulation of experiences that they gain from the home, child-care center, school, community, and other contexts.

Children develop and learn through interactions of one sort or another that take place in the environment. Sometimes the activities may be solitary interactions with objects and at other times with another person or persons. There are times when adult-child interaction must occur if children are to develop and learn to their potential. Sometimes, however, it is only necessary for adults to provide the time, space, and materials for children to use in exploring and experimenting. At those times, adult participation is not required. However, adults must know each child in their care and be good observers to know when their participation enhances rather than hinders the child's progress. (Chapter 2 contains information about observation methods.) When a child has a specific handicap or has problems in some area of development, this is particularly important.

When designing an interactive curriculum, there must be a link between the content presented and children's developmental level. The curriculum should build on the experiences and interests of the children (Jalongo & Eisenberg, 2000). Children need consistent, positive interactions throughout their experiences and activities to develop constructive relationships with other people (Bredekamp & Copple, 1997). Interactions are helpful both in promoting learning and in strengthening relationships.

✑ BASIS FOR RECIPROCAL INTERACTION: THREE THEORIES

Although various theorists may interpret **reciprocal interaction** somewhat differently, it is usually defined as a two-way interaction among various combinations of participants and/or contexts, with each one having the potential of changing or of being changed by the other. Three theories that feature reciprocal interaction as an integral part are now explored with representative examples.

T. Berry Brazelton

The theory of T. Berry Brazelton has parent-child interaction as its focus (Brazelton, 1992; Brazelton & Cramer, 1990). Viewed as a process, interactions reflect a cluster of behaviors from both parent and child. The adult and child take cues from each other, and both have the potential for fostering change in the other. The cues may be verbal or nonverbal. There are cycles of engagement and disengagement, which help to protect a child from too much stimulation. The quality of the interaction can be intrusive and violating or empathetic and reciprocal. This model assumes a mutual influence between parent and child. Here is an example of a positive reciprocal parent-child interaction with cycles of engagement and disengagement.

Billy (age eight weeks) is sitting in an infant seat. Even though he is not using words yet, his mother talks with him. He responds to her voice with a cooing sound, and his mother talks again. Billy responds again. After several rounds of initiation and response, his mother slows and stops before Billy turns away. After a few seconds, Billy turns back to her, and the interaction can resume. Billy's mother observes her child's behavior and makes sure that the interaction is not too stimulating.

Sometimes parents or caregivers do not realize the importance of the child's need to regulate an interaction to avoid overstimulation. When this happens, the interaction may become negative instead of positive.

Urie Bronfenbrenner

Bronfenbrenner's work (1979) concerning the reciprocal relationship between adult and child is similar to that of Brazelton. However, Bronfenbrenner's broader definition of reciprocity includes the ecological context and the culture of the child. He believes that the actions of a child can change the environment in addition to the environment changing the child. The human ecosystems in Bronfenbrenner's theory consist of nested structures (described in chapter 1) on four different levels.

The following example illustrates how each level or system can be influenced, and in turn, influences the others.

Delia (age four years) lives in a low-income housing project in an urban area. Her small home is crowded; her parents and three siblings share four rooms. There are continual interactions (level 1) in the home. Delia learns that she has little control over her home environment. She attends a Head Start program. Her participation extends her envi-ronment so that she can interact (level 2) with interesting objects and with adults and children outside her family. She can choose activities in which to participate. Her parents can also participate and learn ways to enhance their home setting. In the community agency that manages the program, decisions (level 3) are made concerning such things as the educational program, staffing, and nutrition. These decisions can make a difference in Delia's environment. At the highest level (4), government decisions can affect each of the previous systems.

Bronfenbrenner believes the reciprocal interaction between children and their surroundings is continuous. A family's culture is transmitted through interactions between family members and others in the extended family. It may also include people and influences in the greater community.

Richard M. Lerner

The developmental contextualism of Lerner (Ford & Lerner, 1992; Lerner, 1978, 1982, 1984), although similar to Bronfenbrenner's, offers yet another viewpoint related to the reciprocal relationship. According to Lerner, human development occurs through the interactions between a person and the context in which the individual exists. Everything in the context is important, such as people, climate, lighting, furniture, and activities. The biological heritage of the child also plays a part.

Jared (age seven years) will begin to attend a new school tomorrow. He has just moved to a different neighborhood. Although it will be a new classroom and will undoubtedly change him in some ways, the environment in that classroom will also change because of his presence. What will change? There will be one additional student. Groups within the class will change as he is included in activities. He will bring his own talents and skills to the new setting, and there will be a different dynamic in the environment.

The context influences or changes the child, but the child also influences and changes the environmental context. This reciprocal relationship is sometimes called *bidirectional.* In a unique way, children are both products and producers of their own ecology and development (Ford & Lerner, 1992).

The preceding theories describe three ways in which interactions can affect the development and learning of a child. In the first, Brazelton (Brazelton & Cramer, 1990) looks primarily at the complex interactions occurring between parent and child. Bronfenbrenner (1979) focuses on the contexts where interactions can occur that affect the child. He also considers interactions related to the cultural context. Lerner (Ford & Lerner, 1992) describes the interaction of the child's biological inheritance with various organizational contexts. This theory has implications for the study of interactions related to problems in a child's development. Each theory includes reciprocal interaction and mutual causality as an integral part of the theory.

INTERACTION WITH PEOPLE

Reciprocal interactions between people are essential in a child's life. This begins for the infant with parent-child interaction. These kinds of interactions then may extend to caregiver-child, teacher-child, and a variety of other adult-child interactions. Another type of reciprocal interaction that is usually found in children's settings is peer interaction, which consists of exchanges between children who are similar in age. Older children may also interact with younger children.

Parent-Child Interaction

Parent-child interaction is the first and one of the most crucial reciprocal relations in the young child's life. Like all other interactions, this type of exchange takes place in some kind of environmental context. It reflects the background experiences of each parent and the relationship of the parents to each other (Vondra & Belsky, 1993). Both the interaction between the participants and the physical and/or social setting are important aspects of such an interaction. Each interaction has the potential of being positive or negative.

For example, if the interaction takes place with an infant, what is the state of this young child at the time? Is the infant dry, hungry, wide awake, or distressed? Is the interaction taking place in a bedroom of the home, in the car, in the backyard of the home, at a grandparent's home? What is the state of the parent? Is the parent feeling good or tired, hungry, and stressed? The quality of the interaction may be related to the answers to these questions.

Consistency in parent-child interactions is important for a child's development. Parents cannot always have perfect, positive interactions. The "goodness of fit" between the child's temperament and the temperament of each parent may make a difference (Lerner & Lerner, 1983; Thomas & Chess, 1980). Even when there is a problem with the fit between temperamental styles, the parents must try to be positively responsive and relatively consistent in their interactions with the child. This will assist the child in understanding that the world is basically a good place (Erikson, 1963). Here is an example of different temperaments in a parent and child.

June (four years old) goes to a child-care center while her parents work. She has a "slow-to-warm-up" temperament (Thomas & Chess, 1980). She needs time to accomplish a task. Her mother has a

higher activity level. In the evening, when her mother stops at the child-care center to get her, June is slow in getting her coat on. Instead of being upset and doing the task for her, her mother sings a song about putting on the coat. Both are satisfied with the interaction. Her mother understands June's behavior, and June is getting positive information from her parent. As June gains experience in putting on the coat, she will become faster in completing the task.

Sometimes the parent, or other adult, must provide structure in the interaction for it to become successful. This is called **scaffolding.** It supplies a framework in which children can expand their knowledge and skills (Wood, Bruner, & Ross, 1976). The more skilled partner, an adult or a more competent child, estimates the child's actual level of development (the level at which the child can do a particular task unaided). This support person then assists as necessary so that the child can complete the task successfully (Vygotsky, 1978). For a new task, more support is offered, and as the child's competence grows, less support is necessary. The child moves toward independent mastery (Berk & Winsler, 1995). The child must be allowed to experiment with a task as assistance is given. Sometimes the child will be able to figure out how to do it alone, with a few suggestions.

This example demonstrates the concept of scaffolding.

Robby (age four years) wants to help his father fold the clean laundry. Robby's father shows him how to sort and fold the different articles of clothing in piles. Robby practices that and follows his father's suggestions. As he works, he folds each sock individually and puts all of the socks together in a pile. Robby's father then shows him how to match two socks by color and type and then fold them together.

With experience, Robby's competence in the task of sorting and folding laundry improves, and his father gives him fewer suggestions. Soon, he is able to do the task independently.

Adult-Child Interaction

Beginning early in a child's life, adults other than the parents may have important roles in the care of the child. These adults may include relatives (such as a grandparent), a baby-sitter, or a caregiver in a child-care center, and then, as the child gets older, a teacher, recreation leader, or librarian.

Each of the adults in a child's experience can have positive or negative interactions with the child. Both knowledge of child development and information concerning the child's family background, temperament, and capabilities help to promote positive relations. Positive interactions are supportive and give children a sense of security and well-being (Erikson, 1963).

In planning activities, adults should match the child's developmental level with the experience (Hunt, 1961). The match should be at the child's actual developmental level as defined by Vygotsky (1978). As he theorized, there is a difference between the child's actual problem-solving level and the level if given assistance, called the zone of proximal development. At that point, the adult must decide whether to intervene to assist the child. Sometimes children have the skills necessary to finish tasks without help. At other times, adults can provide a scaffold, with appropriate coaching to enable children to experience success; an example follows.

Lupita is in the second grade. She is measuring different objects with a yardstick. Since the yardstick does not bend, she is having trouble measuring

some curved surfaces. As the teacher observes her problem, she asks, "How might you measure without the yardstick?" Lupita indicates that she does not know. The teacher then suggests that she cut a string the length of the yardstick and try that. The child tries it and then figures out that she can find the length with the string and then measure the string with the yardstick to find the length in inches. The teacher's suggestion enabled Lupita to extend her thinking and try out a new idea.

As children build their expertise in different content areas, they may have difficulties in understanding one or another aspect of the information or skill. Sometimes children can watch and imitate an adult to learn. The adult can provide feedback so that the child will know how things are going (Gardner, 1993). At other times, the adult can use questioning strategies or counterexamples to extend the

Girls read a book together.

child's thinking (Piaget, 1948/1973). Positive adult-child interactions foster positive self-esteem in both adult and child (Aldridge, 1993).

Child-Child Interaction

Children engage in activities with peers but also with children who may be several years older. This can occur in the home, neighborhood, or school setting.

Interaction with Peers   Young children usually play with others of their own age. They learn social interaction skills, but they also improve their cognitive abilities. New roles can be practiced. They learn to share, cooperate, and collaborate. They learn from each other, develop their physical skills and imagination, and gain a sense of competence (Millar, 1968; Rogers & Sawyers, 1988).

Children learn informally from each other through play. However, a more formal coaching of a skill may occur as an outgrowth of play with a more competent peer (Vygotsky, 1978). For instance, two 5-year-olds are playing. One has a two-wheeled bicycle, which he can ride. The other is still riding a tricycle. The one with the bicycle offers to teach the other child to ride it. The inexperienced child wants to learn. The experienced child gives him some suggestions. With a minimum of effort and practice, the inexperienced child learns to ride the two-wheeler.

Sometimes more support and practice are required. However, through play and free-choice activities, children learn a great deal from each other, formally and informally.

Interaction with Older Children   In both home and school, older children sometimes interact with those several years younger. The older child may assist the younger child in learning information or in performing a specific skill.

There is an increasing interest in having older students help younger students with such subjects as creative writing, problem solving, or project development. The older students become role models for the younger children. For example, students in the fourth or fifth grades might spend a period of the day in a kindergarten or first-grade classroom. They could assist the younger students in brainstorming topics and subtopics for a class project. The project approach is well suited to teaching children of different ages in one classroom (Katz & Chard, 1989). While working in teams on separate subtopics, the older students assist the younger students with research for the chosen subtopic.

Children from both age groups have strengths that they can bring to the project. However, the older students have the opportunity to teach something with which they have already had some experience. Teaching should help them to understand it better. Thus, both the younger and the older students can profit from this interaction.

✍ OTHER INTERACTIONS

Children have reciprocal interactions with people, but they also have interactions with objects, activities, and environmental settings or contexts. These kinds of interactions may or may not include people. However, they can be just as important to child development and learning.

Child-Object Interaction

Young children begin playing with objects soon after they are born. They find out what things are and how they work. This interest in objects extends past toys to other things in the environment. They explore, become familiar with, and develop an understanding of the properties of different objects (Garvey, 1977). Children tend to use objects realistically, at first, in their play. They enjoy toys that look like objects in the environment, such as play dishes, cars, animals, or people. At three and one-half to four years of age, children begin to substitute one object for another. By then, a toy need not be realistic. For example, a block can represent a telephone, or a broom can represent a horse (Rogers & Sawyers, 1988).

How does reciprocal interaction take place between children and objects? The use of objects and solving problems with them can change the way a child thinks. Objects can also change: blocks and other builders can be put together in new ways. Play dough can change shape. Objects can also take on imaginary roles that form in the mind of the child. Sometimes a change is caused by something breaking or being damaged in some way. A toy may be interactive: After a child's action, another action follows. For instance, when a toy xylophone is struck with a mallet, a tone can be heard; when a crank is turned, a toy clown emerges from a jack-in-the-box.

From an early age, some children prefer to interact with objects instead of people. They tend to be somewhat more introverted, and they have a desire to analyze properties of objects. They are the experimenters, and they look for order. Others are more interested in interactions with people. They tend to be more extroverted and are interested in actions and adventures. They are more likely to engage in pretend play and enjoy maintaining contact with others. There is a continuum between the two extremes. Most children have a unique combination of these interests (Storr, 1988).

Interaction in Activities

Young children are continually engaged in one activity or another. Sometimes children initiate the activities. Parents in the home and caregivers or teachers in group programs may also plan activities for children. Activities must be selected with the developmental level of the child in mind. Group activities should include a variety of activities that match the needs of the individual children. Each child has strengths and areas of lesser ability (Gardner, 1993). When given a choice, children select an activity in which they are interested and with which they think they can succeed. The adult provides the materials and helps to organize and evaluate the experience.

Activity-oriented interactions are usually rather complex. They may include a single child working alone, a small group of children working together, or some kind of adult-child activity. Each activity takes place in a particular context, such as the home, a classroom, a specific room, or a particular part of a room. Many activities for young children take place outdoors in a play area or various parts of the community.

All of the factors in an activity have the potential of being changed by the action that takes place. Not only the physical interaction but also the participants' perception of the interaction is important (Bronfenbrenner, 1979).

—————————— ——————————

A first-grade class is doing a cooking activity. They are working in small groups to make vegetable soup. Jamie says that he does not like vegetable soup. The teacher suggests that he can help make it even if he does not like to eat it. During the activity, Jamie's task is to help peel carrots and potatoes. As he works at that, he begins to understand that vegetable soup is made of different individual vegetables. When the soup is finished, he tries some and likes it. His perceptions have changed during this activity.

—————————— ——————————

There are as many activities and interactions within them as there are people in the world. Each participant brings past experiences to a new activity. Sometimes an activity is repeated for practice or consolidation. At other times, one participant assists a less experienced one in learning a part of the activity. These activities should be positive experiences.

The Child in Context

The **environment** is the setting, or context, in which reciprocal interactions take place. It is the physical setting, which in a room may include such things as the location, size, spacing of windows and doors, temperature, light, water source, and electrical outlets. The furniture, furnishings (i.e., draperies, curtains, cushions, pillows), pictures, and children's equipment and their placement in the room must also be considered (Feeney, Christensen, & Moravcik, 1996). Sounds and smells are also factors. In addition to these physical attributes, the context includes the people (and animals) and interactions that take place.

Possible characteristics of one rather simple setting have been described. However, the environment is not limited to a single immediate setting. Rather, it includes interconnections between single settings and the factors from outside these contexts that may influence them. Socialization practices and cultural patterns also are a part of a setting (Bronfenbrenner, 1979).

A context may also include the heredity and previous experiences of the participants, their behavior within the setting, personality and temperament characteristics, and family patterns (Ford & Lerner, 1992; Thomas & Chess, 1980). The amount of space within a setting can also influence interactions.

A context is not static; it is always evolving and changing, depending on the participants and the interactions taking place (Dewey, 1938). In evaluating changes in development, behavior, and learning, the context in which the changes occurred and the time at which they took place must be considered and understood.

🕮 INAPPROPRIATE INTERACTION

Many types of reciprocal interaction have been described. They are important in many ways for the young child's development and learning. Although interactions take place continuously, there are times when children do not need adult-child interaction. Those who care for and teach young children must know when interaction is not necessary. In fact, at times, it can hinder children instead of helping them (Trawick-Smith, 1994).

Young children need to develop independence, which is basic to their normal development. Independence begins with their mobility as infants. They need safe environments in which to explore. Adults can be important in planning appropriate spaces and activities. However, children should have the freedom to discover things on their own, so that they gain the ability to solve problems and develop self-reliance. If a child indicates by actions or words that assistance is needed, then the adult should be available as a resource (White, 1975).

Sometimes it seems as though a child is unnecessarily repeating a task. An adult may perceive the skill as easy, but the child may not think that it is. Children like to practice skills that they are learning. For example, when children learn to zip a zipper, they may repeat the action over and over again; it is best to let them do it. In this case, children are the best judges of their competence in doing the task.

All too often, when young children are engaged in a task, they are interrupted, possibly as a result of a scheduling problem when the activities are changing for a group or class. At other times, the adult is just trying to be helpful. Adults should understand that they can contribute to inattention and distractibility when they do not allow children to have the time to solve a problem or complete a task (Jacobvitz & Sroufe, 1987).

Another difficulty that adults cause for children is not giving them enough time to respond to a question. Children's thought processes sometimes do not move as fast as those of an adult. They need time to understand the question, think of the answer, and then respond (Donoghue, 1990).

The creative process requires materials, space, time, and experimentation. Usually, if the adult organizes the materials in the setting, children are able to work creatively with little assistance. Since the process should be more important than the product, the adult needs to be a good observer and available for assistance only when needed.

There are many times when interaction is appropriate, but there are also times when it is better for the adult to stand back and not become involved in the child's activity. A knowledge of child development, information concerning the individual child's abilities and/or needs, and good observation skills are necessary for the adult to know when to interact and when to refrain from interacting with a child.

🕮 EXAMPLES OF INTERACTIONS IN EACH DEVELOPMENTAL AREA

A variety of interactions is possible in each of the developmental areas. Examples are described for the selected strands in each area of development. Each interaction takes place in some environmental context. The context should always be considered when evaluating the success of an interaction.

Personal-Social Interactions

In the area of personal-social development, positive reciprocal interactions between adults and children are particularly important. Through these interactions, parental and other adult behaviors become predictable for children. Children have a growing understanding that adults can be trusted to provide a stable environment that meets their needs. This begins with positive parent-child interaction, and later other caregivers or teachers are able to extend the process.

Parents become predictable in providing for the basic needs of food, clean clothing, shelter, nurturing, and security (Maslow, 1970). Parents assist children in gaining independence from them and in developing confidence and self-control. Parents provide role models for interaction with others, and they teach the social skills necessary in the culture. Caregivers and teachers extend the support of the parents. This might take place in the home setting when parents are absent or in a family child-care home, child-care center, or school.

Trust   In Erik Erikson's theory (1963), trust is promoted by the parents' provision of stable care. The child accepts the care and gives positive feedback to the parent. The parent then continues the care in a predictable environment. This process can be extended in the school classroom by the teacher's providing a predictable daily schedule. Occasionally, the schedule might change, but generally children should know when certain activities occur during the school day. The schedule should be posted on the wall, and children told in advance of changes. The following vignette is an example of this kind of experience:

Interaction: Adult-Child

Setting: First-Grade Classroom

Children in a first-grade class (six-year-olds) have learned that the teacher will read them a story after they have returned from the lunchroom each day. Today, a resource person from the local zoo will give a presentation for them in their room after lunch instead. At the beginning of the school day and again before lunch, the teacher tells the class that there will be a change in the schedule. They

discuss the alternate plans and are reminded that the story will be read again as usual on the next day.

The schedule change described in the preceding vignette will have little effect on the behavior of the children in the class. However, when there is no classroom schedule or it is largely unpredictable from day to day, similar activities may take place at different times on succeeding days. When that occurs, many young children may experience feelings of insecurity (Bredekamp, 1987; Seefeldt & Barbour, 1994).

An environment with little predictability and few expectations by the adults in charge may cause anxiety, apathy, low productivity, and aggression in children. Not all children, however, react to the same circumstances in the same way (Shaffer, 1989). Daily routines and adult behaviors need not be rigid, but there should be consistency. Trust is promoted when children have some idea of what to expect of the adults with whom they interact daily.

Attachment/Separation   Beginning at birth, the attachment/separation process is ongoing between parent (or permanent primary caregiver) and child. It usually begins with an attachment between mother and child. A bond based on mutual respect and trust develops between the parents and child (Brazelton & Cramer, 1990). As the child grows older, ambivalence usually occurs between the child's necessary dependence on the parent and a struggle for independence. Children who have experienced a secure environment have few problems moving away from the parent and adjusting to separation experiences. However, it is a gradual process. The parent provides experiences in which the child moves away and then returns to the parent for support. A child who has just recently learned to walk may exhibit the following behavior.

Interaction: Parent-Child

Setting: Friend's Home

Rachel (age one year) has just begun unassisted walking. She walks away from her mother and investigates a box in the corner of the room. Every so often, she looks back to be sure that her mother is still in the area. She walks back and touches her mother, and her mother talks with her. Then Rachel starts out again to look at something else. If another adult in the room talks to her, she smiles, but she also checks to be sure that her mother is still there. She continues to move out and then back to her mother, but she stays away longer each time and checks on her mother less often.

If the child in the preceding example had been in her own home, she may have been more secure in her exploration. However, her mother understood her need for support in the new setting. Young children need many experiences to feel comfortable outside the presence of a parent (or primary caregiver) to whom they have an attachment. However, caring interactive support allows them to attain some independence. Little by little, children learn to function with less adult assistance.

Young children have different reactions to separation, depending on both their early experience with attachment and their temperament. For example, one child may be extremely timid concerning new experiences. Another may have little fear in relation to exploratory behavior. Adults caring for these children should understand the differences and be appropriately supportive when children have separation problems (Brazelton, 1987).

Self-Esteem Positive interactions usually enhance self-esteem. Self-esteem represents the feelings that one has about oneself, and de-

veloping it is a lifelong process (Curry & Johnson, 1990). Self-esteem is a mirror of how others see a person. Young children begin developing self-esteem through interactions with their parents. As the child develops, other caregivers, teachers, and peers contribute to feelings of self-worth. Self-esteem requires a sense of belonging in a family or group and a sense of individuality that includes both strengths and weaknesses. It is expressed through knowledge, talents, and skills (Aldridge, 1993). The development of self-esteem is a gradual process and can change, depending on the situation. Here is an example of a positive interaction.

Interaction: Adult-Child

Setting: Kindergarten Classroom

Billy (age five years) comes into the classroom. As the teacher greets him, he asks, "Hey, do you know what I got?" The teacher observes him as he looks down toward his feet. Together they say, "New shoes!" The teacher and Billy both smile. He feels good about the shoes, and he is also happy to share the news with his teacher. The teacher's reaction is one of warmth and acceptance.

In the preceding example, the teacher has taken time to share the child's good feelings. If adults are too busy, or do not realize the importance of this kind of interaction, children may learn that adults do not think their information or feelings are important. When children are continually given negative feedback from parents and other adults, they begin to believe that they have no value. This can cause them to look elsewhere for ways to bolster their self-esteem. Adults need to value and support children's interests. Activities should be planned that allow each child to be successful each day.

Self-Control In the area of self-control, it might seem that reciprocal interaction has no place. However, parents or other adults can assist children in developing autonomy (the governing of one's own behavior) by setting up experiences that require choices and have consequences, depending on the choice made. In addition, adults can assist young children in resolving conflicts through the use of words rather than physical confrontation (Kamii, 1982). Here is an example of a child who is given a choice.

Interaction: Child-Child

Setting: Child-Care Center

Ruby (age four years) is having difficulty with self-control. George has all of the play dough at the table. Ruby tries to take some, and George hits her. The caregiver has observed the situation. He sug- *gests that Ruby talk to George about the problem. Ruby then says to George that he has all of the play dough and is not sharing. She asks him to give her some, "please." George looks over at the teacher and then hands Ruby some play dough.*

Children being cared for in a group come from all kinds of environments and have had many kinds of experiences. If adults maintain order with direct control and punishment, they are promoting **heteronomy** (being governed by someone else). When adults promote heteronomy, young children are not able to develop self-control or become autonomous (Kamii, 1982). In the preceding example, the caregiver did not directly intervene. He gave suggestions and let the children try to solve the problem. However, the caregiver's presence helped to foster the appropriate response.

Group of preschoolers interact in associative play.

The development of self-control is a gradual process that must take place over time. Experiences to develop self-control should begin in the early years, if children of high school age (and older) are to be expected to make wise choices and solve their problems peacefully. Adults should provide opportunities for children in their care to make choices.

Social Interaction   Young children begin their interactions with parents and other members of their families. Hopefully, the majority of the interactions are positive. Positive interactions with others foster self-esteem and teach a skill that is important throughout life. Adults can model appropriate interactions so that children can learn from them. Human interactions take place between children and their parents, caregivers, teachers, older children, and peers. Children should have social interaction experiences with a variety of people. The following example shows a positive interaction between a young child and an elderly man.

Interaction: Adult-Child

Setting: Grandmother's Home

Carl (age three years) is visiting his grandmother, whom he knows well. A friend of his grandmother stops by with her father (90 years old) for a short time. The man greets Carl and then sits down to read a magazine. Carl comes close to the man and says, "Hi, I want to talk to you." The man puts down the magazine and says, "How old are you?" Carl tells him and then goes to get a favorite book. He hands the book to the man and says, "Read it to me." The man reads the book to Carl.

The preceding example was a positive interaction. However, interactions will not always be positive. Everyone has negative interactions at one time or another. The elderly man may have ignored the child. The child may have had a "slow-to-warm-up" temperament, and he may not have pursued an interaction with the older man.

Interactions also vary according to cultures. For example, Native American children may not make eye contact with the person with whom they're talking. Teachers who do not understand this may think these children are being disrespectful. Facilitating positive interactions depends on knowledge and requires practice. Adults should provide a variety of situations in which children can experience positive social interaction.

Social Skills   All societies have rules. Some rules are written laws and others may be social or safety rules that aid order and predictability. Rules usually have their basis in the predominant culture of the area. Children learn the rules of the family and society through interactions with others. Whether formal or informal, rules and social convention can be transmitted only through interaction. The following example shows the importance of learning a safety rule.

Interaction: Parent-Child

Setting: Outside Child's Home

Shamika (age four years) has just moved into a house that has no sidewalk on her side of the street. To ride her tricycle, she must cross the street. It is not a busy street, and her parents want her to learn how to cross it safely. Her mother shows her how to look both ways carefully before crossing the street. They practice at different times of the day until both her mother and Shamika think she can manage the crossing alone.

Some parents may think that teaching a four-year-old child to cross the street alone is inappropriate. The decision would depend on many factors within the context. Rules are related to many things. Some rules contribute to safety, and others may be related to manners. Children understand rules better when they help to make them. In both the home and in group programs, children can help in establishing rules and determining the consequences when a rule is broken. Adults can assist children in understanding the reasons for laws and rules. When children do not learn rules, it can cause problems and a loss of self-esteem.

Physical Interactions

Interactions in the motor development area may be between people. However, for this area of development, children should have many experiences, including interactions with objects and individual activities to enhance their physical skills. Adults, and children who are competent in a specific motor skill, can provide coaching. This assists children in reaching the highest level of which they are capable (Vygotsky, 1978).

Physical development includes gross motor and fine motor skills. Practice in both begins early in life. Infants are interested in looking, listening, and touching. By the middle of their first year, they are striving for mobility. Reaching, crawling, and walking are gross motor skills. Children need space that is safe for the practice of these skills. Fine motor skills include grasping with the hand, and then the thumb and fingers. Again, much practice is necessary with different objects and physical activities for a child to become competent. As children grow and develop, they want to learn many physical skills. Some skills require coaching, and all require practice.

Gross Motor Bodily movement has a clearly defined developmental schedule across cultures (Gardner, 1993). However, children vary in their ability to learn gross motor

skills. Some have a better bodily kinesthetic sense than others (Engstrom, 1971). One child may take longer to develop the same skill that another child of the same age masters much earlier. There is a wide range of individual differences in gross motor development. Some differences may be hereditary, and others may be cultural (Gardner, 1983). Although most children learn to walk with little coaching, other skills may take some demonstration or assistance.

------------------ ------------------

Interaction: Parent-Child

Setting: Child's Home

Chester (age three years) would like to learn how to skip. No matter how hard he tries, it just does not work. Chester's mother demonstrates how to hop on one foot. She then shows him that skipping is first hopping on one foot and then hopping on the other foot. He tries that out and finds that it works. He then spends a lot of time practicing his newly learned skill.

------------------ ------------------

In the preceding example, the adult assisted the child in learning the parts of the skill and then helped him to put the parts together. Afterward, the child practiced on his own. It was not something that he was told to do. He was interested in improving his skill. The desire to learn the skill matched the child's ability to learn it at that time. Sometimes the child is not motivated to learn a skill. When that is true, it is better not to impose a practice schedule on the child. Without the child's interest, little progress is made.

To help children learn gross motor skills, adults need to understand a child's abilities and interests. If a child needs assistance, it can be helpful to break the larger skill down into parts that can then be introduced in a sequence.

Fine Motor   Small muscles are used in the development of fine motor skills. Eye-hand coordination is also achieved through practice with fine motor movement. The adult must know the history of the child's motor development so that appropriate activities may be introduced. Fine motor skills are necessary for the successful completion of many tasks (e.g., buttoning, writing). Sometimes interaction with adults or children may be necessary. However, many fine motor skills are learned through child-object interaction. Again, as in the development of gross motor skills, practice is essential. An example of a child-object interaction follows.

Interaction: Child-Object

Setting: Family Child-Care Home

Serena (age two years) is playing with a large plastic bottle and 1-inch colored plastic chips. She has learned how to grasp the chip between thumb and forefinger. She drops each chip into the bottle and dumps them out. Then she starts again. She works at it over and over.

The child in this example is practicing a fine motor skill that also enhances her eye-hand coordination. She must line up the chip with the mouth of the bottle to drop it in. Although it may seem like an easy task, a two-year-old needs practice to do it well. Young children need many tasks like this one to develop their small muscles. Both parents and caregivers in child-care programs should provide a variety of fine motor experiences for young children. Young children may have difficulty with a new task and lose interest. When an adult observes this, supportive interaction in teaching the skill can be helpful.

Cognitive Interactions

Interactions that facilitate **cognitive development** may be between people, but adults should provide children with opportunities for interactions with objects as well. Time needs to be allotted for young children to explore and investigate things on their own. After providing a safe, stimulating environment, adults should stand back and observe children in their activities. Sometimes the children may be figuring out how objects work. They may be engaged in activities by themselves or with other children.

At times, the adult may want to assist in extending a child's thinking through suggestions, questioning, or providing counterexamples (Piaget, 1948/1973; Vygotsky, 1978). For example, if a four-year-old child is painting and notices that mixing blue and yellow paint makes green paint, the adult might ask what would happen if red and blue paint were mixed. Over the years, this kind of interaction, sometimes termed the *teachable moment*, is very important in cognitive development.

Parents and other adults can assist young children in the development of attention skills and help them to complete tasks. They can set up problems for children to solve and provide opportunities for choices. Through the use of questioning strategies, adults can promote thinking skills. Although the adult has an important role in promoting cognitive development, young children must also have the freedom to solve problems of their own making.

Development of Attention   The ability to focus attention is one of the most important skills that a person can attain. Although there is a predisposition to attend from birth, it must be learned through interactions with both people and objects. Some children have a more difficult time than others with this skill. No matter what the cause of the difficulty, however, they must still learn to attend. Young children need both the motivation and the skills necessary to be able to do a task. If they do not, they will lose interest. Parents and teachers should assist children in extending their level of attention behavior. An example of such an interaction follows. This child had previously been observed having problems attending to tasks.

Interaction: Adult-Child

Setting: Kindergarten Classroom

Lanty (age five years) has moved to the manipulative shelf during free-choice time. He selects a tub of small plastic builders and dumps them out on the floor. The teacher observes him from the other side of the room. He begins to put two blocks together and is unsuccessful. He picks up two more, and again he is unsuccessful. He starts to leave the activity. The teacher moves in and says, "Let me show you how these work." He watches as she puts two together. She then asks him to take two of the blocks. She holds his hands to show him how they snap together. She says, "Now, you try it." He tries and is successful. He continues to work with the blocks.

In this example, the child did not have the skill to work with the task long enough to gain satisfaction from it. With just a little coaching, the child was able to gain the skill. There are many times when a little assistance solves an attention problem. However, usually there is a pattern of inattentiveness in a child. That is when the adult must provide added assistance to help the child in maintaining attention in different contexts.

Adults can assist children by keeping them interested in a topic or activity. This can be done when adults ask them questions, point out similarities and differences, and as-

sist them in learning the skills necessary to do a particular task.

Problem Solving Children need time to solve problems. An adult can set up a problem for the child to solve, or the problem can evolve from the child's play. In either case, the child should be able to try to solve the problem without intervention. Many times, there is more than one solution to a specific problem. This is when an adult can interact by asking questions to help the child better understand the problem or by suggesting possible alternative solutions. An example of a problem that evolved out of a child's play follows.

Interaction: Child-Object

Setting: Child-Care Center

Rosa (age four years) is working at the sand table. She is trying to make a tunnel in the sand, but it keeps falling in when she digs through it. The caregiver observes her for a while. The caregiver asks, "Why is the sand falling in? What's wrong?" The child thinks a little and then says, "It's not sticky enough." The caregiver asks, "How can we make the sand stickier?" The child decides that it needs more water. The caregiver gives her a pitcher of water and suggests that she add a little at a time until the sand holds together. The child experiments with the water.

In this example, it may have been easier for the caregiver to add the water to the sand herself. By letting the child do it, the child may learn more about sand consistency and that too much water is as bad as not having enough. Some children have trouble solving problems because they do not think about possible solutions. This is when an adult or more competent child can make a difference.

Children can be assisted in solving problems when adults ask questions such as, "What would happen if . . . ?" Adults should help children find solutions that they can do by themselves.

Making Choices Young children need opportunities to begin making choices early. Parents and other adults can assist by planning activities that children can choose. Most people working with young children in group childcare programs and schools recognize this need. They may set up learning center areas within the classroom where children can choose to play and work during specific time periods. The adult sets up the environment, and the children choose activities. The adult can assist a child in making a choice when necessary. This example shows a teacher assisting a child to make a choice within a learning center.

Interaction: Child-Context

Setting: Second-Grade Classroom

Donald (age seven years) has selected the social studies center during the time for center activities. He has not decided what he will do there, but there are several choices. The teacher asks, "What are you interested in learning about?" He looks at a list of possibilities posted in the center and says, "Antarctica." The teacher suggests that he begin with the encyclopedia, look at books on the topic, and then check for further information on the computer. The child has narrowed his choices in the center to one topic.

Some children have little difficulty in making choices. The earlier they have the opportunity, both at home and in group programs, the easier it is for them. In this example, the teacher provided some choices within the context. When children do not have prac-

tice, they find making choices difficult. They should be given support while they are learning. If children are just beginning to learn to make choices, adults should limit the number of possible choices until the child has had some practice. For example, only two choices may be given at first, then more choices can be added little by little.

Asking Open-Ended Questions Young children should have opportunities to both ask and answer open-ended questions. They need to know that questions do not always have only one answer. Questions promote interaction between people. Parents and other adults should begin to ask these kinds of questions early. They should encourage children to do the same. When children are asked open-ended questions, they learn to ask similar kinds of questions. This aids them in developing complex verbal skills (Heath, 1983, 1989). Here is an example of a parent asking a young child an open-ended question.

Interaction: Parent-Child

Setting: Child's Home

Barbara (age three years) is sitting at the table in the kitchen. Her mother says, "What are some vegetables that we could eat?" The child responds with "Carrots, celery, beans, and I forgot the rest." Her mother continues, "Tomatoes, potatoes, peas, and squash." Barbara responds with, "Corn."

In this example, there are many possible answers to the question. If, however, the mother had shown the child a carrot and then asked, "What vegetable is this?" the child would have had only one choice. Adults working with children should think about the questions they ask. They should encourage children to ask questions with more than one answer.

Kindergarten teachers help children learn to ask questions during whole-group time.

Completion of Tasks   To succeed, children must learn the importance of completing tasks or activities that they begin. Some children are good at this, and others need some assistance. Encouragement and support are important when there is a problem. Sometimes children can be grouped together to do a project, and they can assist each other in the completion of the tasks. Following is an example of children working together to complete a project in a school-age child-care context.

Interaction: Child-Child

Setting: School-Age Child Care

Four children (ages six to eight years) are making a large papier-mâché piñata for Cinco de Mayo. They have covered a large balloon with strips of newspaper dipped in wheat paste. The piñata is dry and needs to be painted. One of the girls does not want to paint. A boy says, "If we all paint it, we'll get done faster." The other two children agree, and the girl says she will help.

When children learn the importance of completing tasks, they are more likely to want to try. They need to get satisfaction from completing a task as well as they can. Adults can assist children in learning this skill by encouraging them. For example, the adult might say, "You will be so happy to be all finished." Sometimes the adult may give assistance when there is difficulty in completing a task. An adult might say, "I'll help you put the blocks away." Adults must understand the child's developmental level. Expectations of what can be accomplished should match the child's ability.

Communication Interactions

All areas of communication development require adult-child interaction for the child to learn the language. Parents are the first adults to provide a model of language for their child. Older children and peers can also play a part. Later, other adults from the child's culture give their support. Generally, the interactions are between people. However, books, tapes, and other media may contribute to the development of communication skills.

Communication development includes listening, speaking, writing, reading, and non-verbal interaction. Children begin listening to others early in life. As they hear the sounds of their language, they begin to make sounds themselves. These sounds evolve into verbal language. In the predominant culture of the United States, children are exposed early to printed language. They see it outdoors and on television. As they gain experience with drawing, children begin to make letters. When parents and other adults read to children, they are presenting a model for the child's future reading. Adults can provide a supportive, interactive environment that helps children become literate.

Listening   Listening is the first of the communication skills that an infant encounters. To listen, a child must be able to hear. Listening is the selection from sounds that are heard, combined with the ability to process them for meaning. Young children need listening experiences in different contexts. Adults must provide good speaking models for children to understand the meaning. Tapes can be used to provide listening experiences in group programs. The following example shows this type of activity.

Interaction: Child-Activity

Setting: Child-Care Center

Joe (age four years) has selected the listening center during free-choice time at the child-care center. A tape has been placed in the listening station of the story Mike Mulligan and the Steam Shovel *by Virginia L. Burton (1939). Joe is able to look at the book as he listens to the story.*

In this example, a tape was used. This is one way that media can be used to provide lis-

tening experiences. Videotapes, films, sound filmstrips, records, and computers can also be used. In addition to such media, adults can provide a variety of listening experiences for children. They can read or tell stories and have discussions in groups or with individual children. Parents and other adults or older children can come to the classroom and make a presentation. To provide a good speaking model, adults must speak clearly. When speaking to an individual child, it can be helpful if the adult stoops down to the child's level so the child has no difficulty in hearing.

Speaking   From the time young children can say a few words, they enjoy speaking. They try out new sounds and new words. They need people to talk with, both adults and other children, and they should have environments that encourage oral language. Parents should talk with their children. Talking should be a major focus in child-care programs, and teachers should encourage talking in school classrooms. Oral language is a foundation for writing. Here is an example of an oral interaction between a parent and child.

Interaction: Parent-Child

Setting: Child's Home

Carrie (age one year) is talking a little. She is making sounds and some words. Her mother wants her to learn the names of objects that are used each day; she points to something and says its name, such as "chair" or "doll." Then Carrie tries to say it, too. Sometimes she says the whole word. She is learning what things are and their names.

Carrie's mother is helping her to develop the underlying concepts for the word labels that are used in their language. Children learn to speak the language that is spoken in their homes. Sometimes the language in the group program or school is different from the one the child uses in the home. When this occurs, adults should assist the child in learning the new language.

Writing Writing begins when a child picks up a pencil or crayon and begins to scribble. Drawing is a foundation for writing. To be able to write, children need lots of these kinds of experiences, along with speaking activities. As they draw and have experiences with print, they incorporate letters into their drawing. Dictation occurs when the teacher writes down what the child says about a drawing. When an adult uses dictation in interaction with a child, the child begins to understand that thoughts can become words. Children also need lots of drawing experiences to become good writers. This example shows a caregiver interacting with a child through dictation.

Interaction: Adult-Child

Setting: Family Child-Care Home

Andrea (age four years) is drawing with crayons at a small table. As she finishes her picture, she holds it up to show the caregiver. The caregiver says, "Would you like to tell me about your picture? I will write what you say on the back." Andrea says, "This is my new baby brother. He is very little. His name is Robert." The caregiver writes it down and then reads it to Andrea. She reads it along with the caregiver.

Writing is a process that takes much practice in different kinds of activities. Adults can assist children in activities like the one in the example. They can provide the materials for drawing, and they can provide for many oral language experiences so that children learn to organize their thoughts.

Reading Young children are exposed to print in the environment earlier and earlier. It is not surprising to hear a two-year-old calling out the names "McDonald's" (hamburgers) or "Baskin-Robbins" (ice cream) while passing these restaurants. This is the beginning of reading (Aldridge et al., 1996). Reading to children reinforces this information. They begin to understand that print has meaning and that they can learn to read, too. Many children are reading before they begin kindergarten. The individualized reading approach can assist children in allowing them to begin where they are reading and continue at their own pace. Books are objects that have a message written by someone. In that regard, the interactions are child-object. However, adults can be effective at interacting in this reading process. Here is an example of a teacher interacting with a child in an individual reading conference.

Interaction: Adult-Child

Setting: Third-Grade Classroom

Barry (age eight years) has just finished reading a book. He brings it to his reading conference with his teacher. She asks him some questions about the book. Then she asks him to read several of his favorite paragraphs aloud. He tells her that he would like to recommend the book to others in the class. They decide that he will make a short summary presentation, but he won't tell the ending. He discusses with her the next book he plans to read.

The teacher in the preceding example has personalized her reading lesson with the child. She has learned a lot about his reading progress and that he can comprehend at his reading level. This method requires accurate records for each child. Books that have been read, oral reading ability, and answers to comprehension questions are all important aspects of a child's reading progress. Children who are having difficulty in learning to read should meet with the teacher more often than those having few problems.

Nonverbal Communication There are many ways to communicate without using words. Much creative work is nonverbal. Parents and adults use nonverbal communication in their interactions with young children. These might be facial expressions or gestures. Adults should also provide experiences where children can use nonverbal communication through art media, music, dance, and mime. A mime activity follows:

------------------ ------------------

Interaction: Child-Activity

Setting: Kindergarten Classroom

A group of kindergarten children (age five years) engages in an activity using mime. They each have a turn to act out their favorite community helper. The teacher has given them guidelines and now sits back to observe the activity. The first child has selected firefighter. *He pretends to jump off the fire truck and then holds his hands as though holding a hose directed toward a fire. He pretends to wipe his face. The rest of the children guess who he is pretending to be.*

------------------ ------------------

When a child in a classroom is hearing impaired or deaf, sign language may be needed. The teacher can assist the other children in the class in learning this means of interactive communication with the deaf child.

Creative Interactions

Many interactions in **creative development** are between children and objects or materials. The objects may be such things as plastic builders, blocks, dolls, dress-up clothes, and

puppets. Materials might be a variety of types of paper, pencils, crayons, paints, dough, or clay. These activities sometimes take place with other children, and sometimes a child works alone.

Creativity is the ability to see things in new ways or to combine unrelated objects and ideas into something new (Schirrmacher, 1993). The adult provides the place and the equipment or materials and then observes the children. Although creative interactions can produce a product, the process young children go through in creating is far more important. Children need many experiences in the use of different media in which no specific product is required.

Children may have difficulty in using some materials, and the adult may need to provide assistance. At other times, the adult may interact to help the child think about different possibilities. Children must learn to take risks in trying out new ways of doing things.

Parents and other adults can help children with creative development by providing

Girls manipulate play dough alongside one another.

sen-sory/art experiences, music and movement activities. Creative dramatics includes the use of role playing, flannel board, puppets, and plays. Another part of creative development is creative writing, in which adults, older children, and peers can interact in different phases.

Sensory/Art   Sensory art experiences are important for many of the areas of development. They may encompass social and motor skills or cognitive and communication abilities. Parents may not allow their young children to engage in creative sensory/art experiences in the home setting as a result of a lack of understanding regarding the creative process, the perception of a potential mess, or a lack of available space. Group-care programs and schools should include these kinds of activities on a daily basis. The setting must be aesthetically alive and conducive to creative endeavor (Schirrmacher, 1993). Here is an example of a child-child activity.

Interaction: Child-Child

Setting: Second-Grade Classroom

Eight second-grade children (seven years old) cooperate in planning and making a mural related to a unit on "Summer Fun." During a discussion, they talk about things they hope to do during the summer. They include activities such as playing, swimming, traveling, reading, gardening, helping at home, eating ice cream, and celebrating the Fourth of July. They decide to make a collage of their planned summer activities. Each child has a space on the mural to depict one activity. The mural is a creative group project.

Children need the opportunity to work in the sensory and visual arts individually and in groups, such as in this example. They should have a wide variety of experiences, and adults should value their creative efforts. When children have not had sensory/art opportunities, they need a great many experiences before they feel competent. The later that children begin the process, the less comfortable they are and the less independent they will be.

Music   Music should be a part of a child's life from birth. Parents sing to infants and then, as children become verbal, they sing along. Simple instruments can be used so that young children can make their own music. Sometimes adults interact with children by playing an instrument with them. At other times, the adult provides the equipment, time, and space and stands back to observe (Andress, 1989). Here is an activity in which the adult is interacting with a child.

Interaction: Adult-Child

Setting: Child-Care Center

Thad (age three years) is tapping a rhythm with two rhythm sticks. The caregiver joins him with a shaker. She shakes her instrument in time to his rhythm. He varies the rhythm, and she follows along.

Some children have a better musical sense than others. In this example, the child was able to change his rhythm easily. Some children have more difficulty with this kind of activity. They need experiences that give them practice. Adults can provide a variety of individual and group experiences related to music.

Movement   Young children love to move in their environment, no matter where they are. Adults may interact through movement activities but more often they just participate with the children. Creative movement can take place with or without a music background.

The environment can contribute to movement activities. An example of a spontaneous group movement activity is given here.

——————— ———————

Interaction: Child-Context

Setting: Child-Care Center

Several children (age two years) are playing in a large child-care room. The caregiver puts a record on the phonograph while they play. When the music starts, first one child and then another starts to dance around to the music. The change in the environment has caused a change in their behavior.

——————— ———————

Movement activities can include both motor and creative abilities when children are allowed to interpret the movement possibilities as they wish. It is not a creative activity when children are told exactly how to move.

Dramatics Creative dramatics includes a wide variety of possible experiences. However, in each, the participants assume another role. The interpretation of the role is a major part of the creative process in this type of experience. Children interact with props. The role of the parent, or other adult, is to provide the space and props for the children to use. However, sometimes the adult can assume one of the roles or parts in interaction with children. The following example shows a parent assuming a role in interacting with his child.

——————— ———————

Interaction: Parent-Child

Setting: Child's Home

Cadalia (age six years) is playing with blocks. She has built an elaborate garage for her cars. She invites her father to play with her. She drives a car around a "road" on the rug and then parks it in the garage. Her father drives another car around like she did, and parks his car in the garage. She then suggests that they take a "trip" to a local park. Her father plays with her, interacting with some suggestions of his own.

——————— ———————

Young children play in dramatic activities alone, with other children, and sometimes with adults. They use different kinds of props in different ways. When props are not available, they may improvise with whatever is there.

Creative Writing Creative writing is a process that is based in part in oral language. Children should be encouraged to make up stories orally before they are expected to put words onto paper. Parents and other adults can assist children in organizing their thoughts. As the children gain experience, the interaction will change to sharing their writing. Sometimes this is done for a group. The authors read their work to the other children. Here is an example of this kind of activity.

——————— ———————

Interaction: Child-Child

Setting: Second-Grade Classroom

Carly (age seven years) has finished a draft of a story that she has been writing. She wants to read it to the class so that they can give her suggestions concerning ways that it could be improved. The teacher has a time each day that this kind of activity can occur. Carly reads her story and gets several suggestions from the group.

——————— ———————

When given the opportunity, children take the responsibility of becoming an author seriously. Both adults and other children must respect a child's work at whatever level they are functioning. Within a supportive atmosphere, children can thrive in this type of activity.

❧ SUMMARY

Young children develop and learn through a variety of daily interactions in different contexts. There are three theories in which reciprocal interaction plays a major role. The theory of T. Berry Brazelton focuses on the interactions that take place between parent and child. Social and cultural interactions both within and among environmental contexts are emphasized by Urie Bronfenbrenner. Richard M. Lerner examines biological influences as they relate to organizational contexts in society.

A variety of types of interactions are described in the chapter. Interpersonal interactions include those between parent and child, between adult and child, and between children of various ages. Other interactions that children may have with objects, activities, and environmental contexts are examined. The times that interactions may be inappropriate for young children are discussed.

The developmental areas discussed are the personal-social, physical, cognitive, communication, and creative areas. The chapter concludes with examples of interactions for each strand in each developmental area. Examples are described for children from birth to eight years old in differing settings.

QUESTIONS AND PROJECTS FOR THE READER

1. Select an age level and describe an appropriate interaction for each of the five developmental areas.

2. Select one strand in each developmental area. Describe an interaction that is different from those found in the chapter.
3. Think of ways in which interactions might be different when children have special needs (e.g., blind or motor-impaired children). Write several of your ideas to share with the class.
4. In small groups, class participants can assume the roles of characters in several of the interactions found in the chapter. They should try to make the dramatization as realistic as possible.
5. Think of an inappropriate interaction in each of the five areas of development. Then describe each one and tell how it could be changed to become an appropriate positive interaction.

FOR FURTHER READING

Brazelton, T. B., & Cramer, B. G. (1990). *The earliest relationship* (chapters 10–13). Reading, MA: Addison-Wesley. Chapters 10 through 12 include an overview of studies related to parent-infant interaction. Brazelton's four stages in early interaction are described in chapter 13.

Bronfenbrenner, U. (1979). *The ecology of human development* (Chapter 2). Cambridge, MA: Harvard University Press. Basic concepts and definitions related to the different systems in Bronfenbrenner's theory are described.

Ford, D. H., & Lerner, R. M. (1992). *Developmental systems theory: An integrative approach* (Chapter 3). Newbury Park, CA: Sage. Chapter 3 discusses developmental contextualism, emphasizing the relationship of biology and context. Also included is a description of dynamic interactionism as it relates to reciprocal causality.

Chapter Six

Personal-Social Development

O b j e c t i v e s

After reviewing this chapter, you will be able to

- Identify six key strands of personal-social development.
- Indicate ways that traditional subject matter areas connect to personal-social development.
- Discuss the role of adult-child interaction in developing the six key strands of personal-social development.
- Identify critical elements for providing continuity of care for children in various child-care settings.
- Select developmental, age-appropriate activities for promoting personal-social development for a particular child or a specified group of children.
- Discuss the impact of diverse cultural expectations on the development of social interaction skills and social conventions.
- Generate examples for adapting activities for interactions with special needs children that promote personal-social development.

❧ INTRODUCTION

In infancy, a focus on personal-social development may be critical for survival. Terms such as the "failure to thrive syndrome" and the "vulnerable child syndrome" were coined to reflect disorders of mothering in relation to early bonding and attachment (Green & Solnit, 1964; Brody, 1956). Since the early 1960s, medical practices related to birthing and the premature infant's care have changed dramatically to reflect a concern for physical contact and early parent-child bonding (Brazelton & Greenspan, 2000; Schwartz & Schwartz, 1977). Throughout early childhood, parents, teachers, and caregivers significantly influence a child's personal-social development.

The key strands of personal-social development selected for discussion include trust, attachment/separation, self-esteem, self-control, social interactions, and social skills. Each strand relates to interactions in a variety of contexts in a young child's life. Interactions may take place between an adult and a child, between two or more children, or even between objects or activities and children.

The following sections provide a more detailed description of each strand of personal-social development. Activities that promote each strand are suggested for six age levels, from birth through age eight. Although an appropriate age level is suggested, many of the activities can be adapted for children older or younger than the specified age level.

Activities may also promote a second or third area of development. For example, helping a one-year-old child learn to eat independently promotes self-control, which is a strand in personal-social development. The same activity can also be viewed from the frameworks of physical development, communication development, cognitive development, and even, at times, creative development. The interaction during feeding and eating involves fine motor control, speaking, listening, nonverbal communication, problem solving, and role-playing. Whenever possible, cultural differences are discussed, which helps parents, teachers, and caregivers view elements of personal-social development from different perspectives.

Later in this chapter, a matrix of all the suggested activities (Table 6.1) precedes the activities, which are grouped by strands of development. These activities are referred to in the text. A section on curricular implications is included at the end of the chapter. Ties to alternate methods of curricular planning are discussed, giving specific examples of development-based activities.

❧ KEY STRANDS OF DEVELOPMENT

Trust

The development of basic trust is fostered by the ability of parents and caregivers to create a predictable environment for infants and to maintain that sense of order throughout childhood (Erikson, 1963). To learn to trust, infants must first know that their basic needs for physical and psychological survival will be met consistently. Basic human needs include food, shelter, clothing, love and affection, intellectual stimulation, and provisions for health and safety.

The sensitive adult soon learns to respond to the undifferentiated crying of a newborn with a routine of strategies. Is the baby likely to be hungry? Wet or soiled? Too cold or too warm? Is the infant in discomfort because of an illness, a protruding diaper pin, or an irritating fabric? Does the infant just need to be held or rocked? After a few months, the parent or caregiver can respond to the differences in the infant's cries with greater success. The adult has learned what works to soothe this particular infant, and the infant has learned that her basic needs will be met. The stage for basic trust has been set by the reciprocal interaction between adult and infant, each influencing and being influenced by the other (Brazelton & Greenspan, 2000).

Since infants cry for many reasons, the caregiver must first determine if a crying infant is in pain or needs to be changed or fed. Magda Gerber emphasized the critical need for adults to respect and appreciate infants as individuals. Through observation, the adult tunes in to the infant's rhythms and interacts with the infant on the basis of the infant's cues. Gerber stressed the importance of talking to babies during normal caregiving tasks, such as diapering and feeding. Trust in adults and in the environment is built on this foundation of respect for the infant as an individual. Activity 6.1 lists suggestions for soothing infants.

Caregiver soothes infant who has stranger anxiety.

Early caregiving must be provided on an individualized and personalized basis. Although some infants adapt readily to the routine of the family or the caregiver, individual differences are clearly seen. Family schedules that vary greatly from day to day often interfere with the development of predictable routines. A lack of continuity of caregivers may also impede personalized care. Knowing when and what an infant last ate, when and for how long she or he has slept, or how he or she likes to be soothed is essential to successfully meeting the basic needs of the infant. Caregivers in family child-care homes often develop informal routines for transmitting information about children's individual needs. Group child-care homes and full-day child-care centers are more likely to use a more formal means of keeping track of the daily schedules of the children under their care (Activity 6.2).

Differences in temperament likewise have a profound influence on establishing basic trust. The "slow-to-warm-up" infant is characterized by an initial negative reaction to new stimuli (Thomas & Chess, 1980; Chess & Thomas, 1996). Unless the parent is familiar with this behavior pattern and has identified the infant as having this particular temperament style, the parent might abandon caregiving techniques that meet with initial negative responses. On the other hand, a parent who is alert to a child's tendency to be "slow to warm up" will continue to try new stimuli gradually and patiently.

Children also vary in their willingness to take risks and their cognitive ability to make safe choices. As infants and toddlers increase in their mobility, it is essential for indoor and outdoor environments to be safe places in which to explore (Activity 6.3).

The "difficult" infant presents the greatest challenge to parents and caregivers. Fussy and overly sensitive infants tend to add to a parent's sense of failure as a caregiver. It is difficult to care for an infant who seemingly rejects attempts to meet his or her needs. A parent or caregiver who is aware of the infant's temperament style establishes a sense of trust with consistent, positive caregiving strategies. Experienced parents and caregivers more readily recognize the "difficult" infant. First-time parents are likely to be filled with self-doubt, which can easily reinforce a negative parenting pattern or avoidance.

Although basic trust versus basic mistrust is the first step within Erikson's (1963) framework of psychosocial development, parents and caregivers should not limit a concern for development of trust to infancy. The child's sense of inner security needs to be maintained. As in all areas of development, basic trust does not always follow a pattern of growth. Parents and caregivers need to reestablish trust during a child's illnesses and emotional crises (Brazelton & Greenspan, 2000). The seemingly poor timing of children's illnesses in relation to a parent's adult schedule adds to the frustration encountered by working parents. The child readily senses this frustration. Children need to be reassured that the inconvenience is an adult problem, not a child's problem (Activity 6.4).

The sense of security that routines provide for children (and adults) is well-known to caregivers and teachers. Adults who build realistic routines into their daily schedules find that children thrive on knowing what to expect and when to expect it to happen. Not being able to predict a routine leads some children to test their limits in the classroom. Similarly, classroom management is facilitated by organizing recurring activities into routines that can be maintained with minimal teacher intervention (Activity 6.5).

Parents may intuitively understand the need to provide predictability in the lives of young children dealing with stress. Moving often creates stress for children and their families. Packing a child's favorite toys and other security objects last, and unpacking them first, may add a sense of familiarity to new surroundings. Enrolling in a new school or changing child-care arrangements are two additional examples of events in the lives of young children that require parents to reestablish a sense of trust. Allowing children to observe a new setting in the presence of their parents before beginning a new venture helps them anticipate what to expect in the new situation (Activity 6.6). Certainly, changes in the family resulting from divorce, separation, or new siblings are also periods in a child's life when maintaining trust is critical.

Attachment/Separation

Early bonding sets a foundation for a secure attachment between infants and their parents or infants and their primary caregiver. A secure attachment is built on mutual respect and the infant's knowledge that his or her needs will be met (Brazelton & Cramer, 1990). As infants mature in cognitive ability, they begin to notice when they are separated from their attachment figure and tend to object by fussing or crying (Sroufe, 1996). For example, an infant can be playing happily on the kitchen floor while her mother prepares a meal, only to look up and notice that her mother has left the room. She may begin to cry but at first does not look around or crawl out of the room to look for her mother. As she develops **object permanence,** or a knowledge that an object does not cease to exist when it is out of sight, she will search out the attachment figure.

Parents and caregivers can interact with infants to help them develop object permanence (Activity 6.7). Parents can continue to talk to their infants as they go out of sight into an adjoining room. Infants can begin to attend to the changing sounds of the moving voice. For example, a father is seated next to his infant on the family room floor, folding laundry. The baby is playing contentedly with some plastic rings. The father stands up, picks up the laundry basket, and walks to the adjoining bedroom, saying, "I'm putting away your clothes, Joey. I'll be right back." The father continues to carry on a conversation from the next room. As the father leaves, Joey looks up, concerned, but does not cry.

At her neighbor's house, Mrs. Wang notices that fifteen-month-old Tam clings to her instead of going up to Mrs. Le. Mrs. Le had agreed to watch Tam for a few hours while Mrs. Wang goes to her dentist appointment. Mrs. Wang sits down to visit for a few minutes before leaving. She pulls Tam's favorite blanket out of the diaper bag and hands it to her. After a few minutes, Tam leaves her mother's side, dragging the blanket over to where Mrs. Le's two children are playing.

Many children are better able to separate from their parents when the transition is not forced and the parents are aware of their child's needs for familiarity. Security objects are often favorite blankets or soft toys that parents use to help children make transitions (Caplan, 1978). Children may cuddle the object at naps or bedtime or on a car trip. The object that feels and smells familiar helps children cope with separation from their parents (Activity 6.8).

Separation issues should also be considered when young children enroll in child-care programs. Children may separate more readily from one parent than another. Children who ride in carpools may be accompanied by siblings or other children, which may make the separation from the parent less stressful. Children who are "slow-to-warm-up" may find that coming to the center a little earlier than the rest of the group gives them a few extra minutes of individual time with the teacher or caregiver. Parents who have part-time jobs outside of the home may find that their children separate more easily for a half-day working schedule over a 5-day week than for a 2-day schedule of 10 hours each. Many

individual differences are seen in attachment/separation styles of children.

Child-care centers and schools can also do their part in easing separation difficulties. Activities 6.9 and 6.10 illustrate ways that teachers can strengthen parent-child attachments and support parental efforts in creating positive separation routines. The goal of parents and teachers is to create a climate of security. The focus can then become the child's learning to separate from parents without disintegrating emotionally.

As with maintaining a sense of trust, situations related to attachment and separation continue throughout childhood. When children become attached to their teachers, they may have trouble adjusting to unfamiliar adults in the school environment. Substitute teachers are frequently challenged by students to run the classroom just like the regular teacher. A young child with severe attachment/separation difficulties may refuse to enter the classroom when an unfamiliar person is in charge. Activity 6.11 depicts a strategy for widening a child's exposure to other adults and teaching the child how to interact with unfamiliar adults.

Spending the night away from home without a parent or close family member can sometimes be as anxiety-ridden for the parents as it is for the child. Whether children are spending the night with a friend or attending summer camp, the most difficult time of the day tends to be going to sleep. The activity and excitement of the day are forgotten when children realize they must fall asleep in new surroundings without the support of a parent. Children can use security objects to re-create the safety of the home environment. Preparation is the key. Children who have discussed the possibility of feeling lonely and who know some techniques for coping with this feeling are more likely to deal with their fears. The age when children are ready to spend the night with peers varies greatly (Activity 6.12).

Self-Esteem

Children's mental self-images influence their perceptions of the outside world and the ways in which they behave. A positive self-image develops from interactions directly with adults and indirectly with the environment mediated by those adults (Aldridge, 1993). Children with a positive self-image feel a sense of self-worth as it is reflected in the eyes of their caregivers.

Infants with an "easy" temperament have numerous daily opportunities to see their self-worth reflected by parents and caregivers. Positive reciprocal interactions convey messages to easy infants that they are wonderful and messages to the adults that they must indeed be wonderful parents and caregivers. In contrast, infants with "difficult" and "slow-to-warm-up" temperament styles often give messages of doubt to their caregivers. These infants tend to be at risk for developing a negative pattern of interaction. When babies fuss and react negatively to their parents' actions, the parents perceive themselves as incompetent and tend to withdraw.

Feelings of self-esteem are also enhanced when adults respond to infants' individuality. Parents who recognize the causes of an infant's distress and respond differentially to the causes send the message that they are attending to the infant's individual needs. Helping the infant communicate those needs by labeling feelings begins this process (Activity 6.13). Activity 6.14 extends the concept by matching facial expressions to emotions.

In our society, the use of a person's name often conveys a message that fosters self-worth. Young children like to be acknowledged by name. A child's name can also be a source of personal and cultural pride. The child who proclaims, "My name is Maria Isabella Torres Hernandez," and then adds "I am named after my grandmother, who lives in Puerto Rico," conveys the value she places on

her name. Caregivers and teachers can maintain a sense of cultural pride when they take the time to learn how to pronounce names correctly and when they refrain from calling children by an anglicized version of their name. Activity 6.15 illustrates a strategy for teaching young toddlers to recognize their names.

Teachers frequently use the activity of drawing self-portraits as a means of building a child's sense of self-worth. Attending to the details of their own image by looking in the mirror helps children articulate and represent their individuality. Making life-sized portraits of an entire class can also help children visualize their size and unique features in relationship to their peers. Providing art media to more accurately represent skin tones sends the message to children that a teacher values diversity (Activities 6.16 and 6.17).

Self-esteem has several critical dimensions that are enhanced through interactions with adults, peers, and the environment (Trawick-Smith, 2000). One dimension is a child's feelings of self-worth; a second dimension is a child's sense of individuality (Curry & Johnson, 1990; Harter, 1990). Parents and teachers who truly treat children as individuals are more likely to be sensitive to their strengths and weaknesses in a variety of areas. Gardner's (1993) schema of multiple intelligences is one way of categorizing individual and unique abilities (see chapter 1). Young children need ample opportunities to explore potential giftedness in a variety of areas.

A third dimension of self-esteem is the sense of belonging. Children and their families are often simultaneously members of many cultures, although not all elements of culture are equal in importance at any particular time. Some examples of cultural elements are ethnicity, religion, nationality, gender, region, ability, age, and socioeconomic class. For example, a woman who is a 50-year-old first-generation Mexican American Roman Catholic with a low level of income living in San Diego may have a

Kindergarten teacher helps children work through a problem.

decidedly different cultural background than a 16-year-old girl who is middle-class, third-generation Mexican American, Roman Catholic, and living in Denver, Colorado. Teachers and caregivers must acknowledge the role of culture in a family's values, beliefs, and behaviors and celebrate that diversity. Equally important, teachers and caregivers should not place limitations on children based on a stereotypical view of their cultural background (Curry & Johnson, 1990; Trawick & Smith, 2000). Activity 6.18 taps into children's sense of self-esteem, which can be **nurtured** by connecting with their cultural background.

Self-Control

Autonomy, the psychosocial milestone of the second year of life, according to Erik Erikson (1963), lays the foundation for self-control and future decision-making abilities. Children who are allowed to express choices and who are taught self-help skills move toward independence (Kamii, 1982). This striving for independence is neither smooth nor continuous. Parents must be extremely perceptive to bal-

ance their children's need for care with their need for independence. Certainly, helping children learn to be independent places demands on parents' patience and time. It takes much longer to teach young children how to do things by themselves and wait while they do them than to simply complete tasks for them.

The stage for independence is set in infancy when babies achieve mobility. Parents soon discover that infants can get into anything. Some parents question the validity of baby-proofing the house at this time. They believe that young infants should be taught *not* to touch valuable or dangerous objects. In the guise of discipline, some parents create a home environment that restricts exploration. The focus of many parent-child interactions becomes a power play between the infant's desire to explore and the parent's need to control (Honig, 1996). The pattern of negative interaction between infant and parent is characterized by repeated verbal admonitions of "No, don't touch." These same parents are often surprised when the most frequently heard word in a toddler's vocabulary is "No,

No, No." Parents and caregivers can begin to teach children safety rules by stating the safe behavior and the reasoning behind it. Older infants and toddlers are introduced to safely rules when parents say, "Please sit while you are drinking. I don't want you to choke." Activity 6.19 illustrates the need to create an environment for safe explorations.

Adults frequently use praise to reinforce a child who is practicing a skill or carrying out an adult request. As an external motivator, praise may be used to reinforce successful performance of a skill. A caregiver may praise a toddler's success at putting a puzzle piece in correctly by commenting, "Nice boy, you make me proud of you." Weiser (1991) suggests a subtle but vital difference between praise and encouragement. Encouragement allows children the freedom to try again if first attempts at learning a skill are unsuccessful. However, Weiser (1991) asserts, praise may inadvertently suggest to children that their worth to the "praiser" depends on successful performances. The caregiver may encourage the toddler in the preceding example by changing his comment to "I notice you kept turning that puzzle piece around, trying to figure out how it fit, Jason. Nice job!" This connection to self-worth may also be tied to the use of generic praise rather than specific praise. Some child caregivers frequently use generic or global term of praise, such as "good," "super," or "good boy (or girl)." In addition to pairing success with self-worth, global praise may leave children with the uncertainty of not knowing what it was that they did that was "good." Specific praise that reinforces effort, as well as success, may be more useful. Adults might say, "Great job! You kept trying to pull on your gloves until you did it," to emphasize the child's sense of accomplishment and effort.

Teaching children self-help skills also leads to autonomy and self-control. When children feel pride in their abilities to do things by themselves, feelings of self-worth are enhanced. *Cleversticks* by Bernard Ashley (1991) is the story of a kindergarten child's first days at school. Ling Sung observes other children being applauded for being able to tie their shoes, write their names, button their jackets, and even put on their paint smocks correctly. He can't accomplish any of these tasks and wonders why he can't be good at something. His feelings of self-doubt even lead him to want to stay home from school. By accident, Ling Sung discovers the one thing he can do well that no one else can—use chopsticks. The pride of accomplishment and sense of autonomy created by learning self-help skills are the focus of Activities 6.20 through 6.22.

Teachers and caregivers should also be aware of cultural differences related to gender that affect a child's sense of autonomy (Trawick-Smith, 2000). For example, in some cultures, it is the role of women and girls to serve food to men and boys. In mainstream American culture, this practice is frequently viewed as inappropriate. Teachers and caregivers committed to gender equity may be personally challenged to help children cope with differing expectations in school and home environments

This infant is gaining independence through self-feeding.

without sacrificing a child's sense of worth or imposing the teacher's own cultural values.

Self-control is also nurtured when a child learns that he or she can influence social interactions with peers (DeVries & Kohlberg, 1987). Verbal children have access to social interaction techniques that help them maintain emotional control and resolve conflicts with peers. Early childhood educators can encourage children to use words by making specific suggestions to them. The child-care provider might say, "Tell Gina it hurts when she pinches you." A child who can vent frustrations and express needs and desires verbally instead of physically is perceived much more positively by peers and caregivers. The child's patterns of interactions are more positive, again contributing to self-esteem (Activity 6.23).

Involving children in making classroom rules adds a new dimension to self-control (DeVries & Kohlberg, 1987). Children who feel that they have some say in making rules in the classroom are more likely to respect the rules. Children also learn decision-making rules when they are modeled by adults. The adult has the experience and knowledge that helps children consider variables and perspectives that are not readily apparent to them. The classroom rules become "our" shared rules for acting safely and for treating others with respect rather than rules that the teacher imposes to control the students in the classroom. The focus of control is internal rather than external (Activity 6.24).

Social Interaction

Opportunities for playful social interactions between infants and adults abound in daily routine caregiving activities (Snow, 1998). A foundation for positive social interaction can be based on an infant's need to be fed, changed, bathed, and soothed on a frequent and regular basis. These times together can be viewed by adults as occasions for joyful, verbal interactions or as necessary chores. In child-care settings, caregiver-to-child ratios may limit available time for socially interacting with individual infants, unless the caregiver takes advantage of these routine daily activities (Activity 6.25).

A child's temperament can also affect the type and frequency of social interactions. A toddler with an "easy" temperament tends to see the world as a land of opportunity. It is pleasurable for the child and the adult to go places and try new experiences. In contrast, parents and caregivers of "slow-to-warm-up" and "difficult" children may be reinforced to limit exploration by initial negative responses to novel situations and experiences or by a child's general negative mood. A perceptive parent or caregiver can expand the child's world by allowing time for the child to warm up to new activities without feeling the pressure to become immediately involved. The parent or caregiver of the "difficult" child should be cautioned to be patient and not to take the child's negativity personally. All children thrive on positive social interactions, even if the feedback is not immediate (Activity 6.26).

In Parten's (1932) classic research on children's play, she identifies three types of social play where children are influenced by one another (see chapter 5). **Parallel play** is described as play in which a child plays near other children with the same type of toys but does not interact. The next stage of social play is labeled **associative play.** Children share toys and interact with one another but with no common goal or assignment of roles. During **cooperative play,** children interact to achieve a common goal, using a division of labor. Activity 6.27 may promote parallel social play or the beginnings of associative play. Cooperative play is the focus of the play setting in Activity 6.28.

Opportunities for learning social interaction skills occur in a variety of contexts. Children learn and practice different social skills when they interact with peers, older or younger children, and various adults. Social interactions are also influenced by the places where the interaction takes place. Interacting with Uncle Pete on a picnic blanket at a family outing on Sunday afternoon may differ significantly from participating in a church service next to Uncle Pete on Sunday morning. Children learn from modeling and from participating in experiences. A social skill learned from an adult interaction can be transferred to a peer interaction (Activity 6.29).

Playing informally with other children does not guarantee that children learn how to take turns and to play fairly. For young school-aged children, learning to play a simple game with a partner may be a first step in learning to treat others fairly (Activity 6.30). Teachers and parents can model social behaviors that make game playing fulfilling rather than frustrating for the participants. Teachers and parents can emphasize the mental challenge of developing strategy and the positive social aspects of playing with a partner or playing in a group. Children can learn how to be good winners and losers in games requiring skill or chance, or a combination of each (Kamii & DeVries, 1980). Card games and board games may also provide opportunities for adult-child interaction or family interaction in the home.

Social Skills

The final strand of personal-social development under discussion is learning social skills that relate to societal conventions. Rules in society add order and predictability to social interactions. Rules about health and safety may be essential to survival in our social and physical environments. Although some children learn social conventions by imitation, a more directed approach is usually taken by parents and teachers. In addition to modeling, adults are likely to teach and reinforce rules and explain the rationale for particular rules (Cole & Cole, 2001).

The focus for teaching social conventions for infants and toddlers may be teaching habits that, in the long run, lead to rules that are understood by children. Parents and caregivers occasionally reinforce behaviors in infants and toddlers that are difficult to extinguish in older children. As a parent, it may sometimes be difficult to judge whether a behavior exhibited by an infant or toddler is developmental (i.e., something they will outgrow) or the beginning of a habit, or pattern of behavior. For example, the age-appropriate emotional outbursts (temper tantrums) of early toddlerhood can be frightening to parents. Parents may fear that children who bang their heads on the floor will hurt themselves. Rather than ignoring toddlers, parents may rush to comfort them and give in to their demands.

Brazelton (1989) reminds parents that setting limits is necessary, whether toddlers respond with a tantrum or not. Ignoring the tantrum and giving comfort to toddlers after the tantrum has subsided allows toddlers to learn to deal with this emotional outburst, which is likely to result in a decrease in the number of tantrums. Setting reasonable, age-appropriate limits to behavior also sets the stage for learning about social conventions. Activity 6.31 illustrates teaching an eating habit that later becomes part of the category of social conventions known as table manners.

Rules related to the use of objects can also be taught as those items are introduced to young children. Sometimes parents and caregivers restrict infants and toddlers from using objects because a child may not fully understand when and where these objects are to be used. Infants and toddlers may be prohibited from using crayons, felt pens, paints, play dough, and so on because they cannot be trusted to use them in the manner in which they are intended to be used. Without supervision, children may put art media in their mouths or "decorate" walls or their clothing. Similarly, some parents do not allow three- and four-year-old children to use scissors and knives. Using art media and cooking equipment has benefits for physical, cognitive, and creative development. A parent or caregiver should teach children the rules for using objects long before children are ready to use them without supervision (Activity 6.32).

Activities 6.33 and 6.34 illustrate safety rules for playing with sand and riding tricycles and bicycles. Safety rules are developed to ensure personal well-being and to protect others from harm. In addition, many safety rules are founded in common courtesy and a need for order. The five-year-old child who learns to stop and help a toddler to cross the driveway rather than trying to race to get to the sidewalk first has learned that it is important to protect younger children.

Similarly, rules that protect one's own health can also protect the health of others. For example, table manners often relate to a health practice. Children are taught to use utensils for removing food from serving dishes rather using their hands, to keep their germs away from the food eaten by other people. Even in cultures where hands are used for eating,

there are rules, such as restricting which hand may be used. Learning to cover your mouth when coughing and using a tissue for sneezes are other examples of health rules that have social elements. In a group setting, hand washing may be critical to the well-being of the group as a whole and to the health of a particular child (Activity 6.35).

Last, social skills relate to learning mainstream American societal values, such as truth, justice, and equality. In learning social skills, group cultural differences may conflict. For example, in some cultures, telling the truth, even if it embarrasses a member of one's family, is more important than being personally dishonest; in another culture, saving face may be valued more highly than honesty. Some cultures have a low incidence of common theft. For example, in Japan, a person need not worry about leaving a purse on a bench while playing in the park or locking up a bicycle when entering a store. Activity 6.36 illustrates a social convention based on a mainstream American social issue, but the issue may not have relevance for a recent immigrant who has different cultural values.

Table 6.1 is a matrix correlating all the activities described in Chapter 6 with the appropriate ages and developmental strands.

First graders demonstrate social skills during lunch.

Table 6.1 Personal-social development activities matrix.

Ages (years)	Trust	Attachment/Separation	Self-Esteem	Self-Control	Social Interaction	Social Skills
Birth to one	Comforting Infants Activity 6.1 Adult-child	Peek-a-boo Activity 6.7 Adult-child	Labeling Feelings Activity 6.13 Adult-child	Safe Explorations Activity 6.19 Adult-child	This Little Piggy Activity 6.25 Adult-child	Rules for Eating Activity 6.31 Adult-child
One to two	Communicating Schedules Activity 6.2 Adult-adult	Security Objects Activity 6.8 Child-object	Recognition of Own Name Activity 6.15 Adult-child	Self-Feeding Activity 6.20 Child-object	Swinging Fun Activity 6.26 Adult-child	Using Crayons Activity 6.32 Child-object
Two	Climbing Safety Activity 6.3 Adult-child	Family Photos Activity 6.9 Adult-child	Matching Faces Activity 6.14 Child-object	Helping Dress Myself Activity 6.21 Child-object	Playing with Peers Activity 6.27 Child-child	Simple Rules for Playing Activity 6.33 Adult-child
Three and four	Comforting Ill Children Activity 6.4 Adult-child	Making Transitions Activity 6.10 Adult-child	Self-Portraits Using Mirrors Activity 6.16 Child-object	Using Words Activity 6.23 Child-child	Row Your Boat Activity 6.29 Child-child	Hand Washing Activity 6.35 Adult-child
Five and six	Opening Routine Activity 6.5 Child-object	Running Errands Activity 6.11 Adult-child	Life-Sized Portraits Activity 6.17 Child-child	Making Rules Activity 6.24 Adult-child	Role Playing with Blocks Activity 6.28 Child-child	Traffic Safety Rules Activity 6.34 Child-object
Seven and eight	Entering a New School Activity 6.6 Adult-child	Sleepovers Activity 6.12 Adult-child	Family Connections Activity 6.18 Adult-child	Helping at Home Activity 6.22 Child-object	Games with Partners Activity 6.30 Child-child	Respecting the Property of Others Activity 6.36 Child-child

❧ AGE-APPROPRIATE ACTIVITIES FOR PERSONAL-SOCIAL DEVELOPMENT: BIRTH THROUGH EIGHT YEARS

A c t i v i t y   6 . 1

Comforting Infants

Level Birth to one

Area Personal-Social

Interaction Adult-child

Strand Trust

Materials Needed Rocking chair (if available)

Directions for Implementation

- Hold and rock the infant. Movement often soothes babies.
- Talk or sing quietly to the infant as you rock back and forth.
- Understand that infants vary in the ways they like to be held and in the pace at which they like to be rocked.
- Observe the infant to learn how to match the infant's rhythm.

Extensions

Older children like the closeness that is ensured by being held and rocked. It is also a good time for storytelling or reading a book.

A c t i v i t y   6 . 2

Communicating Schedules

Level One to two

Area Personal-Social

Interaction Adult-adult

Strand Trust

Materials Needed Sample Daily Communication Form (see chapter 4, Figure 4.1)

Directions for Implementation

- As parents drop off their infants and toddlers each day, ask them to jot down a few notes about their child's recent eating, sleeping, and toileting experiences and related health concerns.
- During the day, keep brief notes of the child's activities, for example, what, when, and how much the child ate, the length and time of the child's naps, and any accomplishments or special experiences.
- Give the note to the parents each day or allow them to look at the form each day when they pick up their child. Alert the parent's attention to a particular item by saying, "Jessica was not very hungry this afternoon. She only ate one bite of her applesauce."

Extensions

Daily communication between parents and caregivers concerning schedules is essential for infants and toddlers. Older children are more likely to be able to verbalize their needs and past experiences to caregivers and parents. Prompting discussions by posting menus and daily schedules for parents to read as they bring their children to the center each day aids this communication. Remind children as they are leaving to tell their parents about the day's activities.

A c t i v i t y   6 . 3

Climbing Safety

Level Two

Area Personal-Social

Interaction Adult-child

Strand Trust

Materials Needed Indoor/outdoor slides

Directions for Implementation

- Children who take a high level of risks need close supervision and must be taught safety rules for using slides. For example, a caregiver might say, "One person on the ladder at a time" or "Slide down on your bottom, Julie. It's safer to land on your feet than your head."

- Children who exhibit a low level of risk-taking need the security of rules and gentle encouragement to take small risks, one at a time. For example, a parent can support a young toddler on the way down the slide and catch the child at the bottom or teach her how to spread her legs to slow down her descent.

Extensions

Trust in oneself is built on little successes. Toddlers and young children need to trust the adults in their lives to provide an environment for safe exploration. Most children do not climb past their limits. Encourage, but do not tease or allow others to goad children into taking excessive risks. Many centers and schools have the following rule: A child who is big enough to get on climbing equipment alone is big enough to use it safely.

Comforting Ill Children

Level Three and four

Area Personal-Social

Interaction Adult-child

Strand Trust

Materials Needed Favorite objects (blanket, stuffed toys)

Directions for Implementation

- Observe the child to individualize comforting strategies. Like adults, children react differently to illness. Some children become overly dependent when they are sick, and they want to be continually held. Others prefer to sleep and be left alone.

- Provide a child's favorite objects and capitalize on giving the individual attention on which all children thrive. Children regain independence faster when they can rely on the adults in their lives to provide security when it is most needed.

Extensions

The inability of infants and toddlers to verbalize their needs requires increased observational skills among parents and child-care providers. Physically comforting the young child by holding or rocking is especially comforting. An older child may prefer being in the parent's presence rather than being isolated. A sense of security is maintained by knowing the parent is available when needed.

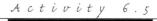

Opening Routine

Level Five and six

Area Personal-Social

Interaction Child-object

Strand Trust

Materials Needed Attendance board (see Appendix D), circular key tags with metal rim

Directions for Implementation

- As they enter the classroom each morning, teach children what to do by planning a routine that, once taught, needs little teacher intervention.
- An efficient way to take attendance and a lunch count is to write each child's name on a round key tag. The key tags can be hung on cup hooks attached to a board near the door. At the beginning of the day, every child's tag is on its hook. As children enter the classroom, they remove their tag and drop it in the appropriate lunch count container. For example, children can order milk or hot lunch or indicate they have

brought their entire lunch from home. The teacher can scan the board and readily see who is absent and then quickly count the tags in each container to complete the lunch count.

- The children then hang up their coats and backpacks and begin work. Some teachers prefer a short seat-work activity to start the day; others plan for children to choose specially designated manipulatives. The goal is to select an activity that does not require teacher assistance.
- The teacher is then free to greet children and communicate briefly to parents.

Extensions

Although child-care facilities are more likely to have children arriving at different times, it is still important to set a simple routine for children to follow as they make the daily transition from home to the center, or, in the case of school-aged children, from school to child care. Children are more secure when they know what to expect. Older children can be taught to share responsibilities in the classroom, such as taking attendance and recording the lunch count. School-aged children in child care can profit from a routine that allows them to relax and eat an afternoon snack before beginning the afternoon's activities.

Activity 6.6

Entering a New School

Level Seven and eight

Area Personal-Social

Interaction Adult-child

Strand Trust

Materials Needed None

Directions for Implementation

- Teachers can foster a sense of trust in young children by planning activities and

schedules that help create a predictable environment for all children.

- Children who enter a new classroom during the school year are particularly challenged to adjust to the new peer group and the academic program. When teachers take time to get to know the new children and their families, the children more readily cope with fitting into a place where everyone else seems to know what is going on.
- In addition to gaining the support of the parents, the sensitive teacher can also help new children make new friendships in the classroom. For example, a teacher can assign a buddy for the day or encourage the children to share information about their previous school or experiences.

Extensions

Teachers of younger children can sometimes build a sense of security by giving parents the opportunity to stay and observe in the classroom if the children seem to have difficulty adjusting to new surroundings. Gradual transitions are also helpful for many children.

Activity 6.7

Peek-a-Boo

Level Birth to one

Area Personal-Social

Interaction Adult-child

Strand Attachment/Separation

Materials Needed None

Directions for Implementation

- Variations of peek-a-boo are played around the world. After making eye contact with the infant, cover your face with your hands. After a brief moment, uncover your face and exclaim, "Peek-a-boo."
- Initially, the infant appears puzzled. Gradually, the infant learns to anticipate the

reappearance of your face and gurgles with delight.

- Vary the activity by keeping your hands in front of your face and peek out over the side. Some children may imitate the adult by putting their hands in front of their faces.

Extensions

Another strategy to reinforce the concept that objects continue to exist when they are out of sight (object permanence) is by playing a hiding game with young children. Begin by having the infant watch you cover up a toy with a small blanket. Encourage the infant to look for the hidden object by saying, "Where did it go?" If the infant does not try to look for the object, demonstrate lifting up the blanket and rehiding it with an edge of the toy showing.

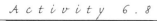

Security Objects

Level One to two

Area Personal-Social

Interaction Child-object

Strand Attachment/Separation

Materials Needed Blanket or plush toy

Directions for Implementation

- At bedtime, encourage independent self-quieting behaviors by establishing a bedtime routine that includes a security object. As part of the bedtime ritual, place the security object next to the toddler, saying, "It's time for you to sleep. You can hug your teddy bear if you want. I'll see you in the morning."
- Firmly and consistently express your expectations that toddlers learn to settle themselves down.
- If needed, allow the child to use the security object during nap times and in coping with new situations.

Extensions

Most children gradually outgrow the need for a security object. In child-care settings, many children can be encouraged to leave security objects in their cubbies by suggesting that the object might get dirty and reminding them that they can have the article whenever they need it. The parent of an older child might tape a picture of the family on the inside lid of a pencil box or include a brief note in a lunch box to convey a sense of security or connection with the home environment.

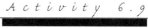

Family Photos

Level Two

Area Personal-Social

Interaction Adult-child

Strand Attachment/Separation

Materials Needed Photographs of family members, pets, and so on

Directions for Implementation

- In child-care settings, display photographs of children with their family members on a bulletin board at the child's eye level.
- During the day, toddlers can be encouraged to show and talk about the people in their families. For example, the caregiver might ask Eduardo, "Where's Mama?" or say, "Show me José," as they discuss the fact that Mama is at work and that his older brother, José, is in school at the moment.

Extensions

Make or have parents involved in making "baggie books" (see Appendix D) for the book corner. Each book may include five to six photographs of the child. Include labels or a narrative to assist new caregivers or volunteers in reading to the child. Personalized books are often favorites in a book corner, and they help young children make connections between home and child-care settings. Infants and toddlers can look at photographs that are enclosed in a single, self-closing plastic bag. Older children can use family photographs to illustrate autobiographies.

A c t i v i t y   6 . 1 0

Making Transitions

Level Three and four

Area Personal-Social

Interaction Adult-child

Strand Attachment/Separation

Materials Needed People puppets or dolls

Directions for Implementation

- Role play difficult transition times with individual children or in small groups. Use a puppet to represent a parent, and give the child a puppet to represent a student. Pretend to greet the child and his father as they enter the classroom in the morning: "Good morning, Tran. Good morning, Mr. Hong. How are you this morning?" Encourage Tran to put away his coat while his father is signing him in for the day: "Tran, I've put out your favorite puzzle this morning. Please tell your father good-bye before you begin to play."
- Encourage brief good-byes by directing the child to a specific activity and reminding him that his father will pick him up that afternoon after they have played outdoors.

Extensions

Encourage parents whose children have difficulty separating in the morning to establish a brief, positive routine as they enter the classroom. Some children need to remain in physical contact with the teacher to make a smooth transition to the classroom, especially after long weekends or absences. Be aware that occasionally it is the parent who has trouble separating. Children who are sensitive to their parent's needs to maintain contact bounce back quickly to the expectations of the center after their parent has left. Older children can also have difficulties separating from parents. Continue to focus on firmly setting a positive routine that allows children to accomplish the separation and verbalize their feelings.

A c t i v i t y   6 . 1 1

Running Errands

Level Five and six

Area Personal-Social

Interaction Adult-child

Strand Attachment/Separation

Materials Needed Notes, attendance sheets

Directions for Implementation

- Create the job of messenger as one of the classroom responsibilities. Rotate jobs on a regular basis.
- Hand a child the attendance form, and instruct him or her to take it to the office. Remind the child to walk on the way and greet the secretary. You might say: "Tell Mrs. Ramirez good morning."
- Informally during the day, use the messenger to get or return supplies to other teachers or staff members.

Extensions

Children who have difficulty separating from familiar adults can fulfill messenger responsibilities with a more confident partner who models the appropriate behavior for them. Children who leave the classroom for auxiliary services, such as speech therapy, may also need support when they separate from the classroom teacher. Older infants and toddlers can learn to find familiar objects and bring them to the adult. An adult might say, "Your ball is in a basket next to the back door. Please go find it so we can play catch."

A c t i v i t y   6 . 1 2

Sleep Overs

Level Seven and eight

Area Personal-Social

Interaction Adult-child

Strand Attachment/Separation

Materials Needed: Ira Sleeps Over by Bernard Waber (1972), teddy bear

Directions for Implementation

- Introduce the story by showing the children a well-loved teddy bear or other plush toy. If possible, relate a story about a favorite toy that you had as a child and ask, "How many of you have a favorite stuffed toy?" Allow a few children to share personal experiences. Say, "Today, we're going to hear a story about a boy named Ira who has to make an important decision."
- Read the children's literature selection.
- Lead a discussion on the story. For example, "Why did Ira hesitate to bring his teddy bear to his friend's house when he went to spend the night?" "How did Ira feel when he found out that his friend slept with a teddy bear named Foo Foo?" "Why do people like to sleep with teddy bears?" Encourage children to share stories about spending the night with friends or sleeping with security objects.

Extensions

Read *The Velveteen Rabbit* by Margery Williams (1983), another story about a well-loved toy. Allow the children to write in their journals

about their favorite stuffed toy. Attitudes about sleep overs with friends vary greatly among individual families and cultural groups. Remind children that common practices in some cultures are considered unusual in other cultures.

A c t i v i t y   6 . 1 3

Labeling Feelings

Level Birth to one

Area Personal-Social

Interaction Adult-child

Strand Self-Esteem

Materials Needed None

Directions for Implementation

- At different times during the day, respond to an infant's varied emotional states by commenting on his or her reactions. For example, when the baby is smiling or cooing, say, "I can see rubbing your tummy makes you happy," or "You sure like to hear me sing to you."
- Parents and caregivers begin to differentiate an individual infant's different cries. The cry that indicates that a baby is hungry may differ from the cry that indicates severe pain or even the whimpering and fussy cry that may mean that the infant is tired or bored. Verbalizing the infant's probable emotional states pairs the feeling with a label.

Extensions

Since receptive language (language that a child understands) far outpaces expressive language (language a child uses), it is imperative to carry on conversations with young infants, in spite of the fact that they are unable to "talk." Part of the frustration that toddlers express in personal-social interaction relates to their inability to verbally express their needs and wants. Older children also need the opportunity and vocabulary to accurately express their feelings to caring adults. Reading books with children, such as Arnold Lobel's *Frog and Toad Are Friends* (1970) or James Marshall's *George and Martha Rise and Shine* (1976) may open a dialogue about how feelings get hurt even among friends.

A c t i v i t y   6 . 1 4

Matching Faces

Level Two

Area Personal-Social

Interaction Child-object

Strand Self-Esteem

Materials Needed Photographs (from magazines) of three large faces depicting happy, sad, and neutral expressions. Photocopy each face twice and laminate or cover them with clear contact paper.

Directions for Implementation

- Create a matching game by spreading all six photographs of the faces on the floor in front of the child.
- Point to one of the photographs and ask the toddler to hand you the face that matches it. Cue as needed to establish the concept of matching happy, sad, and neutral expressions.

Extensions

Create paper plate masks of different facial expressions (see Appendix D for specific directions). Cut out eye holes for the child to look through. Pass out the plates to a group of children and ask them to sit in a circle. Ask children to describe the facial expressions (e.g., puzzled, surprised, shocked, scared, pleased). Encourage the children to mimic the expressions. Younger children may enjoy imitating

an adult's facial expressions in a mirror. Older children can discuss situations in which they were puzzled, surprised, pleased, or had other emotions.

A c t i v i t y   6 . 1 5

Recognition of Own Name

Level One to two

Area Personal-Social

Interaction Adult-child

Strand Self-Esteem

Materials Needed None

Directions for Implementation

- During the various daily caregiving routines, such as feeding, diapering, and bathing, call the infant by name.
- Talk with the infant, using her name, "I see you are just waking up, Meg," or "Are you hungry, Meg?"
- The infant will gradually learn to respond to her name.

Extensions

Preschool-age children benefit from seeing their personal articles and supplies labeled in manuscript print, using capital and lowercase letters, for example, "Janelle" not "JANELLE." Modeling the type of writing that is later taught and then practicing reading that same type of writing is helpful as children make the transition to more formalized school settings. Child-care providers may wish to consult local school teachers about which model of manuscript writing is used in the nearby schools.

A c t i v i t y   6 . 1 6

Self-Portraits Using Mirrors

Level Three and four

Area Personal-Social

Interaction Child-object

Strand Self-Esteem

Materials Needed Drawing paper, crayons, or felt pens, including multicultural skin tones, and individual mirrors or mirrors to be shared with partners.

Directions for Implementation

- Ask the children to look in the mirrors and describe the color of their hair and eyes. Have the children find crayons that are close in color to their own eyes and hair.
- Talk about the richness and variety of skin tones.
- Have children draw self-portraits.

Extensions

Date the children's self-portraits and have them repeat the activity in 6 months. Keeping a portfolio of children's work helps in assessing children's strengths and opportunities for growth and in communicating with parents. Older children can read and discuss the similarities and differences between people illustrated in Peter Spier's *People* (1980).

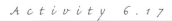

A c t i v i t y   6 . 1 7

Life-Size Portraits

Level Five and six

Area Personal-Social

Interaction Child-child

Strand Self-Esteem

Materials Needed Butcher paper, tempera paint (including multicultural skin tone colors), pencil

Directions for Implementation

- As an individual or small-group activity, create life-sized self-portraits. Instruct the child to lie on his or her back on a large piece of butcher paper. Trace around the

child, and then have the child help complete the outline by sketching in clothing and hair.
- Children need some supervision to complete the portraits using tempera paint. (To prevent spilled jars of paint, use small, sturdy shoeboxes to hold the jars.)
- When the portrait is dry, cut out the figure and display. Many children are amazed to see how big they look.

Extensions

The self-esteem of young children is also enhanced when the classroom equipment and supplies reflect cultural and ethnic diversity. For example, school supply catalogs now carry art media, such as crayons, paints, and paper, and books, dramatic play props, dolls, and other materials that reflect the cultural richness of American society. Classroom environments should not be limited to the cultural backgrounds of the particular children in that classroom.

A c t i v i t y   6 . 1 8

Family Connections

Level Seven and eight

Area Personal-Social

Interaction Adult-child

Strand Self-Esteem

Materials and Person Needed Chart paper and felt pen, a classmate's grandparent

Directions for Implementation

- Invite one of the children's grandparents into the classroom for an interview. Ahead of time, have the children think of questions that can be asked to help them learn about the childhoods of their grandparents. Assign particular children to ask each question. To help children remember details, audiotape or videotape the interview.

- After the interview, write a class story about something mentioned in the interview. Duplicate the story on regular-sized paper to add to a class book on "Our Grandparents."
- As homework, have each child interview a grandparent, an extended family member, or an old family friend.

Extensions

Another way to have children make historical connections is through children's literature. In *The Patchwork Quilt* by Valerie Flournoy (1985), a family's history is told through scraps of fabric. Tanya's grandmother retells events in the lives of her children and grandchildren as she stitches. Consult the children's librarian in a local library for other grandparenting stories from various cultural perspectives. Grandparents and other family members have much to add to the lives of young children. Some child-care centers and programs plan for intergenerational contacts by using volunteers from retired citizens' organizations.

Activity 6.19

Safe Explorations

Level Birth to one

Area Personal-Social

Interaction Adult-child

Strand Self-Control

Materials Needed Safety devices (e.g., electrical outlet covers, latches)

Directions for Implementation

- Analyzing the space from the infant's perspective can create a safe, healthy learning environment. Find and remove hazardous substances and eliminate potential dangers. An infant's mobility changes rapidly. A normal, curious infant can get into anything! Children thrive on sensory explo-

ration, and anything that can be put in their mouths, will be.
- Redirect an infant's need to explore, rather than trying to prohibit the infant from learning from the environment. A family child-care provider might say, "Scott, I see you really like to push the door open and crawl through it. I'm going to latch the door open so that you won't pinch your fingers." Reserving the firm "no" for dangerous situations tends to encourage children to heed those admonitions and focus attention toward what and where the child is supposed to play.

Extensions

A sense of autonomy can be developed when parents and caregivers set consistent, realistic limits. A balance between overcontrolling the environment and failing to set limits on exploration creates a learning environment that is both safe and healthy. The stage for independence is set in early childhood as children gradually gain more self-control by being allowed to accomplish tasks by themselves, while trusting adults to keep them safe. Older children need to participate in safety-rule discussions by figuring out why situations or objects are potentially hazardous and by helping to develop safety rules. Children who understand the need for safety rules and participate in developing them are more likely to follow the rules.

Activity 6.20

Self-Feeding

Level One to two

Area Personal-Social

Interaction Child-object

Strand Self-Control

Materials Needed Child-sized, sturdy dishes and utensils

Directions for Implementation

- Feed toddlers during family mealtimes to get them interested in making the transition from baby food to table food. Serving finger foods in small quantities at a time encourages toddlers to begin feeding themselves while other family members are eating.
- Enhance success by choosing flat bowls and cups that are not easily tipped over. Assume that spills will occur as toddlers learn to master fine-motor control. Capitalize on toddlers' desire to imitate by involving them in cleaning up spills and by modeling appropriate eating behaviors.

Extensions

To prevent choking and to minimize spills, teach children to remain seated while they are eating. Pouring skills (which can be practiced at the sink or in the water play area of a child-care center) can be used in family-style meals. Juice and milk can be transferred to smaller pitchers for ease of pouring for preschool and young school-aged children. Serving healthy foods and encouraging (rather than forcing) children to eat allows them to learn to exert control and to learn healthy eating habits. In some families, children learn to use food as a means of controlling adults. Viewing a daily menu as five to six nutritious small meals rather than three large meals with two to three snacks is more realistic for the needs of young children.

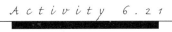

A c t i v i t y   6 . 2 1

Helping Dress Myself

Level Two

Area Personal-Social

Interaction Child-object

Strand Self-Control

Materials Needed Children's clothing, chosen for ease of dressing (e.g., pull-ons, ample size)

Directions for Implementation

- Allow toddlers to help with dressing themselves by limiting the selection to two items of clothing appropriate to the weather and the occasion. For example, hold up two shirts, saying, "Would you like to wear the red shirt or the green shirt today, Andy?" Learning to make choices without needing to consider a wide range of variables is a first step in decision making.
- Encourage active participation in removing and putting on articles of clothing. Ample-sized, pull-on clothing is much easier to put on than clothing that is a little snug and fastens in the back. Allow extra time to complete the task, and praise the effort, even when it doesn't measure up to adult standards. Remember that toddlers in the process of toilet training often need to be able to remove pants and underpants quickly. Build success by choosing clothing that facilitates independence in dressing.

Extensions

Design storage areas for clothing to help young children select and put away clothes whenever possible. A routine that is well taught pays huge dividends in the future. Capitalize on young children's desire to exert independence by allowing them to make simple decisions and by taking the time to teach them how to accomplish simple tasks. Older infants and young toddlers can be encouraged to go get diapers or other articles of clothing when they are stored within reach.

A c t i v i t y   6 . 2 2

Helping at Home

Level Seven and eight

Area Personal-Social

Interaction Child-object

Strand Self-Control

Materials Needed Trash bag

Directions for Implementation

- Teach children how to accomplish tasks in a simple step-by-step manner rather than assuming they can complete the chore to a parent's expectations without instructions. For example, in a home with wastebaskets in each room, a child might be instructed to use a large trash bag and begin to empty the wastebaskets into the bag in the room furthest from the outdoor garbage receptacle. The first time, the parent and child can complete the task together. The second time, the parent might watch the child complete the task, and the third time, the parent can check to see that the task is completed.
- Praise the child for helping with family chores by saying, "We all have more time to play when we work together to get the housework done. Thank you for helping, Russ." Sometimes it seems easier for parents to complete chores by themselves than to teach their children how to do something or to accept chores that are not done completely to adult standards. In the long run, assuming responsibilities builds a sense of independence.

Extensions

Helping with family chores is a natural extension of building independence skills in toddlerhood. Children feel a sense of inner strength when they accomplish tasks by themselves. Other family chores might include putting soiled clothes in laundry containers, setting and clearing the table, making beds, and sweeping outdoors. In child-care and school settings, children may also have responsibilities for maintaining the indoor and outdoor environments. Some of these individual responsibilities include cleaning up one's table area after eating, checking the floor for paper scraps after an art activity, or even making sure that paper towels in the rest rooms are properly thrown away. A second category of classroom responsibilities is one that contains tasks that create a sense of community among children and adults. Classroom chores might include passing out supplies, taking equipment outdoors, feeding pets, or serving as a messenger.

Activity 6.23

Using Words

Level Three and four

Area Personal-Social

Interaction Child-child

Strand Self-Control

Materials Needed None

Directions for Implementation

- When children act out physically to resolve conflicts, it is often because of their inability to verbalize their frustrations, needs, and desires. As parents and caregivers observe children playing, they are wise to intervene before one or both children totally lose control. Suggesting acceptable verbal behavior can help teach children to resolve conflicts. For example, Nicole is riding the center's favorite tricycle around the bike path. Jennifer is behind her, riding another tricycle. Jennifer has stopped Nicole's tricycle and is trying to push Nicole off the seat. The caregiver might suggest, "Jennifer, tell Nicole you would like a turn on the red tricycle when she is done."
- Suggesting a strategy for sharing the two tricycles gives the children another option. "Nicole, you can tell Jennifer that you'd be willing to trade tricycles each time you

pass the storage shed. That sounds like a fair way to solve this problem."

Extensions

Older, more verbal children can be directly involved in coming up with possible solutions to conflicts. A teacher might mediate by saying, "You both want to use the computer to play a math game during free time. How might we solve this problem?" Children grow in independence when adults take their ideas and opinions seriously and when adults expect children to resolve problems, rather than assuming that the adults will always make the decision.

A c t i v i t y   6 . 2 4

Making Rules

Level Five and six

Area Personal-Social

Interaction Adult-child

Strand Self-Control

Materials Needed Poster or chart paper, felt pen

Directions for Implementation

- Involve the children in making the classroom rules at the beginning of the school year or as a new group forms. Discuss the purpose of rules, such as those that ensure safety and those that help people get along fairly. For example, a rule that states: "Walk indoors" relates to safety; "Keep your hands and feet to yourself" is more directly related to learning how to get along with peers.
- Emphasize the behaviors children should exhibit, keeping the focus positive rather than merely stating what children should not do. When children are involved in creating the rules by which they live, they are more likely to respect them. Discussing the consequences of failing to follow rules

lessens some of the types of behavior known as *testing limits*.

- Post the classroom rules, reinforce them consistently, and communicate them to parents.

Extensions

Self-control behaviors are reinforced when children make personal choices to follow or not follow classroom rules. For example, four-year-old Brian disrupts story time by poking his neighbor in the back. The teacher can say, "Brian, please sit with your hands in your lap and listen to our story quietly or go to the back table and look at a book by yourself." She encourages Brian to take responsibility for his own behavior when she forces him to choose to stay with the group or be excluded. If he continues to be disruptive, he loses his opportunity to make a choice.

A c t i v i t y   6 . 2 5

This Little Piggy

Level Birth to one

Area Personal-Social

Interaction Adult-child

Strand Social Interaction

Materials Needed Words to the nursery rhyme "This Little Piggy" (see Appendix C)

Directions for Implementation

- Place the infant on his or her back while being dressed. Gently grab the baby's largest toe while reciting, "This little piggy went to market"; hold the second toe while saying, "This little piggy stayed home"; and so on.
- Repeat the rhyme several times each day when the child is being dressed. Infants soon learn to anticipate the joyful play when a parent or caregiver asks, "Where are those little piggies?"

Extensions

Nursery rhymes have been enjoyed by generations of young children. Hand motions and body movements can be incorporated in the recitations of the rhymes. For example, in "Twinkle, Twinkle Little Star," adults can open and close their hands to simulate the twinkling stars for the first and last lines, point to the sky for the appropriate line, and form a diamond shape with the index fingers and thumbs for that portion of the rhyme. Older children use chants and songs in clapping games and while jumping rope. The culture of childhood and elements of ethnic culture are passed on in these social interactions among children in neighborhoods, schools, and playgrounds.

A c t i v i t y   6 . 2 6

Swinging Fun

Level One to two

Area Personal-Social

Interaction Adult-child

Strand Social Interaction

Materials Needed Tire swing or other baby-safe swing

Directions for Implementation

- Push the baby gently, and watch for her reaction. Most infants enjoy swinging on outdoor swings.
- Talk to the infant about what she is doing and seeing as she swings back and forth.
- End the activity on a positive note as the infant loses interest or begins to fuss.

Extensions

Most young children love being taken to playgrounds and parks. These trips can be excellent opportunities for children and adults to play together.

A c t i v i t y   6 . 2 7

Playing With Peers

Level Two

Area Personal-Social

Interaction Child-child

Strand Social Interaction

Materials Needed Empty plastic containers, sand

Directions for Implementation

- Provide two to three containers per child.
- Encourage the children to talk about what they are doing.
- Expect that the toddlers may imitate each other but will play alone.

Extensions

Set up activities in the classroom for young children to do in pairs. A sensory exploration table may have a large flat tub that can be filled with water. Have a variety of plastic bottles and measuring cups available for filling and pouring. Allow two children to use the tub at a time. As children practice social interaction skills, it is often easier for the child to work with one child rather than in a group. With continued practice, cooperative learning groups can effectively be implemented in the primary grades by building on the pairs structure. Pairs can be joined, with each child in the group of four fulfilling a role. In a cooperative learning group activity, one child might be the reader, another the writer, another the reporter, and the fourth person the supply monitor.

A c t i v i t y   6 . 2 8

Role Playing with Blocks

Level Five and six

Area Personal-Social

Interaction Child-child

Strand Social Interaction

Materials Needed Large blocks, props for a shoe store (such as shoe boxes, various sizes and styles of shoes, measuring devices, cash register, play money, paper, pencils, or paper bags)

Directions for Implementation

- Create a shoe store in the block area, involving the children in its design. This is an excellent follow-up to taking a field trip to a shoe store.
- Allow small groups of children to choose to play in that center during activity time.
- Encourage children to exchange roles from customers to salespersons.

Extensions

The dramatic play area can be adapted to other stores and services when students are learning about their local community. The teacher will need to assess each child's knowledge of the community to plan the most appropriate learning activities, because children with limited knowledge of particular occupations have difficulty role playing those jobs. Younger children usually need time to explore the props before moving into cooperative play. Dramatic play props should be left in an activity center long enough for children to move through stages of play.

Activity 6.29

Row Your Boat

Level Three and four

Area Personal-Social

Interaction Adult-child

Strand Social Interaction

Materials Needed Words to "Row Your Boat" (see Appendix C)

Directions for Implementation

- Parents or caregivers can play this game with a child.
- Sit on the floor with the child, place the child facing you, between your outstretched legs and hold hands.
- As you sing "Row Your Boat," rock back and forth gently.

Extensions

The activity can be varied for older children by changing the pace of the song, for example, faster or slower. Two children can be encouraged to play together. Younger children also enjoy this activity. Toddlers mimic the motions and begin to pick up some of the words or tune but will have difficulty singing and moving at the same time.

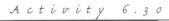
Activity 6.30

Games With Partners

Level Seven and eight

Area Personal-Social

Interaction Child-child

Strand Social Interaction

Materials Needed Beans or other small things to count, 10 per person

Directions for Implementation

- Introduce a "less than, greater than" math game by demonstrating it with a partner. The object of the game is to try to guess whether your partner has fewer or more beans in his hand than you do.
- Give each child five beans and assign a partner. Each person hides from one to five beans in his or her right hand and then puts that hand on top of the table.
- One person begins by saying, "I have less than you" or "I have greater than you." If the child guesses correctly, she or he gets to

keep all of the beans the partner had. If the guess is incorrect, the child gives those beans to his or her partner. If the amounts are equal, it is the partner's turn, and no beans exchange hands.

- Continue the game until one person has all the beans or time is called. At that point, the person with the most beans wins.
- When students master the game using five beans each, have each player begin with 10 beans.

Extensions

Math games are usually designed to give students needed practice with concepts that have been previously taught. Extend this game by having students write down the problems illustrated by the game with the correct less than (<), equal to (=), or greater than (>) symbol. The social skills learned in playing games can be as important as practicing an academic skill. Noncompetitive games that emphasize playing hard, playing fair, and challenging oneself are also appropriate for young children. (Chapter 8 contains more information concerning group games.)

A c t i v i t y   6 . 3 1

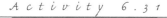

Rules for Eating

Level Birth to one

Area Personal-Social

Interaction Adult-child

Strand Social Skills

Materials Needed Food, feeding tables or high chairs

Directions for Implementation

- Since the goal in the interaction is to teach a routine or reinforce a habit, parents and caregivers should encourage eating behaviors that will be expected when the infant is

older or in other settings. Introduce a bowl (one with a suction cup works best) and a baby spoon to the older infant. Add a small amount of food, such as applesauce, to the bowl. Continue to feed the infant from a bowl that is out of the infant's reach.

- Encouraging infants to keep their food on the tray pays off in the long run. Conversely, laughing at infants who throw food or encouraging them to drop food to animals is likely to reinforce that behavior. Balance children's need to explore and learn fine motor skills with the need to learn eating habits that are socially acceptable.

Extensions

The adage that "you cannot spoil babies but that you can certainly teach them some bad habits" relates directly to the strand of social conventions. One type of social convention is table manners, which may sometimes vary, depending on the context. For example, a baby banging on a feeding tray with a cup may be tolerated in the home but not in a restaurant. Giving children mixed messages by applauding a particular behavior at one moment and correcting it at another confuses young children. Eating habits are also embedded in ethnic cultural contexts. Some cultures strongly prohibit any attempts to play with food. Older children profit from explanations of why they should follow rules. Although detailed explanations are usually lost on infants and toddlers, brief and simple reasons lay the foundation for understanding the purpose of rules.

A c t i v i t y   6 . 3 2

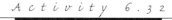

Using Crayons

Level One to two

Area Personal-Social

Interaction Child-Object

Strand Social Skills

Materials Needed Large crayons, paper

Directions for Implementation

- Set up a specific table surface area for using the crayons on paper.
- Put out one crayon to begin, and encourage the toddler to color on the paper. Demonstrate if needed. Emphasize coloring on the paper.
- Remove the crayons from the child's reach when the child loses interest. If the toddler tries to chew on the crayon, remove the crayon, saying, "Crayons are for coloring." Children who continue to put the crayons in their mouths are not yet ready for the experience.

Extensions

Older toddlers may have the physical strength needed to color on an easel with crayons. Markers and paints tend to work better on easels. Even nontoxic art supplies should be stored out of reach until children fully understand where and when they should be used. Older children should also be taught the courtesy rules related to using and sharing supplies in a group. For example, preschoolers can be expected to share supplies as partners. School-aged children can be expected to return supplies to a common area to facilitate their use by other children in the classroom.

Activity 6.33

Simple Rules for Playing

Level Two

Area Personal-Social

Interaction Adult-child

Strand Social Skills

Materials Needed Sandbox and containers

Directions for Implementation

- Sandbox rules generally focus on keeping the sand in the box and using it for digging. Toddlers who persist in putting sand in their mouths should be redirected to another area.
- Toddlers are also likely to experiment with sand by throwing it or dumping it out of the sandbox. Caregivers might say, "Sand is for digging, it hurts when you throw it." In another situation, the caregiver might state, "The sand needs to stay in our sandbox. If you dump it on the sidewalk, we might slip and fall."
- Toddlers who continue to break the sandbox rules can be removed from the area.

Extensions

Older children need to be encouraged to verbalize why a particular rule has been set. A child who has gotten sand in her eye on an earlier occasion is likely to remember that it hurts. When a child throws sand and it gets in another child's face, caregivers can involve the child who threw the sand in taking care of the injured child by having the thrower hold the box of tissues or help brush the sand off of the child's clothes.

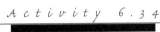

Activity 6.34

Traffic Safety Rules

Level Five and six

Area Personal-Social

Interaction Child-object

Strand Social Skills

Materials Needed Traffic cones, tricycles and bicycles, safety helmets, stop signs

Directions for Implementation

- Discuss the traffic safety rules for riding tricycles and bicycles in your community.

Talk about the role of police officers in enforcing traffic safety rules.

- Set up an obstacle course in a parking lot to teach safe riding habits.

Extensions

Young children have difficulty conceptualizing the danger that cars pose to them as they play. Teaching children never to play around cars and not to use cars as play spaces helps them develop an understanding that rules are often made for safety reasons.

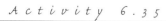

Hand Washing

Level Three and four

Area Personal-Social

Interaction Adult-child

Strand Social Skills

Materials Needed Soap, paper towels, sturdy step stool (if needed)

Directions for Implementation

- Parents and caregivers need to directly teach young children how to wash and dry their hands before meals and after toileting.
- Demonstrate hand washing to a few children at a time, and then supervise the children as they practice hand washing. Show the children how to adjust the water temperature if needed and wet their hands before adding soap. Children can practice washing their palms and the backs of their hands and in between their fingers. After they rinse thoroughly and turn off the water, have them show you how to dry their hands and throw away the paper towel.

Extensions

Health habits can be taught without the child fully understanding the purpose of the activity. Pictures reminding children to wash their hands may serve as useful reminders. Science lessons for older children can focus on germs and how diseases are spread.

Activity 6.36

Respecting the Property Rights of Others

Level Seven and eight

Area Personal-Social

Interaction Child-child

Strand Social Skills

Materials Needed None

Directions for Implementation

- When teachers establish a sense of community in their classrooms, a foundation is set for learning about joint ownership and responsibility. Care of the equipment and supplies in the classroom is viewed as everyone's responsibility. In turn, this climate of pride and responsibility for school property sets a tone for students' learning to respect the property rights of others.
- At the beginning of the school term, the teacher might say, "The extra pencils I keep in this jar are for you to use if your pencil breaks during the morning. If you need to borrow a pencil, put it back after you've sharpened your own. I'll remind you when it is time to sharpen pencils after lunch." Or "If you need to take a pencil home to do your homework, I'd be glad to let you borrow one. You just need to ask."
- Children often bring items from home to share with the class and need to feel that it is safe to do so. Teachers can help children take care of their own property and ensure that items brought from home will not be damaged or taken by another student.

Extensions

Preschool children sometimes put school items in their pockets to bring them home. Alerting parents to this possibility and suggesting a joint course of action can provide a valuable lesson to children without shaming or labeling them in front of their peers. Discussions about making moral decisions can be initiated by children's literature. In *Too Many Tamales* by Gary Soto (1993), Maria tries on her mother's wedding ring while they are making tamales for a family gathering. She faces a moral dilemma when she realizes the ring is missing. Thinking about what one might do in a similar situation can help a child make a real-life decision.

✎ CURRICULAR IMPLICATIONS

Connections to Subject Matter Areas

A traditional method of curricular planning, which ties activities to subject matter areas, is frequently used in preschool and elementary school settings. Subject matter areas such as language arts, mathematics, social studies, and science may be considered the core curriculum. In some programs and schools, art, music, drama, physical education and movement, and health may likewise be viewed as essential subject matter components; in other programs and schools, these same components are supplements to the core curriculum. It is relatively simple to connect activities and learning experiences that are based on developmental areas to subject matter.

Many activities and learning experiences in the personal-social developmental area connect directly to social studies. The personal-social developmental strands of self-control, social interaction, and social skills relate directly to common goals of a social studies curriculum, namely, to become responsible for oneself and others in the social and physical environment. For example, learning to feed, dress, and express oneself promotes self-control. Learning experiences, which promote in-

dependence and responsibility are depicted in Activities 6.20 (Self-feeding), 6.21 (Helping Dress Myself), and 6.23 (Using Words).

Reciprocal interactions with parents, caregivers, teachers, and peers are the focus of all the activities listed in the strand of social interactions. Preschool children are encouraged to team with a peer as they sing and move to the rhythm of "Row, row, row your boat" in Activity 6.28. In a similar manner, other child-child interactions are promoted in Activity 6.27 (Playing with Peers), Activity 6.28 (Role Playing with Blocks), and Activity 6.30 (Games with Partners). Learning to interact in positive ways with peers and adults supports a long-term outcome of the social studies curriculum.

Social conventions can be developed in learning experiences, such as those illustrated in the social skills strand of personal-social development. Learning to follow rules may be different from cultural practices that are taught in homes related to Activity 6.31 (Rules for Eating) to health practices in Activity 6.34 (Hand Washing). Children soon learn that they need to follow rules for participating in group settings with other children as in Activity 6.33 (Simple Rules for Playing) and Activity 6.36 (Respecting the Property of Others). Although the most directly connected activity to the wider community may be learning Activity 6.35 (Traffic Safety Rules), all of the suggested activities for developing social skills lay a foundation for future citizenship, the promotion of which is an important outcome of a social studies curriculum.

Other subject matter areas can similarly be connected to activities selected to enhance growth in the personal-social developmental area. Mathematics is the subject of Activity 6.30 (Games with Partners). Children practice the concept of more than and less than by participating in a game with beans as markers. Art is the focus of learning to make self-portraits using mirrors (Activity 6.16) and life-sized portraits (Activity 6.17). Oral language is an essential component of various suggested activities such as playing peek-a-boo (Activity 6.7) between an infant and an adult, talking about facial expressions in "Matching Faces" (Activity 6.15), and discussing the anxieties of staying overnight at a friend's house in "Sleepovers" (Activity 6.12).

Connections to Thematic Planning

Thematic planning is also a popular approach to planning early childhood programs. A single unifying theme gives caregivers and teachers the opportunity to tie learning activities and experiences to a topic of interest to children. One theme that logically connects to the personal-social area of development relates to families. A theme for a group of three-year-old children might be stated as simply as "families take care of us." The same topic might be expanded for kindergarteners to include the notion that families take care of both physical and emotional needs. A class of eight-year-old children is ready to consider other dimensions of the role of families. The theme for this age group might be articulated as "families provide for our safety and our physical and emotional well-being".

In the personal-social area of development, numerous activities support the use of a family-related theme. The role of parents in building trust, an essential component of establishing emotional well-being, is evidenced in Activity 6.1 (Comforting Infants), Activity 6.4 (Comforting Ill Children), and Activity 6.6 (Entering a New School). Building feelings of security and attachment is promoted in infants and toddlers in Activity 6.8 (Security Objects), and in older children as they discuss the continued use of comforting items in Activity 6.12 (Sleepovers). Caregivers and teachers can include visual representations of families by providing books of family photos (Activity 6.9) made from self-closing plastic bags. In Activity 6.18 (Family Connections), teachers can incorporate cultural dimensions of families in classroom discussions.

SUMMARY

Six strands of personal-social development in children have been identified. Basic trust is nurtured by personalized caregiving and continuity of care. Infants develop a sense of trust when their needs for physical comfort and emotional well-being are met.

A second, related strand is attachment/separation. The securely attached infant or toddler gradually learns to separate from parents and primary caregivers when transitions are built on predictability.

The third strand of self-esteem has as its base feelings of self-worth as an individual and as a member of various cultures. Self-control, or autonomy, is the fourth strand of development. Growing in independence and being able to accomplish tasks without help also add to feelings of self-worth.

The fifth strand concerns social interactions with children and adults. The focus of the sixth strand, social skills, is learning social conventions and rules.

Interactions with adults, peers, and objects can enhance personal-social development. Although activities focus on particular age ranges, most can be adapted to younger or older children. Sample activities are included to suggest possible interactions and to illustrate strands of development. Teachers, caregivers, and parents should adapt activities to meet the individual or group needs of the children under their care.

QUESTIONS AND PROJECTS FOR THE READER

1. Pick one strand of personal-social development (i.e., trust, attachment/separation, self-esteem, self-control, social interactions, social conventions) and create a new activity for interaction for each of the six age groups.

2. Make a diagram of the six strands of personal-social development, using a picture or symbol to represent each strand. For example, cut a photograph out of a magazine of a father feeding an infant to symbolize trust, or perhaps, draw a picture of a teddy bear and a blanket to symbolize attachment/separation.

3. Using the personal-social development strand of autonomy, plan activities for interactions for each of the following contexts: family or extended family, home visitor, family child-care home, parent interaction program, group child care, kindergarten or primary classrooms, or before-school and after-school care.

4. Discuss the six strands of personal-social development in a small group setting, defining each strand and giving examples of the types of interactions that promote each strand of development. In a large group setting, you can work with others to use a cooperative learning group strategy of "jigsawing expert groups." For example, members of the large group count off by sixes. All of the "number ones" are assigned to become "experts" in the trust strand of development. They meet in a small group to discuss the topic. The "number twos" are assigned the attachment/separation strand, and so on. After 5 to 10 minutes, the experts go back to their original places to form groups, with a "number one," through "number six" in each group. Each member of the large group now leads a discussion of one strand of personal-social development in the small-group setting.

FOR FURTHER READING

Brazelton, T. B. (1989). *Toddlers and parents: A declaration of independence.* New York: Delacorte Press/Seymour Lawrence. Brazelton discusses separation issues throughout the text. Specific examples from his practice illustrate strategies for helping children and their parents work through separation difficulties.

Curry, N. E., & Johnson, C. N. (1990). *Beyond self-esteem: Developing a genuine sense of human value.* Washington, DC: National Association for the Education of Young Children. This book begins with an in-depth discussion of self-esteem as it relates to all areas of development in the first 8 years of life. It then suggests practices that adults will find helpful in assisting young children in learning to value both themselves and others.

Kamii, C. (1982). *Number in preschool and kindergarten: Educational implications of Piaget's theory.* Washington, DC: National Association for the Education of Young Children. The appendix contains a thoughtful essay entitled "Autonomy as the Aim of Education: Implications of Piaget's Theory." Dr. Kamii discusses the relationship between autonomy and a child's motivation to learn and behave morally and the role of educators in this vital process.

Chapter Seven

Physical Development

o b j e c t i v e s

After reviewing this chapter, you will be able to

- Discuss the role of adult-child interaction in promoting gross and fine motor development.
- Define the principles of cephalocaudal and proximodistal development.
- Identify genetic and environmental factors that may influence variations in patterns of development over time and among children.
- Discuss safety precautions that should guide the selection of appropriate toys and equipment and the arrangement of the home or school environment.
- Identify equipment and activities that promote physical development in each of the six age groups.
- Indicate ways that traditional subject matter areas connect to physical development.

🙠 INTRODUCTION

The rapid physical growth and maturation that occur during infancy and childhood correspond to increases in fine and gross motor control. Fine motor skills in infancy may include flexing fingers, reaching, grasping, and eye-hand coordination. A four-year-old child's manipulative skills may include buttoning and zipping clothes, building with plastic builders, drawing with crayons, and lacing shoes, which are all evidence of fine motor control. By age eight, most children have sufficient fine motor control to master manuscript handwriting, to explore art media from watercolor painting to collage, and to complete craft projects, such as stitchery and weaving.

Likewise, rapid changes occur in gross motor control. Two-month-old infants can hold their heads off the ground when placed on their stomachs. By one year of age, many children are beginning to walk. At age three, children may be able to jump and to ride a tricycle. Seven-year-old children may be observed riding bicycles, roller-skating, or playing soccer.

Individual differences in the development of fine and gross motor skills may be related to temperament, physical attributes, health, and the experiences provided by parents, caregivers, and teachers. The repetition and practice that facilitate development of physical skills can be influenced by the temperament categories of persistence, attention span, and approach or withdrawal to new situations (Chess & Thomas, 1996; Chess, Thomas, Birch, Hertzig, & Korn, 1983). The persistent young toddler may repeatedly climb up and down stairs, rejecting parental assistance and safety admonitions. Even a child's activity level may affect the development of fine and gross motor control. The highly active infant may achieve gross motor skills at a faster pace than the passive infant. However, parents and caregivers are cautioned to remember that rapid growth in one developmental area is often not matched with similar rates of growth in other developmental areas.

Physical development is also influenced by a child's health, physiological attributes, and handicapping conditions, if any. Ill health often delays the development of physical skills (Bornstein & Lamb, 1992). Premature birth may be associated with developmental delays; however, prematurity has variable effects on development. Each child reacts differently, with consequences dependent on many factors (Fogel, 1991). Developmental delays in the areas of fine or gross motor skills may be caused by a variety of physical or mental conditions. Some infants who are heavy in proportion to their height may tend to be slower in developing locomotor skills (Snow, 1998). The context can also make a difference. For example, blind infants, like sighted babies, reach and grasp early in life when they hear a sound. If they are not provided with an environment in which the reach of the hand produces a sound and an object to be discovered, blind infants stop reaching (Fraiberg, 1975). Thus, a child's rate of development is affected by environmental and genetic factors.

Finally, the development of fine and gross motor skills can be influenced by the equipment and materials provided by caregivers and parents and the opportunities scheduled for their use (Gerber, 1981). Young infants who are allowed to play on their stomachs on the floor practice physical skills that may lead to learning to crawl. When simple puzzles are introduced to toddlers, they learn to pick up and manipulate puzzle pieces. Preschool-aged children and young school-aged children develop strength and coordination when they are given time to play on climbing equipment. Parents and teachers who demonstrate skills and encourage children to participate in craft activities are more likely to observe children refining fine motor skills.

Although caregivers and parents should have a general notion of developmental milestones for infants, toddlers, and children, they should remember that children vary greatly in their developmental paths (Bornstein & Lamb, 1992). Motor development also varies among cultures (Trawick & Smith, 2000). Rapid growth in one area of development may be compared to a slower rate in another area of development. Knowledge of normative behavior is useful to parents and caregivers because it guides the observation of individual children and may alert parents and caregivers to extreme deviations, which may be indicative of developmental problems. Knowing when an infant is likely to be able to pick up small objects with an **ulnar grasp** or **pincer grip,** for example, enables adults to know when to increase safety precautions or when to introduce finger foods that encourage self-feeding behaviors. Similarly, knowing that the average five- to six-year-old child is able to jump rope or ride a small bicycle enables adults to provide interactions with equipment to learn these skills. Support and encouragement can enhance children's abilities to master physical skills. Likewise, keen observation skills on the part of parents and caregivers can lessen a child's excessive frustrations at being unable to accomplish a physical milestone at a particular time (Benelli & Yongue, 1995). Waiting and reintroducing the activity at a later date often leads to greater success.

A matrix of all the suggested activities precedes the activities, which are grouped by strands of development (Table 7.1). Suggested activities follow general guidelines for age appropriateness. Age recommendations should be viewed as a range rather than a specific chronological age (Frankenberg & Dodds, 1990).

A section on curricular implications is included at the end of the chapter. Ties to alternate methods of curricular planning are discussed and specific examples of developmentally focused activities are given.

✖ KEY STRANDS OF DEVELOPMENT

Motor control follows two principles of development. In general, development proceeds simultaneously in two directions in the body. Development that proceeds downward, literally from head to toe, is called **cephalocaudal development.** Control of neck muscles, needed by infants to hold up their heads, precedes control over the muscles required for sitting without support or the leg muscles needed for standing and walking. The second principle of development is the generalization that development proceeds from the center of the body outward to the arms, hands, and fingers. This direction of development is labeled **proximodistal,** which literally translates as "near to far" (Shaffer, 1989; Tanner, 1990). Fine motor control, illustrated by reaching and grasping skills, begins with batting at objects at three months, successfully grasping an object at five months, and picking up a small object with a pincer grip at nine months of age. In this chapter, interactions that promote the development of gross motor skills are first discussed for each age grouping, followed by discussions of interactions that encourage fine motor development. The continuity of gross motor behaviors leading to locomotion (skills used in moving from place to place) follows the cephalocaudal trend in development. In general, control over muscles follows a head-to-toe order.

Gross Motor

An infant's first voluntary attempts at locomotion are the movements of rolling from side to side. As early as the fourth month of life, infants roll from side to side and may even roll from stomach to back (Fogel, 1991). Firm, flat surfaces provide opportunities for practicing rolling skills. Placing an infant on a blanket on the floor may serve this purpose. As a safety precaution, infants and children should never

Table 7.1 Normative milestones related to physical development.

Ages	Gross Motor	Fine Motor
Birth to one	Lifts head off surface Lifts head and chest off surface Balances head in midline Rolls side to side Sits with support Rolls over Crawls Sits without support Creeps, stomach off floor Pulls self to stand Walks with support Stands alone	Reaches and bats at objects Grasps objects Uses ulnar grasp Lets go of objects Bats at objects even when hand is not in visual field Pincer grip develops Uses fill and spill toys efficiently
One to two	Walks alone with arms out for balance Throws with jerky sidearm motion Stops and stoops while working Uses bouncing while jumping, steps off bottom step with one foot Moves rapidly when walking, does not lose contact with ground	Block tower of two cubes Uses spoons and other utensils First sign of spontaneous scribbling Block tower of four cubes Begins to undress self
Two	Jumps off bottom step, lands with two feet Kicks balls from stationary position Walks up stairs with two feet on each step Sits on riding toys pushing with feet Throws facing target using arms with little body movement	Abel to manipulate simple puzzles Scribbling patterns of circular, horizontal, and vertical lines Strings large-holed beads
Three and four	Walks on a straight line Balances on one foot for 3–4 seconds Catches to chest; turns head to avoid impact Jumps over objects; may jump off steps with two feet Pedals tricycle Climbs up and down ladders Throws overhand, uses some body rotation Walks up stairs, alternating steps; walks down stairs with two feet on step Balances on one foot for 10 seconds Hops on one foot	Puts on shoes Copies circles Zips connected zippers Uses scissors Buttons large buttons Laces shoes Strings small beads Copies across

Table 7.1   *(continued)*

Ages	Gross Motor	Fine Motor
Five and six	Catches bounced ball Jumps vertically, two-footed takeoff and landing Throws with forward step on same foot as throwing arm Throws from elbow Gallops Skips Hops proficiently Jumps rope Catches small ball Climbs ladders in adult manner, hand over hand May ride small bicycle Walks on balance beam	Copies squares and triangles Zips coats and jackets with separating zippers Ties shoe laces Uses manuscript writing
Seven and eight	Runs with increased speed and control Dribbles ball Can use individual jump ropes Throws with trunk rotated, steps forward on foot opposite of throwing arm, releases with fingers and wrist Rides bicycle with skill Can kick a ball while running Catches balls more effectively Can roller-skate	Able to make uniformly sized letters and numbers Able to complete simple crafts successfully, e.g., origami, stitchery, weaving Copies diamond shapes

be left unsecured on a high counter or table or be left unattended on a potentially unsafe floor surface. Many an unwary parent has been surprised at a young infant's ability to move across a room by continued rolling. Activity 7.1 illustrates an adult-infant interaction that encourages rolling from side to side.

A second area of gross motor development for young infants involves strengthening the neck muscles and upper body muscle groups (Fogel, 1991). The newborn's head must be fully supported when lifted from a prone position or it bobs. Gradually, the head bobbing decreases as infants learn to balance and maintain the head in a midline position when they are brought to a sitting position or held upright on an adult's shoulder. When placed on a firm, flat surface, infants also practice lifting their heads to a nearly vertical position, which permits maneuvering their arms out in front of their faces. Reaching from the stomach position is promoted when visual

Older infant practices crawling to reach a toy.

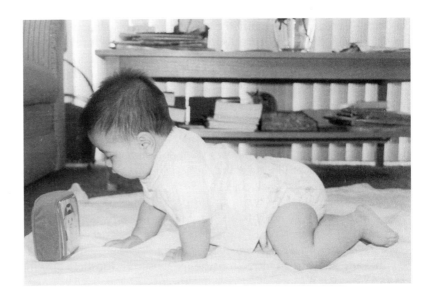

and auditory senses lead infants to pay attention to an object. Attractive objects placed just beyond a young infant's reach, described in Activity 7.2, may catch his or her attention and increase the likelihood of stretching to reach.

Learning to sit follows the cephalocaudal principle of development as motor control proceeds from head to toe. A young infant must be fully supported to sit. Infant seats and front-carrying packs provide the full support of a child's head and torso in the earliest days of life and permit parents and caregivers to vary the infant's visual and auditory environment. With the use of infant seats and front-carrying packs, infants can be readily moved from room to room as parents and caregivers conduct their day's activities. Sitting also provides a change of position for the infant from lying on the stomach or back, before being mobile. Later opportunities to strengthen head, neck, shoulder, and back muscles occur when babies are propped in sitting positions on laps, in swings, or with pillows. Since the head is proportionally heavy in comparison to the body, infants are extremely top-heavy at this age. As a safety pre-

caution, infants should never be left unattended in a propped position.

Sitting also permits the use of the infant's hands and arms. Fingerplays and action songs can be used with infants as they sit in the laps of adults or sit supported in infant seats and other similar equipment. Patty-cake and peek-a-boo variations have been played with children across many cultures and generations (Activity 7.3).

By six months of age, infants may sit unassisted for brief periods; however, they are often bent over at the waist, supporting their weight on their hands and arms. At this stage, they are less able to manipulate objects in their hands. When infants attain the balancing mechanism to sit unassisted, the hands are free to explore. As a safety precaution, it is still wise to place a pillow behind an infant who has just learned to sit unassisted. This prevents the baby from falling backward on the head. Most babies can reach out to catch their falls when they go forward or to the side. Near the end of their first year, many infants pull themselves up to standing, holding onto crib rails, chairs, and even the backs of parent's and caregiver's legs. Gradually, the infant practices taking steps by cruising around, holding on to objects for support. Endless hours are spent practicing this type of walking to achieve coordination and balance. Each infant seems to have a unique timetable for learning to walk (Fogel, 1991). Providing a safe environment, free of sharp edges and free of equipment and furniture that easily topple, allows the necessary repetitions of pulling to stand, collapsing to sit, and squatting to reach objects.

When infants first walk unsupported, they usually hold their arms out for balance and toddle forward with stiffened knees. Their legs are spread apart to balance their weight, and they frequently stop themselves by falling or grabbing on to objects. Infants use their new-found freedom to explore the environment as they practice walking. Gradually, they learn to slow down, stop in the middle of the room, and change directions. Their

arms are lowered to their sides when they are no longer needed for balance. Infants who are soon to be toddlers are often ready for pushing, pulling, and carrying toys on their journeys. Giving children a small pail or basket, as suggested in Activity 7.4, permits them to integrate stooping and reaching for objects as they practice walking.

The toddler's growing agility in walking involves learning to walk backward and sideward. Push toys and pull toys may provide opportunities to practice these changes in direction. Activity 7.5 uses a hula hoop to support walking infants or young toddlers in moving their feet backward and sideward. Toddlers also increase the speed at which they walk. Although older toddlers may appear to be running, especially to a parent or caregiver who is trying to catch them, technically they are still walking because their feet never actually leave the ground at the same time. When

Caregiver encourages infant to take first steps.

toddlers kick balls, they begin by either walking into the ball or kicking the ball from a standing position. Parents and caregivers can interact with toddlers by passing a ball back and forth between them with their feet as described in Activity 7.5.

Upper body movements can be encouraged with a variety of activities. Different-sized balls require slightly different upper body movements. Toddlers usually throw objects over their heads with two hands, generally without shifting their weight to compensate for the motion. Toddlers and preschool-aged children also practice tossing objects at this age from a sitting position. Inappropriate throwing behaviors can be redirected. For example, a parent may stop a child from throwing blocks by admonishing, "Blocks are for building. If you'd like to practice throwing, let's go get a ball." In a toddler group-care setting, caregivers and teachers may use cardboard blocks as a safety precaution.

Preschool children learn to throw a hand-sized ball in stages. At first, children use a stiff, simple arm extension. Next, they twist the shoulder slightly as they throw to follow the arm's throwing motion, but they do not move their feet or shift their weight. Gradually, children learn to step forward with the leg that is on the same side of the body as the throwing arm, which capitalizes on the momentum that is created. A mature throw involves stepping forward with the opposite foot of the throwing hand. Teach the child to step, turn toward a target, and throw the ball (Benelli & Yongue, 1995).

Dance and other movement activities also provide opportunities for gross motor development. Activity 7.7 illustrates one technique for encouraging children to gain upper body control. Different types of music may inspire different types of movement. Although studios with wall-sized mirrors may inhibit movement for some children and distract others, they can also increase body awareness.

Watching other children and adults participate in movement activities can also challenge children to imitate and experiment with a variety of motions.

Before the age of two, children are likely to step off stairs, keeping one foot in contact with the ground. Between the ages of two and three, many children learn to jump off a bottom step with two feet. The stiff-legged toddler style of walking gradually changes to a style using flexed knees. Bouncing on floor cushions and mats provides experience in bending knees to absorb the bounce. Two-year-olds can also be encouraged to jump off low objects into the waiting arms of parents and caregivers. Gradually decreasing the amount of physical support for children's movements builds a sense of confidence and personal safety (Activity 7.8).

Toddlers balance themselves while walking by spreading their legs apart to create a wider base of support. Eventually, children learn to walk and then run with their legs and feet closer together and directly underneath their bodies. It is particularly challenging for young children to walk with their feet directly in front of one another in a heel-to-toe fashion. Older toddlers and young three-year-olds can practice tightrope walking on a rope placed in a straight line on the ground (Activity 7.9). Falling off the line to regain balance is easily remedied by returning to the line for more practice. Older three- and four-year-olds can adapt to curved lines with practice. Low, wide balance beams are available in some centers and schools for additional experience in learning to balance.

Learning to hop, skip, and gallop are all milestones in physical agility. By three and a half years of age, children can hop several times on one foot (Fogel, 1991). Activity 7.10 describes an activity for encouraging preschool children to practice hopping. The five-year-old is likely to be able to hop across a small room. Galloping and skipping are more difficult skills to master; both require shifts in balance and a high degree of coordination. The ability to gallop usually appears earlier than the ability to skip (Gabbard, 1992). This is because skipping is a movement pattern requiring children to use alternate feet, but the leading foot remains forward in galloping. Many children cannot skip until they are almost six years old (Cratty, 1986). Kindergarten teachers can present activities designed to help children learn to skip (Activity 7.11).

For many children, individual differences in temperament styles are readily observed through differences in climbing styles. Some children are reluctant, hesitant climbers. Other children are highly adventurous, even to the point of climbing seemingly beyond their apparent abilities. When this occurs, the adult can usually verbally direct these children to retrace their steps to climb down from the climbing apparatus. Among early childhood educators, a general rule states that children seldom climb farther than they can climb down, as long as they are not challenged by peers or older children. The unwritten message for the teacher or caregiver is not to lift children up to a climbing structure that the children cannot get on by themselves. For most groups of children, this tends to be a feasible rule.

Teaching children to think about their personal safety can build their sense of confidence in their caregivers and themselves. Loose clothing and slippery shoes impede a child's ability to climb safely. Waiting at the bottom of the ladder for the person at the top of the slide to sit down and begin to slide lessens the competition to go up the ladder in a reckless manner and slide down before being ready. Verbally walking children out of a tight spot rather than physically rescuing them can build their sense of individual strength and pride in their accomplishments. Activity 7.12 describes a playground interaction that promotes a sense of confidence in climbing ability.

The ability to catch a ball progresses in stages. Infants can trap a ball that is rolled in between their legs. Older toddlers and young preschool children tend to stick their arms out stiffly when a ball is thrown to them (Gabbard, 1992). Sometimes the ball bounces off the child's chest because he or she has not closed his or her arms to catch it. Catching involves the ability to visually follow an object and anticipate accurately when the ball has reached the target. The right equipment can enhance the success of the practice session (Pangrazi, 1998). Large balls tend to be easier to catch than small balls, and beanbags are sometimes easier to catch because they are more readily grasped. Helping a child learn to catch takes many practice opportunities and a skilled thrower as a partner. It is much less frustrating for a child to play catch with a skilled partner than with a novice. Activity 7.13 illustrates an adult-child interaction for learning to catch.

Learning to throw accurately may be as challenging to a young school-aged child as learning to catch. Throwing beanbags at an attractive target can be a valuable learning activity. Beanbags are easier to catch than balls, and they do not roll far away when the target is missed. They also lessen the need for the catcher to have to fetch an errant throw. Children need to coordinate several cognitive and physical skills in learning how to throw (Pangrazi, 1998). Aiming accurately requires eye-hand coordination, and knowing when to release the object demands predictive abilities. Coordinating the rotation of the shoulder with the movements of the arm and the corresponding leg develops with experience and is influenced by physical maturation (Activity 7.14).

Public and school playgrounds introduce activities to children that have been popular for generations in many cultural groups. Outlines for hopscotch games can be found painted on schoolyards and drawn in chalk on neighborhood sidewalks. Often an older child passes on the rules of the game to younger children. Adults can observe as children participate in the physical and social aspects of the game. Building the skill levels of less physically coordinated participants may also influence their personal-social development. Activity 7.15 involves one form of hopscotch.

Jumping rope is another example of a skill frequently practiced in school and child-care settings. Successful rope jumping requires the coordination of several physical skills when it is done individually. It also builds endurance and promotes cardiovascular health. A long jump rope that is turned by experienced, skilled adults can enhance practice sessions. A child must know how to jump and learn to anticipate when to jump (Activity 7.16). Individual jump ropes can be used in group instruction so that all children practice jumping skills instead of waiting in line for a turn with the long rope. Learning stations staffed with parents or older student volunteers can also be used to lessen waiting times.

Children participate in organized sports at increasingly younger ages. Soccer tends to be less competitive at the beginning stages than many other sports in the United States. Community soccer programs provide children with opportunities to become physically fit by giving all children equal opportunities to participate. Competition between teams is de-emphasized when a score is not tallied. As a sport, soccer requires running, which is good for general health and fitness, and ball control skills, which require coordination (Activity 7.17).

In the final sample interaction, using a parachute promotes gross motor development as a group activity. Depending on the size of the parachute, this activity may involve from eight to over thirty children. It is an activity that integrates developmental areas. Physically, children coordinate the use of arms and legs as well as use strength. Socially, children must cooperate to achieve a common goal. Children can use both verbal and nonverbal means to communicate with the other participants. In the cognitive area, problem-solving skills are enhanced when challenges are presented to the group

Second-grade boy refines his kicking skills.

that require children to predict and test different methods of moving the parachute. Finally, creativity can be promoted when children are asked to discover alternative ways of using the parachute. Activity 7.18 suggests a strategy for using the parachute that promotes strength and gross motor, arm movements.

Fine Motor

An early fine motor behavior for young infants might be batting at objects suspended at the infants' midline within their reach. Objects with high-contrast colors, such as patterns of black and white, are particularly visually attractive to young infants. In the beginning, infants may wave their arms in the air in the direction of the object. Later, they seek to reach and grasp objects or at a minimum cause the object to move or make a noise. The infant's arms must be free to bat at the object. Activity 7.19 allows infants to lie on their backs beneath the suspended object. At around five months, infants begin to reach for objects when their hands are not in their visual field.

There are endless ways to create fill-and-spill activities for infants. Infants repeatedly practice taking objects out of containers and putting them back in the container. Each exploration may involve grasping an object, rotating the wrists to examine it visually or orally, and then learning to release the object consciously. Activity 7.20 contains one version of a favorite homemade fill-and-spill piece of equipment. Small objects for exploration must be nontoxic, free of sharp edges, and large enough not to be swallowed. Objects that are no smaller than plastic golf balls make good choices for fill and spill activities.

An infant's first technique for picking up tiny objects is the ulnar grasp. Infants surround the object with their hand and press it into their palm (Snow, 1998). Parents can observe infants trying to pick up food using this technique without much success. Infants may try to shove their fist and the food particle into their mouth at the same time. By nine months of age, many infants have developed the pincer grip, where the opposing thumb and the finger work together to pinch the object (Shaffer, 1989). A strategy for encouraging self-feeding behaviors is illustrated in Activity 7.21. Parents and caregivers may also observe infants trying the pincer grip to pick up particles of lint from the carpet or even trying to lift off minute designs from fabric.

A young toddler's first blocks can be made out of cardboard or another lightweight material. This is especially recommended for children in group child-care settings, because of the likelihood that blocks may be thrown or knocked over on another child. Much of the time, parents and caregivers can redirect inappropriate throwing behaviors. Building block towers requires eye-hand coordination and fine motor control (Activity 7.22).

Commercially made puzzles for infants and young toddlers may have pieces with knobs attached. Puzzles are excellent tools for promoting fine motor control at any age because they require manipulation of small objects. Simple puzzles can be made for older infants and young toddlers with free or inexpensive materials. Suggestions for using such a puzzle with a young toddler are outlined in Activity 7.23.

Scribbling also proceeds in developmental stages, which are frequently used by early childhood educators to assess levels of development or individual patterns of variation. The spontaneous scribble occurs at approximately one year of age. Since infants and toddlers vary greatly in their mouthing behaviors, the use of even nontoxic crayons should be closely supervised.

Setting up a safe and healthy painting activity for children under the age of two is also challenging for the parent or caregiver. Allowing infants and toddlers to "paint" with water promotes fine motor and sensory exploration. Activity 7.24 is a painting experience for the older infant or young toddler outdoors or on the kitchen floor.

Early childhood centers often provide a variety of tools that children can manipulate. In the water-play area, the teacher may include spoons, whisks, and even an eggbeater. The carpentry center may have child-sized hammers, screwdrivers, and pliers. Scissors, hole punches, and paintbrushes are readily added to art centers. A popular tool for the manipulative center in the toddler classroom or in the home is tongs. A variety of different types may be used. Activity 7.25 is a sample activity for using tongs. The fine motor control needed for using scissors is similar to the skills developed in tong use.

Cube blocks make an excellent table or tray activity. The eye-hand coordination that is needed to stack 1-inch cubes on top of one another is promoted in Activity 7.26. Refined hand movements are also needed to stack the blocks and to move fingers away from the tower without knocking it over in the process. Manipulating cube blocks can also set a foundation for future math concepts.

Although fingerplays and action rhymes can be introduced at an earlier age, two-year-olds seem to be enthralled with this language and fine motor play activity. A teacher or parent can begin with simple fingerplays that children will ask to have repeated at regular intervals. The Beehive Fingerplay (Activity 7.27) is a favorite of toddlers because of the buzzing sound and the tickling motions made by the bees.

Bead stringing (chapter 8, Activity 8.3) requires eye-hand coordination and control of small muscles (Weiser, 1991). Normally, the younger the child, the larger the bead. Macaroni necklaces can be made inexpensively in homes and schools and do not need to be dismantled at the end of the play period. Activity 7.28 includes instructions for setting up a macaroni bead stringing activity.

Scissors are found in most preschool centers and programs for young school-aged children. Child-safe, blunt-tipped scissors with sharp cutting edges are a wise investment for homes, child-care, and school programs. Dull-edged scissors frustrate even patient children. Left-handed scissors and adaptive scissors should be provided for children who need them. Many three-year-olds have difficulty mastering even the simplest cutting tasks. Multiple opportunities for practicing cutting skills should be provided. Free cutting of thin paper precedes the development of skills needed to cut forms of a child's own devising. With continued practice, children can extend their developing cutting skills to thicker paper

Kindergarten girl concentrates as she practices handwriting.

and to cutting on pre-drawn straight and curved lines. A beginning scissor experience is described in Activity 7.29.

Random scribbling is replaced by efforts to draw circular shapes and various styles of lines. Games can be played with preschool-aged children to expand their awareness of different types of drawn figures. In the adult-child interaction described in Activity 7.30, children and adults take turns copying the shapes made by the other. Describing and labeling the shapes adds to the language development possibilities of the activity.

Manipulative skills are enhanced by activities that require children to fit objects together by pushing, pulling, prying, twisting, and otherwise coordinating the muscles of the fingers and hands with the eyes. Commercially available manipulatives are readily available to parents, child-care providers, and teachers. Some of these materials include Duplos, Legos, Lincoln Logs, erector sets, and wooden trains. Numerous other manipulatives can be created from household objects, such as the nuts and bolts experience described in Activity 7.31.

Most self-help skills, which range from feeding to dressing and toileting, involve some type of fine motor control. Taking clothes off and attempting to dress independently promote gross and fine motor control and eye-hand coordination. Using zippers, snaps, and buttons efficiently requires practice. In the age of Velcro fastening and slip-on shoes, some children may not have a personal experience with learning how to lace and tie shoes by the age of five. Few children learn to tie bows by simply observing other people or by trial and error. Direct instruction is usually required for most children to develop this fine motor skill. Lacing cards and lacing frames can be designed by child-care providers and teachers to give children practice in self-help skills, such as lacing, snapping, zipping, buttoning, and tying (Activity 7.32).

Arts and craft activities are commonly found in most schools or child-care settings for preschool-aged and young school-aged children. Creative activities are discussed in chapter 10. A major purpose of craft-type activities in early childhood programs is development of fine motor control and eye-hand coordination. Many of the process skills learned by completing crafts can later be used in more creative endeavors. Tearing paper appears to be a simple activity at first, but creating desired shapes by tearing paper requires practice and well-developed fine motor skills. A torn-paper collage experience is described in Activity 7.33.

Young school-aged children enjoy preparing snacks and simple foods. The use of kitchen utensils requires fine motor control and coordination. The task of spreading butter on a piece of bread involves holding the bread in the hand or on a plate and using a knife to spread butter with the other hand. Cookbooks are available that suggest a variety of snacks and meals suitable for preparation by children. A popular snack is peanut butter–filled celery stalks (Activity 7.34).

The last two suggested activities in this chapter involve crafts. Origami (Activity 7.35), the ancient art of Japanese paper folding, has been practiced by children and adults for centuries. To successfully demonstrate paper folding, teachers and parents should practice the activity before presenting it to children. Stitchery (Activity 7.36) is also a craft that is practiced in many cultures. In the past, very young children were expected to participate in sewing clothes or household linens. Although some parents and teachers believe that stitchery is too difficult for preschool and young school-aged children, both origami and stitchery projects can be adapted to young children and are valuable activities for enhancing fine motor skills. See Table 7.2 for a matrix correlating all the activities described in chapter 7 with the appropriate ages and developmental strands.

Table 7.2 Physical development activities matrix.

Ages (Years)	Gross Motor			Fine Motor		
Birth to one	First Moves Activity 7.1 Adult-child	Stretches to Reach Toy Activity 7.2 Child-object	Patty-Cake Activity 7.3 Adult-child	Batting at Objects Activity 7.19 Child-object	Simple Fill and Spill Activity 7.2 Adult-child	Cereal Pick Up Activity 7.21 Child-object
One to two	Picking up Objects Activity 7.4 Child-object	Walking Backward Activity 7.5 Adult-child	Kicking Balls Activity 7.6 Adult-child	Milk Carton Blocks Activity 7.22 Child-child	One-Piece Puzzle Activity 7.23 Adult-child	Handprints with Water Activity 7.24 Adult-child
Two	Moving Arms to Music Activity 7.7 Adult-child	Jumping off Stairs Activity 7.8 Adult-child	Walking on a Line Activity 7.9 Adult-child	Using Tongs Activity 7.25 Child-object	Towers of Cube Blocks Activity 7.26 Child-object	Beehive Fingerplay Activity 7.27 Adult-child
Three and four	Hopping on One Foot Activity 7.10 Child-child	Climbing Fun Activity 7.12 Child-object	Playing Catch Activity 7.13 Child-Child	Macaroni Necklaces Activity 7.28 Child-object	Using Scissors Activity 7.29 Child-object	Drawing in a Salt Tray Activity 7.30 Adult-child
Five and six	Beanbag Toss at a Target Activity 7.14 Child-object	Skipping Activity 7.15 Child-Child	Hopscotch Activity 7.15 Child-object	Nuts and Bolts Activity 7.31 Child-object	Dressing Skills Activity 7.32 Child-object	Torn Paper Collage Activity 7.33 Child-object
Seven and eight	Jumping Rope Activity 7.16 Adult-child	Dribbling a Soccer Ball Activity 7.17 Child-object	Parachutes Activity 7.18 Child-child	Ants on a Log Activity 7.34 Adult-child	Origami Activity 7.35 Child-object	Stitchery Activity 7.36 Child-object

❧ AGE-APPROPRIATE ACTIVITIES: BIRTH THROUGH EIGHT YEARS

A c t i v i t y   7 . 1

First Moves

Level Birth to one

Area Physical

Interaction Adult-child

Strand Gross Motor

Materials Needed Rattle or other noisemaker

Directions for Implementation

- Lie the baby on a blanket on the floor on his or her back.
- Shake a rattle on one side of the baby, and try to get the baby to turn to that side.
- Encourage the baby to turn toward the sound of the rattle by saying, "Do you hear the rattle? Roll this way."
- Change the rattle from one side to the other to encourage the baby to turn.

Extensions

Lay the baby on the floor on his or her side. Lie down next to the baby, facing his or her back. Whisper to the baby to encourage rolling over to see you. Between four and five months of age, a baby may roll from stomach to back, and by the end of the sixth month, be able to roll from back to front (Caplan, 1993). Rolling becomes a form of locomotion used to expand the environment for exploration. Preschool children can practice various types of body rolling, for example, arms down to the sides, arms over the head, or even curled up into a ball. Young school-aged children can practice the forward roll from a squatting position.

A c t i v i t y   7 . 2

Stretches to Reach

Level Birth to one

Area Physical

Interaction Child-object

Strand Gross Motor

Materials Needed Small toy

Directions for Implementation

- Place the infant on the floor on the stomach.
- Put a small toy just beyond the infant's reach.
- Encourage the infant to reach for the toy.

Extensions

Fill a clear, liter-size soda bottle with colored water about one-fourth full. Securely screw on cap. Place the bottle on its side just beyond the baby's reach. The bottle will roll slightly when it is touched, and the water will move back and forth, catching the baby's eye. Younger infants (approximately two months of age) may be stimulated to lift their head to gaze at an interesting object (Caplan, 1993). Older infants will use a form of locomotion to grasp objects out of their immediate reach.

A c t i v i t y   7 . 3

Patty-Cake

Level Birth to one

Area Physical

Interaction Adult-child

Strand Gross Motor

Materials Needed None

Directions for Implementation

- Sit facing the infant.

- Chant the nursery rhyme as you guide the infant's arms through the hand motions.

Patty-cake, patty-cake, baker's man,
(Clap the baby's hands together.)
Bake me a cake as fast as you can.
(Continue clapping.)
Pat it and roll it and mark it with a B,
(Pat imaginary cake with both hands palms down, roll hands together, and write a B in the air.)
And put it in the oven for baby and me.
(Pretend to put the cake in the oven and point to baby and yourself.)

Extensions

Throughout history, children of many cultures have encountered numerous variations of peekaboo. One variation involves parents or caregivers covering their eyes. Another method is draping a cloth over the head of the infant and saying, "peekaboo" as the cloth is whisked off. The clapping motions dictated by the patty-cake nursery rhyme can also be extended for toddlers by other singing games. A simple song that can be changed to fit a variety of motions is called "Clap, Clap, Clap Your Hands." (Appendix C contains the entire song with suggested variations.) This action song can be further adapted by young school-aged children.

A c t i v i t y   7 . 4

Picking Up Objects

Level One to two

Area Physical

Interaction Child-object

Strand Gross Motor

Materials Needed Small pail or basket with a handle, hand-sized objects that are too big to be swallowed

Directions for Implementation

- Spread small objects around the room.
- Give the toddler a pail, and encourage the child to stoop and collect the objects in the pail.
- Dump the objects out, spread them around, and begin again.

Extensions

Play the game outside with a bucket of small plastic golf balls. Involve even the youngest of toddlers in picking up toys and other cleanup activities. Older children might experiment using the bucket as a catching device.

A c t i v i t y   7 . 5

Walking Backward

Level One to two

Area Physical

Interaction Adult-child

Strand Gross Motor

Materials Needed Hula hoop or other stiff, lightweight object

Directions for Implementation

- In an indoor or outdoor open space, have the toddler stand up, holding one edge of a hula hoop with both hands.
- Stand, holding the opposite edge of the hoop.
- Begin by having the toddler walk forward while you walk backward.
- Change directions by saying, "Let's go back." Slowly walk forward as the toddler steps backward. Try walking sideways and around in a circle, holding the hula hoop.

Extensions

Enlist the help of an older child to play Follow the Leader. Model various actions including walking backward. Remember to announce changes of direction when the child cannot see what you are doing.

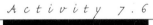

Kicking Balls

Level One to two

Area Physical

Interaction Adult-child

Strand Gross Motor

Materials Needed Rubber ball, approximately 6 inches in diameter, old pair of pantyhose, and a rope

Directions for Implementation

- Create a tetherball-like piece of equipment by placing the ball inside the panty area of the panty hose. Use the legs to secure it firmly in the pantyhose and tie a rope to it.
- Stake or tie the other end of the rope securely to a post or other object to create a grounded tetherball experience.
- Demonstrate kicking the ball.
- Encourage the toddler to kick the ball back and forth to you.

Extensions

Older children can experiment with various-sized balls and with balls that are not tethered.

Moving Arms to Music

Level Two

Area Physical

Interaction Adult-child

Strand Gross Motor

Materials Needed Music from a radio or other source

Directions for Implementation

- Encourage older toddlers to move their arms to the music.
- Demonstrate shaking, waving, clapping, and other movements in response to the music.
- Watch toddlers and imitate their ideas of moving to the music.

Extensions

Find wide ribbons or scarves. Draw circles in the air with the ribbons. Experiment with other ways of using arms to make the ribbons dance. Encourage older children to add leg motions or other types of locomotion to the activity. Infants can also move their arms to music. Attach short ribbons to bracelets or wristbands.

Jumping Off Stairs

Level Two

Area Physical

Interaction Adult-child

Strand Gross Motor

Materials Needed Low stairs

Directions for Implementation

- Hold the toddler's hands when he or she is first learning to jump off a bottom step.
- Help the toddler land softly and safely while practicing jumping with both feet rather than stepping off the stair.
- As confidence in jumping ability grows, support the child with one hand and then gradually encourage jumping alone.

Extensions

Toddlers can also practice jumping up and down while standing or jumping on two feet over flat objects such as ropes. Many young infants and toddlers like to be bounced up and down. An adult can hold an infant or toddler securely as the adult jumps up and down. Older children should be helped to identify resilient surfaces that are safer for jumping and should be instructed to bend their knees to absorb the impact.

A c t i v i t y   7 . 9

Walking on a Line

Level Two

Area Physical

Interaction Adult-child

Strand Gross Motor

Materials Needed Chalk or a rope

Directions for Implementation

- Create a flat balance beam by drawing a chalk line on the sidewalk or placing a rope on the grass or dirt.
- Demonstrate walking heel to toe on the line with your arms out to balance.
- Play a game of "Follow the Leader", rotating the roles with the child.

Extensions

Walking curved lines is more challenging because it requires both balance and the ability to turn the body. Use a long rope to create arcs, circles, and "S" curves. Older children find walking on curbs a challenge.

A c t i v i t y   7 . 1 0

Hopping on One Foot

Level Three and four

Area Physical

Interaction Child-child

Strand Gross Motor

Materials Needed Line markers

Directions for Implementation

- Mark two parallel lines with ropes or tape, approximately 10 feet apart. (The distance should be determined by the experience and skill level of the child.)
- Demonstrate how to hop on one foot from one line to another.
- Challenge the child to hop on one foot in one direction and return on the opposite foot.

Extensions

Older children can make up patterns of gross motor movements for adults and other children to copy that begin and end on the same spot. For example, the child might demonstrate two hops forward, jump once to the left, jump once to the right, and finish with two hops backward. The home spot can be marked with a flat plastic lid or disk. This extension integrates cognitive and physical skills.

A c t i v i t y   7 . 1 1

Skipping

Level Five and six

Area Physical

Interaction Adult-child

Strand Gross Motor

Materials Needed None

Directions for Implementation

- Skip around an open space holding a child's hand, hopping in rhythm first on one foot and then the other.
- Once the child has mastered the skill, exaggerate the pace by skipping slowly and then quickly or change from little skips to big skips.
- Play "Follow the Leader," using skipping and other forms of locomotion.

Extensions

Find music or songs for skipping, such as "Skip to My Lou." Older children can create patterns for their peers to copy. For example, seven- or eight-year-olds can begin by creating a movement pattern of three different elements, such as jumping twice, skipping five times, and then turning three circles with the arms out. The leader models the pattern, and then the rest of the group re-creates the pattern. Remind children to count as they create their patterns. The preceding example might be remembered as two, five, three (i.e., jump, jump, skip, skip, skip, skip, skip, turn, turn, turn). This activity combines elements of physical, cognitive, and creative development.

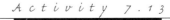

A c t i v i t y   7 . 1 2

Climbing Fun

Level Three and four

Area Physical

Interaction Child-object

Strand Gross Motor

Materials Needed Climbing structure or jungle gym

Directions for Implementation

- Encourage children to develop climbing skills on an individual basis. "Tam, I see you climbed all the way to the third platform today. You must be getting stronger."
- Safe climbing behaviors can be taught by verbally guiding children to accomplish difficult moves. "Han, if you move your hand to the next bar and then move your feet, it may be easier to cross that space."

Extensions

Climbing strengthens both upper body and leg muscles. Using portable equipment, set up an obstacle course using the children's ideas to create safe climbing challenges. Large card-

board boxes from furniture and appliance stores can be used for temporary obstacle courses.

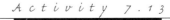

A c t i v i t y   7 . 1 3

Playing Catch

Level Three and four

Area Physical

Interaction Adult-child

Strand Gross Motor

Materials Needed A 10- to 12-inch rubber ball

Directions for Implementation

- Position the child several feet away, facing you.
- Cue the child to prepare for catching the ball by saying, "Arms out. Are you ready? Here it comes."
- Gradually increase the distance between the two participants as the child becomes more successful in catching the ball.

Extensions

Older infants can learn the basics of playing catch by having someone roll a ball to them as they are seated on the floor. Toddlers can practice throwing beanbags or Nerf balls in a game of catch. Older children can use objects to catch the ball, such as a plastic laundry basket or use smaller balls in playing catch with a partner.

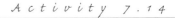

A c t i v i t y   7 . 1 4

Beanbag Toss at a Target

Level Five and six

Area Physical

Interaction Child-object

Strand Gross Motor

Materials Needed Several beanbags, target made from a large cardboard box

Directions for Implementation

- Cut several holes in the cardboard box that are at least twice the size of the beanbag.
- Have the child stand 4 to 6 feet from the box and attempt to throw the beanbags through holes in the box. Adjust the distance if the task seems too difficult or too easy.

Extensions

Younger children can throw the beanbags at a large target that does not have holes or into a large laundry basket. Older children like to challenge themselves by thinking of alternative targets. Empty cans for stacking or an empty plastic milk container might be provided as props to extend the activity.

Activity 7.15

Hopscotch

Level Five and six

Area Physical

Interaction Child-child

Strand Gross Motor

Materials Needed Chalk, small rock for a marker

Directions for Implementation

- Outline a game of hopscotch on a sidewalk or other hard surface. (See Appendix C for a diagram and directions.)
- Most games of hopscotch involve hopping in the single spaces and landing on two feet in the double spaces. Practice hopping and jumping by playing hopscotch.

Extensions

Hopscotch is a game played in some form by children all over the world. A children's book by Mary Lankford, *Hopscotch Around the World* (1992), illustrates the variations in diagrams and rules. Experiment with playing hopscotch games from other cultures.

Activity 7.16

Jumping Rope

Level Seven and eight

Area Physical

Interaction Adult-child

Strand Gross Motor

Materials Needed Long jump ropes

Directions for Implementation

- Ask an experienced child or another adult to help turn the rope.
- Instruct the child to stand on one side of the rope, facing you, in the middle of the rope.
- Without turning the rope, ask the child to jump up and down with both feet at your command.
- Begin turning the rope evenly. Help the child anticipate when to jump by listening to your commands.
- Saying, "Jump, jump, jump" at an even pace helps children pick up the rhythm of rope jumping.

Extensions

Children who have learned to jump with a long rope can practice with individual ropes, which require skills in turning the rope and jumping. In addition to learning to jump while turning the rope forward, children can practice jumping while turning the rope backward, jumping by alternating feet, skipping across the room while jumping rope, and other variations.

Activity 7.17

Dribbling a Soccer Ball

Level Seven and eight

Area Physical

Interaction Child-object

Strand Gross Motor

Materials Needed Soccer ball or another kicking ball, cones or other playground markers

Directions for Implementation

- Set up a cone about 30 feet from a starting point.
- Demonstrate how to kick the ball by using small kicks from the insides of alternating feet while running slowly.
- Emphasize controlling the ball with the feet (rather than trying to kick the ball as hard as possible) as the child runs down to the cone, goes around it, and comes back.
- Continue to emphasize control rather than the speed or distance of each kick.

Extensions

Set up a line of cones that are about 20 feet apart. Encourage the children to dribble, weaving in and out of the cones. Younger children can be encouraged to run to a designated location on the playground as they kick and chase the ball.

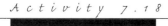

A c t i v i t y   7 . 1 8

Parachutes

Level Seven and eight

Area Physical

Interaction Child-child

Strand Gross Motor

Materials Needed Parachute or blanket, lightweight ball

Directions for Implementation

- Spread out the parachute on the grass and have children sit around it, spaced equally.
- Demonstrate how to hold the edge of the parachute firmly with both hands to keep it taut.
- Have the children practice lifting up the parachute while remaining seated on the

grass. Remind the children to hang on tightly as the parachute goes up and down. Emphasize working together by counting, "One, two, three, lift!" Allow the parachute to billow and fall back down to the grass each time.

- Suggest that the children rise to their knees and repeat the lift. Place a lightweight ball in the center of the parachute when it is on the ground. Challenge the children to shake the parachute up and down to bounce the ball. The object is to bounce the ball as high as possible, without allowing it to fall off of the parachute.
- Repeat the activity with the children standing.

Extensions

Younger children also enjoy using a parachute. A favorite activity of five- and six-year-olds is to call the names of two children standing on opposite sides of the parachute. With the rest of the children standing, billow the parachute, and tell the two children to exchange places by running under the parachute. The object is to run under the parachute and find their new places before it drops.

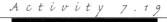

A c t i v i t y   7 . 1 9

Batting at Objects

Level Birth to One

Area Physical

Interaction Child-object

Strand Fine Motor

Materials Needed Black and white pom-pom made from yarn (see Appendix D)

Directions for Implementation

- Securely suspend the pom-pom from another object so that it will be within reach when the young infant is lying on the back. (Safety precaution: This activity is only for non-mobile infants and should be removed when not in use.) A piece of elastic used as the tether will allow the object to bounce when it is hit. For example, a ribbon could be tied between two kitchen chairs, and the elastic could be securely sewn to it.

- Place the baby directly under the pom-pom so that it is midline in relation to the baby.
- Gently touch the object to catch the baby's attention. Watch to see if the baby attempts to bat at the object. Babies usually fuss when they are ready for a change of activity.

Extensions

Pom-poms and lightweight balls can also be suspended as a tetherball-type activity for infants who can sit without needing support or for infants securely fastened in infant seats or strollers. Infants and toddlers should never be left unattended with strings and cords that may cause strangulation. Older children recognize this activity as a type of tetherball.

Activity 7 . 2 0

Simple Fill-and-Spill

Level Birth to one

Area Physical

Interaction Adult-child

Strand Fine Motor

Materials Needed Metal or cardboard can with plastic lid (see Appendix D), a dozen plastic golf balls

Directions for Implementation

- Show the infant how to drop the balls down the center hole.
- When the can is full, take off the lid, dump them out, and begin again.

Extensions

Fill-and-spill activities can be created from any size container that has a plastic lid. Objects for filling the container must be durable, nontoxic, and too large to be swallowed. Younger infants can participate in filling containers with no lids. Also consider using objects that do not roll with nonmobile infants. One variation is to cut a rectangular slit from sample formica tiles. Another variation of the activity is to cut two holes for the objects, one that is too small and one that is just right.

Activity 7 . 2 1

Cereal Pick Up

Level Birth to one

Area Physical

Interaction Child-object

Strand Fine Motor

Materials Needed Bite-size breakfast cereal

Directions for Implementation

- Place a small handful of cereal on the high chair tray or other feeding surface.
- Observe the infant's technique of picking up and eating the cereal.
- Talk to the infant. You might say, "You're getting really good at picking up those pieces of cereal."

Extensions

Provide other finger foods to promote self-feeding skills. Cooked peas, cooked cubed carrots, fish crackers, banana slices, and similar foods are good for beginners. However, hot dog pieces, popcorn, and peanuts are likely to cause choking in infants and toddlers. A valuable safety habit to reinforce for all children is to always sit while eating to lessen the danger of choking.

A c t i v i t y   7 . 2 2

Milk Carton Blocks

Level One to two

Area Physical

Interaction Child-child

Strand Fine Motor

Materials Needed Milk carton blocks (see Appendix D)

Directions for Implementation

- Milk carton blocks work best on a hard surface. Build towers of blocks with the toddlers.
- Allow toddlers to knock them over and begin again.
- If a toddler attempts to throw the blocks, you can redirect his behavior by saying, "Blocks are for building. Let's see how high we can stack them up."

Extensions

Add props to the block play for older children. Vehicles and animals can stimulate a different type of block play as children build structures and enclosures.

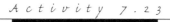

A c t i v i t y   7 . 2 3

One-Piece Puzzle

Level One to two

Area Physical

Interaction Adult-child

Strand Fine Motor

Materials Needed A homemade puzzle made from layers of corrugated cardboard, a photograph of the child or colorful picture from a greeting card, and the plastic lid from an aerosol can for a puzzle piece (see Appendix D)

Directions for Implementation

- Allow the young toddler to play with the simple puzzle by saying, "What's under the lid?"
- After he has removed the lid and discovered the picture, cover it up, and have him find it again.
- Encourage the young toddler to fit the missing piece into the puzzle form.

Extensions

Older toddlers may be challenged by a puzzle with various-sized holes for matching sizes of plastic caps. Pictures under the caps give caregivers added opportunities to talk to the toddlers as they play together.

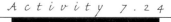

A c t i v i t y   7 . 2 4

Handprints with Water

Level One to two

Area Physical

Interaction Adult-child

Strand Fine Motor

Materials Needed Flat pan (e.g., an aluminum pie pan) filled with water, towels

Directions for Implementation

- Find a fairly smooth concrete surface outdoors, such as a sidewalk or a cement block wall. Place a shallow, flat pan on a towel, and fill it with a small amount of water.
- Put your hand in the water, and start to make handprints on the sidewalk or wall. Encourage the toddler to experiment making prints with his hand.
- Water paint together, finding different ways to make prints. For example, use just one finger, close the fingers on a flat hand, make a fist, or use the side of the hand.

Extensions

Two- and three-year-olds like to paint with water using a small pail and a wide paintbrush. This is an ideal activity for a day when the warm sun helps evaporate any water accidentally spilled on clothing.

A c t i v i t y 7 . 2 5
Using Tongs

Level Two

Area Physical

Interaction Child-object

Strand Fine Motor

Materials Needed Tongs, large cotton balls, or chenille pom-poms in a bowl, empty egg carton

Directions for Implementation

- Ask the child to pick up individual balls and drop them in each section of the egg carton.
- Demonstrate as needed.

Extensions

Several styles of tongs are available to build strength and refine hand muscle coordination. Older children can be taught to use chopsticks.

A c t i v i t y 7 . 2 6
Towers of Cube Blocks

Level Two

Area Physical

Interaction Child-object

Strand Fine Motor

Materials Needed 1-inch cube blocks

Directions for Implementation

- Encourage the toddler to stack the blocks to make a tower.
- If necessary, model putting the blocks evenly on top of one another to balance them.

Extensions

Create three-dimensional structures by filling in layer by layer. Challenge older children to build a cube house of cubes. Explain that each side of the cube house must be a square.

A c t i v i t y 7 . 2 7
Beehive Fingerplay

Level Two

Area Physical

Interaction Adult-child

Strand Fine Motor

Materials Needed None

Directions for Implementation

- Demonstrate the Beehive Fingerplay by using hand motions as you say the rhyme.

Here is the beehive.
  (Make a fist with one hand, and place it in the palm of the other hand.)
But where are the bees?
  (Pretend to look inside your fist.)
Hidden inside where nobody sees.
  (Shake your fist slightly to pretend that bees are inside the hive.)
They're coming out now; they're all alive.
  (Shake fist harder.)
One, two, three, four, five, bzzzzzzzzzzzz.
  (Open your fist, and count each bee by raising another finger. Pretend to make the bees fly away, and tickle the toddler.)

- Repeat often, encouraging the child to say the poem and act out the words.

Extensions

Collections of fingerplays and action rhymes can be found in most libraries and teacher supply stores. Older children become more skilled at combining oral language and movements.

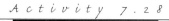
A c t i v i t y   7 . 2 8

Macaroni Necklaces

Level Three and four

Area Physical

Interaction Child-object

Strand Fine Motor

Materials Needed Large pieces of uncooked macaroni, string (about 24 inches long)

Directions for Implementation

- Tie one piece of macaroni near the end of the string. Wrap a piece of masking tape around the other end to stiffen it.
- Show the child how to thread macaroni onto the string.
- Tie ends together when finished to make the necklace.

Extensions

Macaroni can be precolored in a plastic bag with drops of food coloring and a small amount of rubbing alcohol. Shake the macaroni gently to distribute the color and spread on waxed paper to dry. Children may also use paint or felt pens to decorate the beads, either before or after they are strung.

A c t i v i t y   7 . 2 9

Using Scissors

Level Three and four

Area Physical

Interaction Child-object

Strand Fine Motor

Materials Needed Blunt-tipped scissors, strips of thin paper (1 inch by 8 1/2 inches)

Directions for Implementation

- Young children can learn to use scissors by cutting up strips of paper that are easy to hold.
- As their skills progress, children can practice cutting straight lines that are drawn on small sheets of paper.
- Muscles used in cutting with scissors can be strengthened by cutting ropes of play dough.

Extensions

Older children can practice cutting shapes (squares, circles, and triangles) drawn on construction paper for craft projects. Limiting the size of the paper and demonstrating turning the paper as you cut are helpful to many children. Several types of adaptive scissors are available for children with special needs.

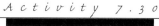
A c t i v i t y   7 . 3 0

Drawing in a Salt Tray

Level Three and four

Area Physical

Interaction Adult-child

Strand Fine Motor

Materials Needed Sturdy, shallow box approximately 9 to 12 inches in length and 6 to 8 inches in width, one-half cup salt or fine sand

Directions for Implementation

- If the inside color of the box is white, glue a piece of colored construction paper to the inside bottom to provide contrast with the salt or sand.
- Pour the salt into the box, and shake the box slightly from side to side to spread out a smooth layer of salt.

- Draw a circle in the salt with your finger, and ask the child to make one just like it. Erase the drawings by gently shaking the box back and forth.
- Repeat the exercise by drawing Xs, rectangles, and triangles.
- Ask the child to draw a shape, and then copy it.

Extensions

Process skills used in creative activities can be developed with craft-type fine motor activities. Toddlers may be interested in this activity as a sensory experience, using one or both hands to create designs. Older children may enjoy practicing writing their names or other words in the salt.

A c t i v i t y   7 . 3 1

Nuts and Bolts

Level Five and six

Area Physical

Interaction Child-object

Strand Fine Motor

Materials Needed A collection of various-sized bolts with corresponding nuts

Directions for Implementation

- Set out two different-sized bolts and their matching nuts.
- Observe children figure out how to put the items together. Offer assistance if requested to support their efforts. Try to guide them verbally without doing the task for them.
- If the children are interested in the activity, offer other nuts and bolts from the collection.

Extensions

This activity is inappropriate for children under the age of three because it contains small parts that could be swallowed. Four-

year-olds may be able to twist nuts on some of the larger bolts. Older children can bolt together pieces of wood that have holes drilled in them. Smaller-sized pliers and screwdrivers can also be offered to older children.

A c t i v i t y   7 . 3 2

Dressing Skills

Level Five and six

Area Physical

Interaction Child-object

Strand Fine Motor

Materials Needed An old pair of cutoffs or shorts that have been modified to provide practice in zipping, buttoning, lacing, and tying (See Appendix D for equipment directions)

Directions for Implementation

- Show the child the specially designed cutoffs.
- Encourage the child to undo all of the fasteners and then redo them.
- Offer assistance as needed. For example, many five-year-olds are still learning how to tie a bow. Show the child the technique step-by-step, by tying the bow on one pant leg of the shorts while the child ties the bow on the other.

Extensions

Older children can practice tying bows by wrapping presents. Other opportunities to practice dressing skills can be offered in the dramatic play area of the classroom.

A c t i v i t y   7 . 3 3

Torn-Paper Collage

Level Five and six

Area Physical

Interaction Child-object

Strand Fine Motor

Materials Needed Scraps of colored construction paper, a sheet of background paper, glue sticks, paste

Directions for Implementation

- Show the child various techniques for tearing different shapes. Holding the paper close to where it is being torn may lead to a more controlled tear.
- Allow the child to create a torn paper collage by gluing torn shapes to a background paper.

Extensions

Younger children can tear paper as a process. Demonstrate to older children how to create three-dimensional effects by combining tearing paper with rolling or folding. For example, rolling the ends of torn strips can create "curly hair."

A c t i v i t y   7 . 3 4

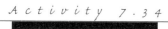

Ants on a Log

Level Seven and eight

Area Physical

Interaction Adult-child

Strand Fine Motor

Materials Needed Celery stalk, peanut butter, raisins, table knife or plastic knife

Directions for Implementation

- Have the child wash hands thoroughly and then wash the stalk of celery, removing any bad spots. Dry with a paper towel.
- Have the child cut the celery into 3- to 4-inch pieces.
- Have the child fill the celery stalk with peanut butter and add a few raisins (ants) to each stalk. Enjoy!

Extensions

Younger children can also do this activity, but the celery may need to be cut for them. Children can make toast and spread peanut butter on it. Older children can cut the toast into halves, fourths, and eighths.

A c t i v i t y   7 . 3 5

Origami Book

Level Seven and eight

Area Physical

Interaction Child-object

Strand Fine Motor

Materials Needed An 8 1/2 × 11 inch piece of paper (or larger), scissors (see Appendix C for directions)

Directions for Implementation

- Create a small four-page book to use for writing and illustrating a story.
- Use a larger scale model to demonstrate to a group of children.
- Emphasize the need to fold accurately and to crease the edges sharply.

Extensions

Origami is the Japanese art of paper folding. Consult community resources for guest artists or books on origami for other projects suitable for children of this age. Remind children that all crafts require practice.

A c t i v i t y   7 . 3 6

Stitchery

Level Seven and eight

Area Physical

Interaction Child-object

Strand Fine Motor

Materials Needed Rectangles of loosely woven fabric, such as burlap; scraps of various colors of yarn; large-eyed tapestry needles; pencils and paper

Directions for Implementation

- Have the child sketch a simple design first on paper, and emphasize that different stitches create different effects.
- Practice threading the needle, knotting the yarn, and making several types of stitches, such as the running stitch and the satin stitch, on a scrap of fabric.
- Use chalk to draw the design on the burlap if desired.
- Stitch the design, and hide loose ends of yarn on the back.

Extensions

Younger children may need some assistance in threading needles. Lacing boards can be used to practice stitching skills.

❧ CURRICULAR IMPLICATIONS

Connections to Subject Matter Areas

Within the framework of a traditional approach to curriculum planning, the age-appropriate activities promoting physical development are aligned most directly to the subject matter area of physical education and movement. Each activity promotes either gross motor or fine motor development. In gross motor development, the youngest infants learn to turn toward sounds (First Moves, Activity 7.1) and later to stretch for objects (Stretches to Reach Toy, Activity 7.2). As older infants and young toddlers become increasingly mobile, activities can be planned to take advantage of children's natural tendencies to move to music (Moving Arms to Music, Activity 7.7) and to untiringly repeat physical tasks (Jumping Off Stairs, Activity 7.8).

Preschool-aged and young school-aged children benefit from planned activities to develop gross motor skills. Parents and caregivers of three- and four-year-old children can create numerous opportunities for children for Playing Catch (Activity 7.13) with a variety of types and sizes of balls. Physical endurance and refined gross motor skills are developed when teachers and other adults include regular opportunities for locomotion as in Skipping (Activity 7.11), Parachutes (Activity 7.18), Jumping Rope (Activity 7.16) and Dribbling a Soccer Ball (Activity 7.17).

Although fine motor skills are not as likely as gross motor skills to be considered as a component of a subject matter–based physical education program, they are equally as important. In early childhood education settings, caregivers and teachers may label the activities that promote fine motor physical development as manipulatives. Teachers in the early elementary grades may view the development of fine motor skills merely as the outcome or benefit of planning arts and crafts activities and lessons for young children. Too often, teachers expect all children to have already mastered fine motor skills before elementary school, or perhaps, they even equate a general lack of fine motor skill to an inherited inability. With the increased emphasis on literacy and mathematics, elementary school teachers tend to limit planning to core subjects. Given the decreased emphasis in highly technological societies on craft or trade apprenticeships, young children no doubt have fewer opportunities to practice using tools and participating in crafts, which promote fine motor development.

Thus, early childhood educators can expand their promotion of physical development by consciously including activities and experiences for developing fine motor skills in the curriculum for all children from birth through age eight. Activities such as a Simple Fill and Spill (Activity 7.20) or one-piece puzzles (Activity 7.23.) facilitate an infant's grasping and eye-hand coordination skills. Tool use can be developed by Using Scissors (Activity 7.31), Nuts and Bolts (Activity 7.31), Ants on a Log (Activity 7.34), or Stitchery (Activity 7.36).

Physical development activities, which require that children follow verbal and nonverbal directions, can be linked to the language arts. In addition, most activities having either a child-child or adult-child interaction component involve conversation, another valuable opportunity for developing an oral language. More structured language arts experiences, such as learning fingerplays and action rhymes, Patty-Cake (Activity 7.3), and the Beehive Fingerplay (Activity 7.27), allow infants and two-year-olds to combine words and physical actions. Preschool-aged and school-aged children extend oral language skills by singing as they learn Skipping (Activity 7.11) and Jumping Rope (Activity 7.16); these activities combine three subject matter areas, physical education and movement, language arts, and music.

Connections to Thematic Planning

The physical developmental area also lends itself for use as a basis for thematic planning. One theme that connects several physical development activities is the topic of community building. In planning for a kindergarten class, a teacher may assist children in carrying out the theme that working together helps us learn better and builds our classroom community. Extensions of Activity 7.4 (Picking up Objects) are the foundation of learning to be responsible for the clean-up of the classroom. Several activities require cooperation in large or small groups to be successful. Playing follow the leader is suggested as part of skipping in Activity 7.11. A multicultural version of Hopscotch (Activity 7.15) involves partner or small group play, as does Jumping Rope (Ac-

tivity 7.16). The success of the Parachute activity (7.18) depends an entire group working well together. Even promoting Dressing Skills (Activity 7.32) is a valuable lesson in helping peers with coats, shoes, and painting shirts. The interactive focus of the developmental activities greatly enhances the theme of working as a community of learners.

✒ SUMMARY

Rapid changes in both gross and fine motor development occur in the first eight years of life. The neonate with limited mobility develops into the eight-year-old who can run, skip, and ride a bicycle. Within the same eight-year period, the child may develop from the young infant who bats at a toy to a child who can thread a needle. Although normative data suggest a general timetable for the development of particular fine motor and gross motor skills, there are vast individual differences. Some of the differences in physical development are related to temperament, genetic-based physical attributes, and health factors. Other differences may be related to the experiences that have been provided by parents, child-care providers, and teachers in the child's early years.

Adults play key roles in providing appropriate equipment, in planning suitable activities and environments, and in interacting directly with infants, toddlers, and young children as these children mature and develop increasingly refined physical skills. The general principles of development that guide growth patterns in cephalocaudal (head to toe) and proximodistal (midline to extremities) directions give parents, teachers, and caregivers a working knowledge to support these key roles. A knowledge of normative behaviors is useful in planning appropriate activities and in identifying children whose behaviors suggest that they may need further evaluation for determining developmental delays.

Children need interactions with adults, peers, and objects to reach their potential in the two strands of physical development. The activities in this chapter are each designed for a specific age level. However, many can be adapted for younger or older children. Teachers, caregivers, and parents should adapt activities and design new ones to meet the individual and/or group needs of particular children.

QUESTIONS AND PROJECTS FOR THE READER

1. Choose several activities suggested in the chapter, and use them with an appropriate-age child. Observe the child participating in the activities, and keep a log of your observations.
2. Create a homemade piece of equipment that promotes fine motor development. Identify the developmental age for which you think the equipment is most appropriate.
3. Observe three different children in a classroom setting. Describe their abilities to write, draw, and cut with scissors.

4. List five factors that may account for individual differences in development.

FOR FURTHER READING

Cratty, B. J. (1986). *Perceptual and motor development in infants and children.* Upper Saddle River, NJ: Prentice Hall. This book is an excellent resource for the development of both gross and fine motor skills in young children. It addresses the range of developmental levels found among children.

Gabbard, C. (1992). *Lifelong motor development.* Dubuque, IA: Wm. C. Brown. Two chapters in this textbook, chapter 8, "Early Movement Behavior," and chapter 9, "Motor Behavior During Early Childhood," describe motor development from birth to age six. Diagrams and charts illustrate sequences in the development of locomotor skills and fine motor control.

Weiser, M. (1991). *Infant/toddler care and education* (2nd ed.). Upper Saddle River, NJ: Merrill/ Prentice Hall. An overview of fine and gross motor development in the first three years of life is included in a chapter entitled, "Nurturing Motor Skill Development." The author describes numerous activities to promote the development of gross motor, fine motor, and self-help skills.

Chapter Eight

Cognitive Development

o b j e c t i v e s

After reviewing this chapter, you will be able to

- Identify five key strands of cognitive development.
- Discuss the role of adult-child interaction in developing the five key strands of cognitive development.
- Identify the different levels in Bloom's taxonomy.
- Select developmentally age-appropriate activities for promoting cognitive development for a particular child or a specified group of children.
- Develop open-ended questions for use with young children.
- Discuss problems that individual children might have in each strand of cognitive development.

INTRODUCTION

Cognitive development in early childhood is the basis for much of the learning that humans engage in throughout life. As infants interact with their environment, they develop concepts of objects, people, and conditions and begin to accumulate knowledge. They build a framework of information that can be used in solving problems and making decisions. Young children learn what things are and how they work. Their inherent curiosity can help them to remain with a task long enough to gain meaning from it. They need opportunities and the time to extend their thinking in new ways.

Adults can assist children by having interesting equipment and activities for them to choose from and explore. Children need large amounts of uninterrupted time and the freedom to experiment on their own. However, sometimes children need assistance from the adults to focus their attention or to extend their thinking. Adults can interact with young children and model the imaginative use of materials or equipment (Bredekamp & Copple, 1997). The observant adult offers suggestions, asks questions, and provides counterexamples so that a child or several children are able to proceed with a task or problem (Piaget, 1948/1973; Vygotsky, 1978).

The key strands of cognitive development selected for discussion are development of attention, problem solving, making choices, asking open-ended questions, and completion of tasks. Adults can support young children in each of these strands in the different contexts in which children play and learn each day. Sometimes children are able to function without assistance. At other times, some help is necessary so that they can experience success and develop to their potential.

The following sections provide a more detailed description of each strand of cognitive development. A matrix of all the sample activities introduces the activity section of the chapter. Activities that promote each strand are then suggested for the six age levels of birth through age eight. An appropriate age level is suggested for each activity. However, the activities can be adapted for children who are older or younger than the recommended age. Activities can also promote other areas for development. For example, asking a child an open-ended question (no single answer) can assist the child's thinking and speaking skills (communication development). Helping to develop rules for the classroom can be a problem-solving activity. It can also support the development of autonomy and social skills (personal-social development). Children with different cultural backgrounds and those with special learning needs are included in the discussion. The final section of the chapter discusses curricular implications of cognitive development. Strategies for connecting a subject matter and a thematic approach to cognitive development activities are offered.

KEY STRANDS OF DEVELOPMENT

Development of Attention

The ability to pay attention is important for all learning. A child must be able to attend to an experience long enough to be able to gain some understanding from it. At times, something catches a child's attention, such as a contrast in color, movement, or sound, but the attending behavior is not sustained for long. Although most humans have the potential for sustained attention from the time they are born, the ability is not innate. It is a skill that must be learned in interaction with objects and people in the environment (Aldridge, Eddowes, & Kuby, 1998; Yendovitskaya, 1972).

A range of attention behaviors are considered normal. Within the range, attention ability may vary widely among children or even one child among different tasks. Many children who are identified as having attention problems may be within the normal range (Landau & McAninch, 1993; Rosenberg, Wilson, & Legenhausen, 1989) (Figure 8.1).

When children have abnormally low level of attentive ability, attention is usually at a low level in all of the contexts in which the child is found: These children cannot attend long in any situation. They tend to move rapidly from one activity to the next. In contrast, a child with a high level of attentive ability can sometimes become so engrossed with a problem or activity that there is little awareness of anything else in the environment. This behavior can become a withdrawal from or avoidance of interaction with others, and it is then considered abnormal (Storr, 1988).

Both age and context should be examined if children have trouble sustaining attention to a task or in a situation. Sometimes children are asked to engage in an activity that is not appropriate for their age or developmental level (Bredekamp & Copple, 1997). An inappropriate environment is one in which too much is expected of children too soon. For example, the amount of time children should be able to sustain attention in large-group activities is about double their age in years as expressed in minutes (Guddemi, 1988). A two-year-old usually can attend for 4 minutes and a six-year-old for 12 minutes in a teacher-directed whole-group activity. However, children who are engaged in tasks of their own choosing will likely attend for a longer time.

When children are engaged in individual or small-group activities, they must have the skills to do the task and a long enough period of time to finish it. Sometimes adults decide on arbitrary rotating time periods such as 10 or 15 minutes each. At a given signal, children are expected to put away their equipment and materials and move to a new activity. Sometimes children are more insightful than the adults in a program. For example, a child (age four) was observed moving to a block area after a bell had been rung for a 10-minute rotation. He sat on the floor leaning against a shelf. When asked why he did not build something, he replied, "There is not enough time to get the blocks out and build something before I have to put them away again."

If children do not have time to really get involved with an activity before they are asked to stop, the interruption creates fragmentation. The practice limits the opportunity for sustained attention and the potential for thinking on a higher cognitive level. When a child is engaged in a task, adults should be careful not to disrupt the ongoing activity. They should intervene only when a child is having some kind of difficulty (Aldridge, Eddowes, & Kuby, 1998; Jacobvitz & Sroufe, 1987).

Temperament is always an important factor to consider. The kind of interaction that occurs between a child's temperament and the environment contributes to differences found in children (Rosenberg et al., 1989; Thomas & Chess, 1980). Three behavioral characteristics closely related to attentive ability in young children have emerged from temperament research: activity, distractibility, and persistence.

Children with a high level of activity may have trouble in attending, because they move so fast from one activity to the next that they never learn to focus their attention. **Distractibility** is the ease with which a child can

Figure 8.1   Attention behavior.

be diverted from an ongoing activity. Some children are easily distracted from what they are doing because they are trying to attend with more than one of their senses at a time. For example, a child is asked to look and listen to something simultaneously. Some children have more difficulty in attending under these circumstances. Adult intervention may be needed to help such children focus on using one of their senses at a time. Persistence is the ability to continue an activity even though distractions are present (Chess & Thomas, 1973). It is important to know each child and assist those who are easily distracted.

Parents, child-care personnel, and teachers can all assist young children in the development of their attention ability. Infants and young children need interaction with both objects and people to begin to develop sustained attention. To attend successfully, several things must take place. A person must (1) come to attention, (2) focus attention, (3) maintain attention, (4) extend attention, and (5) resist distracters (Eddowes & Aldridge, 1990). Adults can assist young children in all of these points by talking with them, pointing things out to them, and devising simple activities that help them sustain their attention. Activity 8.1 illustrates how this might work for a young infant.

As children become mobile, they like to practice the skills of crawling, standing, and walking. These can also help them in developing attention skills. Their interest in becoming good at a skill keeps them motivated to continue. Children of this age are learning the names of different objects. Pictures of things that children see in the environment help them move from the three-dimensional object (with height, width, and depth) to the two dimensions found in a picture (height and width). Adults can use activities that include motor skills along with sensory activities to maintain children's interest in an activity. Activity 8.2 is an experience that is interesting to newly mobile young children.

Two-year-olds like to learn new skills. For them to sustain their attention in a task, they must have the ability to do the task. This can be difficult without some assistance in developing a skill. The thought processes must work together with the physical skills for success to occur. Chapter 7 provides many examples of both fine and gross motor development. When children have learned how something works, they enjoy practicing until they become really good at it. They are learning the process of how to do the task. Children need large amounts of uninterrupted time to persist in activities and perfect their developing skills (Bredekamp & Copple, 1997). These kinds of activities can relate to any of the areas of development. Activity 8.3, a beginning stringing activity, is a physical skill that two-year-olds enjoy.

If children understand the skills necessary to do an activity and how objects can be used, the experience can assist them in their sustained attention because they will continue with the activity for a longer time. However, children's interest often subsides when the task is mastered, if there is no further way it can be extended.

As young children begin to develop fine motor skills, they are interested in using the skills in building with small plastic builders that snap together. Many different kinds of structures can be made from them, using both cognitive and creative skills. When children understand how the builders fit together and the possibilities for their use, the activity can assist them in their sustained attention. Some children need a little coaching to gain enjoyment from the experience. Adults may need to show children how to reposition a block for it to fit (Bredekamp & Rosegrant, 1992). Activity 8.4 is such an experience.

Children who have not had assistance in learning to focus their attention before entering kindergarten need extra assistance. Sometimes the interests of other children in the group will help with this. Simple card and

Young preschooler uses plastic builders to create an airplane.

board games can assist children to focus attention. When several children select a game to play, they usually all want to finish it. Activity 8.5 assists five- and six-year-olds in their attention development.

Primary-aged children can usually focus their attention for longer periods of time than younger children can. They need activities that extend their attention over time. Individual or group projects may assist them (Helm & Katz, 2001; Katz & Chard, 1989). Having children begin **collections** may be helpful. This activity assists them in focusing and maintaining their attention on one topic, extending their attention as they expand the collection,

and helping them to resist distractions. A collection can be useful for a year or two, or it can be developed throughout a lifetime. Collections begun in early childhood can be very educational. Activity 8.6 provides suggestions for developing a collection.

All children need assistance in developing their attention ability. This should begin early in the child's life. Each child has an attention style. Some are able to attend well in different contexts. Others may have difficulty with large group activities but are able to focus on activities of their own choosing. Yet others have difficulty in any context: These children tend to move from one activity to another, never really engaging in any.

Some children are more interested in objects. Those children are more likely to block out distracting information, and they can be persistent in completing tasks. Other children are more people-oriented. They seek interpersonal contacts and are likely to change their activities to coincide with what their friends are doing. These children may need more help in maintaining their attention in an activity.

Recently, an increasing number of children have been diagnosed with **attention deficit hyperactivity disorder (ADHD).** These children are consistently viewed as too active, based on both age and circumstances. They are outside the normal range of attention and activity behavior. ADHD is difficult to diagnose in young children because a typical three-year-old is likely to be very active (Aldridge, Eddowes, & Kuby, 1998; Rosenberg et al., 1989).

When ADHD is suspected, both the behavior and the context in which it is taking place must be examined. Sometimes the context makes children "activity hyper" (Eddowes & Aldridge, 1990). Children diagnosed with ADHD may be given a medication to control their activity level. The medication does not teach the children to attend. It only assists them in acquiring the skill. Adults must help these children learn to attend.

Problem Solving

The ability to be good at solving problems enables an individual to resolve practical difficulties as they arise. The effective problem solver also finds or creates problems that are the basis for new knowledge. Sometimes the solution to a problem requires a new product to be generated (Bruner, 1966). Problem-solving abilities may differ among cultures in regard to the types of problems that are considered worth solving (Gardner, 1983).

Steps must be followed to solve a problem. First, the problem must be identified. Then possible solutions can be formulated and tried out. Sometimes additional information is necessary to find a successful solution. After the problem is solved, conclusions are drawn and summarized. Then what has been learned can be applied in new situations.

Solving problems requires reflection and experimentation. It is necessary to think in new categories. The effective problem solver is usually very creative. Activities that encourage problem solving should be available for young children early and often. They should have the freedom to solve all kinds of problems with little intervention from adults. However, the parent or teacher can be an active participant in the process by suggesting problems and by observing the process that the children go through to arrive at a solution. Intervention should be sparing but supportive (DeVries & Kohlberg, 1987).

Problem-solving abilities can be useful in many ways. The obvious one is in the logical-mathematical area, in which children learn to solve arithmetic problems or do science experiments. However, there are many other kinds of dilemmas for which solutions may be necessary. Sometimes a problem evolves through play: an object that is not available may be needed. The children then must decide on a substitute item, or they may change the play sequence to fit an item that is available.

Solving problems in the creative arts can be very challenging and overlaps with the area of creative development. How much water is necessary for paint? What can be used as a background for a mural? How can certain musical tones be made from existing equipment? What ways can materials be fastened attractively? The varied answers to these kinds of questions expand the thinking of young children.

Problem-solving skills are also important in the resolution of conflicts. This strand overlaps with the area of personal-social development and particularly the development of autonomy and social interaction. As children become more autonomous and guide their own behavior, conflicts may arise with others. Problem-solving strategies can be helpful in resolving those kinds of difficulties.

Children develop their cognitive abilities through the experiences that they have as they grow. One milestone reached during the early years is termed object permanence. As infants become aware of the people and things in the environment, they begin to understand that they are separate from them. When something disappears, babies do not realize that it still exists out of sight. Little by little, they begin to develop this concept (Bodrova & Leong, 1996). They learn that people or objects still exist, even though they cannot be seen. Before children realize this, they can have difficulty separating from a parent because they think that the parent will not return. This relates to the strand of attachment/separation, as described in Chapter 6. Various activities can promote the ability to develop the understanding of object permanence. Activity 8.7 describes such an experience for an infant.

It takes time for children to develop object permanence. As children get older, other kinds of hiding games may be of interest. Activity 8.8 is a game that one- and two-year-olds enjoy.

Many activities promote problem-solving abilities. Young children need to have experiences in which they figure out how things go together or how they work (Bodrova & Leong, 1996). Simple puzzles can be helpful. Shape sorters in which the right-sized shape fits through a similar-shaped hole can also be of interest. Fitting hollow blocks together is another activity that promotes problem solving. Finding out how things work in the world provides a basis for future learning. A beginning science experiment is described in Activity 8.9.

As children get older, they continue to like to figure things out. Sometimes they want to take something apart to see how it works. Then the trick is to put it back together again. Adults should allow for children's curiosity but should also teach them about safety and responsibility.

One such activity that interests children is using a latch board. Different kinds of latches are mounted on a board for children to explore and learn to open and close. Adults should explain the reasons for using latches and why opening a latched or locked area can be dangerous. Activity 8.10 describes a problem-solving experience for three- and four-year-olds.

Another problem-solving activity is mapping, the basics of which can be learned early through simple experiences. Mapping requires spatial ability and is valuable in promoting thinking skills (Gardner, 1983). A map is a representation of an area. It could be a room, a building, or a geographical place. The representation can be drawn or printed, such as a road map. It can be a representation that is made of blocks (Hirsch, 1996) or a graphic map on a computer screen (Char & Forman, 1994). Activity 8.11 is a mapping activity that five- and six-year-old children can do.

One of the most difficult tasks confronting society is conflict resolution. Young children can begin to learn how to solve conflicts relatively early in life. The first rule in conflict resolution is the use of words instead of more violent actions to solve problems. Children must learn to try out different strategies in this kind of activity. Adults can assist children by having group discussions concerning what to do in different situations. The children can take turns role-playing to experience how the strategies might work. The experience in Activity 8.12 assists primary children in learning some useful methods.

Sometimes children have difficulty in solving problems. When this happens, the

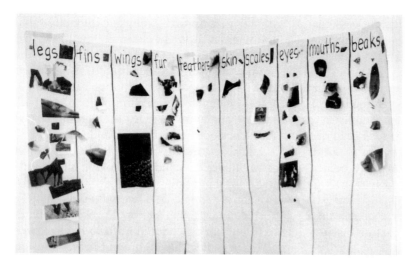

Children classify animal characteristics in a study of animal adaptations.

adult should determine the children's level of problem-solving ability. Problems of appropriate difficulty that match the child's developmental level should be suggested. Then, if the child continues to have difficulty, the adult or a more capable peer can supply a little guidance to enable the child to solve a problem and then attempt another individually. In this way, the child will develop the skills necessary to advance to a higher level (Vygotsky, 1978). The trick is to find an activity that matches the child's ability—not too easy or it will be boring and not too difficult, or the child will lose interest (Hunt, 1961).

Making Choices

Making choices and decisions can be regarded as a part of problem solving (Ford & Lerner, 1992). However, because the ability to make wise decisions is so important as children develop, we consider it as a separate strand. If young children are to become good decision makers as adults, they first need lots of practice in making simple choices. When adults continuously direct the behavior of children and structure their learning, children are unlikely to become autonomous decision makers (DeVries & Kohlberg, 1987; Kamii, 1982).

Adults can assist children by allowing them to make choices. Even in infancy, children can begin to choose if they are given the opportunity. In the home, young children can choose the toys with which they will play. They can select clothing to wear, food to eat, and how to spend their time. In classroom settings, they can select from available materials, equipment, and activities (Bredekamp & Copple, 1997).

When young children are able to make simple choices, they also learn that they must live with the consequences of a particular choice. For example, if a three-year-old child selects blue pants to wear, instead of red pants, when she is getting dressed in the morning, she can't change her mind after she gets to the child-care center. She must wear those blue pants for the rest of the day.

As children begin to make choices, the number from which to choose should be limited. Very young children should choose from only two alternatives. As they gain experience in choosing, more options can be added. The adult's role is to provide choices that match the child's level.

Adults should be cautioned to offer only acceptable choices. If an adult is unable to accept a child's choice, then no alternatives should be presented. Asking a child to choose and then invalidating the child's choice by not accepting it does more harm than good. As children develop the ability to make wise choices, they can begin to make decisions of a more abstract nature. They can do this as individuals as well as within a group. Children make decisions in different ways than adults do. Their decisions are more intuitive and less reasoned (Kohlberg & Lickona, 1987; Seefeldt & Barbour, 1998; Vygotsky, 1978).

In group programs, children can contribute to decisions concerning their classroom community. One way they can do this is by voting and living with the decision of the majority (Kamii, 1982). Of course, they must learn how voting works and that they can vote only once for one of the choices. When given many opportunities to vote, children begin to understand how the process works. Children can vote on many different kinds of things. They might decide on the name of a new classroom pet, what to plan for the snack tomorrow, or how well they liked a book read to them or an activity in the classroom. In this process, the teacher must also abide with the decision of the majority. This transfers some of the teacher's power to the children and promotes the development of their autonomy, as described in Chapter 6.

In addition to voting, children can make other kinds of group decisions related to life in their classroom. Although this process takes time, patience, and persistence on the part of the teacher, children can gain a sense of responsibility for their own actions in the group. This can be related to the children deciding on the rules and the consequences that govern behavior in the classroom. Children who take part in making the rules are more likely to respect them. It gives them a sense of membership in a community. This also contributes to the development of social-moral reasoning and the behavior of individual children (DeVries & Kohlberg, 1987).

Very young children can begin to make a choice between two objects even before they are able to talk. The choice must be limited, and there should be an assurance that the child is attending to the activity. Activity 8.13 describes this kind of simple choice by an infant.

As children have experiences with pictures and books, they can point to pictures. A book that might be interesting for toddlers is *The Baby's Catalog* by Janet and Allan Ahlberg (1983). Toddlers can choose the picture they like best from a book or an assortment of pictures. The pictures can be on a similar topic such as flowers or vehicles, or they can be varied as to subject. A variety might include pictures of different family members, toys, or furniture. Activity 8.14 demonstrates this type of activity for a toddler.

As children have experiences in making choices, they can begin to choose the clothes they will wear. At first it is wise to limit the choices and to discuss what articles of clothing go together and the appropriate dress for different occasions. In that way, the child will be able to make a more informed choice of clothes. Another way that children can make choices is related to the food they eat. A parent can give a child a choice among foods, before the meal is prepared. There can also be a choice of both food and the quantity of the food when eating. Family-style serving allows young children to serve themselves the quantity of food

they choose to eat. Then they should be able to eat that amount. Young children can also help in a family decision about where they might eat out at a restaurant. When their wishes are considered, children believe their ideas are valued. Activity 8.15 is an experience that allows a child to make suggestions about the food to be prepared for lunch.

When children attend group child-care and school programs, they should be able to choose the toys, equipment, and materials that they are using. One way in which adults can organize the environment is by the use of interest or learning centers (Chapter 3). When materials are available in specific centers, children can choose the center to use and also materials and equipment available in the center. When children choose the activity they will engage in, they are likely to attend to it for a longer time than if it is assigned by someone else. Children need time to really get involved in an activity (chapter 4). Activity 8.16 demonstrates this.

One of the most difficult tasks that confronts adults working with young children is that of teaching them how to handle situations of personal safety with strangers. Young children are usually friendly. Many choose to willingly talk with strangers in different contexts. Usually, this is acceptable. However, there are times when it would be better if they were not so friendly. Sometimes talking with strangers can be dangerous. Children must be alerted to this kind of danger without scaring them. They must learn how to distinguish strangers from persons they know, so that they can choose wisely with whom they will interact. Usually, if a trusted person, such as a parent, caregiver, or teacher, says a situation or person is all right, it is. However, if children are in an unfamiliar context and do not know the person, they should never talk with the person or accept a ride, treat, or present.

Sometimes local police departments have a staff member who visits group programs to

Teacher helps children solve problems in block-building center.

talk with the children. Films are also available. Discussions in class with a role-playing activity can likewise be of assistance. Activity 8.17 is a useful experience for five- and six-year-olds.

When children have had experience making choices in different situations, they are better able to begin making decisions about somewhat more abstract ideas. Children of school age can participate in group decision making. This may be related to making rules, resolving conflicts, deciding on a class project, planning a field trip, or some other class activity. When children are involved in group decision making, they begin to understand ideas from another person's point of view. They develop an understanding that they must sometimes compromise for the good of the group. This enhances both their social and moral development. Activity 8.18 is an experience in selecting a class project in which all children participate.

When they begin early in life, most children are able to learn to make wise choices.

Sometimes children have not had the opportunity to make any choices. When this is true, no matter what the age, the number of items from which to choose should be narrowed. Even inexperienced six- to eight-year-old children should begin by picking between two choices. After they have some practice in both choosing and living with the consequences of the choice, they can be given a broader selection from which to choose. As children grow older, they must make more complicated decisions. The more practice they have, the better able they are to make informed decisions.

Asking Open-Ended Questions

Questioning skills are directly related to cognitive development. Adults must understand the types of questions that they are asking young children. Many questions have one answer. When children are asked those kinds of questions, they tend to focus on details and do not do any analytical thinking (Donoghue,

1990). They realize that there is just one answer, and they may not know what it is. When they are continually unable to answer literal questions, children can have feelings of failure and begin to have the idea that adults know all answers to all questions.

This gives adults power that is really not theirs. No one knows the answers to all questions. Children do need to know some facts. However, with so much knowledge available, it is far better for adults to use the approach that much information is known and some is not. Children need to learn ways to seek information that is available. They also should learn that there are questions with no answer. These kinds of activities promote thinking and creative approaches to problem solving.

The ability to both answer and ask open-ended questions helps to extend thinking. Bloom's taxonomy of the cognitive domain (Bloom et al., 1956) can be helpful to adults working with young children. It includes six different levels of cognitive complexity that can be used in helping children to develop their thinking skills and questioning ability. Bloom's method is particularly useful in assisting adults to ask a variety of questions in their interactions with young children.

Knowledge questions require specific answers. These kinds of questions often are asked of children. Such a question might be, "What is the color of that block?" There is only one answer to the question. The answer to a **comprehension** question shows an understanding of meaning. The answer to this question would show a child's understanding of rabbits: "Can you describe the rabbits that Jane brought to class yesterday?" When a person understands the **application** of a concept, it means that the information can be used in new situations. After learning about zoo animals, a question might be, "What could happen if a tiger escaped from the zoo?" Information concerning tigers would be used in the answer.

Answers to **analysis** questions show the ability to see parts and relationships. Such a question might be: "What rooms would you like to have in your house, and where would they be located?" In **synthesis,** parts of some kinds of information are used to create an original whole. After studying fish and learning about their parts and habits, a question might be, "Can you design a new type of fish?" At the **evaluation** level, judgments are made based on criteria. Questions might be, "What is your favorite book? Why?" Figure 8.2 supplies the type of question appropriate for each level on one topic.

Asking children different types of questions increases their ability to think through problems. It assists them in asking their own open-ended questions. They realize that they can find out information by themselves, independent of parents and teachers. Asking children different types of questions also encourages group cooperation in searching for information that provides answers to questions. It promotes not only cognitive development but also communication and creative development.

Before children can talk, adults can ask them questions. During the routines of feeding and diapering, parents or caregivers can pose questions such as, "How are you feeling today?" "What will you wear?" "Which toy do you want to play with?" Even though the children can't respond, they hear the question and can begin to understand what the words mean. Adults tend to ask young infants questions that require one-word answers. However, a variety of questions should be asked. Activity 8.19 illustrates this type of questioning.

Although infants cannot respond in words, sometimes their understanding permits them to act on a question. For example, a child (14 months old) is looking at a book with a caregiver in the living room of the child's home. When they finish, the adult asks, "Do you have another book that you like?" The

Transportation Project

1. Knowledge (recalling information)

   What kinds of transportation are there?

2. Comprehension (understanding meaning)

   Describe a kind of boat.

3. Application (using learning in new situations)

   If you had a car and came to a river with no bridge, what could you do?

4. Analysis (seeing parts and their relationships)

   What would happen if the parts of an airplane were not put together correctly?

5. Synthesis (using information to create a new original)

   How would you design a mural that includes all kinds of transportation?

6. Evaluation (making judgments based on certain criteria)

   What is the best kind of transportation to use in different situations?

Airplanes, Boats, Trains, and *Trucks,* four books by Byron Barton (1986), may be helpful on this topic.

Figure 8.2 Example of questioning strategies using Bloom's taxomony.

child runs to her nearby bedroom and returns with another book. She has understood the question and is responding with an action instead of words. Only when given this kind of opportunity will children be able to respond. Activity 8.20 is an example.

As children become verbal and hear questions, they begin to ask them. It may start with a one-word question such as, "How?," meaning, "How does it work?," or "What?," meaning, "What is it?" As they have experience and their verbal skills improve, they expand the number of words in their questions. At this time, it is good to discuss the answers with them. In the discussion, the adult may want to ask another question to encourage the child to think of a possible answer. Activity 8.21 describes this kind of an experience for a verbal child.

Children need ways of applying information that they have acquired. For example, if they know the rainbow colors, they should be able to apply the information. They should be able to point to various items that are red. As they have experience with different concepts, they need to extend that information. Adults can use open-ended questioning strategies to assist children. The application of knowledge is practiced in Activity 8.22.

As children get older, they continue to have great curiosity concerning how things work or the different uses for things. Adults can stimulate their thinking by employing open-ended questioning strategies. Many times there is more than one use for an object, even when the object was designed to be used in a specific way. For example, a yardstick is designed to measure things. However, it could also be used to point to something or to knock down a hat that blew into a tree. A pan lid is designed to be used on a pan. However, two pan lids can become a pair of cymbals for a rhythm band. Children can be creative in thinking of new ways to use things. Activity 8.23 illustrates this.

Child explores wood shavings in the outdoor play area.

Completion of Tasks

There is satisfaction in the completion of tasks. It is also important to complete the mental functioning necessary for doing the task to enhance cognitive abilities. Adults can help children in this activity by providing support, assisting them in focusing their attention, and providing verbal encouragement (Bredekamp & Copple, 1997). Children must develop an intrinsic need to complete things they begin (Montessori, 1912/1964). However, the task must match both the ability and interest of the children (Hunt, 1961).

Infants and toddlers have no understanding or need to complete what they begin. They are engaged in activities as a process to learn about their world. They use an object for a long enough time to gain some small bit of information from it. This is their way of completing an activity, and they move on to something else. However, when children reach Erikson's (1963) third stage, i.e., initiative versus guilt (four- and five-year-olds), they shift to a more relaxed and purposeful participation in activities (see chapter 1). They engage in some planning and begin a task with a purpose in mind. At that time, children are more likely to finish activities by themselves.

Even though infants and toddlers usually are not interested in completing activities, adults can sometimes help provide closure. Adults can take the responsibility for helping children finish a task and can support children in its completion. For example, an adult can assist a child in focusing attention on the task of putting all of the objects into a container. When looking at a book, the adult can make sure that both the contents and length of the book will hold the child's interest. Very young children are developing their gross motor skills. Many times, they stay with this type of activity to practice the skill.

When children reach the preschool and kindergarten years, they should be able to

As children have experience working with open-ended questions, they should be able to consciously think of those kinds of questions on their own. Parents and teachers can encourage them to ask open-ended questions. Activity 8.24 is an example of this kind of activity.

When children have had little or no experience in either being asked or being encouraged to ask open-ended questions, they will have difficulty unless given some coaching and support. As in other areas of learning, these children must begin at the beginning. First, they must be exposed to the concept of open-ended questions. Then they must learn to both answer and ask them. This takes the time and patience of those working with children.

complete tasks that match both their age and individual developmental level. Children who are unable to do this may have limited sustained attention. They may also see little intrinsic value in completing a task. At times, it may not be important to finish something that has been started, depending on the reason for the activity.

When adults interact with very young children, they must use a flexible approach to assisting children in completing tasks. It is practice for the future, not a concept that these children will be able to learn at the time. Activities 8.25 through 8.27 assist infants and toddlers in completing tasks with adult support.

One of the tasks that both parents and teachers of young children consider important is the ability to put away toys after play is finished. If children are to do this, they must understand the reasons and be supported as they learn. Toys must be put away for safety reasons and to make room for other activities. It will be helpful to the child if toys and spaces are organized so that there is a place for everything (chapter 3).

As children learn to put their things away, adults can be supportive by helping them at first. It is a lot easier to complete such a task with help. As children learn, they also begin to understand that they should not take everything out at once, only things that they are playing with at the time. This makes it easier to put things away later. In classrooms, children can work together to put things away (see Activity 8.28).

Cooking activities provide many different cognitive experiences for young children. Food selection, menu planning, use of recipes, and measuring are skills they can learn. They also learn how food is processed and how it changes when it is prepared. For example, many young children have no idea where peanut butter comes from, other than from a jar. A good food preparation experience would be having them shell peanuts and then use a blender to grind the peanuts into peanut but-

ter. (Add a little oil and salt as you blend them.)

Two-year-old children can begin simple food preparation experiences. They can wash vegetables, mix dips, spread cheese, and make instant pudding. As children get older, they can assist (with supervision) with simple cooking activities, such as using an electric skillet or a toaster oven. A food preparation or cooking activity encourages completion of tasks, because the food cannot be eaten until it is prepared. This keeps most children on task (see Activity 8.29).

As children get older, they can take more and more responsibility for their own learning and the completion of their work in school. One way of doing this is by using contracts (see chapter 4). Contracts can be helpful in assisting children to plan what they will do and when they will do it. A weekly contract for seven- and eight-year-olds has some activities that are required, such as reading, math, writing, and perhaps time to work on a project. Children can choose other activities as they wish, such as crafts, woodworking, or **dramatics.** However, all activities on the contract must be completed by the end of a specified time. When children use contracts, they become very good at planning their time and completing tasks. Contracts can be used at home and at school (Activity 8.30).

Children who have had little responsibility in the past could have problems using contracts. The adults must work with them on an individual basis until they learn to do it. These children should be given classroom duties or tasks to do so that they can gain practice in responsible behavior. They can learn to take responsibility for something that belongs to the class as a whole or as a community. Examples include feeding a pet, helping with a snack, straightening up the library center, or completing some other activity.

Table 8.1 is a matrix correlating all the activities described in Chapter 8 with the appropriate ages and developmental strands.

Table 8.1 Cognitive development activities matrix.

Age (Years)	Development of Attention	Problem Solving	Making Choices	Asking Open-Ended Questions	Completion of Tasks
Birth to one	Follows Objects with Eyes Activity 8.1 Child-object	Looks for Dropped Toy Activity 8.7 Adult-child	Choosing Toys Activity 8.13 Child-object	Adult Asks Questions Activity 8.19 Adult-child	Crawls Up a Ramp Activity 8.25 Child-object
One to two	Big Box Crawl Through Activity 8.2 Child-object	Hide the Shell Activity 8.8 Adult-child	Points to Pictures Activity 8.14 Adult-child	Ask Child to Respond Activity 8.20 Adult-child	Climbs Down Stairs Activity 8.26 Child-object
Two	Stringing Beads Activity 8.3 Child-object	Sink and Float Activity 8.9 Child-object	Mealtime Choices Activity 8.15 Adult-child	Encourage Questioning Activity 8.21 Adult-child	Build a Tower Activity 8.27 Child-object
Three and four	Plastic Builders Activity 8.4 Child-child	Latch Board Activity 8.10 Child-object	Pick an Activity Center Activity 8.16 Child-object	Things that are Round Activity 8.22 Child-child	Put Toys Away Activity 8.28 Child-child
Five and six	Concentration Activity 8.5 Child-child	Mapping the Classroom Activity 8.11 Child-child	Stranger Danger Activity 8.17 Child-child	How Can We Use This? Activity 8.23 Child-child	Cooking Vegetable Soup Activity 8.29 Adult-child
Seven and eight	Collections Activity 8.6 Adult-child	Conflict Resolution Activity 8.12 Child-child	Choosing a Project Activity 8.18 Child-child	Thinking of Open-Ended Questions Activity 8.24 Child-child	Completing a Weekly Contract Activity 8.30 Adult-child

🙠 AGE-APPROPRIATE ACTIVITIES: BIRTH THROUGH EIGHT YEARS

A c t i v i t y   8 . 1

Follows Objects with Eyes

Level Birth to one

Area Cognitive

Interaction Adult-child

Strand Development of Attention

Materials Needed Mitt puppet (see Appendix D)

Directions for Implementation

- Place the baby on her back on a flat surface.
- Use the puppet to get the baby's attention.
- When you are sure the baby is looking at the puppet, move it slowly from left to right.
- Repeat, being sure the baby's eyes are following the puppet from one side to the other.
- Talk to the baby as you play.

Extensions

Older children enjoy tracking a moving object with their eyes. It might be a bird, a person, a car, or an airplane.

A c t i v i t y   8 . 2

Big Box Crawl Through

Level One to two

Area Cognitive

Interaction Child-object

Strand Development of Attention

Materials Needed Large cardboard box (see Appendix D)

Directions for Implementation

- Put the box on the floor near the child.
- Say, "Look at this box. Can you crawl inside?"

- When the child crawls into the box, ask, "What do you see?"
- The child will look at the pictures in the box. The child can also look out of holes cut in the sides of the box or can stand up and look out a hole cut in the top.
- Stand back, and let the child play, crawling in and out of the box.

Extensions

Change the pictures in the box from time to time. Older children enjoy a box that they can pretend is something else. For example, a box can become a vehicle or a house. Older children can help put pictures on the sides of the box.

A c t i v i t y   8 . 3

Stringing Beads

Level Two

Area Cognitive

Interaction Child-object

Strand Development of Attention

Materials Needed Large wooden beads (1-inch) and laces

Directions for Implementation

- Put a container of beads on the floor.
- Show the child how to put a bead on the lace. String a couple of beads.
- Ask the child to try it.
- Observe the child stringing the beads, and assist if necessary until the child can do it alone.
- When a lace is full, show the child how to take the beads off and begin again.

Extensions

Older children enjoy stringing smaller beads. They can make patterns with different colors or shapes of beads. Older children can also string macaroni (see Activity 7.28) and similar materials (see Chapter 7).

A c t i v i t y 8 . 4

Plastic Builders

Level Three and four

Area Cognitive

Interaction Child-object

Strand Development of Attention

Materials Needed Small plastic builders that snap together

Directions for Implementation

- Show the child how the builders fit together.
- Be sure the child knows how to use them.
- Talk with the child about what can be made with the builders.
- When the child begins building, leave her or him to do it alone.
- If the child loses attention, talk about what is being built. Talk about what might be built. Suggest props, such as small vehicles, that the child might use along with the builders.

Extensions

Younger children may be able to use larger-sized builders. Older children enjoy using small toy houses, trees, and people in play with the builders.

A c t i v i t y 8 . 5

Concentration

Level Five and six

Area Cognitive

Interaction Child-Child

Strand Development of Attention

Materials Needed Selected pairs of matching playing cards from two decks (two or more children)

Directions for Implementation

- The adult selects from the two decks a number of pairs of playing cards that are exactly alike. They are arranged face down on a table or on the floor. The number of pairs depends on the age and experience of the players.
- The players take turns turning up two cards, one at a time, trying to make pairs.
- A player who selects two cards that match can keep the pair.
- The object of the game is to concentrate on where the cards are, so that matches can be made.
- The adult observes as the children play.
- Children can play the game without supervision when they learn the rules.

Extensions

With young children, the game works best when picture cards are used. These can be made by gluing pairs of pictures to individual pieces of cardboard. For older children, the number of pairs of cards can be increased as players become proficient at the game. Kamii and DeVries (1980) describe many other games for preschool- and primary-aged children. The book includes information concerning the value of games, and winning and losing.

A c t i v i t y 8 . 6

Collections

Level Seven and eight

Area Cognitive

Interaction Adult-Child

Strand Development of Attention

Materials Needed An example of a collection (e.g., shells, bottle caps, stamps)

Directions for Implementation

- Discuss collections with the child. Give the definition of a *collection:* an accumulation of similar objects.
- Show an example of a collection.
- Discuss collections in which the child may be interested. Encourage children to create individual or group collections.
- Children can keep collections in the child-care center or school classroom in boxes on a shelf designated for the purpose.
- From time to time, discuss how the child's collection is progressing.

Extensions

Younger children may enjoy beginning with a group or class collection to learn how it is done. Some children may be interested in having several collections at one time. Others focus on one collection and accumulate as many objects as possible in that collection.

Activity 8.7

Looks for Dropped Toy

Level Birth to one

Area Cognitive

Interaction Adult-child

Strand Problem Solving

Materials Needed Small toy

Directions for Implementation

- Hold the child on your lap.
- Show the toy to the child.
- Drop the toy on the floor.
- Say, "Where did it go?"
- Look down for the toy with the child.
- Pick up the toy and drop it again.

Extensions

Ask the child to drop the toy, and then look for it together. Older children enjoy looking for hidden objects.

Activity 8.8

Hide the Shell

Level One to two

Area Cognitive

Interaction Adult-child

Strand Problem Solving

Materials Needed Two plastic butter tubs and a medium-sized sturdy shell

Directions for Implementation

- Sit on the floor with the child.
- Put the shell under one of the butter tubs.
- Say, "Where did the shell go?"
- The child looks for and finds the shell.
- After the child understands how to play the game, use two butter tubs and hide the shell under one of them.
- The child looks for the shell.

Extensions

Older children can play the game with more butter tubs. They can take turns hiding and finding the shell (or a block). Older children may also enjoy playing the game of "hide and seek."

Activity 8.9

Sink and Float

Level Two

Area Cognitive

Interaction Child-object

Strand Problem Solving

Materials Needed Several waterproof items that float and several that sink in water, a plastic tub

Directions for Implementation
- Put some water in the tub.
- Sit at a table with the child.
- Demonstrate that one of the items floats and another one sinks.
- Tell the child to put one of the items in the water to see what happens.
- Allow the child to experiment to see which floats and which sinks.

Extensions

A somewhat older child is able to predict which items will sink or float before trying them in the water. Older children also enjoy a different experiment, in which they work with a magnet to see which items are attracted to it and which ones are not.

A c t i v i t y   8 . 1 0

Latch Board

Level Three and four

Area Cognitive

Interaction Child-object

Strand Problem Solving

Materials Needed Latch board (see Appendix D)

Directions for Implementation

- Put the latch board on the table in front of the child.
- Show the child how one of the latches works.
- Let the child experiment with the different latches to figure out how they work.
- Explain that the child must have permission to open latches that are in other places.

Extensions

Older children can use a board on which small doors can be locked and unlocked with keys.

They must figure out which key goes with which lock.

A c t i v i t y   8 . 1 1

Mapping the Classroom

Level Five and six

Area Cognitive

Interaction Child-Child

Strand Problem Solving

Materials Needed Unit blocks

Directions for Implementation

- Explain to the class that they will be making a map of the classroom using unit blocks.
- Discuss how they might do that. (One way is to measure the classroom, figure out the scale necessary in using the blocks, and then build the model. However, the class may have different suggestions on how to proceed.)
- The children divide the tasks and then collect the information.
- They build the model of the open floor plan (e.g., doors, walls, tables, chairs).
- Assist the children in solving problems, if necessary, by questioning and making comments to extend their thinking.

Extensions

Older children may be able to draw a two-dimensional linear map on paper of their classroom or the whole school.

A c t i v i t y   8 . 1 2

Conflict Resolution

Level Seven and eight

Area Cognitive

Interaction Child-Child

Strand Problem Solving

Materials Needed None

Directions for Implementation

- Discuss the problem of conflict with the whole class.
- List some personal conflicts that might need to be resolved (e.g., two people not agreeing, someone cutting in on a line, or two people wanting to use the same thing at the same time).
- Discuss word sequences that might work in resolving the problems. For example, instead of arguing, a person might say, "I know you don't agree with me, but I will listen to your ideas, and I hope that you will listen to mine."
- Divide the class into small groups, and give each group one of the problems to solve.
- Move around the classroom, meeting with each group as they think of a solution or solutions.
- Come back into the large group, and share the solutions.

Extensions

After the groups share the solutions, they may want to act out the conflict with their solutions. As children learn the rules of behavior in specific settings, they will have some conflicts. Younger children can begin to use words to solve their conflicts with others. They may use puppets in role-playing a solution to a conflict. Adults can assist children in learning to solve their own problems involving conflict.

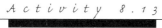

Choosing Toys

Level Birth to one

Area Cognitive

Interaction Child-object

Strand Making Choices

Materials Needed Two different small toys

Directions for Implementation

- Lay the baby on the floor.
- Hold the toys within the baby's reach.
- Say, "Which one do you want?"
- As the baby reaches for one of the toys, move the other one out of sight.
- Play the game again until the baby begins to lose interest.

Extensions

Older children are able to choose between toys for play.

Points to Pictures

Level One to two

Area Cognitive

Interaction Adult-child

Strand Making Choices

Materials Needed A stack of pictures cut from magazines and mounted on construction paper or poster board

Directions for Implementation

- Sit on the floor or at a table with the child.
- Lay a few of the pictures out for the child to see.
- Say, "Look at the pictures."
- Point to and name each picture.
- Say, "You point to the one that you like best."
- When the child does it, change the pictures and begin again.

Extensions

Children who are talking may be able to tell why they have chosen a picture from the group. They may also be able to tell why they did not choose one of the other pictures.

Activity 8.15

Mealtime Choices

Level Two

Area Cognitive

Interaction Adult-child

Strand Making Choices

Materials Needed None

Directions for Implementation

- Discuss with the child two possibilities for fruit that will be eaten at lunch. (Choices might be applesauce and bananas.)
- Ask, "Which of those fruits would you like to eat today?"
- Let the child help in preparing the fruit chosen.

Extensions

Older children are able to choose more items in a meal. They are also able to plan for meals that take place at a later time. They can make choices that follow the nutrition food pyramid.

Activity 8.16

Pick an Activity Center

Level Three and four

Area Cognitive

Interaction Child-object

Strand Making Choices

Materials Needed Several learning centers in a classroom

Directions for Implementation

- Explain to the group that it is center time.
- Tell the group about any special activities available in any of the centers.

- Remind the children to watch to see the number of children who may use a center at one time. (This can be noted in the center by using stick figures, clothespins in a can, or some similar means.)
- Tell the children they can move quietly to the centers.
- Observe to make sure that all children have made a choice both of a center and of an activity within a center.
- Move around the classroom observing and interacting as appropriate.

Extensions

Older children may have certain assigned activities within different centers that they must complete during a block of time. It is usually their responsibility to be sure that those are completed and choose other free-choice activities.

Activity 8.17

Stranger Danger

Level Five and six

Area Cognitive

Interaction Child-child

Strand Making Choices

Materials Needed None

Directions for Implementation

- Lead a discussion concerning possible situations that could arise regarding personal safety.
- Divide the children into groups, and role-play different situations. (For example, two children are playing in front of one child's house. Someone stops in a car to ask them a question. What should the children choose to do?)
- After the various role-plays, answer any other questions the children may ask.

Extensions

Repeat the activity at intervals. Be open to any stranger problems the children may have. Plan another discussion concerning this topic.

A c t i v i t y   8 . 1 8

Choosing a Project

Level Seven and eight

Area Cognitive

Interaction Child-child

Strand Making Choices

Materials Needed A chalkboard or chart paper

Directions for Implementation

- Discuss potential projects with the group. (Some suggestions: conservation, homes, plants, wheels)
- List several of the most popular ideas on the chalkboard.
- Discuss resources that might be available for each.
- Delete projects for which few resources are available.
- Reach a consensus concerning the project that is chosen.

Extensions

Younger children may participate in choosing a unit or theme that they want to learn about. Toddlers and three-year-olds may be able to suggest a topic of interest to them, such as balls or pets.

A c t i v i t y   8 . 1 9

Adult Asks Questions

Level Birth to one

Area Cognitive

Interaction Adult-child

Strand Asking Open-Ended Questions

Materials Needed None

Directions for Implementation

- Child has just awakened from a nap.
- As you change a diaper, ask, "How are you feeling this afternoon? Are you feeling sleepy, or hungry, or happy?"
- Even though the child cannot really respond, continue with, "What should we do now? Should we have a snack, or go for a walk?"
- Continue to talk with the child and ask questions whenever there is an opportunity.

Extensions

Verbal children will begin to be able to answer the questions. Ask them what they think about different things.

A c t i v i t y   8 . 2 0

Ask Child to Respond

Level One to two

Area Cognitive

Interaction Adult-child

Strand Asking Open-Ended Questions

Materials Needed None

Directions for Implementation

- Sit with child as she is playing.
- Ask, "Can you find your favorite toy?"
- Observe the child to determine if the question was understood.
- If the child has trouble finding a toy, give assistance.

Extensions

Verbal children are able to answer questions that are asked. They can be encouraged to engage in a discussion in which questions are asked and answered by both the adult and the child.

Encourage Questioning

Level Two

Area Cognitive

Interaction Adult-child

Strand Asking Open-Ended Questions

Materials Needed None

Directions for Implementation

- When a child asks a question, encourage thinking of an answer.
- Repeat the question, expanding on the words if necessary. (For example, if the child asks, "What?" and points to a bird, say, "What is that?")
- Then say, "Watch it. What do you think it might be?" Depending on the child's experience, a counterquestion might be asked, such as: "Is it a dog?"
- Before telling the child it is a bird, have the child observe it and see what it can do.
- Use the opportunity to expand the child's thinking skills and knowledge.

Extensions

Older children are able to go to additional resources, such as books or a computer database, to learn more about something for which they have a question. Whenever possible, children should be encouraged to do their own thinking and not just look for easy answers.

Things That are Round

Level Three and four

Area Cognitive

Interaction Child-object

Strand Asking Open-Ended Questions

Materials Needed A classroom and several rounded shapes, such as a circle, oval, sphere

Directions for Implementation

- Have the children discuss roundness and things that are round (spherical, globular, ball-shaped, circular, having a curved edge, not flat or angular).
- Show them examples of roundness.
- Have the children look for things in the room that are round.
- Discuss the differences in round things.

Extensions

Younger children might enjoy playing with different kinds of round objects that are located in the same place (e.g., a box of round objects). Older children can make comparisons between different-shaped objects.

How Can We Use This?

Level Five and six

Area Cognitive

Interaction Child-child

Strand Asking Open-Ended Questions

Materials Needed Several objects that could have different uses (e.g., stick, block, scarf, glass jar)

Directions for Implementation

- Discuss how an object sometimes can be used for a purpose differing from its intended purpose.
- Ask, "Can you think of something that can be used in a different way?"
- Talk about any objects the children mention.
- Show them the objects that are available to look at and think about.

- Divide the class into groups of three or four children, and give each group one object.
- Ask each group to think of different ways the object could be used. Later they can share their ideas in the large group.

Extensions

All children enjoy making things out of found objects, or "beautiful junk." They can realize that the original purpose of the object is not the one for which they are using it. Older children might enjoy writing down an alternative use for a particular object and then asking the other children in the class to guess which object they mean.

Activity   8.24

Thinking of Open-Ended Questions

Level Seven and eight

Area Cognitive

Interaction Child-Child

Strand Asking Open-Ended Questions

Materials Needed None

Directions for Implementation

- Discuss the value of open-ended questions.
- Have the group as a whole think of a question and then answer it.
- Divide the class into small groups, and have group members think of several open-ended questions to ask the rest of the class. The questions should be written down.
- Have the class discuss answers to at least one question from each group.

Extensions

The children can think of questions on one topic that they would like to have answered. If appropriate for the group, the children can be introduced to the levels of Bloom's taxonomy and can think of questions for each level.

Activity   8.25

Crawl Up a Ramp

Level Birth to one

Area Cognitive

Interaction Child-object

Strand Completion of Tasks

Materials Needed A low ramp (not more than 18 inches high)

Directions for Implementation

- Place the infant who is able to crawl at the bottom of the ramp. Position yourself at the top.
- Say, "Can you crawl up here?"
- Encourage the child to try to climb up to you.

Extensions

As the child becomes more proficient, crawling down and then up again becomes possible. Somewhat older children who are walking are able to climb up stairs but may be unable to climb back down.

Activity   8.26

Climb Down Stairs

Level One to two

Area Cognitive

Interaction Child-object

Strand Completion of Tasks

Materials Needed Stairs

Directions for Implementation

- Allow the child to climb up several steps.
- Say, "I will help you come down."
- Show the child how to sit on one step and then slide down to the next one.

- Assist until the child is down all of the stairs.
- Let the child try again.

Extensions

As children are able to maintain their balance, they can practice walking down the stairs. This is a necessary skill that is frightening for some children. However, there is a motivation to succeed and thus to finish the task.

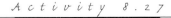

Build a Tower

Level Two

Area Cognitive

Interaction Child-object

Strand Completion of Tasks

Materials Needed A set of graduated nesting blocks

Directions for Implementation

- Take the set of blocks apart, and put them on the floor or a table.
- Demonstrate to the child how the blocks can fit together to make a tower.
- Assist the child in building the tower.
- After some practice, the child will be able to complete the task alone.

Extensions

Younger children can build a tower with similar-sized blocks. Older children enjoy designing towers from existing materials in the classroom. Children can also "nest" the blocks, one inside the other.

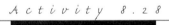

Put Toys Away

Level Three and four

Area Cognitive

Interaction Child-child

Strand Completion of Tasks

Materials Needed Toys to put away

Directions for Implementation

- When the children are finished playing, say, "It's time to put the toys away."
- The class might sing a clean-up song. (For example, "This is the way we clean up the room, clean up the room, clean up the room. This is the way we clean up the room, so early in the morning" to the tune of "Here We Go 'Round the Mulberry Bush.")
- Encourage the children who have been playing in a certain area to work together to finish. (For example, they could make a "conveyor" line to put the blocks away.)
- Assist children who need help.
- Plan something for the children to do when they complete the task. (This might be moving to a large group activity or getting ready to eat lunch.)

Extensions

Older children can assist in organizing materials both at home and in a classroom.

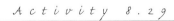

Cooking Vegetable Soup

Level Five and six

Area Cognitive

Interaction Adult-Child

Strand Completion of Tasks

Materials Needed Slow cooker, assorted vegetables, bouillon cube, vegetable peelers, recipe poster, crackers

Directions for Implementation

- Show the children the recipe poster and discuss it.

- Discuss each of the vegetables that will go into the soup.
- Divide the tasks of washing and peeling the different vegetables among the children.
- The vegetables must be prepared early in the day so that the soup will be ready to eat before the children leave.
- Put the vegetables, some water, and the bouillon cube into the slow cooker.
- When the vegetables are cooked, eat the soup with crackers.

Extensions

Children can plant a garden and grow the vegetables to use in the soup. In that way, they see the food process from seeds to eating. Many different kinds of food and cooking experiences are possible for young children to complete. They can also learn good nutrition practices at the same time. The preparation of various ethnic foods can help children learn about different cultures. Children's books that go with this activity are *Stone Soup: An Old Tale* by Marcia Brown (1947) and *Everyone Serves Soup* by Norah Dooley (2000).

A c t i v i t y   8 . 3 0

Completing a Weekly Contract

Level Seven and eight

Area Cognitive

Interaction Adult-Child

Strand Completion of Tasks

Materials Needed Individual contracts for each child (see chapter 5)

Directions for Implementation

- Explain the meaning of a contract to the group and how it works.
- Give each child a copy of a class contract. Assist each child in writing it for the first few weeks. (Depending on the group and

its previous experience with contracts, it may be good to begin with a daily contract and work up to one that is completed in a week or more.)
- Keep a copy of each child's contract.
- Observe the children throughout the time frame of the contract. If they appear to be having trouble completing it, give them extra support. (Some children may need to be monitored at intervals during the contract time.)
- At the end of the time, check to see how the children are doing in completing the task.

Extensions

Younger children can make oral plans concerning their activities during a period of time.

CURRICULAR IMPLICATIONS
Connections to Subject Matter Areas

Among all of the developmental areas, cognitive development is the domain that is clearly embedded in all subject matter categories. Although the novice caregiver or teacher may connect cognitive skills primarily with the core subjects of mathematics, science, and social studies, the strands of development in an interactive curriculum also encompass language arts, music, drama, art, and physical education, and health. In addition, there are cognitive skills, which can be classified as generic, that are not directly associated with a particular subject matter area. When an infant learns to track objects as in "Follows Objects with Eyes" (Activity 8.1) or begins to establish object permanence as in "Looks for Dropped Toy" (Activity 8.7) or "Hide the Shell" (Activity 8.8), these activities go beyond connecting to a specific topic. Similarly, a kindergarten child who focuses attention on a task and develops visual memory by playing a game of Concentration (Activity 8.5) is learning and practicing a cognitive skill that can be used in all subject areas.

For curriculum planners seeking to use a subject framework in developing daily plans, there are suggested activities tied directly to a particular subject. Preschool children participating in using Plastic Builders (Activity 8.4) or exploring the shapes of objects in "Things that are Round" (Activity 8.22) are learning geometric concepts found in the mathematics curriculum. The science area includes activities such as "Sink and Float" (Activity 8.9) for two-year-olds, and an exploration of the principles of simple machines in the Latch Board apparatus for preschool-aged children (Activity 8.10). Mapping the Classroom (Activity 8.11) is a common exercise for first-grade students who begin a study of the community by looking first at the classroom, the school, and the neighborhood.

In the language arts area, there is a heavy incidence of reciprocal interactions in developing speaking and listening skills. Open-ended questions invite conversation between adults and children and among children. All of the activities listed under the developmental strand of Asking Open-Ended Questions promote oral language skills. For young school aged children, the question-asking activity (Activity 8.24) extends to written language. Oral language and role-playing can be integrated in "Stranger Danger" (Activity 8.17), which assists children in learning to make choices, an essential component of more sophisticated decision-making skills in later childhood. Similarly, several of the activities selected to illustrate strategies for helping children develop task completion abilities focus on the physical education area of curriculum. Infants and toddlers can be encouraged to complete selected tasks, such as crawling up a ramp (Activity 8.25), crawling down stairs (Activity 8.26), and building a tower (Activity 8.27).

Connections to Thematic Planning

Advocates of thematic planning can develop themes within the cognitive developmental area. One theme that readily connects many of the suggested activities is the topic of inventions. For many age groups, the theme could be articulated as "learning to make something from nothing." A strategy for introducing the theme to children is to read aloud a version of a well-known Jewish folktale. Sims Taback's (1999) rendition of this tale, *Joseph Had A Little Overcoat*, was awarded the Association for Library Service to Children's coveted Caldecott Medal for the best picture book of 2000. The storyline features an inventive tailor who satisfies his grandson's need to preserve the past by transforming what begins as a child's favorite blanket into increasingly smaller articles of clothing. The blanket changes to an overcoat, a jacket, a vest, a scarf, a necktie, a handkerchief and finally a cherished covered button. When the button gets lost, there's still enough material left to create a story. The message of the story is that one can truly invent something out of nothing. An earlier version of the folktale, *Something from Nothing* (Gillman, 1992) is equally compelling.

Young school-age children can be encouraged to invent a new use for a common object in "How Can We Use This" (Activity 8.23). A follow-up activity could be designed to assist children in figuring out the intended use of another child's invention. An adaptation to the classic game of "20 Questions", which requires that participants only ask questions that can be answered by "yes" or "no", could be to limit student's questions strictly to those that require more than one-word answers (Activity 8.24). Other activities that easily connect to the theme are "Choosing a Project" (Activity 8.18) and "Completing a Weekly Contract" (Activity 8.30). Both of these activities focus on skills that are essential to independent project work, which is valuable in cognitive development.

✒ SUMMARY

Five strands of cognitive development have been identified. The first strand, the development of attention, is enhanced when young children are helped to focus their attention on a task and maintain it. The second strand is problem solving, which requires reflection and experimentation. Problem solving draws on many cognitive abilities. It is related to the third strand, making choices. To make the best choice, children often need to be good problem solvers. Children must learn to make wise choices before they can become effective decision makers. The ability to ask open-ended questions is the fourth strand. This is particularly important in assisting children in thinking in different categories and understanding that most questions have more than one answer. The last strand concerns the ability to complete tasks. It is necessary to complete most tasks to learn from them.

Children need interactions with adults, peers, and objects to reach their potential in the various areas of cognitive development. The activities included in the chapter are examples to illustrate the selected strands of cognitive development for specific age levels. However, many can be adapted for younger or older children. Teachers, caregivers, and parents should adapt activities and design new ones to meet the individual and group needs of children.

QUESTIONS AND PROJECTS FOR THE READER

1. Select an age group and develop a new activity for each of the strands of cognitive development (development of attention,
problem solving, making choices, asking open-ended questions, completion of tasks).
2. Develop strategies that you could use to work with a kindergarten child who has difficulty with sustained attention.
3. Using the cognitive development strand of problem solving, plan activities for interactions for each of the following contexts: family or extended family, home visitor, family child-care home, parent interaction program, group child care, kindergarten and primary classrooms, and school-aged child care.
4. Using Bloom's taxonomy, select a theme and develop a question for each of the levels.
5. Discuss how the five strands of cognitive development are related (development of attention, problem solving, making choices, asking open-ended questions, completion of tasks).

FOR FURTHER READING

Aldridge, J., Eddowes, E. A., & Kuby, P. (1998) *No easy answers: Helping children with attention and activity level differences.* Olney, MD: Association for Childhood Education International. This book has theoretical information concerning children's attention development and activity levels. There are practical suggestions to use in working with attention problems.

Hirsch, E. S. (Ed.). (1996). *The block book* (3rd ed.). Washington, DC: National Association for the Education of Young Children. All aspects concerning the use of unit blocks in preschool and elementary school classrooms are thoroughly covered in this book. Chapters relate to many curriculum areas, such as science, math, social studies, and dramatic play. The stages of block play are described.

Kamii, C., & DeVries, R. (1980). *Group games in early education: Implications of Piaget's theory.* Washington, DC: National Association for the

Education of Young Children. The rationale for using a variety of group games with young children is included in this book. It has many examples of games with instructions. The discussion of how games may be used in teaching includes a section on competition in games.

Kohlberg, L., & Lickona, T. (1987). Moral discussion and the class meeting. In R. DeVries & L. Kohlberg (Eds.), *Constructivist early education: Overview and comparison with other programs* (pp. 143–181). Washington, DC: National Association for the Education of Young Children. This chapter includes information concerning the benefits of group decision-making and the use of the spontaneous interpersonal conflicts of the classroom to promote social-moral development.

Chapter Nine

Communication Development

objectives

After reviewing this chapter, you will be able to

- Identify five key strands of communication development.
- Discuss the role of adult-child interaction in developing the five key strands of communication development.
- Differentiate between receptive and expressive language skills.
- Indicate ways that traditional subject matter areas connect to communication development.
- Select developmentally age-appropriate activities for an individual child from each communication strand.
- Generate strategies for promoting nonverbal communication skills and give examples of culture-specific body language and gestures.
- Identify two critical elements in the development of written communication skills.

223

INTRODUCTION

Helping children learn to communicate is both our easiest and most challenging task as parents and educators. Most infants and toddlers learn to understand and use language without direct instruction (Lenneberg, Rebelsky, & Nichols, 1965; Snow, 1998). Further evidence of this seemingly natural process may be found in the rapid growth in communication skills that occurs in early childhood. At birth, an infant begins to communicate with undifferentiated crying, and by the age of three, a young child can speak in simple sentences. However, this process is unlikely to occur outside of a language-rich environment, and it is the adult who for the most part controls the environment. A language-rich environment includes interactions with adults and other children and interactions with materials, activities, and experiences provided by adults (Schickedanz, 1986; Snow, 1998).

Communication development is divided into five strands: listening, speaking, reading, writing, and nonverbal communication. Communications skills can also be categorized in terms of receptive and expressive skills (Adamson, 1995; Donoghue, 1990). Receptive skills involve receiving and understanding messages verbally, nonverbally, and in written form. Listening, reading, and interpreting nonverbal language, such as gestures, facial expressions, and other forms of body language, are considered to be **receptive language** skills. In contrast, speaking, writing, and using body language are defined as expressive communication skills.

Ideas and feelings are expressed orally, nonverbally, or in written symbols. The development of receptive language precedes the development of expressive language. Infants understand much of what is said to them long before they are able to express those same concepts and feelings. Likewise, receptive vocabulary exceeds oral expressive vocabulary, and, in general, the words used in speaking also exceed those used in writing.

Human languages share basic organizing principles. All languages combine a set of sounds, are governed by grammatical rules, and enable expression of ideas. In this respect, no one language is more advanced than another. Normal infants are capable of learning any language to which they are exposed (Diaz-Rico & Weed, 1995). The pace of language learning also follows a universal schedule. Babies learn languages at a similar pace, replicating sounds in the first year of life, using single-word utterances in the second year, and combining words by the third year. By the age of five, a child's patterns of speech generally approximate adult forms and are readily understood (Donoghue, 1990; Trawick-Smith, 2000).

Although there are universal stages of language acquisition, the rates at which individual children learn to communicate vary considerably, as in other areas of development (Glazer, 1989). Most concerns about children's communication skills, particularly articulation and unconventional grammatical patterns, are remedied with time. Legitimate causes of language delays that should be a concern for parents and caregivers involve hearing loss, including temporary losses related to frequent inner ear infections. Infants and toddlers who appear to fail to develop receptive language may also be candidates for further testing by physicians and speech and language development specialists. Although second language learners, i.e., those who learn a primary language first and then a second language, may have some challenges learning a second sound system, Arnberg (1987) suggests that children who are exposed equally to two languages from birth often become quite proficient in speaking both languages by the age of five. When young children grow up in a **bilingual** home, they may initially experience some temporary confusion between the two languages. One sign of this confusion is mixed-language utterances (Trawick-Smith, 2000). In general, children learn to talk when people speak and listen to them. Providing an environment rich in oral and written language may be the key to a child's development of communication skills.

This chapter's organization parallels the structure of chapters 6–10. The next section presents the five key strands of communication development: listening, speaking, reading, writing, and nonverbal communication. The matrix of all of the suggested activities, which promote this developmental area, follows and then the suggested activities themselves are presented. These are organized sequentially by age and by the intended strand of development. The final section of the chapter focuses on curricular implications including integrating activities with traditional subject matter areas and with a thematic planning framework.

❧ KEY STRANDS OF DEVELOPMENT

Listening

Informal conversations are valuable tools for acquiring a language. The focus is on communicating to others and understanding other people's ideas and feelings. The context is the here and now, and the language used is personalized and functional. Routine caregiving tasks, such as bathing, diapering, and dressing, provide opportunities for parents and caregivers to interact verbally with individual infants and children. Conversation topics can include a discussion of what the parent or caregiver is actually doing. For example, the parent might say, "I'm going to put on these red booties. First one foot and now the other." Sometimes parents and caregivers feel self-conscious carrying on these supposedly one-sided conversations with young infants. Other parents and caregivers think that it is useless

to talk to infants until the infants begin to respond by making sounds.

An infant learns a language by hearing it and connecting the spoken language to actions, which facilitates learning. The patterns of language found in poems and songs can also be useful in promoting listening skills. Nursery rhymes are excellent conversation starters that infants and young children have enjoyed for countless generations. Regional and ethnic cultures have traditional rhymes and songs that are passed down in families and communities. Activity 9.1 includes a rhyme that might be made up by an adult while dressing a young infant.

Outdoor environments provide a wealth of natural and manmade sounds for expanding listening experiences. Pointing out sounds during walks or outdoor play helps toddlers listen. Asking children to point out the location of the sounds and, if possible, helping them visually discover the source of the sound helps develop critical listening behaviors. Parents and caregivers also expand vocabulary and other language patterns during these types of conversations. Parents and caregivers may use Activity 9.2 to expand listening experiences to the outdoor environment.

Some families and family child-care homes keep televisions or radios on during most of a child's waking hours. Excessive loud noise is damaging to hearing and should obviously be avoided. However, constant background noise may also keep children from attending to specific sounds and differentiating sounds from one another (Heft, 1985). Continuous music may hinder opportunities for conversations. Parents and caregivers can provide a variety of listening experiences by playing different kinds of music. Some communities have outdoor concerts that expose children to various types of music and do not require children to sit still and listen for extended periods of time. Music appreciation experiences promote listening skills, as in Activity 9.3.

The focus in this chapter is on listening as a means of acquiring a language and on listening as a means of paying attention to the auditory elements of a child's environment. Listening is also the foundation of effective interpersonal relationships. In an urban society, listening has social and communicative aspects. Similarly, listening functions as a vital learning process in a technological age. Television and radio are major sources of information and recreation in today's world.

Direct instruction to promote listening skills improves a child's ability to develop appreciative and critical listening abilities (Donoghue, 1990). Adults should model active listening in interactions with children and should provide opportunities for children to listen to each other (Jalongo, 1995). Teachers and caregivers can plan activities that improve a child's ability to listen for information and use it to solve problems. Activity 9.4 combines listening and observing skills.

Children are often required to respond to requests from parents, teachers, and caregivers by hearing, understanding, and following directions. Frequently, academic tasks require children to listen attentively as individuals and as members of small or large groups. Likewise, the classroom management styles of many teachers and caregivers depend on children following directions. Attentive listening skills can be improved with specific instruction and practice. Activity 9.5 can be used as a specific lesson or employed as a transitional activity. Teachers and caregivers can make optimal use of class time by filling the waiting of transition time with activities that require no materials and a minimum of planning. Listening activities are readily incorporated into this format.

Preschool teacher reads to a child in the library corner of the classroom.

Donoghue (1990) categorizes listening skills according to three main types: appreciative, attentive, and critical. The example of listening to music described in Activity 9.3 is appreciative listening. Attentive listening skills focus on listening for details, such as the type of listening skills promoted in Activities 9.4 and 9.5, entitled "I Spy" and "Following Directions." Critical listening demands that children evaluate what they've heard before reflecting or acting on that information. Young children tend to take what they hear literally. Their lack of experience or sophistication with language may prevent them from understanding that what they heard may not be what was meant. A young child watching a commercial on television may have difficulty evaluating the authenticity of the promotion. Teachers and parents can informally help children develop critical listening skills by asking questions or, formally, by planning activities to meet these goals (see Activity 9.6).

Speaking

The second strand of communication development is speaking. Speaking is considered to be expressive language because ideas and feelings are conveyed to other listeners. In infancy, speaking or oral language is primarily prelinguistic; that is, it contains no actual words. The earliest vocalizations of young infants are labeled undifferentiated crying. Later, infants differentiate their cries, communicating varied messages to their caregivers, ranging from hunger and pain to boredom. Cooing, the first noncrying vocalization, is described as primarily extended vowel-like sounds, such as "ooooos" and "aaahs."

Babbling, chains of repeated consonant and vowel sounds, follows cooing at approximately five months of age (Caplan, 1993). At this stage, infants also begin to use intonation, varying the pitch of these babbled syllables. By twelve months, many infants have short-

ened their babblings to one or two syllables, such as "mama," "dada," and "baba," and they consistently use these expressions to refer to a particular person or object.

Parents and caregivers may question the use of "baby talk" as a means of communicating with infants and children. Certainly, consistently responding to infants' vocalizations by mimicking their sounds does not provide an appropriate language model for infants and young children. However, when a parent reinforces a young baby's vocalizations in play by replicating them, the interchange between baby and adult is more likely to have a positive effect on language development. For example, if the baby makes the sound "ga, ga, goo," the adult could repeat it in a conversational way.

Responding to the young infant's cooing and babblings by imitating the sounds in an infant-adult conversation differs from calling a bottle a "ba-ba" just because that is the sound combination a toddler uses to refer to the bottle. In this case, the adult should say "bottle" and not repeat "ba-ba." Adults who continue to use baby talk beyond the first year of an infant's life may find the toddler and young child trying to imitate that pattern of speech.

Activity 9.7 is a reciprocal interaction between adult and child, with each responding to the cues of the other. The conversation interaction should take place when the infant begins to make cooing sounds. For many babies, this is a time during the day when they are neither hungry nor tired.

Infants speak their first word at an average age of 12 months. By 24 months, toddlers may have a 50- to 100-word vocabulary and may begin to put two words together to convey extended meaning. Many of the first words are nouns, specific or general names of objects in their personal environments. These nouns also tend to be objects that can be acted on (Nelson, 1973; Waxman & Hall, 1993).

Children tend to be interested in animals and the sounds that they make, as illustrated in Activity 9.8.

Simple fingerplays, action rhymes, and songs promote oral language in young children. Acting out the words through gesture and body movements helps connect meaning to new vocabulary. Singing and acting at the same time may be challenging for two-year-olds, but through repetition, they generally master the task. Sometimes parents and caregivers may observe a child who, although reluctant to speak or sing in a group setting, repeats a favorite rhyme or song when alone. Activity 9.9 is an example of an action rhyme.

Children can be encouraged to practice speaking in the natural flow of conversations. When conversations are about topics of personal interest to children, they generally have more to contribute, and most children enjoy having adults talk with them. Some children do not have frequent opportunities to converse with adults on a one-to-one basis. In a child-care setting, activities can be planned to give children individual time with adults. Volunteers can serve as conversation buddies if group sizes prohibit teachers and caregivers from spending time talking to individual children for extended periods.

In Activity 9.10, a tape recorder is used to give children the opportunity to hear their voices on audiotape. Volunteers should be cautioned that correcting a child's articulation or grammar tends to impede conversations. Articulation difficulties and imperfect grammar are normal for preschool children.

Natural conversations can also be promoted by family-style meals in child-care settings where adults sit at tables with children rather than serve or walk around to monitor behavior. Mealtimes can be opportunities to share personal news and to discuss common experiences. Likewise, in the home, family mealtimes can enhance the oral language skills of children. In some families, variable schedules may seem to prohibit regular family gatherings and may take a major commitment to maintain. Keeping mealtime discussions separated from discipline issues is also conducive to pleasant conversation.

Meals are heavily governed by traditional cultural practices. Table manners that are appropriate in one culture may be considered inappropriate or rude in another (Diaz-Rico & Weed, 1995). In some cultures, children may not be permitted to join in extended family discussions at meals. In other cultures, boys and men may be served before women and girls sit down to eat. Family-style meal discussions for school and child-care settings that promote oral language are outlined in Activity 9.11.

Teachers can broaden children's oral skills by creating opportunities for them to speak in front of peers and adults. Many children enjoy participating in dramatic productions when teachers help them develop oral skills in a

Two children enjoy a story together.

stress-free atmosphere. Roles can be assigned to individuals, based on their skill level and previous experience, to ensure success. Practice sessions should be designed to build the confidence of individual players to prevent major stumbling in front of a group of peers (Activity 9.12). Performances encourage children to speak with expression and to take on roles that are outside of their usual styles of speaking.

Writing

The third strand of communication development is the promotion of writing skills. For young children, learning to write has two components. The first component of writing involves the mechanics of handwriting. Children must first have sufficient fine motor control to be able to use tools of writing, such as pencils, pens, and crayons. Later, children develop an understanding of alphabetic principles. They learn that fairly arbitrary but standard symbols represent oral language on paper.

The second component of writing deals with the expression of ideas. The transition from oral language to written language can be conveyed to children as "talk written down." Children can dictate ideas and stories to teachers, parents, and caregivers and then watch them convert these ideas to written symbols. The written symbols can then be read back to children to underscore the natural process of writing.

Long before children write for the first time, they begin to develop the fine motor control that is needed to make alphabet letters, the symbols of language. The young infant learning to grasp and release objects and the toddler learning to use a fork and a spoon as tools are both developing the muscle coordination needed for writing. Activities 9.13 and 9.14 can be considered to be precursors of handwriting.

As early as two years of age, toddlers can be observed mimicking adults who are writing. A toddler may pick up a play telephone, put it to his ear, and pretend to scribble on a pad of paper. This child is demonstrating that he has some conceptual understanding of the purpose of writing (Martens, 1998; McGee & Richgels, 1990). Scribbling can also be viewed as knowing that written symbols in some way represent ideas or language. In addition, parents and caregivers would undoubtedly prefer that children learn that scribbling is something that belongs on paper rather than on walls or other objects. Activity 9.15 helps children learn that scribbling on paper is an acceptable practice.

By the age of four years, many children have begun to include figures in their artwork (Eddowes, 1995). Children usually draw vertical and horizontal lines before drawing circles and other enclosed spaces.

The ability to copy lines, circles, and other figures is useful in learning to write the alphabet. Activity 9.16 is designed to promote the ability to write letters.

The **whole language movement** promoted the idea that writing and reading are complementary processes and that the processes should develop simultaneously (Adams, 1999). Although there is no one universally held definition of whole language, Weaver (1994) asserts that whole language is primarily a philosophy that guides instructional decision-making. Some principles of whole language instruction include making language learning functional, allowing learners to construct meaning from a variety of contexts, and promoting individual choice and individual patterns of learning (Weaver, 1994). Many kindergarten teachers who include journal writing in their weekly planning discover that children are indeed capable of writing in some form and are certainly able to understand that writing is a process of putting thought on paper.

Children with phonemic and alphabetic awareness can be encouraged to use invented or phonetic spelling in the beginning writing stages (Adams, 1990; Yopp, 1992). The idea that must be conveyed to children is that a writer's first concern is not correct spelling. The primary focus should be on thinking and then expressing those thoughts on paper (Schickedanz, 1986; Tompkins, 2001). Teachers can create word banks for young children to use in their writing by brainstorming ideas before writing. Children can also generate a list of words they are likely to use in their stories. Coding the words with quickly drawn pictures or symbols helps children access the list.

When class sizes and teacher-child ratios discourage teachers from planning writing activities, other organizational formats can be explored. Some teachers with large class sizes plan journal writing as a small group activity for a time in the schedule when other children are working independently. With a class of thirty students, a teacher could plan for six children a day to write in their journals. At this age, journal entries most often include illustrations that help children and teachers read their entries (Activity 9.17). Other teachers make use of volunteers to transcribe dictated stories from individual children for journal entries.

Teachers who use the **writing process** to teach writing skills support the premise that writing is foremost the expression of ideas (Olson, 1987). The conventions of writing that include spelling, grammar, and punctuation are taught in context and as editing skills. The first step of the writing process is prewriting. There is a dual focus to prewriting—generating ideas and organizing thoughts. The second step, drafting, involves translating ideas to paper. The third step, revising, requires that writers seek responses to their writing from peers and adults. Writers review the suggestions and revise their work. Editing, the fourth step, applies the conventions of writing to the work. At this stage, writers check for accurate spelling, punctuation, and grammar. The fifth

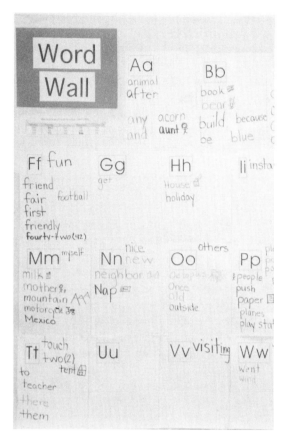

Word wall is used to help children learning to read and write.

and last stage is sharing or publication. The writing may be shared orally or published in a form to be read by others (Andreasen et al., 1980; Tompkins, 2001).

Donoghue (1990) believes that children must learn that their writing is appreciated and useful. Activity 9.18 is the use of an author's chair. The author's chair can be used for seeking responses to a work in progress before its revision. It can also be used to share a finished product with an audience.

Reading

Learning how to read, or becoming literate, is currently viewed as a gradual or emerging process. The term **emergent literacy** has been coined to more accurately depict the manner by which children learn to make sense of written symbols. Many educators no longer view the teaching of reading as a specific process that can begin only after a child has demonstrated various readiness skills (Campbell, 1998; McGee & Richgels, 1990). The focus of emergent literacy is understanding the intimate connection between reading and the other strands of communication development, especially listening, speaking, and writing.

It is obvious that even infants and toddlers have print awareness. A 12-month-old infant may be observed holding a board book and babbling with intonation as he flips through the pages. The toddler sitting on his father's lap looking at a book may impatiently point to the print on the page if his father attempts to turn the pages without talking. An increased awareness of printed symbols is demonstrated by three-year-olds as they point to a fast-food logo in the magazine their mother is reading. It is also demonstrated by four-year-olds who, when seeing a word that begins with the same letter as their name, remarks, "There's my name." In our print-rich society, children come to school with considerable awareness and knowledge of reading processes and functions (Aldridge et al., 1996).

Literacy development begins early in life and is ongoing. In addition to providing an environment that is rich in oral language, parents and caregivers can introduce books to infants by reading aloud. Wells (1986) documents a clear connection between school achievement and early experience with listening to stories. Reading aloud builds a knowledge base for children and introduces them to print (California Department of Education, 2000). Board books designed for infants and toddlers are used in Activity 9.19. The pages of these sturdy books are printed on cardboard, making them easier to turn and more durable for children learning to handle books.

Illustrations are an important component of children's literature and are readily incorporated in storytelling. Children learn to interpret meaning from the illustrations that accompany text when parents and caregivers talk through books (Reynolds, 1998; Schickedanz, 1986). Adults may find that infants and toddlers prefer to point out elements of a picture as it is being described or as a story is being told. Picture cards can be used by adults to tell stories to toddlers and can be used by young children when they retell or write stories. Activity 9.20 can be adapted to many age groups.

Although young children can be taught to handle books carefully, parents and caregivers should try to create books that are easy to handle without being damaged. Books made from self-locking plastic bags fit these criteria. Books are created by stapling five to eight plastic bags together. Plastic tape can be used to cover the staples and create a sturdy binding. Photographs or pictures mounted on construction paper can be put in the bags and sealed to form the pages. A parent might create a family book from photographs by mounting the photographs on note cards to create space for a caption. Illustrated directions for making plastic bag books are in Appendix D ("Baggie Books"). Activity 9.21 uses these books.

The identification of literary elements in fiction such as story line, or plot, is a critical reading task. The actions of the characters are related in an orderly manner, usually with a beginning, middle, and end. Preschool children can be introduced to story line with sequence cards. Details in the illustrations give clues to time sequences, assisting children in placing the pictures in order. Activity 9.22 suggests techniques for using commercially made or teacher-made sequence cards.

Teaching all children to read is a high priority for educators, parents, and the general public (Graves, Juel, & Graves, 2001; Tompkins, 2001). Tompkins (2001) describes a comprehensive, balanced approach to literacy instruction as one that acknowledges the contributions of various theoretical perspectives on learning to read and write and reflects current research in literacy development. The report of the California Reading Task Force, *Every Child a Reader* (1995), suggests a reading curriculum time line for use in developing comprehensive language arts programs for kindergarten through eighth grade. The goal of the balanced, research-based literacy programs that combine skills development with literature and language-rich activities is that all students will read at grade level by the end of third grade and will make significant grade-level progress each subsequent year. Program components include strands promoting phonemic, print, and syntactic awareness at the preschool level and exposure to letter names and the alphabet. Examples of developmentally appropriate activities for preschool children include listening to a variety of books; exposure to environmental print, such as labeling objects in the room; and playing with words and sounds in rhymes and song.

Preschool children can be exposed to letter names by reading alphabet books. Children exposed to a rich, meaning-based language arts program may also express an interest in letter recognition and letter formation. Kindergarten-aged and young school-aged children should learn letter names, letter-sound correspondence, sight words, and basic word families within the context of a literature and language-rich program (California Department of Education, 1995).

Phonemic awareness, for example, can be facilitated by language play in literature and song (Adams, Foorman, Lundberg, & Beeler, 1998; Yopp & Yopp, 1996). Yopp (1995) recommends that teachers read and reread books that make obvious use of rhyme and other forms of sound play, while commenting on the unique use of language sounds. Parents and teachers can also help children make predic-

tions and orally create new verses or versions of the story.

Books with predictable patterns are also particularly attractive to emergent readers (Donoghue, 1990; Tompkins, 2001). Many teachers find that children participate in group reading activities by repeating word patterns. Sometimes predictable books follow a cumulative pattern, such as *The Gingerbread Man* (Kimmel, 1990). As the story progresses, character after character is added to the chain of people and animals trying to catch the gingerbread man. The story also includes a rhyming refrain, "Run, run, as fast as you can. You can't catch me, I'm the Gingerbread Man." Children begin to recognize and associate meaning with particular words and word sequences. Books with word patterns help children predict and anticipate story line and language. A different type of pattern book is included in Activity 9.23.

Although parents commonly read picture books to young children, sometimes these same parents cease reading aloud when their children begin to read on their own. Trelease (1995), in *The New Read Aloud Handbook,* advocates reading aloud to all children no matter what their age. Reading chapter books aloud to young school-aged children helps them make the transition from illustrated books to children's novels. First, although chapter books may have some illustrations, the reader cannot usually depend on those illustrations to follow the story line. Listening to this type of reading helps children paint word pictures of setting and character. Second, chapter books are not usually read in their entirety at one time. The child must sustain interest over a longer time period. Well-written books about a specific set of characters that are published in a series help to create an ongoing interest in the characters and their stories. Teachers and parents can encourage an interest in reading chapter books, such as the one recommended in Activity 9.24.

Second-grade teacher reads aloud to the whole class.

Nonverbal Communication

The fifth strand of communication development, nonverbal communication, includes body language, gestures, and facial expressions. Parents, teachers, and caregivers probably communicate as much nonverbally to young children as they do verbally (Snow, 1998). Even young babies appear to sense the emotional climate of the home or child-care setting. An infant may respond differently to the relaxed body language of a parent that conveys a sense of calm than to body language that expresses tension and stress. Similarly, babies usually imitate facial expressions that they see. Combining nonverbal and verbal communication styles helps young children interpret and label nonverbal behaviors. Activity 9.25 is a reciprocal interaction that focuses on facial expressions.

Nonverbal communication can be a form of receptive language in that it demonstrates understanding of verbal communication. Pointing is an early form of demonstrating receptive language skills that is frequently used by infants and toddlers (Fenson, Dale, Reznick, Bates, Thal, & Pethick, 1994). Parents and caregivers model pointing to objects as they identify and verbally label objects for young children. Activity 9.26 is a game that can be played by parents and older infants or young toddlers to learn to identify body parts.

Young children may use nonverbal communication behaviors as a less threatening means of communicating with others. Forcing a child to verbally respond is often counterproductive. Although many children between the ages of two and three move from telegraphic speech to full sentences, this does not mean that children choose to communicate verbally. A child who is extremely verbal at home may be perceived as relatively nonverbal in a group setting. Shy or "slow-to-warm-up" children are particularly reluctant to carry on conversations with unfamiliar people. Activity 9.27 emphasizes a nonthreatening method of encouraging young children to communicate without forcing them to talk.

Gestures and other forms of body language convey meaning to others but not necessarily the meaning that is intended. In general, gestures and facial expressions are culturally specific (Trawick-Smith, 2000). In some Asian cultures, smiling is reserved for family members and close friends. Smiling may also convey superficiality and a lack of seriousness. Smiling in a school photograph is considered inappropriate in some cultures because it indicates a lack of seriousness about one's role as a student. In contrast, in mainstream American culture smiling tends to be interpreted as acceptance and friendliness.

The interpretation of gestures varies from culture to culture. Beckoning a child "to come here" is signaled in European and American cultures by holding the hand vertically, palm facing the body, and moving the fingers back and forth rapidly. Other cultures interpret this motion as a rude gesture.

The game of charades is modified for young children in Activity 9.28. Teachers and caregivers should be aware of the cultural backgrounds of the families in their schools and centers when planning activities that include gestures and other forms of body language.

Another method of communicating without words involves the use of sounds. Teachers can demonstrate how to communicate directions in movement activities, as illustrated in Activity 9.29. Older children can research historical and current uses of Morse code as well as other sound-based communication systems.

Some types of drama and dance are nonverbal forms of communication. Mime, for example, is a form of acting that does not use words. Portraying a message without using verbal language challenges children to think creatively and critically. Activity 9.30 can be used to introduce children to mime.

Table 9.1 is a matrix correlating all the activities described in this chapter with the appropriate ages and developmental strands.

🦋 AGE-APPROPRIATE ACTIVITIES: BIRTH THROUGH EIGHT YEARS

Activity 9.1

This Little Toe

Level Birth to One

Area Communication

Interaction Adult-child

Strand Listening

Materials Needed None

Directions for Implementation

- Starting at the infant's little toe, gently grab the toe and say, "This little toe is number one." At the next toe add, "The second little toe wants some fun." Touch the third toe and say, "The third little toe is stuck in the middle." At the fourth toe recite, "The fourth little toe is fit as a fiddle." Wiggle the big toe and say, "And if the great big toe has his (or her) way, all the little toes will go out to play."
- Use animated facial features, and vary the pitch of your voice to capture and maintain the infant's attention.

Extensions

Parents and caregivers can also sing nursery rhymes to young children. Singing songs and even singing directions to children catches their attention and creates an alternate avenue for communication. Soothing lullabies are found in all cultures. See Appendix C for sample nursery rhymes, fingerplays, and songs.

Table 9.1 Communication development activities matrix.

Ages (Years)	Listening	Speaking	Writing	Reading	Nonverbal Communication
Birth to one	This Little Toe Activity 9.1 Adult-child	First Sounds Activity 9.7 Adult-child	Holding Rattles Activity 9.13 Child-Object	Board Books Activity 9.19 Adult-child	Facial Expressions Activity 9.25 Adult-child
One to two	Outdoor Sounds Activity 9.2 Adult-child	Animal Noises Activity 9.8 Adult-child	Using Utensils Activity 9.14 Child-object	Picture Cards Activity 9.20 Adult-child	Body Parts Activity 9.26 Adult-child
Two	Listening to Music Activity 9.3 Adult-child	Heads, Shoulders, Knees, and Toes Activity 9.9 Adult-child	Jotting a Note Activity 9.15 Adult-child	Plastic Bag Books Activity 9.21 Adult-child	Identifying Family Photos Activity 9.27 Adult-child
Three and four	I Spy Activity 9.4 Adult-child	Recording Voices Activity 9.10 Adult-child	Drawing Figures Activity 9.16 Adult-child	Sequence Pictures Activity 9.22 Adult-child	Charades Activity 9.28 Adult-child
Five and six	Following Directions Activity 9.5 Adult-child	Table Talk Activity 9.11 Adult-child	Journal Writing Activity 9.17 Adult-child	Pattern Books Activity 9.23 Adult-child	Making Sound Patterns Activity 9.29 Adult-child
Seven and eight	Fact or Fiction? Activity 9.6 Adult-child	On Stage Activity 9.12 Child-child	Author's Chair Activity 9.18 Child-child	Chapter Books Activity 9.24 Adult-child	Mime Activity 9.30 Child-child

A c t i v i t y   9 . 2

Outdoor Sounds

Level One to Two

Area Communication

Interaction Adult-child

Strand Listening

Materials Needed None

Directions for Implementation

- As you are walking or playing outdoors, point out sounds in the environment.
- If you hear an airplane or helicopter flying overhead, you might say, as you scan the sky for its location, "I hear an airplane. Let's look for it. It's getting louder. It must be getting closer to us."
- Insects and other animals are also frequently in outdoor environments. For example, you can point out a dog barking or a fly buzzing.

Extensions

When young babies attend to sounds and vocalizations by looking toward the source of the sound, help them identify the sound by making comments such as, "I think that sounds like the garbage truck coming up our street. Shall we go look?" or "Mommy must be singing in the shower." Older children can be helped to use tape recorders to capture the sounds of a trip to the zoo or to a farm.

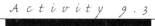

A c t i v i t y   9 . 3

Listening to Music

Level Two

Area Communication

Interaction Adult-child

Strand Listening

Materials Needed Radio, tape or CD player

Directions for Implementation

- When music is played, encourage the two-year-old to listen to various qualities of the music. Contrasts such as loud and soft, fast and slow, and high and low can be pointed out.
- You might say, "I love hearing that man's voice, it is so low." In response to a rhythmic or lively beat, you might say that the music makes you want to dance.

Extensions

Since many adults prefer certain types of music and even dislike others, it may take a conscious effort to provide a variety of musical listening experiences. Libraries often lend tape recordings of interest to children, such as the opera "Peter and the Wolf" or the ballet "The Nutcracker." Local community organizations may also sponsor concerts designed for children.

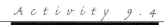

A c t i v i t y   9 . 4

I Spy

Level Three and four

Area Communication

Interaction Adult-child

Strand Listening

Materials Needed None

Directions for Implementation

- Look around the room, and choose an object to describe. Turn your back to the child to give clues as to what the object is and where it is located.
- Encourage the child to listen closely to the clues by saying, "I spy something that is red, round, and in a bowl on the kitchen counter." Hopefully, the child will look around the room, see a bowl of red fruit, and say "apples."

- Build success by choosing objects familiar to the child and increasing the difficulty slowly.

Extensions

The game can be varied for older children by encouraging them to take the role of choosing an object and describing it. Suggest that they do not look at the object when they are describing it to force the other players to listen carefully. Younger children may learn the names of objects during the normal course of the day when adults identify objects by verbally labeling the objects. Curious toddlers may also ask "What's that?" when they encounter new objects. Adults can play an informal game with infants and toddlers by encouraging them to point and talk at the same time. The adult might request "Show me your ears" or "Show me your shoes."

A c t i v i t y   9 . 5

Following Directions

Level Five and six

Area Communication

Interaction Adult-child

Strand Listening

Materials Needed None

Directions for Implementation

- Begin by making up a series of three simple instructions. For example, you can ask the group to "Stand up, turn around, and jump two times."
- Instruct the children to listen first, do the action, and then freeze.
- As children improve their listening and memory skills, you can add more challenging actions, "Slide two steps to your right, clap your hands above your head, turn around on your tiptoes, and jump back to your original place."

Extensions

Older children can become the leaders of a larger group, or teachers can assign children to work in pairs or in small groups. The activity could be adapted for younger children or for English language learners by modeling simple directions.

A c t i v i t y   9 . 6

Fact or Fiction?

Level Seven and eight

Area Communication

Interaction Adult-child

Strand Listening

Materials Needed Illustrated animal stories, chart paper, a felt pen

Directions for Implementation

- Briefly discuss the differences between fact and fiction using several examples. Clifford in *Clifford, the Big Red Dog* (Bridwell, 1985) acts like a loyal and friendly pet who lives with a family. Other events in the story clearly portray his behavior as make-believe.
- Read an animal story, and tell the children to listen for examples from the story that are or could be facts about animals and other examples that are fiction.
- At the end of the story, make a chart about the animals in the story; identify actions and descriptions that are fact and those that are fiction. Ask children to talk about how they determined that something was fact or fiction.

Extensions

Preschool-aged and young school-aged children gradually learn to distinguish between real and imaginary characters. A related listening activity for younger children could be making a tape recording of real animal noises paired with human imitations of those animals. Ask children to identify the real animal noises and the pretend animal noises.

First Sounds

Level Birth to one

Area Communication

Interaction Adult-child

Strand Speaking

Materials Needed None

Directions for Implementation

- With the baby facing you, imitate the baby's vocalizations and mouth movements. For example, the baby may make an "oo" sound like in the word "cool" with the lips rounded.
- In addition to imitating sounds, you might respond to the vocalization by saying, "You sound so happy when you make that sound."
- When the infant turns his or her head or closes his or her eyes to terminate the interaction, look away briefly to keep from overstimulating the baby. Allow the infant to pace the interaction.

Extensions

Routine caregiving activities consume large amounts of time in the lives of young children and their parents or caregivers. Taking advantage of the time spent bathing, dressing, feeding, and traveling in the car to engage children in meaningful conversation is time well spent in developing language skills. Older children enjoy singing favorite childhood songs during routine activities. Songs build vocabulary and language patterns, such as rhyming, and engage children in practicing oral language.

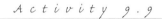
Animal Noises

Level One to two

Area Communication

Interaction Adult-child

Strand Speaking

Materials Needed A variety of stuffed animals

Directions for Implementation

- Choose a stuffed animal, for example a dog, that makes a sound familiar to young toddlers. Pick up the toy, and make barking noises.
- Encourage the child to imitate the sounds made by dogs by asking, "What does the dog say?"
- Play with the child, imitating the sounds that animals make. Suggest reasons for the dog's barking. For example, you might ask, "Is that dog hungry? Does he want to go outside? Is your dog trying to scare that cat?"

Extensions

Many children's songs and stories contain animal noises. "Old MacDonald Had a Farm" requires children to imitate animal sounds. Peter Spier's book *Gobble Growl Grunt* (1971) depicts the sounds of a variety of animals.

Activity 9.9
Heads, Shoulders, Knees, and Toes

Level Two

Area Communication

Interaction Adult-child

Strand Speaking

Materials Needed None

Directions for Implementation

- Sit on the floor or grass with your legs straight out facing the child. Ask the toddler to sit just like you.
- Sing or chant the rhyme, and touch the named body parts:

Heads, shoulders, knees and toes, knees and
    toes.
Heads, shoulders, knees and toes, knees and
    toes.
Eyes and ears and mouth and nose.
Heads, shoulders, knees and toes, knees and
    toes.

- Encourage the toddler to repeat the names of the body parts as they are touched.

Extensions

Young children often have difficulty saying the words and doing the motions to songs at the same time. Older children can stand up and sing this rhyme and keep their knees straight when they bend over. Younger children tend to lose their balance or their place in the song when they cannot see the adult modeling the actions. Older children also enjoy this song by doing the actions but leaving out a word each time through. On the second time through the song, omit the word "toes" each time you come to it. The third time, omit "knees," and so on. By the fifth time the song is sung, the children are doing the motions in order but only singing "Eyes and ears and mouth and nose."

A c t i v i t y   9 . 1 0

Recording Voices

Level Three and four

Area Communication

Interaction Adult-child

Strand Speaking

Materials Needed Tape recorder and a tape

Directions for Implementation

- In a quiet area, sit down and record a conversation between you and the child. Encourage the child to speak clearly and to stay close to the microphone. If the microphone is built into the tape recorder, point out where it is.
- Most children need to be prompted with questions. Start with a topic that is familiar to the child and with questions that require only a short answer. Gradually encourage the child to talk by asking open-ended questions. For example, a conversation about a pet may start out like this: "I remember you told me you have a dog at home. What is your dog's name? Can you tell me where your dog, Rusty, sleeps? How do you get Rusty to play with you? Why do you think dogs make good pets?" Pause between questions, allowing ample time for the child to respond.

Extensions

Older children can practice reading into a microphone or telling stories. To increase the likelihood of success, have children practice reading passages to themselves several times and then to a peer before they read into a tape. Samples of children's oral reading skills taped at regular intervals can be added to portfolios to document and assess emergent literacy.

A c t i v i t y   9 . 1 1

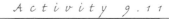

Table Talk

Level Five and six

Area Communication

Interaction Adult-child

Strand Speaking

Materials Needed Adult seated at tables with children

Directions for Implementation

- Initiate discussions about a variety of topics during mealtime. Modeling listening behavior is essential. You might begin a conversation about family ways of celebrating birthdays by saying, "We celebrated my daughter's birthday last Sunday by having a picnic at the park. How does your family like to celebrate birthdays?" Try to include all children in the conversation rather than having a series of dialogues with one child at a time.
- Past and current events at the school or center provide a shared experience to be discussed. You might ask, "What did you think of our experiment with the balloon?" to prompt a discussion of other experiences with balloons at home or school.

Extensions

Staff and parents can help create family-style mealtime discussions in schools and childcare centers. Alerting regular or special guests to the language development benefits of informal conversations is critical to the success of the practice. Small-sized groups also discourage competing to engage the sole adult at the table in a dialogue. Communication skills are enhanced when a pleasant rather than a stressful environment is created. The parents of older children might discuss ways of enhancing mealtime conversations at parent meetings. Sharing personal, local, or national news might be used as a springboard for watching news programs on TV or reading newspapers or magazines.

Materials Needed Reader's theater script or simple plays

Directions for Implementation

- Children need to be given ample opportunity to practice reading or saying their lines before performing in front of others.
- Highlighting children's lines helps them focus on the task, as does rehearsing in small groups rather than large groups.
- Using props and helping children connect language to movements or gestures improves recall of their lines on cue. For example, suggest that a child playing the character of a cashier ringing up groceries hold out a hand and say, "That will be $3.25 please."

Extensions

Younger children can act out familiar stories that have been reread and retold, such as the *Three Little Pigs* (Leonard, 1990) or *The Five Chinese Brothers* (Bishop, 1989). Help younger children get into character by giving them simple costumes, pictures, or puppets to hold. The adult can be the narrator, setting the scene, pacing the story, and prompting as needed. Having the whole group or smaller groups become a character can also help less confident children participate verbally. For example, the teacher may say to a small group of children, "Pretend you are the Chinese brother who swallowed the sea. Tell the judge that you warned the little boy to come back when you signaled."

A c t i v i t y   9 . 1 2

On Stage

Level Seven and eight

Area Communication

Interaction Child-child

Strand Speaking

A c t i v i t y   9 . 1 3

Holding Rattles

Level Birth to one

Area Communication

Interaction Child-object

Strand Writing

Materials Needed Small-handled, lightweight rattle

Directions for Implementation

- Give the baby rattles and other objects to hold. Young infants hold objects with a grasping reflex. They tend to wave the object up and down, often hitting themselves in the face. As a safety precaution, consider the infant's age and size when choosing rattles.
- Provide a variety of baby-proof small objects for the infant to manipulate.

Extensions

The fine motor control that is needed for controlling the movement of writing instruments is gradually developed. Some infants and toddlers show a preference for gross motor activities, others seem to participate mostly in social and language activities. Parents and teachers should observe their children's preferences and provide a balance of activities for enhancing all areas of development. Children who do not choose a manipulative activity on their own often participate when an adult plays with them.

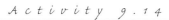
Using Utensils

Level One to two

Area Communication

Interaction Child-object

Strand Writing

Materials Needed Toddler-sized spoon and fork

Directions for Implementation

- Provide a spoon and a small amount of food in a container that is securely attached to a feeding table or high chair. Caregivers and parents can continue to spoon-feed in-

fants while the infants are learning to use a spoon.
- Later, a fork can be added or alternated with a spoon, depending on the foods that are served. Bite-sized servings and finger foods will probably continue to be the preferred mode of eating.

Extensions

Preschool and school-age children like to be involved in food preparation. Table knives and plastic serrated knives can be used to cut objects. Large spoons can used for stirring and mixing. Other utensils that can be incorporated in food preparation experiences, dramatic play areas, or sand tables include tongs, potato mashers, strawberry hullers, wire whips, and spatulas.

Jotting a Note

Level Two

Area Communication

Interaction Adult-child

Strand Writing

Materials Needed Pencil, note pad (approximately 5 × 7 inches), play telephone

Directions for Implementation

- Role-play answering a play telephone. Pretend to listen for a moment, and exclaim, "Just a minute. Let me write that down."
- Pretend to take a note on the note pad by scribbling on the paper. Then hand the toy telephone to the child. When the toddler answers the phone, hand him or her the note pad and the pencil, and suggest writing a note on the paper.
- If the child attempts to chew on the pencil, redirect behavior to writing on the note pad while saying, "Pencils are for writing on paper." If the child persists in putting

the pencil in his mouth, remove the activity and reintroduce it at an older age. Store pencils and other sharp objects out of the reach of toddlers when you are unable to directly supervise them.

Extensions

Although it is easier to scribble with felt pens than crayons, many toddlers continue to explore toys with their mouths. As a safety precaution, nontoxic felt pens with washable ink should be purchased for children's use. Learning to control the movement of paint brushes also enhances the fine motor development needed for writing.

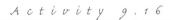

Drawing Figures

Level Three and four

Area Communication

Interaction Adult-child

Strand Writing

Materials Needed Pencils or felt-tip markers, paper

Directions for Implementation

- Draw a circle on a sheet of paper, and say, "Can you make a circle just like mine?" Practice drawing and copying different-sized circles.
- Experiment with other figures and shapes such as an X, a cross, a square, and a triangle.
- Encourage the child to draw a figure, and then copy it yourself.

Extensions

Older children like to draw with other children. In pairs, or in groups of three or four, ask children to work on a drawing cooperatively. Give each child a different-colored felt pen,

and give the group one piece of paper. Choose a subject, such as a house. The first child draws one shape and passes the paper to the next person; the second person adds to the drawing and passes it on. If you ask the children to sign their names with their own color of pen, you can tell what each child drew.

Journal Writing

Level Five and six

Area Communication

Interaction Adult-child

Strand Writing

Materials Needed Handmade journals (wide-ruled paper with space above for pictures, enclosed in a construction paper cover), pencils, crayons, chart paper, or chalkboard

Directions for Implementation

- Gather the whole group or a small group in front of a chalkboard or a piece of chart paper. The teacher can say, "Before you write in your journals, let's talk about yesterday's field trip to the fire station. Who can tell us what you saw or heard at the fire station?"
- Allow several children to share objects, events, or impressions from the field trip. Respond by elaborating details if needed.
- Create a word bank of fire station vocabulary by asking children to think of words they might want to use in their journals. Next to each word, quickly draw a symbol or outline of the object.
- Direct children back to their desks or table to write in their journals using the word bank as a reference or phonetic spelling. Entries should be illustrated when the writing is completed.

Extensions

Teachers and caregivers can also introduce children to writing by creating chart stories. Some teachers use this activity at the beginning of the day to record the date and weather. For example, the children might use the pattern "Today is Monday, March 3, 1996. It is raining today." Other teachers prefer to use chart stories as a closure activity at the end of the day to record class news for parents. With a computer, the sentences written on chart paper can quickly be added each day and printed as part of a newsletter to go home at the end of the week or on Monday morning.

Activity 9.18

Author's Chair

Level Seven and eight

Area Communication

Interaction Child-child

Strand Writing

Materials Needed Teacher's chair or other specially designated chair, sample of child's writing

Directions for Implementation

- Children sign up for presenting a sample of their writing to the class. Many teachers require students to verify that they have practiced reading it to themselves aloud or with a peer. This practice builds fluency before children read in front of the whole class.
- The child reads from the author's chair to an attentive audience. Model constructive comments and praise when this activity is first introduced. You might respond to a child's story about the death of his pet dog by saying, "Your words told me how sad you feel. You might want to write about a time when your dog made you laugh to

help you remember that, too." The goal at this stage is to help children learn to respond to the content rather than merely the technical aspects of writing.

Extensions

The author's chair can also be used to model adult writing. The teacher, staff members, and parents share samples of their writing. Community members can introduce the field of writing as a career choice. Local newspapers, historical societies, and colleges are possible sources of guest writers.

Activity 9.19

Board Books

Level Birth to one

Area Communication

Interaction Adult-child

Strand Reading

Materials Needed Sturdy board books

Directions for Implementation

- With the infant sitting on your lap, share books by talking about the pictures as you turn the pages.
- Point out the objects seen on each page, saying something like, "This baby is playing with blocks" or "I see a big red ball."
- Once you have modeled turning the pages, most infants choose to participate by helping you turn the pages. Sometimes you can read aloud simple text or nursery rhymes accompanying the illustrations before the infant turns the page. Following the infant's pace tends to be less frustrating to the reader and the infant.

Extensions

Children should be exposed to all types of reading materials. One excellent source of children's magazines is the Canus Publishing Company. *Babybug* is a board-book magazine for infants and toddlers ages six months to two years. *Ladybug* (for ages two to six) and *Spider* (for ages six to nine) are monthly magazines containing stories, poems, songs, and games. Appendix E contains a list of publishers of children's magazines.

A c t i v i t y   9 . 2 0

Picture Cards

Level One to two

Area Communication

Interaction Adult-child

Strand Reading

Materials Needed Action pictures and photographs cut from magazines mounted on stiff paper and laminated or covered with clear adhesive vinyl

Directions for Implementation

- Look at the pictures with the toddler sitting on your lap, and tell stories about what you see.
- Involve the toddler in the story by asking him to point to the objects as you discuss them or by asking questions. When looking at a picture card of a family eating a meal, you might begin by saying, "It's time for dinner. I see a daddy handing a bowl to his daughter. I wonder what they are eating for dinner. Looks like rice. What else do you see for dinner?"

Extensions

The pages from inexpensive nursery rhyme books can be cut apart and laminated or covered with clear adhesive vinyl. Usually, this creates a two-sided card. Depending on the age of the child, spread three to five cards on the floor or table. Begin to recite one of the

nursery rhymes, and see if the child can pick out the card and finish the rhyme with you.

A c t i v i t y   9 . 2 1

Plastic Bag Books

Level Two

Area Communication

Interaction Adult-child

Strand Reading

Materials Needed Books made from plastic bags with photographs enclosed (see Appendix D, "Baggie Books," for specific directions on making the book)

Directions for Implementation

- Mount the photograph on a note card, and write a simple sentence on the bottom of each picture. Choose photographs familiar to the child, such as pictures of the children from the child-care center.
- Read the book to the child, pointing to the words written on the bottom of the cards.

Extensions

Have a parent workshop to make plastic bag books for the center. Provide the materials, and model the manuscript printing needed to describe the photographs. Use photographs taken indoors and outdoors at the child-care center and those taken on field trips.

A c t i v i t y   9 . 2 2

Sequence Pictures

Level Three and four

Area Communication

Interaction Adult-child

Strand Reading

Materials Needed Teacher-made or commercially prepared sequence cards (see Appendix D for directions for teacher-made cards)

Directions for Implementation

- Illustrate the story-line concept of beginning, middle, and end by introducing sequence cards that have three cards in the set.
- Ask the child to tell you what is happening on each card.
- Instruct the child to choose the card that shows what happened first in the sequence. Reinforce the concept of beginning by saying, "This story begins with a boy sleeping in a bed, and it is daylight outside." The middle card might show a picture of the same boy eating breakfast in his pajamas. The third card might show a picture of the boy dressed in a jacket and jeans going out the door with a school backpack. The teacher or caregiver might ask, "How do you know which picture ends this story?"
- Ask the child to tell the story from beginning to end.

Extensions

Older children can use critical thinking skills to sequence cards made from folktales and other familiar stories. Inexpensive paperback books can be taken apart and laminated to create sequence cards that are more challenging.

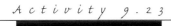

Pattern Books

Level Five and six

Area Communication

Interaction Adult-child

Strand Reading

Materials Needed Literature with a predictable pattern, such as Ed Young's Chinese fable *Seven Blind Mice* (1992)

Directions for Implementation

- Assess the child's prior knowledge of blindness before reading the story by putting an unseen, unfamiliar object in a paper bag. Select a volunteer to reach into the bag and describe the object. Ask the child, "What color is the object?" Briefly discuss what you can discover without seeing objects.
- Read the story once, and then retell the key elements of the story. The use of sentence strips and a pocket chart creates a visual aid for sequencing the story. For example, write on the first sentence strip, "On Monday, the red mouse said, 'It's a pillar.'" The second strip might read, "On Tuesday, the green mouse said, 'It's a snake.'" The story continues until Sunday.
- As a class, adapt the story by choosing a new object to be discovered by the seven blind mice, using the same pattern: "On _____, the _____ mouse said, 'It's a _____.'"

Extensions

Write a class book based on a patterned song, such as "Mary's Wearing a Red Dress." This is a traditional song that is adapted to the children in a particular class and the clothes worn by those children. The pattern of the song is as follows:

Mary's wearing a *red dress, red dress, red dress.*
Mary's wearing a *red dress* all day long.
_____'s wearing a _____, _____,
_____.

_____'s wearing a _____ all day long.

Photocopy the format. A child fills in the blanks as indicated with name and the corresponding article of clothing. After the pages are illustrated, bind the pages into a class book that can be read by many of the children in the class with minimal assistance.

A c t i v i t y   9 . 2 4

Chapter Books

Level Seven and eight

Area Communication

Interaction Adult-child

Strand Reading

Materials Needed A book from a series, such as *Ramona Quimby* by Beverly Cleary (see children's literature list)

Directions for Implementation

- Establish a regular daily read-aloud time.
- Read with expression without unnecessarily interrupting the flow of the story. Unfamiliar vocabulary can be explained briefly in context. In a group setting, encourage children to save questions and comments until the end of the session.
- At the close of the read-aloud time, allow children to make predictions about what might happen next in the story.

A c t i v i t y   9 . 2 5

Facial Expressions

Level Birth to one

Area Communication

Interaction Adult-child

Strand Nonverbal Communication

Materials Needed Large mirror

Directions for Implementation

- Hold the infant up to the mirror, and talk about your images. Say something like, "I see you. Can you find your nose? Look, I can make my nose go up and down."
- Open your mouth, and wait to see if the infant will copy you. If the infant smiles,

copy his smile and comment, "You have a happy smile on your face today."
- Talk about what you feel when you frown, look puzzled, wrinkle your nose, and so on.

Extensions

Most children are attracted to full-length mirrors. Play a mirror-image game by making a statue with your body and asking the child to make a statue just like yours. For example, you could stand with your legs spread apart and your hands clasped over your head. Ask the child to create a statue, and copy it yourself.

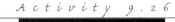

A c t i v i t y   9 . 2 6

Body Parts

Level One to two

Area Communication

Interaction Adult-child

Strand Nonverbal Communication

Materials Needed None

Directions for Implementation

- Sit on the floor opposite the toddler.
- Ask the toddler to touch his or her head. If he or she does not respond or points to another body part, try pointing to your own head, saying, "Here's my head. Where's yours?" Put the toddler's hand on top of his or her head if needed, saying, "There's your head."
- Continue playing the game, asking the child to find ears, nose, toes, and stomach. As a safety precaution, demonstrate how to gently point to eyes.

Extensions

Second-language learners who are in the pre-production stage (Krashen & Terrell, 1983) demonstrate comprehension skills by pointing. Some teachers devalue nonverbal communication skills by insisting on a verbal response. In this first stage of learning a second language, it is more important to include children in the learning setting by making them feel comfortable and allowing them to participate without risking failure. In a group setting, a teacher might ask one child to point to the type of vehicle that can be used to haul dirt to assess understanding rather than to have a child struggle in remembering the words "dump truck" in front of his peers. Another child at a higher fluency level may be asked questions that require a multiword response.

A c t i v i t y   9 . 2 7

Identifying Family Photos

Level Two

Area Communication

Interaction Adult-child

Strand Nonverbal Communication

Materials Needed Scrapbook of photographs of family members from each child's family

Directions for Implementation

- Encourage a shy child to communicate by asking questions that do not require verbal responses, such as, "Can you point to your mommy?"
- Talk about the photographs, suggesting possible scenarios that might involve the people in the photographs. Predictions can be confirmed or denied nonverbally by nodding.

Extensions

Even older children become frustrated when they cannot make themselves understood. Sometimes they do not know or remember the name of the object under discussion. Other times, they cannot articulate the speech sounds of the word they wish to express. Al-

lowing children to show, not tell, often defuses a frustrating situation for children and their parents or caregivers.

A c t i v i t y   9 . 2 8

Charades

Level Three and four

Area Communication

Interaction Adult-child

Strand Nonverbal Communication

Materials Needed A list of gestures and other types of body language that children can act out (e.g., waving good-bye, "come here," "no," "yes," angry, sad, happy, afraid, surprise)

Directions for Implementation

- In a small group setting, select a child to help you talk without using words.
- Whisper in the child's ear what you want him to demonstrate with you.
- Tell the other children to guess what you are "saying."
- Model the body language with the child. For example, "afraid" can be demonstrated with the arms up in alarm and the mouth and eyes wide open.

Extensions

Older children can demonstrate body language without needing the adult to first model it for them. Children who read can choose a message to demonstrate from a container. Instruct the other children in the group to guess the meaning of the body language.

A c t i v i t y   9 . 2 9

Making Sound Patterns

Level Five and six

Area Communication

Interaction Adult-child

Strand Nonverbal Communication

Materials Needed Drum and drumstick, open space for movement

Directions for Implementation

- Tell the children to listen to the beat of your drum. Select a child to demonstrate how to move to the pattern of your beat. After the child has demonstrated how to move slowly when the drum beats slowly and how to move quickly when the drum beats fast, encourage all of the children to move to the rhythm of the drum.
- To more easily manage a movement activity with a group of children, establish a "freeze" signal, such as a single loud drum beat or a loud clap.
- Vary the speed and loudness of the drum beat to encourage different types of movement.

Extensions

Older children can discuss the use of sounds to convey messages that may have been used earlier in history. Establish a nonverbal signal system for the classroom based on the children's suggestions.

A c t i v i t y   9 . 3 0

Mime

Level Seven and eight

Area Communication

Interaction Child-child

Strand Nonverbal Communication

Materials Needed None

Directions for Implementation

- Have children line up in pairs facing each other along a line on the playground or in a gymnasium.

- Describe the line as being an invisible wall that is transparent so that they can see through it but also a solid barrier so that they cannot reach through it. Have one line of children at a time approach the wall to "feel" it. Show them how to position their hands on the pretend flat wall. Reverse groups and have the other line of children touch the pretend wall.
- Assign one line of children to be mimes and the other line to be "mirrors." Make sure the two lines are at least a foot apart.
- Have the children move their hands up and down and side to side on the wall with the children opposite mirroring their actions. Reverse roles.

Extensions

Older children can look up books about mimes in the library. If possible, watch a mime perform on video or in person. Discuss whether it is easier to communicate with words or without words, and why.

✀ CURRICULAR IMPLICATIONS
Connections to Subject Matter Areas

It would be difficult to plan any subject matter area lesson without including at least one strand of communication development. Listening and reading are valuable skills and abilities that allow learners to access new information. Similarly, as learners integrate new information they often use speaking and writing skills to convey their understanding of concepts and processes. The phrases "reading and writing across the curriculum" and "content-area reading" convey the importance of using specialized language art skills to comprehend texts that are written in an expository style. Consequently, most curriculum planners intentionally connect or assume that communication skills are in some way tied to planning activities and experiences for young children.

Although all of the suggested activities in the communication developmental area connect to the broad area of language arts, a number of activities also link to other subject matter areas. The sequencing of pictures found in Activity 9.22 reinforces the concept of ordering based on specific criteria and keen observation, skills related to both mathematics and science. Concepts about community members and community building are usually included in the social studies curriculum of young children. Adults can encourage informal conversations at mealtimes (Activity 9.11) to engage children in thinking about ways that families and the larger community connect to a school or center. The importance of families is also promoted in "Family Photos" (Activity 9.27), in which even shy children are encouraged to communicate.

Music is another subject matter area that is frequently used to build communication skills. Listening skills can be developed in Listening to Music (Activity 9.3) and Making Sound Patterns (Activity 9.27). In particular, learning songs, fingerplays, and action rhymes enhances the oral language skills of English language learners. These learning experiences are valuable for learning new vocabulary and language structures, as illustrated in the extension suggestions found in Activity 9.23, "Pattern Books."

Similarly, drama is a subject area that combines various aspects of communication development. Children's reading fluency is enhanced by the multiple practice sessions inherent in participating in "Reader's Theater" (Activity 9.12). Teachers can readily adapt the dialogue in most narratives to a script that is read by young children rather than memorized. In a small group setting, the more experienced readers can take on the role of main characters and the narrator, and less able readers can successfully participate with shorter parts. Numerous rereadings build both reading fluency and the ability to read with expression. Similarly, plays assist children in developing oral language and nonverbal communication skills. Charades (Activity 9.28) and Mime (Activity 9.30) extend a child's ability to use facial expressions and gestures to communicate.

Connections to Thematic Planning

One theme that would engage many learners is storytelling. Stories or narratives are the foundation of early literacy programs. Preschool children might have the theme expressed as "Books tell stories." Young children are more likely to engage in an extension of this theme that includes the notion that "People tell (and write) stories to represent the past, the present, and the future." This theme can easily be connected to a study of literary genres. Children learn that folk tales, historical fiction, and biography often tell stories of a real or an imagined past. Contemporary fiction is often the basis of chapter books (Activity 9.24), and make-believe worlds found in fiction and science fiction are frequently timeless.

Infants and toddlers can be told informal stories by parents and caregivers. Board books (Activity 9.19) and Plastic Bag Books (Activity 9.21) make books accessible to the youngest children, who are often as interested in the tactile experience as they are in looking at the pictures. Preschoolers can participate in sequencing pictures (Activity 9.22), which is a foundation for learning about storyline, or plot. Adults can introduce this concept by emphasizing the beginning, middle, and end and asking what will happen next.

Young school-aged children frequently learn to read by engaging in predictable text, books that have repetitive language and story structures. When adults read pattern books (Activity 9.23) with them, emergent readers learn sight vocabulary and other word recognition strategies. Early readers practice comprehension skills when they begin to discern the imaginary from the real, as illustrated in

Fact or Fiction? (Activity 9.6). Finally, children can learn to tell stories in their writing. Participating in Author's Chair (Activity 9.18) helps a writer learn about audience. A child's peers make suggestions to improve the writer's story by asking questions related to details or offering ideas to make the story paint a better picture for the reader or listener. In summary, thematic planning heavily emphasizes integrating subject areas. Communication development plays an essential role in both methods of making curricular connections.

ᘰᕈ SUMMARY

The development of communication skills is divided into five interrelated strands: listening, speaking, writing, reading, and nonverbal communication. Listening, reading, and some forms of nonverbal communication are considered receptive language abilities. Receptive skills allow children to understand oral and written forms of language. In contrast, speaking, writing, and most forms of nonverbal communication are identified as expressive language skills. Communication skills are learned within a meaning-based social and cultural context. Children simultaneously learn about language and how to use it in a wide variety of situations.

Most children acquire language skills without direct instruction within an environment rich in oral and written forms of language. The sequence of language acquisition follows universal stages. Infants normally babble by five months of age, speak their first words at 12 months of age, and begin combining words at the age of two. By the age of three, many children use simple sentences and articulate the sounds of their home language in such a way that they are usually understood. Five-year-olds have developed most of the grammatical forms of their first language and continue to learn new vocabulary.

Helping children develop effective communication skills is probably the single most important task of parents, teachers, and caregivers. Informally, natural conversations allow children to practice listening and speaking skills. Adults also help create a language-rich environment filled with experiences and activities promoting oral and written forms of language. Reading aloud to children of all ages builds conceptual understandings and motivates children to want to learn to read for information and pleasure. Learning to write involves both fine motor control and the expression of ideas and feelings. Adults can provide a variety of experiences and activities to promote the mechanics and thought processes of writing. In short, children learn language by actively using it.

QUESTIONS AND PROJECTS FOR THE READER

1. Select an age group. Review the sample activities in each strand from the matrix of activities. Develop a new activity for each strand of communication development.
2. Discuss possible strategies for learning about culturally diverse communication styles. Find someone to interview who learned English as a second language as a child. What factors helped or hindered his or her development of English communication skills?
3. Describe the steps you would use to teach writing as a process. How does this strategy for teaching writing differ from traditional approaches?
4. Justify scheduling time to read aloud to children on a daily basis. Choose an age group, and suggest guidelines for making appropriate literature selections.
5. With a partner, simulate a conference with a parent of a kindergarten-aged student.

As the teacher, generate possible evidence for all five strands of communication development. As the parent, you can develop questions and seek suggestions for enhancing the child's communication skills.

FOR FURTHER READING

Aldridge, J., Kirkland, L., & Kuby, P. (1996). *Jump-starters: Integrating environmental print throughout the curriculum* (2nd ed.). Birmingham, AL: Campus Press. This book gives a rationale for using environmental print in early childhood classrooms and describes activities for all areas of the curriculum.

California Department of Education. (2000). *Prekindergarten learning and development guidelines.* Sacramento, CA: Author. An overview of the rationale for curricular guidelines in all developmental areas, this book includes information on nonverbal and verbal communication practices in culturally diverse communities. Guidelines for teachers and program developers in developing language and literacy are presented.

Trelease, J. (1995). *The new read-aloud handbook* (Rev. ed.). New York: Penguin. This is the most recent edition of this widely read book from a trade publisher. The benefits of reading aloud to children are documented along with numerous suggestions of outstanding books for children of all ages.

Yopp, H. K. & Yopp, R. H. (1996). *Oo-pples and boo-noo-noos: Songs and activities for phonemic awareness.* Orlando, FL: Harcourt Brace. Although the explanation of phonemic awareness and its relationship to reading and spelling achievement is brief, the authors include numerous word play activities, songs that play with sounds, and an annotated list of read-aloud books emphasizing oral manipulation of speech sounds.

Chapter Ten

Creative Development

o b j e c t i v e s

After reviewing this chapter, you will be able to

- Identify five key strands of creative development.
- Discuss stages of artistic development.
- Indicate ways that traditional subject matter areas connect to creative development.
- Select age-appropriate activities for enhancing a specific strand of creative development.
- List guidelines for adult-child verbal interactions that promote or discourage a child's creative behavior.
- Discuss the roles of teachers, caregivers, and parents in planning opportunities for developing creativity.

✌ INTRODUCTION

Creativity may reflect an ability to think divergently, or an ability to seek multiple solutions rather than a single solution to problems (Guilford & Hoepfner, 1971). Guilford (1959) identifies flexible thinking, originality, and fluency in developing ideas as traits shared by creative people. Although creativity may not have a universally accepted definition, creative behavior in both adults and children involves thinking, or cognitive skills.

Another dimension of creative development is behavioral. Getzels and Jackson (1962) noted that creative school-aged children were playful, independent, and readily able to express their feelings. The personal attributes needed to demonstrate creative thought may also tie creative development to personal-social development. Adults can promote creative development by providing open-ended materials and activities that encourage sensory exploration and manipulation of ideas (California Department of Education, 2000). The types of interaction that occur between children and adults can also nurture a child's creative expression. Adults who respect and accept a child's creative efforts may strengthen a child's resolve to express and act on unique ideas (Moyer, 1995). Lasky and Mukerji (1980) found that the courage to break with tradition and express original thoughts is common to creative expression.

For the purposes of this text, creative development has been divided into five strands: sensory/art, music, movement, dramatics, and creative writing. Creative expressions can be found in most areas of a young child's life. Parents, caregivers, and teachers should also consider block play, woodworking, storytelling, social interactions, and mathematical problem-solving experiences as opportunities for the growth of creativity.

The first strand of creative development under discussion is sensory/art. Sensory experiences, especially those related to the senses of touch and sight, may lay a foundation for the visual arts. Similarly, opportunities for sensory development may also promote fine motor skills that enhance a child's ability to use art media. Regular experiences with drawing instruments (e.g., crayons, pencils, felt pens), paint, collage, sculpture, and modeling materials allow children to experiment.

Musical activities are included in the second strand of creative development. Listening and responding to the sounds and the auditory rhythms of the environment stimulate an interest in music for many children. Children can also produce sounds vocally and with instruments. Experiences with music can readily be incorporated into home, child-care, and school settings and integrated with other activities.

Likewise, creative movement activities are easily integrated into the daily routines of most children. Specific movement activities can be planned to help children develop a sense of body awareness, force and time, space, locomotion, and weight (Sullivan, 1982). Creative movement can also be combined with music and dramatics.

Dramatic play, the fourth strand of creative development, consists of pretend play, role-play, and more formalized types of drama. Many children freely use materials and activities, such as blocks, to represent the real world in their dramatic play. An infant may pretend to feed a stuffed animal with a toy bottle. Preschool-aged children may delight in dressing up in costumes to role-play events in their daily lives. Older children can view or participate in dramatic presentations.

The fifth and final strand of creative development is creative writing. Although the mechanics of writing must be mastered to some degree before a child can write independently, the thought processes that undergird creative writing can be developed from infancy. The oral tradition of storytelling can be used by parents, caregivers, and teachers to build a sense of story. Children learn about the literary elements of character, plot, setting, mood, and theme long before they are able to identify them.

✺ KEY STRANDS OF DEVELOPMENT

Sensory/Art

The emphasis in art activities for young children is on process rather than product. Children need to discover how materials work together (Eddowes, 1995). Allowing children to freely create art with open-ended materials, such as paints, felt pens, and modeling doughs, is the most important type of art experience for young children (Schiller, 1995). Many early childhood educators consider product-oriented, pattern-directed activities to be crafts rather than art (Schirrmacher, 1993). The purpose of offering craft activities is to develop fine motor skills. In contrast, the objective of art experiences is to be creative.

Guidelines for adult interactions with children during sensory/art experiences should be founded in a genuine respect for the process orientation of creativity (California Department of Education (2000). Bos (1978) advocates a hands-off approach to working with children in the art area. Bos's "gentle guidance" approach emphasizes setting general safety and management guidelines for the use of art materials and then letting children experiment and create to their own satisfaction. Adults should also avoid making models for children because children tend to feel discouraged when they are unable to copy the adult creation. Models also inhibit a child's creativity by emphasizing uniform responses rather than unique creations.

Likewise, verbal interactions between adults and children can enhance or inhibit creativity (Trawick-Smith, 2000). Schirrmacher (1986) compares traditional approaches to responding to children's art with alternate strategies for creating dialogues with children about their art. One traditional approach focuses on complimenting children with general comments, which may lead children to conclude that all their creative efforts are the same or that the purpose of art is to please an adult. Another traditional approach focuses on the questioning strategies that adults use. Asking a child, "What are you making?" or "What is that supposed to be?" gives the underlying message that all art must be representational. Even the request to "tell me about your picture" can be overused and can intimidate some children. Schirrmacher (1986) advocates commenting on the design elements of art, such as the artwork's color, line, pattern, shape, or texture. He also promotes engaging children in dialogue about their creative efforts by listening and responding to their comments to focus the conversation.

There are two main stages of artistic development, the scribbling stage and the representational stage (Lasky & Mukerji, 1980). Spontaneous scribbling may occur as early as twelve months of age. Young toddlers can be encouraged to scribble with nontoxic felt pens on a large sheet of paper. The scribbling stage may last until the age of four. During this time, scribbling universally follows a general developmental path (Cole & Cole, 2001). The three substages of scribbling are placement patterns, implied shapes, and outlined shapes (Eddowes, 1995). In an exploration of figure-ground relationships, the young scribbler begins to place scribbles in specific places on the paper. The next substage occurs when the child draws implied shapes, for example, shapes that begin to approximate circles and other enclosed figures. With experience, the child begins to make specific shapes, such as circles, crosses, and rectangles, and to use them in patterns. Seefeldt (1995) recommends that adults make specific comments that are geared to a child's developmental level at the scribbling stage. A teacher observing a child in the process of scribbling might remark, "You've moved your marker from top to bottom in this picture."

The design phase is the beginning of the representational stage of artistic development. Most four-year-olds are moving to this first phase of recognizable art. The design phase features shapes that display balance. Suns, mandalas, faces, and other shapes with lines radiating out from them are commonly found in children's art at this phase. The second phase consists of early pictorial art, which is generally recognizable to adults. Children in this phase readily interpret drawings when they are asked to talk about their pictures. Objects in the picture tend to be unrelated to each other. In the third phase of representational art, the child uses the page to tell a story. When the child in this phase chooses to draw abstract art, it is done with relative degree of precision and planning. Seefeldt (1995) recommends that teachers and parents of children in the representational art stage comment on art elements such as line, texture, color, shape, and form.

Before the scribbling stage, however, infants can still participate in sensory activities. Infants begin to use their visual and tactile senses to explore different substances. Foods provide many experiences with texture and shape. Since infants explore most of their environment by mouthing objects, it is critical for parents and caregivers to be vigilant in providing for an infant's health and safety needs. Sensory/art activities must be nontoxic, free from sharp edges, and too large to be swallowed. Activity 10.1 features an adult-child interaction with bubbles.

Further sensory explorations for toddlers can include finger painting and play dough. Although children's paints and regular play doughs are nontoxic, one must assume infants and young toddlers will put their hands in their mouths sometime during the activity and so should be supervised closely. Activity 10.2 is a sensory exploration experience that promotes tactile stimulation.

Another example of an open-ended art medium is clay. Doughs are modeling materials frequently used in child-care and school settings because of their low cost and ease of cleanup. A number of recipes are available for play doughs, varying in texture and durability. Appendix D includes a sampling of play dough recipes. Some dough recipes lend themselves to sculpting objects that will be dried and saved. Other doughs are intended to be used only as a tactile experience. The play dough used in Activity 10.3 has a smooth texture and is readily reused when stored in an airtight container. For older children, implements such as bottle caps, tongue depressors, or a garlic press can be added to play dough activities to extend the creative play. Cookie cutters are commonly included with play dough. This tends, however, to limit the play to making cookies.

Similarly, finger painting activities take many forms. Finger painting can be done while the child is seated on a chair and limited to the tips of the fingers, or performed with gusto by standing next to the table and experimenting with various hand and arm positions. Some formulas call for liquid starch or a homemade soap mixture to which dry or liquid tempera is added. For ease of cleanup, this activity can be done outdoors or on large food service trays. Some children are hesitant and need to be gently encouraged to feel the paint. In contrast, other children volunteer to extend the activity by painting with their feet. Images of finger painting designs can be preserved by making a print with a piece of paper, as in Activity 10.4.

A common art experience involves experimenting with color. Food coloring can be added to jars of water for use in mixing colors. Eye droppers are useful for mixing small

Preschool-aged girls paint with cotton swabs.

amounts of the colored water in plastic lids or on absorbent paper. Dry and liquid tempera paints and watercolor paints can also be used for exploring color mixtures. Teachers may also add white and black paints to the easel to encourage children to discover how to make colors lighter or darker. Mixing colors and the relationships between colors can be an outgrowth of a study of weather and the natural creation of rainbows. In addition, rainbows are popular motifs in the early representational art stage. Activity 10.5 is both a sensory experience and an opportunity to discuss color as an element of art.

Sculpture is a three-dimensional art activity that should be included in the art curriculum for young children. Children can create with wood scraps, found objects, play doughs, and other objects in the art center. In the block area and in sand play, three-dimensional structures are also seen. Seven- and eight-year-olds in the representational art stage may seek guidance on using their developing physical skills to create specific items. A child may ask a teacher how she can make her sculpted figure look like it is kicking a ball. Although many early childhood educators discourage the use of teacher-made models, techniques can be modeled and ample opportunities given to experiment with materials (Seefeldt, 1995). Activity 10.6 incorporates both of these suggestions.

Music

Traditional approaches to music education for young children generally entail teacher-directed large-group sessions of singing, moving in prescribed sequences to sounds, and on occasion playing rhythm instruments. More recent approaches that include both teacher-initiated and child-initiated music activities have been advocated by Andress (1989) and Littleton (1989). Child-initiated activities might

Kindergarten children create sculptures from found objects.

include free play with musical instruments; play with music-related props, such as music stands, microphones, and conductor's batons; and play with recorded music. This type of creative play with music permits children to manipulate and experiment with sounds (California Department of Education, 2000).

Teacher-initiated music activities include large-group teacher-led sessions and sessions in which teachers guide and prompt children as individuals or in small groups (Littleton, 1989). The goal of the teacher is to expose young children to various forms of musical expression and to engage the children's curiosity and interest in musical learning. Parents and caregivers in home settings can informally create opportunities for musical play and also take advantage of free or inexpensive community-based musical opportunities. Likewise, integrating music experiences into the daily programs in child care and school reinforces its importance in the curriculum.

Andress (1989) views parents as the most effective teachers of music for infants and young toddlers. When a bond of love and trust is firmly established, the young child is free to participate with spontaneity and enthusiasm. The interaction is also personalized for the particular needs of the child. In Activity 10.7, infants are introduced to the production of sound. When lying on her or his back, the five-month-old tends to reach for his or her feet. Bell bands placed on the ankles at this stage of development capitalize on the infant's fascination.

The second year of life is characterized by a remarkable rate of growth in an infant's receptive and expressive language skills. A language-rich environment promotes growth in this area. Singing as an alternative to speaking can also serve as an opportunity to expose children to vocal play (Gardner, 1983). The child hears and may even imitate these pleasurable vocalizations. Singing is likewise a means of conveying a family's cultural traditions to children, as suggested in the extensions to Activity 10.8.

Although the tones created by tapping and pinging kitchen equipment and utensils may not always be pleasing to the ears, this exploration of sound production is an easily implemented and readily accessible activity in most homes. Pitch, loudness, duration, and timbre are four characteristics of sound related to musical awareness (Burton, 1989). Parents and caregivers can verbally label sounds that are high and low, loud and soft, long and short, and similar and different as the toddler explores potential instruments for a kitchen band in Activity 10.9 or in the guided listening experience in Activity 10.10.

Young children learn singing skills and language skills through songs. The receptive language skills of listening and reading can be promoted by helping children connect visual symbols to auditory messages. Although learning all songs by combining reading and singing would be frustrating to beginning readers, teaching a few repetitive songs in this manner is one way of integrating the language arts with music. In addition, songs with repetitive patterns are particularly suit-

able for second-language learners, as noted in Activity 10.11.

Acquainting children with the sounds made by musical instruments is a goal of many music education programs. Learning instruments by groups (e.g., wind, strings, percussion) may help children connect the sounds they hear to the mechanics of producing the sounds. Likewise, hands-on experience with instruments is recommended over viewing two-dimensional pictures or photographs of the instruments. In schools without music programs, teachers may be able to tap into parental or community sources for people willing to demonstrate different types of instruments. Music is also an area that offers opportunities for exploring diverse cultures, as noted in Activity 10.12.

Movement

Movement activities can be a natural extension of music appreciation, or they can be viewed as a creative extension of gross motor physical development. Many young children participate in movement spontaneously and without hesitation. Other children, especially older children, may become self-conscious

Children of various ages in a family child-care home play musical instruments.

when others observe their movement activities. Sullivan (1982) has excellent suggestions for teachers who are setting up movement programs that encourage creativity. In planning the environment for movement activities, Sullivan first recommends that teachers and caregivers choose spaces that are not readily accessible to passersby and other observers. She believes that uninvited watchers may sometimes inhibit the creativity of teachers and children.

Second, Sullivan (1982) proposes specific techniques for dealing with children who attempt to ridicule others. A serious look or a quiet word may be sufficient to deter teasing, or a child may need to be taken aside for a private discussion. Since creative movement may involve taking risks, under no circumstances should children be allowed to belittle one another.

In cultures all over the world, dance is a natural outgrowth of the rhythm of music. Dance forms can be inspired by the types of music that are played as well as the social aspects of a culture. Parents, as the primary transmitters of culture, convey their interests and preferences to their children. For most infants, dancing with a parent is a pleasurable activity—no matter what type of music is being played. A parent-child interaction that involves dancing is described in Activity 10.13.

In the second year of life, many children make tremendous strides in physical agility. An infant who takes the first steps at twelve months of age will undoubtedly be walking well by twenty-four months. Although walking becomes the favored means of locomotion, crawling skills may still be employed. As skills are mastered, they have the potential for being used creatively. The skilled crawler is ready for experimenting with different types of crawling movements. Although the movement activity described in Activity 10.14 can be done without music, the use of music may inspire the adult participant to be more creative.

Other daily and classroom activities may inspire movement experiences. A visit to a farm or the zoo may stimulate parents and caregivers to plan movement activities in which children reenact the movements of animals. A discussion of weather may lead to simulating trees being blown by the wind. A ride on a train or a bus may be recaptured as a movement activity. In Activity 10.15, watching popcorn being popped is the stimulus for a creative movement experience.

Props are often added to motivate and enhance movement activities. Metz (1989) found that some props did not enhance movements related to the music being played in a prekindergarten class session. Children needed concrete associations between the prop and the music to connect it to a specific body movement. For example, the ticking of a clock encouraged children to swing back and forth when they viewed a pendulum moving back and forth in a rhythmic pattern. Although young children may use scarves in variety of creative ways, merely adding them to a music learning center does not ensure that they are used for creative movement. Activity 10.16 allows preschool children the opportunity to experiment with various movements using scarves.

Activities developed to build strength empower children and enhance a sense of confidence (Sullivan, 1982). Many young children want to be strong and powerful. The images of movie and television superheroes are based on physical strength. A superhero may also have superior mental powers but may be portrayed as evil or violent. Gender biases may influence the ways that parents, caregivers, and teachers view physical strength and the value they place on planning activities that promote strength. Sullivan (1982) advocates that teachers plan creative movement activities that help children feel personal strength, learn to focus strength, and use it constructively. Activity 10.17 is a strength-building activity.

Children can participate in creative movement activities as individuals and as members of cooperative groups. Young children tend to imitate the movements of others when they experiment with unfamiliar movements. One child's idea may stimulate another child to come up with a totally new idea. Working in groups also benefits personal-social development when children practice problem-solving skills. The teacher can assign a physical challenge that can be accomplished only by working together as a team. Activity 10.18 presents this type of challenge.

Dramatics

Donoghue (1990) distinguishes between children's theater and creative drama. Creative drama, as an informal, process-driven form of behavior, is the primary focus of the dramatic strand of creative development. Children learn to use props, sometimes even imaginary ones, to represent real objects. Behavior and dialogue are spontaneous, allowing any child who has the desire to participate. In contrast, children's theater is considered to be drama performed for children (Donoghue, 1990). The sixth sample activity in this strand, Activity 10.24, approaches the performance arena of dramatics.

Near the end of an infant's first year of life, a parent or caregiver may entice an infant to pretend to replicate a familiar task. Young children tend to be expert imitators. If a father pretending to drink coffee from a cup hands his daughter an empty cup, she may bring it to her lips and pretend to drink. This precursor to dramatics is also promoted in Activity 10.19 in the form of role playing.

With improved walking skills, toddlers can pull, push, and carry objects around with them in their play activities. Toy shopping carts, wagons, and other wheeled vehicles are used to haul items from place to place. At this time, toddlers may also demonstrate an interest in transferring objects in and out of diaper bags, purses, and similar carryalls. These exploratory activities tend to be prohibited by parents and other family members, especially after a toddler has misplaced car keys or other valuable items. In an effort to appease a curious toddler and teach her about personal ownership of property, a parent may give the toddler a carryall for his or her own use, as illustrated in Activity 10.20.

Another possibility for toddlers to participate in dramatic play is the use of puppets. To make use of an object in pretend play, a child must be familiar with it in the real world. Many children are interested in and know about the behaviors of common animals. They may know how animals move, the sounds that they make, and some of their normal habits. Parents and caregivers can lead children to act out this knowledge by using an animal puppet (Activity 10.21).

Home and school settings may also provide areas for dramatic play. A dress-up trunk or an outdoor play house may contain clothing and props suitable for acting out family

Teacher and child pretend to talk on the telephone to one another.

roles. The makeshift fort or the ship made from an appliance box stimulates a different type of action and adventure. In preschool and primary-grade classrooms, dramatic play centers can augment thematic units of study. A field trip to a veterinarian may spark the creation of a stuffed animal treatment center. The large block area might be used another day to re-create a ride on the bus. Children and adults can work together to rotate props and improvise new themes for role playing and creative dramatics. Adults who interact with children in dramatic play should be cautioned to follow the creative lead of child participants rather than try to direct the play. Learning centers for older children may reinforce recently acquired reading, writing, and mathematical skills. A popular dramatic play theme may be a restaurant, as illustrated in Activity 10.22.

In addition to dramatic play and block centers, creative drama may occur in sandboxes. On a limited scale, an indoor sand table may provide space for several children to create a model of a familiar or imaginary scene. Hearing a teacher read aloud *The Boxcar Children* (Warner, 1942) may inspire a group of children to re-create the children's camp in the sand table. In dramatic play, teachers should allow children to take the lead and should support their choices for creating settings and themes in their play. The teacher can also stimulate creative thinking by asking open-ended questions. A large outdoor sand area offers endless possibilities for carrying out dramatic play.

An experience with children's theater as a member of the audience may spark an interest in the performance side of dramatics. Involving children in the creation of an original play or in the reenactment of a traditional story provides opportunities to integrate language arts skills with the performing arts. The practice of reading or speaking with expression builds communication skills. In addition, learning to portray emotions assists in the development of nonverbal communication abilities. Activity 10.24 suggests teaching strategies for helping students learn to write dialogue.

Creative Writing

The fifth and final strand of creative development is creative writing. A critical foundation of this process is to expose children to the art of storytelling. Creative writing captures the imagination of the reader by its ability to paint word pictures. Hearing and understanding stories from an early age builds background knowledge for expressing ideas creatively.

In addition, cultural knowledge is passed down through generations in part by the telling and retelling of family stories. Informally, children learn about values and customs from parents and family members, particularly in cultures that have strong oral traditions (Trawick-Smith, 2000). Oral societies place heavy emphasis on memory skills for remembering what has been told and on group learning settings because the storyteller needs an audience (Diaz-Rico & Weed, 1995).

Infants and toddlers learn language by hearing it spoken in meaningful contexts. Conversing with an infant or toddler by telling stories is one means of conveying knowledge and exposing children to this language form. Activities 10.25 and 10.26 involve parents or caregivers in informal storytelling. A puppet is used as a prop in Activity 10.25, and a board book serves as the springboard for interaction in Activity 10.26. Stories can also be told and retold using felt pieces on a flannel board.

The cognitive and communication components of creative writing may lie in the imaginative expression of ideas. By being authors, children learn that writing is not just meant to be read but to be understood (Adams, 1992; Morrow & Gambrell, 1998). Another component of creative writing concerns the physical ability to write. In turn, the mechanical aspects of writing are built on abilities to use writing tools and to replicate symbols. Activity 10.27 is planned to allow the child to experience both the use of a writing tool and the creation of pictorial symbols.

Books can also be used to teach children about storytelling. Story lines are skillfully developed in text and illustration in many picture books. After children have had experience identifying the beginning, middle, and end of stories, they may be ready to create their own endings for stories that have been read to them. The adult reader can encourage children to think about other ways the stories might have ended and ask children to indicate a preference for an ending. The teacher models the creation of an ending to a story that has been partially read to a group of children in Activity 10.28.

Viewing photographs and pictures can also prompt creative writing. By the age of five, many children are familiar with the process of looking at book illustrations to interpret meaning and add context to a story. When children reach the representational art picture stage, they use their own drawings to tell stories. Teachers can build on a child's ability to analyze and interpret pictures by planning activities such as the one described in Activity 10.29.

Some primary-grade teachers have begun to adopt writing workshop strategies in their language arts curricula (Tompkins, 2001). Atwell (1998) has identified principles to guide teachers as they plan for creative writing. Teachers need to allow extended time for children to write on topics of their choice (Atwell). Children also need children and adults to respond to their writing during the composing process, and children should learn the mechanics of writing in context (Atwell). These and other principles of teaching writing help teachers, parents, and children see that writing is a process rather than an act that produces a finished product in a single session.

Activity 10.30 outlines a plan for teaching writing.

Table 10.1 is a matrix correlating all the activities described in this chapter with the appropriate ages and developmental strands.

❧ AGE-APPROPRIATE ACTIVITIES: BIRTH THROUGH EIGHT YEARS

A c t i v i t y   1 0 . 1

Fun with Bubbles

Level Birth to one

Area Creative

Interaction Adult-child

Strand Sensory/Art

Materials Needed Bubble solution made from tearless shampoo, bubble pipe made from a Styrofoam cup and a straw

Directions for Implementation

- In a margarine tub, mix one capful of shampoo to one-half cup of water. Construct the adult's bubble pipe by using a sharp object to poke a small hole in the side of the cup near the base. Insert a straw.
- Place the bubble solution out of the infant's reach.
- Dip the upside-down cup into the bubble solution. Turn right side up, and blow bubbles.
- Allow the infant to explore the bubbles through the senses of sight and touch.

Extensions

Older children can blow bubbles on their own or try painting with bubbles. Color the bubble solution with food coloring, and allow it to stand overnight. Use the homemade bubble pipe or a purchased bubble wand to blow colored bubbles on white paper. Create several colors of the bubble solution to add interest.

Table 10.1 Creative development activities matrix.

Age(Years)	Sensory/Art	Music	Movement	Dramatics	Creative Writing
Birth to one	Fun with Bubbles Activity 10.1 Adult-Child	Ankle Bell Bands Activity 10.7 Child-object	Dancing with Baby Activity 10.13 Adult-child	Feeding Dolly Activity 10.19 Adult-child	Puppet Stories Activity 10.25 Adult-child
One to two	Texture Box Activity 10.2 Child-object	Sing, Sing, Sing Activity 10.8 Adult-child	Creepy Crawlers Activity 10.14 Adult-child	Carryalls Activity 10.20 Child-object	Tell Me a Story Activity 10.26 Adult-child
Two	Play Dough Activity 10.3 Child-object	Kitchen Band Activity 10.9 Child-object	Popcorn Activity 10.15 Adult-child	Animal Puppets Activity 10.21 Adult-child	Story Starters Activity 10.27 Adult-child
Three and four	Table Painting Activity 10.4 Child-object	Guided Listening Activity 10.10 Child-child	Dancing with Scarves Activity 10.16 Child-object	Restaurant Activity 10.22 Child-child	Group Stories Activity 10.28 Adult-child
Five and six	Rainbow Making Activity 10.5 Adult-child	Sing a Song Activity 10.11 Child-child	Showing Strength Activity 10.17 Child-child	Sand Play Activity 10.23 Child-child	Picture Stories Activity 10.29 Child-object
Seven and eight	Foil Sculptures Activity 10.6 Child-object	Making Instruments Activity 10.12 Adult-child	Building Bridges Activity 10.18 Child-child	Writing Plays Activity 10.24 Adult-child	Stories of My Own Activity 10.30 Child-object

A c t i v i t y   1 0 . 2

Texture Box

Level One to two

Area Creative

Interaction Child-object

Strand Sensory/Art

Materials Needed Cardboard box (approximately 1 × 2 × 2 feet), white glue, variety of fabrics and papers with different textures, such as smooth vinyl, corrugated cardboard, carpet, satin, sandpaper, velvet, corduroy, and foil

Directions for Implementation

- Tape the box closed, and securely glue a variety of materials to the outside of the box.
- Allow young toddlers to freely explore the textures on the box.
- Talk to the toddlers as they touches the textures, supplying verbal labels for the different textures, for example, rough, smooth, bumpy, ridged, soft, hard, grainy, and so on.

Extensions

Fill sensory tables for older children with different textures of sand, cat litter, packing beads, soapy water, and so on. Sometimes individual dish tubs can be set up for solitary or partner play. Props for pouring, lifting, and spooning can be added to various-sized containers to extend the activity.

A c t i v i t y   1 0 . 3

Play Dough

Level Two

Area Creative

Interaction Child-object

Strand Sensory/Art

Materials Needed Homemade cooked play dough (see Appendix D for instructions on making play dough), optional assortment of plastic utensils, small rolling pins, and other tools

Directions for Implementation

- Play alongside of the toddler without making models. Knead, roll, pat, flatten, pinch, and squish the play dough with your hands.
- Vary the experience on other occasions by providing tools.

Extensions

Although cooked play dough can be stored for months in an airtight container, eventually a clean batch is needed. Older children can then use it to create play dough sculptures that can be left in the air to dry. Toothpicks, packing beads, small rocks, and other items can be added for variety.

A c t i v i t y   1 0 . 4

Table Painting

Level Three and four

Area Creative

Interaction Child-object

Strand Sensory/Art

Materials Needed Washable table surfaces or large plastic trays, shaving cream, tempera, paper, and paint smocks

Directions for Implementation

- Squirt shaving cream on the table or tray, and sprinkle a small amount of tempera on the mound.
- Encourage the child to finger paint as desired.
- To make a print of the design, place a sheet of paper directly on top of it, and press

gently. Lift the paper to see a reverse image.

Extensions

Older children can experiment with reverse images that result from this printing process. Have the child write her name on the table in finger paint and make a print. Give the child the opportunity to figure out how to write a word on the table that prints correctly. If the child needs a hint, begin with the word "bob" and then "boy," to encourage the child to think about which letters change, why they change, and what happens to the order of the letters. Focus on the child's discovery of the process rather than on telling the answers.

A c t i v i t y   1 0 . 5

Rainbow Making

Level Five and six

Area Creative

Interaction Adult-child

Strand Sensory/Art

Materials Needed Two quart-sized zip-locked plastic bags, food coloring (red, yellow, blue), goop (see Appendix D for goop recipe)

Directions for Implementation

- Spoon the goop evenly into the two bags. Close the bag, removing most of the air. Carefully spread out the mixture with your hands until it fills the space across the bottom of the bag.
- Carefully reopen the bag, and add the food coloring as follows: center section, four to five drops of yellow; right edge, four to five drops of blue; left edge, four to five drops of red.
- Reclose the bag, and tape shut if necessary.
- Work the food coloring into the goop, creating a rainbow effect when the colors com-

bine (red, orange, yellow, green, blue, indigo, and violet).

Extensions

Younger children can combine small amounts of primary-colored play dough to create secondary colors. Older children can use eyedroppers and colored water to experiment with color mixing.

A c t i v i t y   1 0 . 6

Foil Sculptures

Level Seven and eight

Area Creative

Interaction Child-object

Strand Sensory/Art

Materials Needed Cardboard bases, glue, scissors, aluminum foil

Directions for Implementation

- Provide materials, and discuss alternative techniques for shaping foil. Give suggestions on request about techniques for creating certain features by manipulating scraps of foil.
- Allow time to experiment with crushing, tearing, folding, and bending.

Extensions

Younger children usually prefer abstract art. Provide junk materials for sculpting, such as toilet paper rolls, fabric scraps, yarn pieces, and toothpicks. Creations can be painted or left unpainted.

A c t i v i t y   1 0 . 7

Ankle Bell Bands

Level Birth to one

Area Creative

Interaction Child-object

Strand Music

Materials Needed Pieces of elastic (5–8 inches long × 5/8–3/4 inches wide), four to six jingle bells

Directions for Implementation

- Measure elastic for ankle bands or wrist bands. Sew ends together.
- *Securely* sew bells to elastic.
- When the infant is in a playful mood, put the bands on the baby's ankles or wrists. Talk to the baby about music when the baby moves.

Extensions

Older children can dance to music wearing the bells, or they can shake them in time to the beat while they sing. The cuffs from a worn-out pair of socks can also be used for the ankle or wrist bands. Cut off the cuffs, and sew the bells around the cuffs.

Activity 1 0 . 8

Sing, Sing, Sing

Level One to two

Area Creative

Interaction Adult-child

Strand Music

Materials Needed None

Directions for Implementation

- At times during the course of the day, sing to the baby instead of talking.
- Vary the tempo, pitch, and volume to match the activity. For example, make your voice go up the scale as you go up the stairs, making up words as you climb, "Up, up, up, we climb the stairs."

Extensions

Sing lullabies as you rock children to settle them down for naps or bedtime. See Appendix E for sources of lullabies and other songs for children. Songs are also effectively used during transitions with older children.

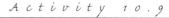

Activity 1 0 . 9

Kitchen Band

Level Two

Area Creative

Interaction Child-object

Strand Music

Materials Needed Kitchen equipment and utensils that are free from sharp edges, such as cooling racks, wooden spoons, saucepans and lids, cookie sheet; music source (e.g., tape recorder, radio)

Directions for Implementation

- Experiment with equipment and utensils that can be tapped, strummed, beat, or otherwise used to create a sound.
- Play music that has a definite beat. March through the house or outdoors, playing one of the newly created instruments for a kitchen band.
- Model tapping to the music and marching to the beat.

Extensions

Older children like to create sound effects for plays and skits. Shaking a piece of aluminum foil might simulate thunder. Empty coconut shells cut in half could be used to create the sound of horse's hooves when they are clapped on a tabletop or the floor. Encourage the children to think of everyday objects that make sounds. Tape-record a skit with sound effects.

A c t i v i t y   1 0 . 1 0

Guided Listening

Level Three and four

Area Creative

Interaction Adult-child

Strand Music

Materials Needed Recorded orchestral music; tape, record, or CD player

Directions for Implementation

- Sit in a circle with a group of children. Space the children far enough apart to allow them to freely move their arms. Use exaggerated arm movements to model fast and slow tempos.
- Stand up and run or walk in pace with the tempo of the music.
- After the concept of fast and slow is established, help the children learn to identify high and low pitches and soft and loud volume changes.

Extensions

Guided listening activities can be developed for older children to identify specific musical instruments. Introduce the actual instruments and the unique sounds each makes. If music specialists are not available on staff, enlist parents and other community members to play for the children.

A c t i v i t y   1 0 . 1 1

Sing a Song

Level Five and six

Area Creative

Interaction Child-child

Strand Music

Materials Needed Pocket chart, sentence strips, felt pens

Directions for Implementation

- Choose a favorite children's song, such as "I Know an Old Woman Who Swallowed a Fly," that has repetitive patterns.
- Make sentence strips for the song. Include symbols next to key words for second-language learners to facilitate comprehension.
- Teach the song visually and by singing it line by line.
- During free time, children can put the strips in the pocket chart and sing their favorite songs.
- As a group activity, create new lines for the song, for example, "I know an old man who swallowed a rabbit. Just by habit, he swallowed that rabbit. I wished he grabbed it."

Extensions

Singing songs is an excellent vocabulary-building exercise for first- and second-language learners. Younger and older children profit from singing activities. Adding creative movements to singing activities likewise increases their comprehensibility.

A c t i v i t y   1 0 . 1 2

Making Instruments

Level Seven and eight

Area Creative

Interaction Adult-child

Strand Music

Materials Needed Clean clay flowerpot with a 6-inch diameter, crepe paper, four thick rubber bands sized to fit tightly around the top of the pot

Directions for Implementation

- Help the child make a Middle Eastern tambour-type drum by having her cut a 9-inch circle from crepe paper.
- Demonstrate carefully stretching the crepe paper evenly to create a thin membrane-like surface for the top of the drum.
- Place the thin paper circle on top of the pot, and secure tightly with the thick rubber bands.
- Hold the drum under the arm with an elbow and beat it with alternating hands for a hollow drum sound to accompany Middle Eastern music.

Extensions

Borrow or collect ethnic folk instruments to use with music and movement activities. See Appendix D for instructions for making other homemade instruments, such as maracas, guiros, and castanets.

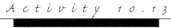

Dancing with Baby

Level Birth to one

Area Creative

Interaction Adult-child

Strand Movement

Materials Needed Radio or tape player

Directions for Implementation

- Hold the baby or carry her in a front pack and dance around the room.
- Depending on the baby's response to the activity, vary your movements. Older babies may enjoy more bouncing movements.

Extensions

Some exercise and dance videos are created for family participation. Older children can

also learn dance patterns that are taught in segments. The use of full-length mirrors allows children to match perceived body motions to actual body motions.

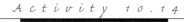

Creepy Crawlers

Level One to two

Area Creative

Interaction Adult-child

Strand Movement

Materials Needed Spooky or suspenseful music; record, tape, or CD player

Directions for Implementation

- Model crawling around the room, pausing in response to the music. Encourage the toddler to follow you.
- Stop and turn from side to side to look around in wonder.
- Experiment with different kinds of crawling, for example, on the stomach, knees, or elbows and knees. Reverse roles, and copy the movements of the toddler.

Extensions

Older children can create movement activities to different types of music. In group settings, teachers sometimes hesitate to plan movement activities that may inspire children to lose self-control. Begin movement sessions by defining physical boundaries and behavioral expectations. The emphasis should be on safety as well as creativity. Establishing an effective "freeze" signal helps teachers and children feel in control. Specific instructions for teaching the freeze signal can be found in *Feeling Strong, Feeling Free: Movement Exploration for Young Children* (Sullivan, 1982).

Popcorn

Level Three and four

Area Creative

Interaction Adult-Child

Strand Movement

Materials Needed Hot-air popcorn popper, popcorn, large clean bedsheet or tablecloth

Directions for Implementation

- Spread the large sheet on the floor, and place the popcorn popper without the lid in the center of sheet.
- Seat the children with their legs crossed around the edges of the sheet without touching it.
- Show the children the unpopped kernels, and discuss how the heat is going to make kernels change. Discuss safety rules including the need to stay off the sheet and to wait until you remove the hot air popper to eat the popcorn.
- Have the children scrunch down and listen for the kernels to pop. When they hear a pop, they pop up and scrunch back down to wait for the next one. The popping starts slowly, proceeds rapidly, and then trails off.
- To end the activity, scoop the popcorn into small paper cups and eat. (Safety note: Children must remain seated while eating.)

Extensions

Older children will be able to think of other ways of popping up to simulate the corn popping. After eating the popcorn, re-create the tempo of popping with a drum to experiment with the children's suggestions for popping movements.

Dancing with Scarves

Level Two

Area Creative

Interaction Child-object

Strand Movement

Materials Needed Scarves for each child, music source

Directions for Implementation

- Introduce the activity by having the children stand in a large circle facing one another, an arm's length apart.
- As the music plays, wave the scarf to the music and watch how other children move their scarves. Imitate a child's idea, remarking, "Kara is circling her scarf above her head. It looks like it's floating in the air."
- Play follow the leader, moving with the scarves, or encourage children to move at will, dancing with their scarves.

Extensions

Streamers attached to short dowel sticks require more coordination as a creative movement prop. Experiment with types of motions that allow the stream to flow rather than getting tangled. Long ribbons are used in a form of Chinese dancing. They are also one of the props in Olympic rhythmic gymnastics.

Showing Strength

Level Five and six

Area Creative

Interaction Child-child

Strand Movement

Materials Needed None

Directions for Implementation

- Before the activity begins, ask the children if they have ever tried to push over a big rock. Have the children think of other objects that are sturdy and difficult to move.
- Ask for a volunteer to help you demonstrate this activity. Tell the children you are going to help them learn to use their strength. Instruct the child to kneel on her hands and knees on the ground.
- Talk about how being close to the ground helps to form a solid base. Tell the child you are going to push on her but that you do not want to tip her over. Ask her to use her strength to resist. Push gently at first until the child understands how to center her energy to resist your pushing. Move around the child, and try to push firmly from other angles.
- Pair children by height and weight for participating in this activity. Have one person be the solid object and the partner, the tester. Tell the children to practice being strong and to remember that the objective is to push hard but not push the partner over. Children then change places.

Extensions

Another activity for testing strength is to build different kinds of walls with people. Form groups of four, matching height and weight as closely as possible. Ask one group to stand on a line, approximately a foot apart. Have them extend their arms and grasp hands as well as spread their legs to touch feet. Ask another group of four to stand side by side on a line with their elbows interlocked. Gently test the strength of each wall. Ask the children to create a solid wall with their bodies that would be very difficult to tip over.

Activity 1 0 . 1 8

Building Bridges

Level Seven and eight

Area Creative

Interaction Child-child

Strand Movement

Materials Needed Open space marked with two long lines made out of rope or tape

Directions for Implementation

- Begin with the lines approximately 18 inches apart. Have the children each think of ways they can bridge the two lines with their bodies. Point out unusual solutions to help children to think creatively.
- Move the lines farther apart to promote physically challenging solutions to bridging the space so that at least one part of the body is touching the other line.
- Allow the children to choose partners, and move the lines farther apart. The challenge is to work as a team to bridge the space between the lines and remain connected to each other.

Extensions

The activity can be adapted for younger children by using hula hoops. Challenge the children to think of ways to make part of their bodies be inside the circle and part outside of the circle. Recognize creative solutions that other children might like to try by saying, "Janelle has her feet inside the circle and is touching the outside of the circle only with her head."

Activity 1 0 . 1 9

Feeding Dolly

Level Birth to one

Area Creative

Interaction Adult-child

Strand Dramatics

Materials Needed Plastic dishes, eating utensils, doll

Directions for Implementation

- Place the doll in a sitting position, and ask the infant to help you feed the baby.
- Pretend to spoon food into the doll's mouth. Hand the spoon to the infant, saying, "He's still hungry, Brian. Can you give him something to eat?"
- Pretend to give the doll a drink out of a cup. Try to engage the infant in role-playing.

Extensions

Infants and toddlers may role-play with everyday objects in familiar settings. Other settings familiar to children in this age group are bathing, sleeping, and comforting routines. Preschool-aged and young school-aged children's role-playing abilities reflect developing cognitive skills and life experiences. Older children can use more abstract props in their pretend play. In multiage group settings, children also learn by observing older playmates taking roles.

A c t i v i t y   1 0 . 2 0

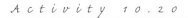

Carryalls

Level One to two

Area Creative

Interaction Child-object

Strand Dramatics

Materials Needed Small containers with handles, such as purses, lunch boxes, brief cases, or tote bags; baby-safe items to put in the container, such as keys, comb, small toy, or paper

Directions for Implementation

- Create a personalized carryall for the young toddler who is confident in walking. Find a carryall that can be opened and closed easily and that is not too cumbersome to carry around.
- Talk to the toddler about the items in the personal container.

Extensions

Children like to imitate older children, especially siblings, by using the same type of objects. An extra lunch box for the toddler who has a lunch box–toting older brother may make morning time transitions from home to school more pleasant for the family. In a group child-care setting where keeping track of personal objects is challenging, the carryall can be stored in the cubbie for the day. Older children can use small suitcases when they pretend to go on a trip or visit a relative.

A c t i v i t y   1 0 . 2 1

Animal Puppets

Level Two

Area Creative

Interaction Adult-child

Strand Dramatics

Materials Needed Hand puppets that depict animals familiar to toddlers (preferably puppets with movable mouths)

Directions for Implementation

- Choose a puppet, such as a dog, that makes a sound familiar to the child.
- Pretend to make the dog bark, saying, "Woof, Woof! Rusty wants inside. Can you open the door?"
- Try to entice the toddler into taking the puppet from you and making animal

noises. You might say, "Oh dear, why is that dog barking now? It must be time to feed Rusty."

- If the child seems interested in using the dog puppet, you could put on the cat puppet to continue the play by adding, "Meow, Meow, your barking woke me up. I was trying to take a catnap."

Extensions

Puppets can sometimes be used to prompt a reluctant child to speak. Asking the puppet a question, rather than the child, relieves the pressure to respond. Puppets can also be used to act out familiar stories. Even when children know the story line, they may need help organizing dialogue. For example, when Little Red Riding Hood and the Wolf meet in the forest, the Wolf might ask, "Why are you picking flowers, little girl?" Prompt the child, if necessary, to think about where she is going and for whom she is picking the flowers.

A c t i v i t y   1 0 . 2 2

Restaurant

Level Three and four

Area Creative

Interaction Child-child

Strand Dramatics

Materials Needed Variety of unused containers from local fast-food restaurants, plastic food props, serving trays, note pads, pencils, cash register, and other restaurant props

Directions for Implementation

- Dramatic play areas can be rotated throughout the year and can fit thematic unit plans. When planning a unit on the community, you might take the children on a walking field trip through the neighborhood to acquaint children with the stores,

restaurants, and other businesses in the area.

- Introduce the new theme to the dramatic play area of the classroom by demonstrating items in the center or by role-playing with small groups of children.

Extensions

Dramatic play areas give older children opportunities to practice written language skills and mathematics. Possibilities for theme-related dramatic play centers include shoe stores, repair shops, buses, fire stations, and post offices. As a health precaution, note that some group programs discourage the use of hats and wigs in dramatic play areas to prevent the spread of lice. Dramatic play centers also give second-language learners informal opportunities to develop vocabulary and practice conversational skills.

A c t i v i t y   1 0 . 2 3

Sand Play

Level Five and six

Area Creative

Interaction Child-child

Strand Dramatics

Materials Needed Outdoor sand area; containers and tools for molding and building with sand; props such as trucks, cars, street signs

Directions for Implementation

- Add water to the play area if the sand is too dry for shaping.
- The addition of props before a play theme develops may lead children to choose a particular theme; observe and wait for the play to begin.
- Children are empowered when adults support their play by making suggestions and verbal observations as requested by the

children. A typical scenario includes a child frustrated by her efforts to tunnel under a mound of sand who exclaims, "This never works!" You might suggest making the sand wetter or supporting the sides of the tunnel with scraps of wood.

Extensions

Sand play for younger children may consist mainly of digging holes and building mounds. Adults and children may interact verbally in this play setting by pretending to cover and uncover hidden objects.

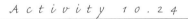
A c t i v i t y   1 0 . 2 4

Writing Plays

Level Seven and eight

Area Creative

Interaction Adult-child

Strand Dramatics

Materials Needed Chart paper and felt pens, props as needed

Directions for Implementation

- An introductory experience to playwriting can involve retelling a familiar historical event, a folktale, or a favorite story. Begin by identifying the characters and describing the setting in detail. Try to create the feeling that the students are actually in the setting before writing the dialogue.
- Write the dialogue between the characters in small group settings. Ask, "Who talks first? To whom is the character speaking? What is the character saying?" as you write the character's name on the chart.
- Listen for suggestions, and paraphrase, if needed, line by line.
- If a classroom computer is available, enlist a parent volunteer or teacher aide to transcribe the dialogue for use in practicing lines.

Extensions

Five- and six-year-olds also enjoy participating in dramas and reenactments. Planning for group responses permits greater participation and allows shy children to take part in the play without the pressure to perform.

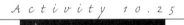
A c t i v i t y   1 0 . 2 5

Puppet Stories

Level Birth to one

Area Creative

Interaction Adult-child

Strand Creative Writing

Materials Needed Hand puppets with movable mouths

Directions for Implementation

- Use the puppet to tell a story to the infant. Make up the story as you go along or retell a recent event.
- Sit in a chair, holding the baby on your lap to one side. Put the puppet on your other hand, and talk to the baby through the puppet, using the baby's name in the story. For example, you might say, "Amanda, you had such a big lunch today, sitting in your high chair eating bananas. First you washed your hands, and then you ate, and then got your hands and face washed all over again. Amanda, you are learning to eat all by yourself."

Extensions

Storytelling has traditionally been an important method of passing on cultural knowledge and promoting creativity. Learning to listen to and understand stories begins in early childhood and continues throughout life. Some families and cultures place a higher value on the art of storytelling than others.

Activity 10.26

Tell Me a Story

Level One to two

Area Creative

Interaction Adult-child

Strand Creative Writing

Materials Needed Simple picture books with limited text

Directions for Implementation

- Many picture books for young toddlers have limited text to accompany the illustrations. Parents and caregivers can use this as an opportunity to make up stories to go along with the pictures.
- Starting stories with "once upon a time" cues children into understanding that someone is making up or retelling a story.
- Look at the picture book, and make up stories based on the illustrations. For example, on one page of a board book, there is a photograph of a father giving his baby a bath; the storyteller might begin by saying, "Once upon a time, there was a daddy and a little boy named Jeremy. Well, the daddy and the little boy were playing outside, and when the daddy turned his head, Jeremy fell right into the mud. This little baby was so dirty that the daddy said, 'Jeremy, you need a bath right now!' He filled up the tub and. . .'"

Extensions

Occasionally, preschool children get the mistaken notion that making up stories is the same as lying. Young children understand language literally rather than figuratively. The difference between being dishonest by making up a story and telling stories as a creative act may have to be explained. Encourage parents to retell favorite family stories to preserve family history.

Activity 10.27

Story Starters

Level Two

Area Creative

Interaction Adult-child

Strand Creative Writing

Materials Needed Bar crayons (see Appendix D for instructions on making crayons), paper, and flat, textured objects, such as leaves

Directions for Implementation

- Tape a leaf to the table. Place a sheet of paper over the leaf. Tape if needed.
- Use the crayon bars to transfer the design of the leaf onto the paper by rubbing back and forth.
- Make rubbings from other flat objects.
- Start a story using the rubbings for ideas. Ask the child to tell you what happens next. For example, "Once upon a time, there was a huge tree in the middle of park. All summer long, the children played under the shade of the big tree. One day (use the child's name) went to the park to play and saw yellow leaves on the ground under the tree. Just then the wind began to blow, and (use the child's name) looked up and. . . .'"

Extensions

Create mystery pictures by gluing flat objects to a sturdy piece of cardboard. Cover the objects with a piece of paper, and tape down securely. Ask the child to identify the unseen objects by rubbing the bar crayons over the surface. Challenge older children to think of objects that could be used in the activity to challenge their peers. Have the children create clues to solve the identity of their mystery objects.

A c t i v i t y   1 0 . 2 8

Group Stories

Level Three and four

Area Creative

Interaction Adult-child

Strand Creative Writing

Materials Needed Chart paper and felt pens, unfamiliar picture book

Directions for Implementation

- Read a story to the children without reading the ending.
- As a group, discuss several possible endings to the story. Choose one to write on the chart paper.
- Finish the story, and compare the author's ending to the class ending. Ask the children to decide which ending they like the best.

Extensions

Creative story starters can be used in the primary grades as journal entries or as prompts in a writing center. Prompts can tie in with thematic planning. A second-grade classroom on the Oregon coast may study a unit on the seashore. A story starter could be written about the secret lives of the animals living in the tide pools, for example, "Oscar was no ordinary crab. He spent his entire life borrowing houses. One day. . . ." Two children collaborate during creative writing.

A c t i v i t y   1 0 . 2 9

Picture Stories

Level Five and six

Area Creative

Interaction Adult-child

Strand Creative Writing

Materials Needed Photographs or other pictures depicting some type of action, writing paper, and pencils

Directions for Implementation

- Cover up one half of a photograph with another piece of paper, and have the children describe what they see.
- Ask the children to make predictions as to what is on the other side of the photograph. Uncover the hidden side, and discuss what is now seen.
- On a chalkboard, record the children's ideas in a story web by listing the main ideas within circles with details branching out from each circle.
- Have the children write or dictate a story about the photograph.

Extensions

Make a class book with the photograph and the students' stories. If the stories were not dictated and printed by an adult, edit the rough drafts, and have children print a final copy for the class book.

A c t i v i t y   1 0 . 3 0

Stories of My Own

Level Seven and eight

Area Creative

Interaction Child-object

Strand Creative Writing

Materials Needed Writing paper, individual folders, and pencils

Directions for Implementation

- As an ongoing creative writing process, have the children write stories on a topic of their own choice. Their stories are kept in their own writing folder. Teaching children to write on every other line makes revising easier.

- During the writing period, rove from child to child to listen to story ideas and make suggestions as needed.
- Since the children will finish their stories at different rates, children can be paired up to practice editing skills.
- Complete the final edits as each story is completed. Save the final copies, and read them to the class or to another audience.

Extensions

As beginning writers, five- and six-year-olds may become frustrated when asked to produce extended stories. The physical mechanics of writing do not usually keep pace with the flow of ideas. Therefore, allowing children to dictate stories becomes a viable alternative for creative writing.

✌ CURRICULAR IMPLICATIONS

Connections to Subject Matter Areas

Creative development focuses on learning to think and respond physically in multiple ways. Although creative development is most closely aligned with the visual and performing art areas of the curriculum, it does connect to core curricular areas. Sensory experiences are topics for scientific study as well as processes with which scientists observe and describe the natural and manmade world. Sensory explorations set the stage for developing the abilities to use the senses of sight, smell, hearing, taste, and touch. Adults can plan activities to help children develop their senses as well as to describe those experiences. Infants and toddlers begin this investigation by attempting to blow bubbles or watch the effects of other experiments with soapy water in Activity 10.1. These youngest children are also introduced to textures in Texture Box (Activity 10.2). Kindergarten students participate in creating color changes by mixing food coloring in

a cornstarch-based goop in Rainbow Making (Activity 10.5).

In the subject area of mathematics, children begin to develop counting skills and number concepts as they order and serve food in the Restaurant (Activity 10.22). Concepts about volume and mass can be introduced to kindergarteners as they experiment with sand and water play in Activity 10.23. Similarly, the social studies curriculum intersects with creative development when teachers use culturally diverse choices for Making (musical) Instruments (Activity 10.12) and choosing songs for Activity 10.11. Young school-aged children learn about the commonalities they share with other children in the United States and in the world, as well as their individual differences.

Creativity is likewise linked to the language arts subject matter areas. Written language skills are promoted in creative writing activities. Preschool children dictate stories to an adult in Group Stories (Activity 10.28) and may dictate or use phonetic spelling to create a story about a partially hidden picture in Activity 10.29. School-aged children write their own stories in the final activity in the creative writing strand, Stories on My Own (Activity 10.30), and create dialogue in Writing Plays (Activity 10.24).

Obviously creative development ties directly to art, music, drama, and movement. Preschoolers are encouraged to use multiple parts of their hands and arms in Table Painting (Activity 10.6) and to experiment with crushing, tearing, folding, and bending foil to shape it for sculpture (Activity 10.6). Various vocal and instrumental experiences promote creativity in the subject area of music. Children of all ages can participate in the Kitchen Band (Activity 10.9). This is an activity, which combines creative thinking with creative movement as children test out different ways of making musical sounds with ordinary kitchen utensils.

Pretend play is a behavior that may have its roots in imitation. Older infants and toddlers can be observed pretending to drink and eat imaginary foods. Parents and caregivers can add simple props to encourage this dramatic use of the imagination, as in Feeding Dolly (Activity 10.19), Carryalls (Activity 10.20), or Animal Puppets (Activity 10.21). Movement activities similarly contain elements of creativity. In Creepy Crawlers (Activity 10.14), toddlers are prompted to move to different types of music. Similarly, listening to and watching popcorn kernels explode promotes creative movement in Activity 10.15. Individuals and groups are encouraged to use creativity to meet the space-spanning challenges of "Building Bridges" (Activity 10.18).

Connections to Thematic Planning

One effective approach to thematic planning in creative development is to choose a theme from an area such as science or social studies. This gives children ample opportunities to stretch their thinking in trying to represent concepts that they normally consider from a single perspective. One topic that meets these criteria is the colors of nature. Preschool-aged and young school-aged children can be given various opportunities to observe and discuss colors that appear in natural objects and phenomena compared with those that are given to manufactured objects. Making field observations is an important skill in learning to use the senses to gather information; it is also an excellent technique for building vocabulary in the language arts area. Adults can assist children in learning to represent what they see in words and pictures.

Within the art curriculum, several activities could be used to tie science concepts to suggested activities. The finger painting experience or food-color mixing activities can be used to introduce the topic of colors in nature (Activities 10.4 and 10.5). School-aged children may be able to come up with categories, such as warm and cool colors, and experiment with making colors on a color wheel. Younger

children can be encouraged to represent the color of leaves they have collected.

Guided listening (Activity 10.10) may focus on tape recordings of the sounds of nature. Children can orally describe the scenes that these sounds portray, draw a scene, and conclude by writing descriptions of the scenes using words that vividly convey colors (Activities 10.28, 10.29, and 10.30). In addition to representing these color observations in art media, children could also brainstorms ways of representing colors in music and movement. The Kitchen Band (Activity 10.9) is easily extended to stimulate children to replicate the sounds that they hear on tape. For example, twisting a cookie sheet might produce a lightning strike type of sound. In the movement area, adults can plan an activity that incorporates dancing with scarves (Activity 10.16) to encourage children to interpret the sounds of nature with colored scarves. In general, a thematic planning approach to curriculum planning may incorporate both the teacher's and the children's imagination and creativity.

✿ SUMMARY

Creativity, as a process, involves learning about the social and physical environment and then using that learning in new and unique ways. Behaving creatively may require certain cognitive processes and personal characteristics to implement creative ideas. Creative endeavors can potentially be found in every aspect of our lives.

For the purposes of this text, creative development has focused on five strands: sensory/ art, music, movement, dramatics, and creative writing. Sensory/art includes activities generally included in the visual arts and the sensory experiences that lead to these artistic expressions. Music as a strand of creative development consists of aesthetic listening and the production of sounds vocally and with instruments. Although some movement activities such as dance are inspired by music, other creative movement experiences are not. Dramatics focuses primarily on informal creative drama rather than on more formal forms of dramatic performance. Creative writing is included to emphasize the relationship between creativity and other areas of a traditional school curriculum.

Parents and teachers promote creative development by helping children acquire knowledge and skills and by establishing social and physical environments that stimulate creative thought and action. Open-ended materials and activities encourage sensory exploration and manipulation of ideas. Interactions with adults can also nurture the development of creativity when adults accept and respect a child's creative efforts.

QUESTIONS AND PROJECTS FOR THE READER

1. How would you justify planning creative activities for infants to an administrator or parent?
2. Choose an art medium such as finger painting or play dough. Plan an age-appropriate activity with this art medium for each of the six age ranges.
3. Describe the two main stages of children's art and detail the various substages.
4. Develop guidelines for parents to use in providing creative experiences for young children. Include suggestions for verbally supporting a child's creative endeavors in sensory/art, music, movement, dramatics, and writing.
5. Plan a series of creative writing lessons using the writing as a process format.
6. Review the activities suggested for the music and movement strands of creative

development in Table 10.1. Choose a specific age group, and suggest three additional activities that combine music and movement.

FOR FURTHER READING

Andress, B. (Ed.). (1989). *Promising practices: Prekindergarten music education.* Reston, VA: Music Educators National Conference. This overview of exemplary university-based, commercially developed, and public school music education programs for young children includes numerous music-related activities. Several articles also suggest developmentally appropriate strategies for integrating music and movement.

Bos, B. (1978). *Don't move the muffin tins: A hands-off guide to art for the young child.* Nevada City, CA: Burton Gallery. A wealth of ideas for visual art activities are focused on developing creativity in young children. The author includes guidelines for planning process art experiences.

Olson, C. B. (1987). *Practical ideas for teaching writing as a process.* Sacramento, CA: California State Department of Education. This is an inexpensive collection of lesson ideas for teaching each step of the writing process: prewriting, writing, sharing/responding, rewriting/editing, and evaluation. Although this publication includes strategies written by classroom teachers (kindergarten through high school), many activities are pertinent for primary-grade teaching and teachers developing a philosophy for teaching writing as a process.

Sullivan, M. (1982). *Feeling strong, feeling free: Movement exploration for young children.* Washington, DC: National Association for the Education of Young Children. This is a practical guide for teaching movement activities to children, ages three through eight. The author effectively describes planning and child guidance techniques for ensuring an effective and valuable movement education program.

Part 3

Resources for Interaction

*A*ppendixes with a variety of resources are included in Part 3. Appendix A contains a matrix of activities in each developmental strand by age. The Child Development Associate competencies and functional areas are listed in Appendix B, with chapters where relevant information can be found noted. Specific directions for selected activities are found in Appendix C. Appendix D includes directions for the construction of selected pieces of equipment. Appendix E includes addresses for obtaining additional information. Part 3 also includes a glossary, children's literature list, and the references cited in the book.

Activities by Age

PERSONAL-SOCIAL DEVELOPMENT					
Trust	Attachment/ Separation	Self-Esteem	Self-Control	Social Interaction	Social Skills
Comforting Infants Activity 6.1 Adult-child	Peek-a-boo Activity 6.7 Adult-child	Labeling Feelings Activity 6.13 Adult-child	Safe Explorations Activity 6.19 Adult-child	This Little Piggy Activity 6.25 Adult-child	Rules for Eating Activity 6.31 Adult-child

PHYSICAL DEVELOPMENT					
Gross Motor			Fine Motor		
First Moves Activity 7.1 Adult-child	Stretches To Reach Toy Activity 7.2 Child-object	Patty-Cake Activity 7.3 Adult-child	Batting at Objects Activity 7.19 Child-object	Simple Fill and Spill Activity 7.20 Adult-child	Cereal Pick Up Activity 7.21 Child-object

COGNITIVE DEVELOPMENT				
Development of Attention	Problem Solving	Making Choices	Open- Ended Questions	Completion of Tasks
Follows Objects with Eyes Activity 8.1 Child-object	Looks for Dropped Toy Activity 8.7 Adult-child	Choosing Toys Activity 8.13 Child-object	Adult Asks Questions Activity 8.19 Adult-child	Crawls Up a Ramp Activity 8.25 Child-object

COMMUNICATION DEVELOPMENT				
Listening	Speaking	Writing	Reading	Nonverbal Communication
This Little Toe Activity 9.1 Adult-child	First Sounds Activity 9.7 Adult-child	Holding Rattles Activity 9.13 Child-object	Board Books Activity 9.19 Adult-child	Facial Expressions Activity 9.25 Adult-child

CREATIVE DEVELOPMENT				
Sensory/Art	Music	Movement	Dramatics	Creative Writing
Fun with Bubbles Activity 10.1 Adult-child	Ankle Bell Bands Activity 10.7 Child-object	Dancing with Baby Activity 10.13 Adult-child	Feeding Dolly Activity 10.19 Adult-child	Puppet Stories Activity 10.25 Adult-child

FIGURE A.1   Matrix of Activities by Age: Birth to One

PERSONAL-SOCIAL DEVELOPMENT					
Trust	Attachment/ Separation	Self-Esteem	Self- Control	Social Interaction	Social Skills
Communicating Schedules Activity 6.2 Adult-adult	Security Objects Activity 6.8 Child-object	Recognition of Own Name Activity 6.15 Adult-child	Self- Feeding Activity 6.20 Child-object	Swinging Fun Activity 6.26 Adult-child	Using Crayons Activity 6.32 Child-object

PHYSICAL DEVELOPMENT					
Gross Motor			Fine Motor		
Picking Up Objects Activity 7.4 Child-object	Walking Backward Activity 7.5 Adult-child	Kicking Balls Activity 7.6 Adult-child	Milk Carton Blocks Activity 7.22 Child-child	One-Piece Puzzle Activity 7.23 Adult-child	Handprings with Water Activity 7.24 Adult-child

COGNITIVE DEVELOPMENT				
Development of Attention	Problem Solving	Making Choices	Open- Ended Questions	Completion of Tasks
Big Box Crawl Through Activity 8.2 Child-object	Hide the Shell Activity 8.8 Adult-child	Points to Pictures Activity 8.14 Adult-child	Asks Child to Respond Activity 8.20 Adult-child	Climbs Down Stairs Activity 8.26 Child-object

COMMUNICATION DEVELOPMENT				
Listening	Speaking	Writing	Reading	Nonverbal Communication
Outdoor Sounds Activity 9.2 Adult-child	Animal Noises Activity 9.8 Adult-child	Using Utensils Activity 9.14 Child-object	Picture Cards Activity 9.20 Adult-child	Body Parts Activity 9.26 Adult-child

CREATIVE DEVELOPMENT				
Sensory/Art	Music	Movement	Dramatics	Creative Writing
Texture Box Activity 10.2 Child-object	Sing, Sing, Sing Activity 10.8 Adult-child	Creepy Crawlers Activity 10.14 Adult-child	Carryalls Activity 10.20 Child-object	Tell Me a Story Activity 10.26 Adult-child

FIGURE A.2   Matrix of Activities by Age: One to Two

PERSONAL-SOCIAL DEVELOPMENT					
Trust	Attachment/ Separation	Self-Esteem	Self-Control	Social Interaction	Social Skills
Climbing Safety Activity 6.3 Adult-child	Family Photos Activity 6.9 Adult-child	Matching Faces Activity 6.14 Child-object	Helping Dress Myself Activity 6.21 Child-object	Playing with Peers Activity 6.27 Child-child	Simple Rules for Playing Activity 6.33 Adult-child

PHYSICAL DEVELOPMENT					
Gross Motor			Fine Motor		
Moving Arms to Music Activity 7.7 Adult-child	Jumping off Stairs Activity 7.8 Adult-child	Walking on a Line Activity 7.9 Adult-child	Using Tongs Activity 7.25 Child-object	Towers of Cube Blocks Activity 7.26 Child-object	Beehive Fingerplay Activity 7.27 Adult-child

COGNITIVE DEVELOPMENT				
Development of Attention	Problem Solving	Making Choices	Asking Open-Ended Questions	Completion of Tasks
Stringing Beads Activity 8.3 Child-object	Sink and Float Activity 8.9 Child-object	Mealtime Choices Activity 8.15 Adult-child	Encourage Questioning Activity 8.21 Adult-child	Build a Tower Activity 8.27 Child-object

COMMUNICATION DEVELOPMENT				
Listening	Speaking	Writing	Reading	Nonverbal Communication
Listening to Music Activity 9.3 Adult-child	Heads, Shoulders, Knees and Toes Activity 9.9 Adult-child	Jotting a Note Activity 9.15 Adult-child	Plastic Bag Books Activity 9.21 Adult-child	Identifying Family Photos Activity 9.27 Adult-child

CREATIVE DEVELOPMENT				
Sensory/Art	Music	Movement	Dramatics	Creative Writing
Play Dough Activity 10.3 Child-object	Kitchen Band Activity 10.9 Child-object	Popcorn Activity 10.15 Adult-child	Animal Puppets Activity 10.21 Adult-child	Story Starters Activity 10.27 Adult-child

FIGURE A.3   Matrix of Activities by Age: Two

PERSONAL-SOCIAL DEVELOPMENT					
Trust	Attachment/ Separation	Self-Esteem	Self-Control	Social Interaction	Social Skills
Comforting Ill Children Activity 6.4 Adult-child	Making Transitions Activity 6.10 Adult-child	Self-Portraits Using Mirrors Activity 6.16 Child-object	Using Words Activity 6.23 Child-child	Row Your Boat Activity 6.29 Child-child	Hand Washing Activity 6.35 Adult-child

PHYSICAL DEVELOPMENT					
Gross Motor			Fine Motor		
Hopping On One Foot Activity 7.10 Child-child	Climbing Fun Activity 7.12 Child-object	Playing Catch Activity 7.13 Adult-child	Macaroni Necklaces Activity 7.28 Child-object	Using Scissors Activity 7.29 Child-object	Drawing in a Salt Tray Activity 7.30 Adult-child

COGNITIVE DEVELOPMENT				
Development of Attention	Problem Solving	Making Choices	Asking Open-Ended Questions	Completion of Tasks
Plastic Builders Activity 8.4 Child-object	Latch Board Activity 8.10 Child-object	Pick an Activity Center Activity 8.16 Child-object	Things that Are Round Activity 8.22 Child-object	Put Toys Away Activity 8.28 Child-child

COMMUNICATION DEVELOPMENT				
Listening	Speaking	Writing	Reading	Nonverbal Communication
I Spy Activity 9.4 Adult-child	Recording Voices Activity 9.10 Adult-child	Drawing Figures Activity 9.16 Adult-child	Sequence Pictures Activity 9.22 Adult-child	Charades Activity 9.28 Adult-child

CREATIVE DEVELOPMENT				
Sensory/Art	Music	Movement	Dramatics	Creative Writing
Table Painting Activity 10.4 Child-object	Guided Listening Activity 10.10 Adult-child	Dancing with Scarves Activity 10.16 Child-object	Restaurant Activity 10.22 Child-child	Group Stories Activity 10.28 Adult-child

FIGURE A.4 Matrix of Activities by Age: Three and Four

PERSONAL-SOCIAL DEVELOPMENT					
Trust	Attachment/ Separation	Self-Esteem	Self- Control	Social Interaction	Social Skills
Opening Routine Activity 6.5 Child-object	Running Errands Activity 6.11 Adult-child	Life-Sized Portraits Activity 6.17 Child-child	Making Rules Activity 6.24 Adult-child	Role Playing with Blocks Activity 6.28 Child-object	Traffic Safety Rules Activity 6.34 Child-object

PHYSICAL DEVELOPMENT					
Gross Motor			Fine Motor		
Beanbag Toss at a Target Activity 7.14 Child-object	Skipping Activity 7.11 Adult-child	Hopscotch Activity 7.15 Child-child	Nuts and Bolts Activity 7.31 Child-object	Dressing Skills Activity 7.32 Child-object	Torn Paper Collage Activity 7.33 Child-object

COGNITIVE DEVELOPMENT				
Development of Attention	Problem Solving	Making Choices	Asking Open-Ended Questions	Completion of Tasks
Concentration Activity 8.5 Child-child	Mapping the Classroom Activity 8.11 Child-child	Stranger Danger Activity 8.17 Child-child	How Can We Use This? Activity 8.23 Child-child	Cooking Vegetable Soup Activity 8.29 Adult-child

COMMUNICATION DEVELOPMENT				
Listening	Speaking	Writing	Reading	Nonverbal Communication
Following Directions Activity 9.5 Adult-child	Table Talk Activity 9.11 Adult-child	Journal Writing Activity 9.17 Adult-child	Pattern Books Activity 9.23 Adult-child	Making Sound Patterns Activity 9.29 Adult-child

CREATIVE DEVELOPMENT				
Sensory/Art	Music	Movement	Dramatics	Creative Writing
Rainbow Making Activity 10.6 Child-object	Sing a Song Activity 10.11 Adult-child	Showing Strength Activity 10.17 Child-child	Sand Play Activity 10.23 Adult-child	Picture Stories Activity 10.29 Child-object

FIGURE A.5   Matrix of Activities by Age: Five and Six

PERSONAL-SOCIAL DEVELOPMENT					
Trust	Attachment/ Separation	Self-Esteem	Self-Control	Social Interaction	Social Skills
Entering a New School Activity 6.6 Adult-child	Sleepovers Activity 6.12 Adult-child	Family Connections Activity 6.18 Adult-child	Helping at Home Activity 6.22 Child-object	Games with Partners Activity 6.30 Child-child	Respecting the Property of Others Activity 6.36 Child-child

PHYSICAL DEVELOPMENT					
Gross Motor			Fine Motor		
Jumping Rope Activity 7.16 Adult-child	Dribbling a Soccer Ball Activity 7.17 Child-object	Parachutes Activity 7.18 Child-child	Ants on a Log Activity 7.34 Adult-child	Origami Activity 7.35 Child-object	Stitchery Activity 7.36 Child-object

COGNITIVE DEVELOPMENT				
Development of Attention	Problem Solving	Making Choices	Asking Open-Ended Questions	Completion of Tasks
Collections Activity 8.6 Adult-child	Conflict Resolution Activity 8.12 Child-child	Choosing a Project Activity 8.18 Child-child	Thinking of Open-ended Questions Activity 8.24 Child-child	Completing a Weekly Contract Activity 8.30 Adult-child

COMMUNICATION DEVELOPMENT				
Listening	Speaking	Writing	Reading	Nonverbal Communication
Fact or Fiction? Activity 9.6 Adult-child	On Stage Activity 9.12 Child-child	Author's Chair Activity 9.18 Child-child	Chapter Books Activity 9.24 Adult-child	Mime Activity 9.30 Child-child

CREATIVE DEVELOPMENT				
Sensory/Art	Music	Movement	Dramatics	Creative Writing
Foil Sculptures Activity 10.6 Child-object	Making Instruments Activity 10.12 Adult-child	Building Bridges Activity 10.18 Child-child	Writing Plays Activity 10.24 Adult-child	Stories of My Own Activity 10.30 Child-object

FIGURE A.6 Matrix of Activities by Age: Seven and Eight

Child Development Associate (CDA) Competency Goals and Functional Areas: Information Locator Guide

CDA Competency Goals	Functional Area	Chapter
I. Establish and maintain a safe, learning environment.	1. Safe	3
	2. Healthy	3
	3. Learning Environment	3, 4
II. Advance physical and intellectual competence.	4. Physical	7
	5. Cognitive	8
	6. Communication	9
	7. Creative	10
III. Support social and emotional development and provide positive guidance.	8. Self	6
	9. Social	6
	10. Guidance	2, 6
IV. Establish positive and productive relationships with families.	11. Families	3, 4
V. Ensure a well-run, purposeful program responsive to participant needs.	12. Program Management	4
VI. Maintain a commitment to professionalism.	13. Professionalism	1, 2, 4, 5

CDA, Child Development Associate
Adapted from Council for Professional Recognition, 1992

 **Directions for Activities**

Songs and Rhymes

This Little Piggy

This little piggy went to market,
This little piggy stayed home,
This little piggy had roast beef,
This little piggy had none,
This little piggy went, "Wee, wee, wee, wee!"
All the way home.

Twinkle, Twinkle, Little Star

Twinkle, twinkle, little star,
How I wonder what you are!
Up above the world so high,
Like a diamond in the sky.
Twinkle, twinkle, little star,
How I wonder what you are!

Row, Row, Row Your Boat

Row, row, row your boat,
Gently down the stream,
Merrily, merrily, merrily, merrily,
Life is but a dream.

Clap, Clap, Clap Your Hands

Clap, clap, clap your hands,
Clap your hands together,
Clap, clap, clap your hands,
Clap your hands together.

Shake, shake, shake your hands,
Shake your hands together,
Shake, shake, shake your hands,
Shake your hands together.
Slap, slap, slap your knees,
Slap your knees together,
Slap, slap, slap your knees,
Slap your knees together.
(NOTE: Continue to create verses using the children's suggestions, such as stomp your feet, knock your knees, twist your hips, shake your head, etc.)

Skip to My Lou

Skip, skip, skip to my Lou,
Skip, skip, skip to my Lou,
Skip, skip, skip to my Lou,
Skip to my Lou, my darling.
Lost my partner, what shall I do?
Lost my partner, what shall I do?
Lost my partner, what shall I do?
Skip to my Lou, my darling.

Peekaboo

Peekaboo, I see you,
Hiding behind that chair,
Peekaboo, I see you,
Hiding behind that chair. Boo!

Faces

Forehead knocker
(Tap gently on the forehead.)
Eye winker, Tom Tinker
(Point to one eye and then the other.)
Nose smeller
(Touch nose.)
Mouth eater
(Point to mouth.)
Chin chopper
(Tap chin.)
Gitchy, gitchy goo
(Tickle gently under the chin.)

Let Everyone Clap Hands

Let everyone clap hands like me.
(Clap twice.)
Let everyone clap hands like me.
(Clap twice.)
Come on and join in the game.
You'll find that it's always the same.
(NOTE: Improvise by substituting different motions for "clap hands" such as shake arms, point heels, tiptoe, turn around, and frog leap.)

Peter Hammers

Peter hammers with one hammer.
(Pound with one fist in rhythm.)
One hammer, one hammer.
Peter hammers with one hammer,
All day long.
(Repeat as follows:)
Peter hammers with two hammers.
(Pound with both fists.)
Peter hammers with three hammers.
(Pound with both fists and one foot.)
Peter hammers with four hammers.
(Pound with both fists, and both feet.)
Peter hammers with five hammers.
(Pound with both fists, both feet and nod head.)
Peter's getting tired now.
(Yawn, stretch and sing more slowly.)

Tired now, tired now.
Peter's getting tired now,
It's time to sleep.
(Pretend to nod off to sleep.)

Ten Fingers

I have ten fingers,
(Hold both hands up to the chest, spread.)
And they all belong to me.
I can make them do things.
(Wiggle fingers.)
Would you like to see?
(Extend hands and arms as if asking a question.)

I can shut them up tight.
(Make a fist.)
I can open them wide.
(Spread fingers apart.)
I can put them together,
(Put hands together, hiding fingers.)
And make them all hide.

I can make them jump high.
(Extend hands above head.)
I can make them jump low.
(Extend hands toward the floor.)
I can fold them together,
(Fold hands in lap.)
And hold them just so.

Hickory Dickory Dock

(Rock back and forth like the pendulum on a clock.)
Hickory dickory dock,
The mouse ran up the clock,
The clock struck one, the mouse ran down,
Hickory dickory dock.

Hickory dickory dock,
The mouse ran up the clock,
The clock struck two, the mouse said, "Who?"
Hickory dickory dock.

Hickory dickory dock,
The mouse ran up the clock,
The clock struck three, the mouse said, "Me!"
Hickory dickory dock.

The Grand Old Duke of York

The grand old duke of York, he had ten thousand
  men,
He marched them up to the top of the hill,
And marched them down again.
And when they're up, they're up,
And when they're down, they're down,
And when they're only half way up, they're nei-
ther up nor down.

Hopscotch

1. Draw a hopscotch pattern on a large flat
   surface using the model suggested in the
   drawing, or use a small stick to outline
   the pattern in dirt. Chalk works well on
   concrete, and masking tape can be used
   on most indoor surfaces.

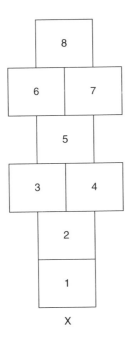

2. The child stands on the "X," and throws
   a marker (a small rock) into square 1.
   (When a marker lands outside the lines
   of the intended square, the player loses
   his turn to hop.)
3. He then jumps through the pattern by
   hopping on one foot in the single squares
   and landing on two feet in the double
   squares, skipping any squares with markers in them. For example, the first time
   through the pattern, a child throws his
   marker accurately into square 1 to begin
   the game. He hops over square 1 to land
   on one foot in square 2. He jumps into
   squares 3 and 4, landing with one foot in
   each square. He hops into square 5 with
   one foot, jumps into squares 6 and 7, and
   hops to square 8.
4. At the end of the hopscotch pattern, the
   child turns to face the beginning. The
   child hops back to the starting point,
   pausing at square 2 to bend down on one
   foot to pick up the marker from square 1.
5. The second time through the hopscotch
   pattern, the child tosses the marker into
   square 2 and hops over square 2 to complete the pattern.
6. The child's turn continues until the
   marker is thrown into the wrong square
   or the child lands in a square with a
   marker or inadvertently touches the
   ground with the other foot while hopping.
7. When a player steps on the line or puts
   both feet down in a single square, the
   child loses a turn and the marker stays in
   place until the next turn.
8. The first person who completes the pattern proceeding from square 1 to square 8
   and reversing the order back to square 1
   wins the game.

Try variations from other cultures detailed
in Mary Lankford's *Hopscotch around the
World*. (See children's literature list.)

Hopscotch patterns from two countries
are shown in the following drawings.

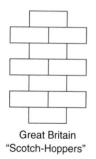

Great Britain
"Scotch-Hoppers"

	cabeza (head)	
brazo (arm)	casa (house)	brazo (arm)
	tercera (third)	
	segunda (second)	
	primera (first)	

Honduras
"La Rayuela" (line)

Origami Book

Step 1: Fold paper in half lengthwise, unfold.	Step 2: Fold in half horizontally, unfold.
Step 3: Fold top & bottom edges to center, unfold.	Step 4: Paper should be creased into 8 rectangles.
Step 5: Fold in half horizontally (repeating Step 2). Cut from the folded edge along the vertical center crease to the horizontal crease. Begin cutting here Fold line Open edges	Step 6: Unfold and refold lengthwise. Cut opening Fold
Step 7: Firmly hold each end. Push ends together, Creating a diamond-shaped opening. Top view: Hold here	Step 8: Collapse to form book, by pushing edges together. (top view of paper)
Step 9: Completed book	Step 10: Use as a horizontal or a vertical book. I like ...... Math Stories

Appendix D

Directions for Making Equipment

This appendix provides list of materials and directions for creating equipment and resources used in the activities in the book's last 5 chapters. Directions are coded with an activity number to assist the reader in matching the equipment to the appropriate activity.

For   Activity   6.5

Attendance Board

Materials

Piece of plywood (approximately 18 × 24 inches for a class of 25 children)
Drill
Sandpaper
Paint or varnish if desired
Cup hooks (one per child)
Circular key tags with metal rim (one per child)

Directions

Sand wood and paint if desired. Drill two holes near the top for hanging, or make a stand for the board. Evenly space cup hooks in five rows of five for a class of 25. Write the names of the children on at least one side of the key ring tags. Label small boxes or plastic containers with lunch options. For example: one container might read "hot lunch," another "milk only," and a third "sack lunch."

For   Activity   10.27

Bar Crayons

Materials

Used, broken crayons
Muffin tin or old metal ice cube tray
Oven

Directions

Peel the paper off the old crayons, and break them into small pieces. Fill muffin tin or ice cube tray with the broken pieces, keeping colors together or combining colors, depending what result is desired. Place in a warm oven to melt the crayons. Turn off the oven, and allow crayons to cool and harden. Before they are completely hard, remove from containers and continue to let them cool.

For   Activity   6.9

Baggie Books

Materials

Six to eight self-locking plastic bags (sandwich or quart size)
Stapler
Colored plastic tape

Directions

For reusable baggie books, staple the desired number of bags together on the edges opposite the openings. Make a sturdier binding by covering the stapled edge with plastic tape. Insert photographs or pictures mounted on heavy paper in each bag. Zip the bags closed. For infants and toddlers, consider making a baggie book that does not open. Insert the photographs, seal bags, and staple the opening edges together. Cover the stapled edge securely with brightly colored plastic tape.

For   Activity   8.2

Big-Box Crawl Through

Materials

Large corrugated cardboard box
Magazine pictures
Utility knife
Scissors
Glue

Directions

Cut one end from the box. Cut a hole in one side of the box big enough for a child to crawl through. (Do not cut out both ends or the box will collapse.) Cut other small holes in the top and sides. Glue pictures of familiar objects, shapes, or colors inside and outside of the box.

For Activity 7.32

Dressing Skills

Materials

Old pair of jeans or shorts that have a zipper
Extra fabric
Buttons
Snaps
Belt
Grommets

Directions

Design a dressing skills garment by adding pockets and flaps to an old pair of denim shorts. Use a variety of types and sizes of buttons and snaps. Attach grommets to the hems of the shorts to use for lacing and tying.

For Activity 7.20

Fill and Spill

Materials

Cardboard or metal can with plastic lid (cans for formula or powdered fruit drinks)
Felt pen
Utility knife
Plastic golf balls

Directions

Put your hand inside the can to check for sharp edges. Cut a round hole in the plastic top the same size as the golf ball.

For Activity 10.5

Goop

Materials

1 cup cornstarch
1/3 cup sugar
4 cups water

Directions

Cook over medium heat, stirring constantly until thick. Cool before using.

For Activity 8.10

Latch Board

Materials

Two pieces of 1/2-inch plywood cut exactly the same size
Four kinds of latches
Four sets of hinges
Several 3/4-inch screws
Saber saw
Drill
Sandpaper
Clear, nontoxic varnish

Directions

Cut four rectangular pieces out of one board with the saber saw for the doors. Sand edges of pieces and the holes from which they were cut. Sand outsides of the boards and edges. Attach a latch and hinges to each piece, and replace them in the board, making sure each door will open, close, and latch. Varnish both sides of each board. Fasten together securely with screws.

For Activity 7.22

Milk Carton Blocks

Materials

Clean gallon or quart milk cartons (two of same size per block)
Scissors or utility knife
Adhesive shelf paper (optional)

Directions

Cut the tops off the milk cartons. Slide two cartons together. Cut the corners of one carton slightly, if necessary to slide the two cartons together. Cover with brightly colored adhesive shelf paper, if desired.

F o r   A c t i v i t y   8 . 1

Mitt Puppet

Materials

Cotton work glove
Brightly colored chenille balls
Needle
Thread
Scissors

Directions

Sew a different-colored chenille ball securely on the end of each finger of the glove.

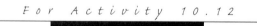

F o r   A c t i v i t y   1 0 . 1 2

Musical Instruments

Castanets

Materials

Walnut shells, intact halves
Drill
Elastic cord

Directions

Drill holes in the top of each half shell. Thread a 5-inch piece of elastic cord through the holes so that the walnut shell appears whole. Securely tie a loop with the excess elastic cord that is big enough to slip over a child's middle finger. Demonstrate how to clap the shell halves together to make the clicking sounds of castanets.

Guiros

Materials

Corrugated cardboard, 6× 12 inches, with ridges running parallel with the 12-inch side
Stapler
Unsharpened pencil
Colored plastic tape (optional)

Directions

Roll the cardboard into a cylinder, and connect the seam securely with staples. Cover the seam with tape to prevent scratches. To play the guiro, slip the hand into the corrugated cylinder and hold. Rub the pencil up and down the ridges with the opposite hand.

Maracas

Materials

Small round balloons
Newspaper, torn in strips approximately 6 × 1 inches
Paper towels, torn in strips approximately 6 × 3/4 inches
Liquid starch
Dried beans or rice
Two 8-inch dowels
Paint
Brush

Directions

Blow up the balloons to about a 3-inch diameter. Papier-maché around the balloons by dipping the newspaper strips in a shallow bowl of liquid starch and smoothing them around the balloons. Allow to dry. Add a layer of torn paper towel strips, and allow to dry. Pop the balloon, and remove it carefully. Add a small amount of beans or rice to the ball. Insert the dowel into the hole and securely tape together. Papier-maché one more layer of paper towels on the maracas. Paint and decorate when dry. Shake one at a time or in pairs.

One-Piece Puzzle

Materials

Four pieces of corrugated cardboard (approximately 6 × 8 inches)
Utility knife
One aerosol can lid
Adhesive shelf paper
Glue
Photograph of child or colorful picture from greeting card
Plastic tape

Directions

Place the lid on the center of one of the pieces of cardboard. Draw around the lid, and cut out the circle with a utility knife. Use the cardboard for a model, and cut out a circle from two of the other pieces of cardboard, making certain that the holes are lined up. The fourth piece of cardboard is the base. Center the photograph or picture directly under the holes, and glue it to the base. Cover the top and bottom boards with adhesive shelf paper. Layer the cardboard pieces, and tape the edges. Cover the hole with the lid.

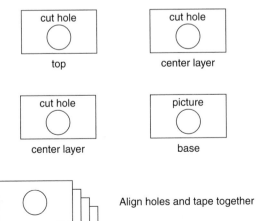

Paper Plate Masks

Materials

Sturdy, solid-colored paper plates
Scissors or utility knife
Felt pens
Hole puncher, yarns (optional)

Directions

With felt pens, create masks with varied facial expressions, for example, happy, sad, surprised, puzzled, angry. Use scissors or a utility knife to cut out eye holes for the child to look through. If desired, punch holes on the edges of the plate to create hair or a beard. Lace or knot lengths of yarn in each hole.

Play Dough

Cooked Play Dough

Materials

Saucepan
2 cups flour
1 cup salt
1 teaspoon cream of tartar
2 tablespoons cooking oil
Food coloring
2 cups water

Directions

Mix all ingredients in the saucepan. Cook over medium heat, stirring constantly until the dough mixture becomes stiff and leaves the sides of the pan. Dump mixture on a piece of waxed paper or foil, and allow to cool slightly. Knead for three to four minutes until smooth. Store in an airtight container. This dough does not need refrigeration and keeps for months.

Uncooked Play Dough

Materials

2 cups flour
1 cup salt
Food coloring
Water
Optional: 1 tablespoon oil for smoother tex-
ture

Directions

Mix floor and salt together. Gradually add
enough water to form a ball of dough. Knead
on floured towel until mixture is pliable but
not sticky.

Cornstarch Play Dough

Materials

1/2 cup cornstarch
1 cup salt
Food coloring
1/2 cup boiling water

Directions

Mix ingredients in a saucepan. Cook over
medium low heat, stirring constantly until
mixture is too stiff to stir. Dump onto waxed
paper or foil, cool to touch, and knead until
smooth.

F o r   A c t i v i t y   7 . 1 9

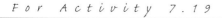

Pom-Poms

Materials

Yarn (3-ounce skein for solid-colored ball)
Cardboard (sturdy, 8 × 5-inch rectangle)
Scissors

Directions

Cut a frame for wrapping the yarn to make a
yarn ball. An 8 × 5-inch frame makes a ball
approximately 8 inches in diameter. Tape the
end of the yarn to the frame, and begin wrapping the yarn tightly in even layers around the

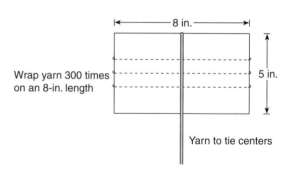

8-inch length of the frame. For a fluffy ball,
wrap the yarn around the frame 300 times. To
make a black and white ball, use 150 wraps of
black yarn and 150 wraps of white yarn. Then
cut a 24-inch piece of yarn, and tie a secure
knot around the center of the back and the
center of the front of the wrapped yarn. Cut
the loops of the wrapped yarn from one end of
the frame, and tie the two centers securely together. Remove the yarn from the frame, and
cut the remaining loops. Fluff into a ball. Trim
the excess yarn, or use it to suspend the ball
from a piece of elastic.

F o r   A c t i v i t y   9 . 2 2

Sequence Cards

Materials

Discarded or inexpensive paperback picture
books
Scissors
Clear adhesive shelf paper or laminate

Directions

Choose pictures from the book to demonstrate
the beginning, middle, and ending of a story.
To make the pictures durable, cover them with
clear adhesive shelf paper or laminate them.
Consider buying extra copies of inexpensive
paperback picture books for children to use in
retelling favorite stories. Mount on tag board
and laminate.

Professional Resources

Associations

Association for Childhood Education International (ACEI)
17904 Georgia Avenue, Suite 215
Olney, MD 20832
301-570-2111 or 800-423-3563
www.acei.org
E-mail: aceihq@aol.com

Council for Professional Recognition (CDA)
2460 16th Street, NW
Washington, DC 20009-3575
202-265-9090 or 800-424-4310

International Reading Association
800 Barksdale Road
P.O. Box 8139
Newark, DE 19714-8139
216-672-4840 or 800-336-7323
www.reading.org

National Academy of Early Childhood Programs
A Division of the National Association for the Education of Young Children

National Association for the Education of Young Children (NAEYC)
1509 16th Street, NW
Suite 400
Washington, DC 20036-1426
202-232-8777 or 800-424-2460
www.naeyc.org
E-mail: naeyc@naeyc.org

National Council for the Social Studies
3501 Newark Street, NW
Washington, DC 20016-3167
202-966-7840
www.ncss.org
E-mail: information@ncss.org

Southern Early Childhood Association (SECA)
P.O. Box 56130
Little Rock, AR 72204-6130
501-221-1648 or 800-305-7322
www.southernearlychildhood.org

Assessment Materials

Brigance® Diagnostic Inventory of Early Development, Revised is available from:
Curriculum Associates, Inc.
153 Rangeway Road
North Billerica, MA 01862-2021
800-225-0248
www.curriculumassociates.com

Denver Developmental Materials, Inc.
P.O. Box 371075
Denver, CA 80237-5075
303-355-4729

Children's Magazines

Canus Publishing Company
315 Fifth Street,
Peru, IL 61354
Babybug (ages 6 months to 2 years)
Ladybug (ages 2 to 6 years)
Spider (ages 6 to 9 years)

National Wildlife Federation
8925 Leesburg Pike
Vienna, VA 22184-0001
Your Big Backyard (ages 3 to 6 years)
Ranger Rick (ages 7 to 12 years)

National Geographic Society
1145 17th Street NW
Washington, DC 20036-4688
800-647-5463
www.nationalgeographic.com
Send magazine orders for *National Geographic World* (ages 6 to 12 years) to:
P.O. Box 63002
Tampa, Florida 33663-3002

Fingerplays and Action Rhymes

Beall, P. C., & Nipp, S. H. (1977). *Wee sing: Children's songs and fingerplays.* Los Angeles: Price/Stern/Sloan Publishers.

Beall, P. C., & Nipp, S. H. (1981). *Wee sing and play: Musical games and rhymes for children.* Los Angeles: Price/Stern/Sloan Publishers.

Glazer, T. (1973). *Eye Winker Tom Tinker Chin Chopper.* Garden City, NY: Doubleday.

Yolen, J. (ed.). (1994). *Sleep rhymes around the world.* Honesdale, PA: Wordsong.

Yolen, J. (ed.). (1992). *Street rhymes around the world.* Honesdale, PA: Wordsong.

Glossary

Ability (or exceptionality): The disabilities and gifts of people who, based on unique social and personal needs and special interests, form cultural groups.

Age cohort: The life experiences, traits, and values that are shared with other people born during the same era.

Analysis: A level in Bloom's taxonomy of cognitive behavior in which the learner is able to see parts and their relationships.

Application: A level in Bloom's taxonomy of cognitive behavior in which learning is applied to new situations.

Assessment portfolio: A collection of a child's work that demonstrates the child's efforts, progress, and achievements over a specified period.

Attachment: The psychological condition of being attached to another person.

Attention deficit hyperactivity disorder (ADHD): A broad category that can include problems of inattention, hyperactivity, impulsiveness, and/or other related conditions.

Autonomy: The condition or quality of being self-governed.

Bilingual: Ability to communicate orally in two languages.

Child initiation: A teaching method in which a child's choices direct the activity.

Child-care center: A facility for children, birth to five years, which may have either a full-day or part-day program.

Child caregiver: A person in a child-care program who cares for children.

Cephalocaudal development: A sequence of development that proceeds from the head to the tail.

Cognitive development: Developmental area that encompasses elements related to attention, problem solving, and thinking.

Collection: An accumulation of similar objects.

Communication development: Encompasses elements of verbal and nonverbal receptive and expressive language.

Completion of tasks: The ability to finish an undertaking that has been chosen.

Comprehension: A level in Bloom's taxonomy of cognitive behavior, in which the learner demonstrates an understanding of meaning; also a term used in reading instruction and assessment.

Concept: An abstract thought, idea, or notion that is generalized from particular knowledge or experiences.

Consistency: Establishing and maintaining routines, methods and practices.

Context: The situation in which an event occurs.

Creative development: Encompasses elements of sensory experience, exploration, expression, and process through discovery.

Creative writing: The process of choosing a topic and putting ideas together in written text.

Creativity: The ability to combine unrelated objects and ideas into something new.

Cruising: The use of furniture as a support for balance by young children who are beginning to walk.

Development: The process by which organisms grow and change over the course of their lives.

"Difficult" children: Children characterized by irregularity of biological functions, negative withdrawal responses to new stimuli, slowness or lack of adaptability to change, and an intense negative mood.

Direct instruction: A teaching strategy with specific instructions and content.

Distractibility: The ease with which a child can be diverted from an ongoing activity.

Dramatics: Using activities or materials to represent the real world.

"Easy" children: Children characterized by regularity of biological functions, positive responses to new stimuli, a high level of adaptability to change, and a mild positive mood.

Emergent literacy: The development of the association of sounds and print with meaning that precedes the development of conventional literacy.

Environment: The external physical setting and any social and cultural conditions that are related to it.

Ethnic group: A cultural group that shares a common history, language, values, behaviors, beliefs, and other characteristics that lead to a sense of shared identity with other members of the group.

Evaluation: Judgment of the teaching and learning process; also refers to a level in Bloom's taxonomy of cognitive behavior, in which judgments are made based on certain criteria.

Exosystem: Interrelationships in one or between settings that do not actively involve persons but can affect them.

Expressive language: The use of speech, writing, or nonverbal communication to convey thoughts and feelings to others.

Extensions: A provision of additional or alternative information; augmenting or expanding an activity.

Family child-care home: A family home in which not more than six children are cared for each day.

Fine motor: Small muscle development and eye-hand coordination.

Formative evaluation: Systematic, ongoing judgment of the teaching or learning process.

Full-day child-care program: A program in which childcare is provided for more than 4 hours per day.

Full-day child-care center: A facility in which child care is provided for more than 4 hours per day.

Gender: Behaviors associated with culturally determined male and female roles.

Goal: Broad aim of a program.

Gross motor: Development of whole-body movement skills.

Head Start: Government-funded educational program for three- to five-year-old children whose family income is at or below the poverty level.

Heteronomy: Being governed by someone other than self.

Implementation: Carrying out planned activities and experiences.

Inclusion: Including all similar-aged children with handicapping conditions in classrooms with non-handicapped children.

Inclusive setting: A school classroom that includes one or more children with handicapping conditions.

Infant: A child between the ages of birth and 12 months.

In-home caregiver: A person employed in the home to care for children.

Kindergarten: A week-day school program for five-year-olds.

Kindergarten-aged child: Five-year-old child.

Knowledge: A level in Bloom's taxonomy of cognitive behavior in which the learner recalls information.

Language (or linguistic background): A shared system of oral and written communication.

Learning: A relatively permanent change in behavior that results from experience or practice.

Listening: Comprehension of the spoken word.

Macrosystem: Interrelationships that can have cultural implications for the whole society.

Making choices: Selecting from a number of possible alternatives.

Maturation: Developmental changes in the body or behavior that result from the growth process rather than from learning.

Mentor: A wise and experienced advisor.

Mesosystem: Interrelations that are linked between two or more settings.

Microsystem: Interrelations within an immediate setting.

Movement: The process of becoming aware of one's body and its capabilities.

Multiage: Children in a group made-up of more than two ages (e.g. 5, 6, 7 years).

Music: Any harmonious combination of sounds.

Nonverbal communication: Conveying meaning without using words.

Nurture: Providing sustenance and care.

Object permanence: The concept that objects continue to exist when they are out of sight.

Objective: A specific behavior that can be observed.

Open-ended questions: Questions with more than one answer.

Parent: A child's guardian, stepparent, foster parent, or adult relative.

Parent Child Center: A government-funded program for parents and children, ages newborn to three years, whose family income is at or below the poverty level.

Parent interaction program: An educational program for parents along with their children in which parents learn about child development and adult-child interaction skills.

Part-day program: A child-care program that operates for 4 hours or less during the day.

Personal-social development: Encompasses elements related to self concept and self-help, emotional stability, social responsibility, and guidance.

Physical development: Encompasses elements of fine-motor, gross-motor, and eye-hand coordination.

Pincer grip: A grasp in which thumb and finger are used together to pick up objects.

Planning: Designing activities and experiences to promote development and learning.

Portfolio: See *Assessment portfolio.*

Preschool-aged child: Three- to five-year-old child.

Primary grades: Levels in a weekday program for first, second, and third grades.

Primary-aged child: Six-, seven-, or eight-year-old child.

Problem solving: Working out a solution to a question or situation.

Proximodistal development: A sequence of development that proceeds from the center of the body to the extremities.

Psychopathology: Abnormal condition of the mind; doesn't always produce abnormal behavior.

Reading: The process of constructing meaning from written text.

Receptive language: The use of listening, reading, or interpretation of others' nonverbal cues in reciprocal communication of thoughts or feelings.

Reciprocal interaction: Mutual interchange between people, a person and an object, or a person and the context.

Religion: A personalized or institutionalized set of beliefs, rituals, and practices related to the worship of God or the supernatural.

Scaffolding: The provision of structure in an interaction to enable a child to expand knowledge or skills.

School-aged child care: A program in which care is provided for children before or after the regular weekday school program.

Self-concept: How the self is thought about, or perceived.

Self-control: Control of emotions, desires, or actions by will.

Self-esteem: How a person feels about the self; pride in the self.

Self-image: The way a person pictures the self.

Sensory/art: The development and expression of the senses through use of a variety of media.

Separation: The act or process of separating from a significant person.

"Slow-to-warm-up" children: Children characterized by a combination of mild negative responses to new stimuli, along with slow adaptability to new situations.

Social interaction: The capacity to read the intentions and desires of other individuals and to act on this knowledge.

Speaking: Producing speech that can be understood by others.

Strand: A specific part of an area of development.

Summative evaluation: Judgment of the teaching and learning process at the end of a specific period or unit of work.

Sustained attention: The ability to select from a range of stimuli and to respond to those that are relevant to the ongoing activity, while disregarding others.

Synthesis: A level in Bloom's taxonomy of cognitive behavior in which the learner uses information to create an orginal, new whole.

Teacher: A person who is employed in a school and has primary responsibility for instruction.

Temperament: Natural disposition.

Toddler: Children between the ages of 13 and 35 months.

Trust: To have confidence in; feel sure of.

Ulnar grasp: An early skill in which objects are held by pressing fingers against the palm of the hand.

Weekday school: A program in public or private school that serves students from kindergarten through third grade.

Whole language movement: A philosophy that the process of communication should occur through use and not through practice exercises.

Writing: Producing written text that can be understood by others.

Zone of proximal development: The difference between a child's actual developmental level and the level of potential development when guided by an adult or more capable peer.

References

Adams, M. J. (1990). *Beginning to read: Thinking and learning about print.* Cambridge, MA: MIT Press.

Adams, M. J. (1999). Why not phonics and whole language? In *Read all about it!: Readings to inform the profession,* (pp. 79–94) Sacramento, CA: California State Board of Education.

Adams, M. J., Foorman, B. R., Lundberg, I., & Beeler, T. (1998). *Phonemic awareness in young children.* Baltimore, MD: Paul H. Brookes.

Adamson, L. (1995). *Communication development in infancy.* Madison, WI: Brown & Benchmark.

Alabama State Department of Education. (no date). *Curriculum guidelines K–6.* Montgomery, AL: Author.

Aldridge, J. (1993). *Self esteem: Loving yourself at every age.* Birmingham, AL: Doxa.

Aldridge, J., Eddowes, E. A., & Kuby, P. (Eds). (1998). *No easy answers: Helping children with attention and activity level differences.* Olney, MD: Association for Childhood Education International

Aldridge, J., Kirkland, L., & Kuby, P. (1996). *Jumpstarters: Integrating environmental print throughout the curriculum* (2nd ed.). Birmingham, AL: Campus Press.

Andreasen, N., Cadenhead, K., Havens, G., Riley, J. F., & Tyra, D. (1980). The child and the composing process. *Elementary School Journal, 80,* 247–253.

Andress, B. (1989). A parent-toddler music program. In B. Andress (Ed.), *Promising practices in prekindergarten music education* (pp. 25–35). Reston, VA: Music Educators National Conference.

Arizona Center for Educational Research and Development. (1973). *P.I.E. Cycle.* Tucson, AZ: University of Arizona.

Armstrong, T. (1994). *Multiple intelligences in the classroom.* Alexandria, VA: Association for Supervision and Curriculum Development.

Arnberg, L. (1987). *Raising children bilingually: The preschool years.* Philadelphia: Multicultural Matters Ltd.

Atwell, M. (1998). *In the middle: New understandings about reading and writing with adolescents* (2nd ed.). Upper Montclair, NJ: Boynton/Cook.

Banks, J. A. (2001). Multicultural Education: Characteristics and Goals. In J. Banks & C. M. Banks (Eds.). *Multicultural education: Issues and perspectives* (4th ed.). New York: John Wiley & Sons, Inc.

Banks, J. A. & Banks, C. M. (2001). *Multicultural education: Issues and perspectives* (4th ed.). New York: John Wiley & Sons, Inc.

Beaty, J. J. (1998). *Observing development of the young child.* (3rd ed.). Upper Saddle River, NJ: Merrill/Prentice Hall.

Benelli, C., & Yongue, B. (1995). Supporting young children's motor skill development. *Childhood Education, 71,* 217–220.

Bentzen, W. R. (1985). *Seeing young children: A guide to observing and recording behavior.* Albany, NY: Delmar.

Berk, L. E., & Winsler, A. (1995). *Scaffolding children's learning: Vygotsky and early childhood education.* Washington, DC: National Association for the Education of Young Children.

Bloom, B. S., Engelhart, M. D., Frost, E. J., Hill, W. H., & Krathwohl, D. R. (1956). *Taxonomy of educational objectives. Handbook I: Cognitive domain.* New York: David McKay.

Bodrova, E., & Leong, D. J. (1999). Play and its role in developing and learning. In M. Guddemi, T. Jambor & A. Skrupskalis (Eds.). *Play in a changing society* (pp. 29–31). Little Rock, AR: Southern Early Childhood Association.

Bodrova, E., & Leong, D. J. (1996). *Tools of the mind: The Vygotskian approach to early childhood education.* Upper Saddle River, NJ: Merrill/Prentice Hall.

Bornstein, M. H., & Lamb, M. E. (1992). *Development in infancy: An introduction* (3rd ed.). New York: McGraw-Hill.

Bos, B. (1978). *Don't move the muffin tins: A hands-off guide to art for the young child.* Nevada City, CA: Burton Gallery.

Brazelton, T. B. (1989). *Toddlers and parents: A declaration of independence.* New York: Delacorte Press/Seymour Lawrence.

Brazelton, T. B. (1987). *Working and caring.* Reading, MA: Addison-Wesley.

Brazelton, T. B. (1992). *Touchpoints: Your child's emotional and behavioral development.* Reading, MA: Addison-Wesley.

Brazelton, T. B., & Cramer, B. G. (1990). *The earliest relationship.* Reading, MA: Addison-Wesley.

Brazelton, T. B., & Greenspan, S. I. (2000). *The irreducible needs of children: What every child must have to grow, learn, and flourish.* Cambridge, MA: Perseus.

Bredekamp, S. (Ed.). (1987). *Developmentally appropriate practice in early childhood programs serving children from birth through age 8* (Rev. ed.). Washington, DC: National Association for the Education of Young Children.

Bredekamp, S. & Copple, C. (Eds.). (1997). *Developmentally appropriate practice in early childhood programs* (Rev. ed). Washington, DC: National Association for the Education of Young Children.

Bredekamp, S., & Rosegrant, T. (Eds.). (1992). *Reaching potentials: Appropriate curriculum and assessment for young children* (Vol. 1). Washington, DC: National Association for the Education of Young Children.

Bredekamp, S., & Rosegrant, T. (Eds.). (1995). *Reaching potentials: Appropriate curriculum and assessment for young children* (Vol. 2). Washington, DC: National Association for the Education of Young Children.

Brigance, A. H. (1991). *Brigance® Diagnostic Inventory of Early Development, Revised.* North Billerica, MA: Curriculum Associates.

Brody, S. (1956). *Patterns of mothering.* New York: International Universities Press.

Bronfenbrenner, U. (1979). *The ecology of human development: Experiments by nature and design.* Cambridge, MA: Harvard University Press.

Bruce, T. (1993). For parents particularly: the role of play in children's lives. *Childhood Education, 69,* 237–238.

Bruner, J. S. (1990). *Acts of meaning.* Cambridge, MA: Harvard University Press.

Bruner, J. (1983). Play, thought, and language. *Peabody Journal of Education, 60*(3), 60–69.

Bruner, J. S. (1960). *The process of education.* Cambridge, MA: Harvard University Press.

Bruner, J. S. (1966). *Toward a theory of instruction.* Cambridge, MA: Harvard University Press.

Burton, L. (1989). Musical understanding through creative movement. In B. Andress (Ed.). *Promising practices in prekindergarten music education* (pp. 97–104). Reston, VA: Music Educators National Conference.

California Department of Education. (1995). *Every child a reader: California reading task force report.* Sacramento, CA: Author.

California Department of Education. (2000). *Prekindergarten learning and development guidelines.* Sacramento, CA: Author.

Campbell, R. (1998). Looking at literacy learning in preschool settings. In R. Campbell (Ed.). *Facilitating preschool literacy* (pp. 77–83). Newark, Delaware: International Reading Association.

Caplan, F. (1978). *The parenting advisor.* Garden City, NY: Anchor.

Caplan, F. (1993). *The first twelve months of life: Your baby's growth month by month* (Rev. ed.). New York: Putnam.

Char, C., & Forman, G. E. (1994). Interactive technology and the young child: A look to the future. In J. L. Wright & D. D. Shade (Eds.). *Young children: Active learners in a technological age.* Washington, DC: National Association for Education of Young Children.

Ceppi, G., & Zini, M. (Eds.). (1998). *Children, spaces, relations: Metaproject for and environment for young children.* Reggio Emilia, Italy: Reggio Children/Domus Academy Research Center.

Charney, R. S. (1992). *Teaching children to care: Management in the responsive classroom.* Greenfield, MA: Northeast Foundation for Children.

Chen, J., Krechevsky, M., & Viens, J. (with Isberg, E.). (1998). *Building on children's strengths: The experience of project spectrum* (Project Zero Frameworks for Early Childhood Education, Vol. 1). New York: Teachers College Press.

Chess, S., & Thomas, A. (1996). *Temperament: Theory and practice.* New York: Brunner/Mazel.

Chess, S., Thomas, A., Birch, H. G., Hertzig, M. E., & Korn, S. (1983). *Behavioral individuality in early childhood.* New York: New York University Press.

Children's Defense Fund. (1999). *The state of America's children yearbook.* Washington, DC: Author.

Cole, M. & Cole, S. (2001). *The development of children.* New York: Worth.

Coplan, R. J., & Rubin, K. H. (1998). Social play. In D. P. Fromberg & D. Bergen (Eds.). *Play from birth to twelve and beyond: Contexts, perspectives, and meanings* (pp. 368–377). New York: Garland.

Council for Early Childhood Professional Recognition. (1992). *Child Development Associate: Assessment system and competency standards.* Washington, DC: Author.

Cratty, B. J. (1986). *Perceptual and motor development in infants and children.* Upper Saddle River, NJ: Prentice Hall.

Curry, N. E., & Johnson, C. N. (1990). *Beyond self-esteem: Developing a genuine sense of human value.* Washington, DC: National Association for the Education of Young Children.

Davidson, S. (1996). Knock down the classroom walls. In M. Guddemi, T. Jambor, & A Skrupskalis (Eds.). *Play: An intergenerational experience* (pp. 35–37). Little Rock, AR: Southern Early Childhood Association.

DeVries, R., & Kohlberg, L. (1987). *Constructivist early education: Overview and comparison with other programs.* Washington, DC: National Association for the Education of Young Children.

Dewey, J. (1916). *Democracy and education.* New York: Macmillan.

Dewey, J. (1938). *Experience and education.* New York: Macmillan.

Diaz-Rico, L., & Weed, K. (1995). *The crosscultural language and academic development handbook.* Needham Heights, MA: Allyn & Bacon.

Donoghue, M. (1990). *The child and the English language arts* (5th ed.). Dubuque, IA: Brown.

Eddowes, E. A. (1991). Review of research: The benefits of solitary play. *Dimensions, 20*(1), 31–34.

Eddowes, E. A. (1992). Children and homelessness: Early childhood and elementary education. In J. H. Stronge (Ed.). *Educating homeless children and adolescents* (pp. 99–114). Newbury Park, CA: Sage.

Eddowes, E. A. (1993a). *Bright ideas—handmade toys: Caring for infants and toddlers.* Little Rock, AR: Southern Early Childhood Association.

Eddowes, E. A. (1993b). Planning retreats for solitary activity in day care. *Day Care and Early Education, 20*(3), 27–29.

Eddowes, E. A. (1995). Drawing in early childhood: Predictable stages. *Dimensions of Early Childhood, 23*(1), 16–18.

Eddowes, E. A., & Aldridge, J. (1990). Hyperactivity or "activity hyper"—helping young children attend in appropriate environments. *Day Care and Early Education, 17*(4), 29–32.

Eddowes, E. A., & Ralph, K. S. (1987). Family day care: Balancing the program for infants and toddlers. *Dimensions, 15*(3), 11–14.

Eddowes, E. E. (1974). *A cognitive model of what is learned during flying training.* Williams Air Force Base, AZ: AFHRL, Flying Training Division.

Edwards, C., Gandini, L., & Forman, G. (1993). *The hundred languages of children: The Reggio Emilia approach to early childhood education.* Norwood, NJ: Ablex.

Engstrom, G. (Ed.). (1971). *The significance of the young child's motor development.* Washington, DC: National Association for the Education of Young Children.

Erickson, F. (2001). Culture in society and in educational practices. In Banks, J. A. & Banks, C. A. (Eds.). *Multicultural education: Issues and perspectives* (4th ed.), (pp. 31–58). New York: John Wiley and Sons.

Erikson, E. H. (1963). *Childhood and society* (2nd ed.). New York: W. W. Norton.

Erikson, E. H. (1980). *Identity and the life cycle.* New York: Norton.

Erikson, E. H. (1972). Play and actuality. In M. W. Piers (Ed.). *Play and development* (pp. 127–167). New York: Norton.

Erikson, E. H. (1977). *Toys and reasons: Stages of ritualization of experience.* New York: W. W. Norton.

Evans, E. D. (1975). *Contemporary influences in early childhood education* (2nd ed.). New York: Holt, Rinehart & Winston.

Eysenck, H. J. (1969). *The biological basis of personality.* Springfield, IL: Charles C. Thomas.

Feeney, S., Christensen, D., & Moravcik, E. (1996). *Who am I in the lives of children?* (5th ed.). Upper Saddle River, NJ: Merrill/Prentice Hall.

Fenson, L., Dale, P., Reznick, J., Bates, E., Thal, D., & Pethik, S. (1994). Variability in early communicative development. *Monographs of the Society for Research in Child Development, 59,* 5, Serial No. 242, pp. 1–173.

Fogel, A. (1991). *Infancy: Infant, family, and society* (2nd ed.). St. Paul, MN: West.

Ford, D. H., & Lerner, R. M. (1992). *Developmental systems theory.* Newbury Park, CA: Sage.

Fraiberg, S. (1975). Intervention in infancy: A program for blind infants. In B. Z. Friedlander, G. M. Steritt, & G. E. Kirk (Eds.). *Exceptional infant* (Vol. 3, pp. 40–62). New York: Brunner/Mazel.

Frankenburg, W. K., & Dodds, J. B. (1990). *Denver II.* Denver, CO: Denver Developmental Materials, Inc.

Frankenburg, W., Dodds, J., Archer, P., Bresnick, B., Mashka, P., Edelman, N., Sharpiro, H. (1992). *Denver II* (2nd ed.). Denver, CO: Denver Developmental Materials, Inc.

Franklin, M. B. (2000). Meanings of play in the developmental-interaction tradition. In N. Nager & E. K. Shapiro (Eds.), *Revisiting a progressive pedagogy: The developmental interaction approach* (pp. 47–71). Albany, NY: SUNY Press.

Freitag, P. J. (2000). Games, achievement, and the mastery of social skills. In D. P. Fromberg & D. Bergen (Eds.). *Play from birth to twelve and beyond: Contexts, perspectives, and meanings* (pp. 303–312). New York: Garland.

Fromberg, D. P., Bergen, D. (2000). Introduction. In D. P. Fromberg & D. Bergen (Eds.). *Play from birth to twelve and beyond: Contexts, peerspectives and meanings* (pp. xv–xxi). New York: Garland.

Gabbard, C. (1992). *Lifelong motor development.* Dubuque, IA: Brown.

Gardner, H. (1983). *Frames of mind: The theory of multiple intelligences.* New York: Basic Books.

Gardner, H. (1993). *Multiple intelligences: The theory in practice.* New York: Basic Books.

Gardner, H. (1998). Are there additional intelligences? In J. Kane (Ed.). *Education, information, and transformation* (pp. 111–131). Upper Saddle River, NJ: Prentice Hall.

Gartrell, D. (1994). *A guidance approach to discipline.* Albany, NY: Delmar.

Garvey, C. (1977). *Play.* Cambridge, MA: Harvard University Press.

Gerber, M. (Speaker). (no date). *Seeing infants with new eyes* (Video No. 852). Washington, DC: National Association for the Education of Young Children.

Gerber, M. (1981). What is appropriate curriculum for infants and toddlers? In B. Weissbound & J. Musick (Eds.), *Infants: Their social environments* (pp. 77–85). Washington, DC: National Association for the Education of Young Children.

Getzels, J. W., & Jackson, P. W. (1962). *Creativity and intelligence: Explorations with gifted students.* New York: Wiley.

Gillespie, C. W. (2000). Six Head Start classrooms begin to explore the Reggio Emilia approach. *Young Children, 55,* 21–27.

Glazer, S. M. (1989). Oral language and literacy development. In D. S. Strickland & L. M. Morrow (Eds.). *Emerging literacy: Young children learn to read and write* (pp. 16–26). Newark, DE: International Reading Association.

Goffin, S. G. (1994). *Curriculum models and early childhood education: Appraising the relationship.* Upper Saddle River, NJ: Merrill/Prentice Hall.

Gollnick, D. M. & Chinn, P. C. (1998). *Multicultural education in a pluralistic society* (5th ed.). Upper Saddle River, NJ: Merrill.

Golod, V. I., & Knox, J. E. (Eds.). (1993). *Studies on the history of behavior: Ape, primitive, and child (L. S. Vygotsky and A. R. Luria).* Hillsdale, NJ: Erlbaum.

Gordon, A. M., & Browne, K. W. (1989). *Beginnings and beyond: Foundations in early childhood education.* Albany, NY: Delmar.

Grace, C., & Shores, E. F. (1991). *The portfolio and its use: Developmentally appropriate assessment of young children.* Little Rock, AR: Southern Early Childhood Association.

Graves, M. F., Juel, C. & Graves, B. B. (2001). *Teaching reading in the 21st century* (2nd ed.). Boston: Allyn & Bacon.

Green, M., & Solnit, A. (1964). Reactions to the threatened loss of a child: A vulnerable child syndrome. *Pediatrics, 34,* 58–66.

Guddemi, M. P. (1988). Understanding children's behavior and encouraging self discipline. In M. H. Brown (Ed.), *Quality environments: Developmentally appropriate experiences for young children.* Champaign, IL: Stipes.

Guilford, J. P. (1959). Traits of creativity. In H. H. Anderson (Ed.), *Creativity and its cultivation* (pp. 142–161). New York: Harper & Row.

Guilford, J. P., & Hoepfner, R. (1971). *The analysis of intelligence.* New York: McGraw-Hill.

Hamner, T. J., & Turner, P. H. (1996). *Parenting in contemporary society* (3rd ed.). Boston: Allyn & Bacon.

Harter, S. (1990). Causes, correlates, and the functional role of global self-worth: A life span perspective. In R. J. Sternberg & J. Kolligan (Eds.). *Competence considered* (pp. 67–97). New Haven: Yale University Press.

Heath, S. B. (1983). *Ways with words: Language, life and work in communities and classrooms.* Cambridge, England: Cambridge University Press.

Heath, S. B. (1989). Oral and literate traditions among Black Americans living in poverty. *American Psychologist, 44,* 367–373.

Heft, H. (1985). High density and perceptual-cognitive development: An examination of the effects of crowding and noise in the home. In J. F. Wohlwill & W. van Vilet (Eds.). *Habitats for children: The impacts of density.* Hillsdale, NJ: Erlbaum.

Helm, J. H., & Katz, L. (2001). *Young investigators: The project approach in the early years.* Washington, DC: National Association for the Education of Young Children.

Hirsch, E. S. (Ed.). (1996). *The block book* (3rd ed.). Washington, DC: National Association for the Education of Young Children.

Honig, A. S. (1996). *Behavior guidance for infants and toddlers.* Little Rock, AR: Southern Early Childhood Association.

Hudson, S. D., & Thompson, D. (1999). Reducing "risk" on playgrounds. In M. Guddemi, T. Jambor, & A. Skrupskellis (Eds.). *Play in a changing society* (pp. 61–62). Little Rock, AR: Southern Early Childhood Assn.

Hunt, J. M. (1961). *Intelligence and experience.* New York: Ronald.

Hunt, J. M. (1964). The psychological basis for pre-school enrichment. *Merrill-Palmer Quarterly, 10,* 209–248.

Isbell, R. (1995). *The complete learning center book.* Beltsville, MD: Gryphon House.

Jacobvitz, E., & Sroufe, L. A. (1987). The early caregiver-child relationship and attention-deficit disorder with hyperactivity in kindergarten: A prospective study. *Child Development, 58,* 1488–1495.

Jalongo, M. R. (1995). Promoting active listening in the classroom. *Childhood Education, 72,* 13–18.

Jalongo, M. R., & Isenberg, J. P. (2000). *Exploring your role: A practitioner's introduction to early childhood education.* Upper Saddle River, NJ: Merrill/Prentice Hall.

Jambor, T. (1986). Risk-taking needs in children: An accommodating play environment. *Children's Environments Quarterly, 3*(4), 23–25.

Jambor, T. W. (1994). Recess and social development. *Dimensions of Early Childhood, 22*(4), 17–20.

Jarrett, O. S., & Young, C. (1999). Play among urban school children: Outdoor games at recess. In M. Guddemi, T. Jambor, & A. Skrupskelis (Eds.). *Play in a changing society* (pp. 63–65). Little Rock, AR: Southern Early Childhood Assn.

Kamii, C. (1982). *Number in preschool and kindergarten: Educational implications of Piaget's theory.* Washington, DC: National Association for the Education of Young Children.

Kamii, C. (Ed.). (1990). *Achievement testing in the early grades: The games grown-ups play.* Washington, DC: National Association for the Education of Young Children.

Kamii, C., & DeVries, R. (1978). *Physical knowledge in preschool education: Implications of Piaget's theory.* Upper Saddle River, NJ: Prentice-Hall.

Kamii, C., & DeVries, R. (1980). *Group games in early education: Implications of Piaget's theory.* Washington, DC: National Association for the Education of Young Children.

Kamii, C., & Kamii, M. (1990). Why achievement testing should stop. In C. Kamii (Ed.), *Achievement testing in the early grades: The games grown-ups play* (pp. 15–39). Washington, DC: National Association for the Education of Young Children.

Katz, L. G., & Chard, S. C. (1989). *Engaging children's minds: The project approach.* Norwood, NJ: Ablex.

Katz, L. G., Evangelou, D., & Hartman, A. (1990). *The case for mixed-age grouping in early education.* Washington, DC: National Association for the Education of Young Children.

Kirkland, L., Aldridge, J., & Kuby, P. (1991). Environmental print and the kindergarten classroom. *Reading Improvement, 28,* 219–222.

Kohlberg, L., & Lickona, T. (1987). Moral discussion and the class meeting. In R. DeVries & L. Kohlberg (Eds.), *Constructivist early education: Overview and comparison with other programs* (pp. 143–181). Washington, DC: National Association for the Education of Young Children.

Kritchevsky, S., Prescott, E., & Walling, L. (1977). *Planning environments for young children: Physical space* (Rev. ed.). Washington, DC: National Association for the Education of Young Children.

Landau, S., & McAninch, C. (1993). Young children with attention deficits. *Young Children, 48*(4), 49–458.

Lasky, L., & Mukerji, R. (1980). *Art: Basic for young children.* Washington, DC: National Association for the Education of Young Children.

Lenneberg, E. H., Rebelsky, F. G., & Nichols, I. A. (1965). The vocalizations of infants born to deaf and hearing parents. *Human Development, 8,* 23–37.

Lerner, R. M. (1978). Nature, nurture, and dynamic interactionism. *Human Development, 21,* 1–20.

Lerner, R. M. (1982). Children and adolescents as producers of their own development. *Developmental Review, 2,* 342–370.

Lerner, R. M. (1984). *On the nature of human plasticity.* New York: Cambridge University Press.

Lerner, R. M., & Lerner, J. V. (1983). Temperament-intelligence reciprocities in early childhood: A contextual model. In M. Lewis (Ed.). *Origins of intelligence: Infancy and early childhood* (pp. 399–421). New York: Plenum.

Linderman, C. E. (1979). *Teachables from trashables: Homemade toys that teach.* St. Paul, MN: Redleaf Press.

Littleton, D. (1989). Child's play: Pathways to music learning. In B. Andress (Ed.). *Promising practices in prekindergarten music education* (pp. ix–xiii). Reston, VA: Music Educators National Conference.

MacDonald, S. (1996). *Portfolio and its use. Book II: A road map for assessment.* Little Rock, AR: Southern Early Childhood Association.

Martens, P. (1998). Growing as a reader and writer: Sarah's inquiry into literacy. In R. Campbell (Ed.). *Facilitating preschool literacy,* (pp. 51–68). Newark, DE: International Reading Association.

Maslow, A. H. (1970). *Motivation and personality* (2nd ed.). New York: Harper & Row.

Mason, J. (1982). *The environment of play: A trilogy of play. Vol. 2. Where.* West Point, NY: Leisure Press.

McGee, L. M., & Richgels, D. J. (1990). *Literacy's beginnings: Supporting young readers and writers.* Boston: Allyn & Bacon.

Meisels, S. J. with Atkins-Burnett, S. (1994). *Developmental screening in early childhood: A guide* (4th ed.). Washington, DC: National Association for the Education of Young Children.

Metz, E. (1989). Music and movement environments in preschool settings. In B. Andress (Ed.). *Promising practices in prekindergarten music education* (pp. 89–96). Reston, VA: Music Educators National Conference.

Millar, S. (1968). *The psychology of play.* Baltimore, MD: Penguin.

Moyer, J. (1990). Whose creation is it, anyway? *Childhood Education, 66,* 130–132.

Montessori, M. (1912/1964). *The Montessori method.* New York: Schocken.

Montessori, M. (1949/1967). *The absorbent mind.* New York: Dell.

Morrison, G. (2000). *Fundamentals of early childhood education* (2nd ed.). Upper Saddle River, NJ: Merrill/Prentice Hall.

Morrow, L. M., & Gambrell, L. B. (1998). How do we motivate children toward independent reading and writing? In S. B. Newman & K. A. Roskos (Eds.). *Children achieving: Best practices in early literacy.* (pp. 144–161) Newark, DE: International Reading Association.

Moyer, J. (Ed.). (1995). *Selecting educational equipment and materials for school and home.* Wheaton, MD: Association for Childhood Education International.

Murphy, K. (1984). *A house full of kids: Running a successful day care business in your home.* Boston: Beacon Press.

National Association for the Education of Young Children. (1998). *Accreditation criteria and procedures of the National Academy of Early Childhood Programs* (Rev. ed.). Washington, DC: Author.

Nelson, K. (1973). Structure and strategy in learning to talk. *Monographs of the Society for Research in Child Development. 38*(1–2, Serial No. 149).

Nieto, S. (2000). *Affirming diversity: The sociopolitical context of multicultural education* (3rd ed.). New York: Longman.

Nicolson, S. & Shipstead, S. (1998). *Through the looking glass: Observations in the early childhood classroom.* Upper Saddle River, NJ: Merrill/Prentice Hall.

Olson, C. B. (1987). *Practical ideas for teaching writing as a process.* Sacramento, CA: California State Department of Education.

Ovando, C. J. (2001). Language diversity and education. In Banks, J. A. & Banks, C. A. (Eds.). *Multicultural education: Issues and perspectives* (4th ed.), (pp. 268–292). New York: John Wiley and Sons.

Pangrazi, R. P. (1998). *Dynamic physical education for elementary school children* (12th edition). Boston: Allyn & Bacon.

Parent Cooperative Preschools International. (2000). *PCPI directory.* Indianapolis, IN: Author.

Parents as Teachers National Center & Missouri Department of Elementary and Secondary Education. (1993). *Program planning and implementation guide* (Rev. ed). St. Louis, MO: Author.

Parten, M. (1932). Social participation among preschool children. *Journal of Abnormal and Social Psychology, 27,* 243–269.

Piaget, J. (1951). *Play, dreams, and imitation in childhood.* New York: W. W. Norton.

Piaget, J. (1955). *The language and thought of the child.* Cleveland, OH: World.

Piaget, J. (1970a). Piaget's theory. In P. Mussen (Ed.), *Carmichael's manual of child psychology* (3rd ed., vol. 1, pp. 703–732). New York: Wiley.

Piaget, J. (1970b). *Science of education and the psychology of the child.* New York: Viking. (Original work published 1969).

Piaget, J. (1972). Some aspects of operations. In M. W. Piers (Ed.), *Play and development* (pp. 15–27). New York: Norton.

Piaget, J. (1948/1973). *To understand is to invent.* New York: Grossman.

Piaget, J. (1978). Preface. In C. Kamii & R. DeVries, *Physical knowledge in preschool education* (pp. vii–viii). Upper Saddle River, NJ: Prentice-Hall.

Piaget, J. (1981). *Intelligence and affectivity: Their relationship during child development.* Palo Alto, CA: Annual Reviews.

Puckett, M. B., & Black, J. K. (1994). *Authentic assessment of the young child: Celebrating development and learning.* Upper Saddle River, NJ: Merrill/Prentice Hall.

Raines, S. C., & Canady, R. J. (1989). *Story stretchers: Activities to expand children's favorite books.* Mt. Rainier, MD: Gryphon House.

Raines, S. C., & Canady, R. J. (1991). *More story stretchers: More activities to expand children's favorite books.* Mt. Rainier, MD: Gryphon House.

Raines, S. C., & Canady, R. J. (1992). *Story stretchers for the primary grades: Activities to expand children's favorite books.* Mt. Rainier, MD: Gryphon House.

Redleaf, R. (1987). *Teachables II: Homemade toys that teach.* St. Paul, MN: Redleaf Press.

Reggio Emilia (1996). *The municipal infant-toddler centers and preschools of Reggio Emilia: Historical notes and general information.* Reggio Emilia, Italy: Reggio Children.

Reggio Emilia (1997a). *The hundred languages of the children* (2nd ed.). Reggio Emilia, Italy: Reggio Children.

Reynolds, B. (1998). To teach or not to teach reading in the preschool . . . that is the question. In R. Campbell (Ed.). *Facilitating preschool literacy* (pp. 155–168. Newark, DE: International Reading Association.

Rivkin, M. S. (1995). *The great outdoors: Restoring children's right to play outside.* Washington, DC: National Association for the Education of Young Children.

Rogers, C. S., & Sawyers, J. K. (1988). *Play in the lives of children.* Washington, DC: National Association for the Education of Young Children.

Roopnarine, J. L., & Johnson, J. E. (2000). *Approaches to early childhood education* (3rd ed.). Upper Saddle River, NJ: Merrill/Prentice Hall.

Rosenberg, M. S., Wilson, R. J., & Legenhausen, E. (1989). The assessment of hyperactivity in preschool populations: A multidisciplinary perspective. *Topics in Early Childhood Special Education, 9*(1), 90–105.

Rubin, K. H. (1977). Play behaviors of young children. *Young Children, 32*(6), 16–24.

Sadker, D. & Sadker, M. (2001). Gender bias: From colonial America to today's classrooms. In Banks, J. A. & Banks, C. A. (Eds.). *Multicultural education: Issues and perspectives* (4th ed., pp. 125–151). New York: John Wiley and Sons.

Sadker, M., Sadker, D., & Klein, S. (1991). The issue of gender in elementary and secondary education. In G. Grant (Ed.), *Review of research in education.* Washington, DC: American Educational Research Association.

Safford, P. L. (1989). *Integrated teaching in early childhood.* White Plains, NY: Longman.

Sanoff, H. (1995). *Creating environments for young children.* Raleigh, NC: North Carolina State University.

Sapon-Shevin, M. (1992). Ability differences in the classroom: Teaching and learning in inclusive classrooms. In D. A. Byrnes & G. Kiger (Eds.), *Common bonds: Antibias teaching in a diverse society* (pp. 39–52). Wheaton, MD: Association for Childhood Education International.

Schaefer, E. S. (1971). Development of hierarchical, configurational models for parent behavior and child behavior. In J. P. Hill (Ed.). *Minnesota symposia on child psychology* (Vol. 5). Minneapolis, MN: University of Minnesota Press.

Schickedanz, J. A. (1986). *More than the ABCs: The early stages of reading and writing.* Washington, DC: National Association for the Education of Young Children.

Schiller, M. (1995). An emergent art curriculum that fosters understanding. *Young Children, 50*(3), 33–38.

Schirrmacher, R. (1986). Talking with young children about their art. *Young Children, 41*(4), 3–7.

Schirrmacher, R. (1993). *Art and creative development for young children* (2nd ed.). Albany, NY: Delmar.

Schwartz, J., & Schwartz, L. (1977). *Vulnerable infants: A psychosocial dilemma.* New York: McGraw-Hill.

Seefeldt, C. (1995). Art—a serious work. *Young Children, 50* (3), 39–45.

Seefeldt, C., & Barbour, N. (1998). *Early childhood education: An introduction* (4th ed.). Upper Saddle River, NJ: Merrill/Prentice Hall.

Shaffer, D. R. (1989). *Developmental psychology: Childhood and adolescence* (2nd ed.). Pacific Grove, CA: Brooks/Cole.

Silin, J. (2000). Real children and imagined homelands: Preparing to teach in today's world. In N. Nager & E. K. Shapiro (Eds.). *Revisiting a progressive pedagogy: The developmental interaction approach* (pp. 257–273). Albany, NY: SUNY Press.

Smilansky, S. (1968). *The effects of sociodramatic play on disadvantaged children: Preschool children.* New York: Wiley.

Smilansky, S., & Shefatya, L. (1990). *Facilitating play: A medium for promoting cognitive, socioemotional, and academic development in young children.* Gaithersburg, MD: Psychosocial & Educational Publications.

Snow, C. W. (1998). *Infant development* (2nd ed.). Upper Saddle River, NJ: Prentice Hall.

Steele, C., & Nauman, M. (1985). Infants' play on outdoor play equipment. In J. L. Frost & S. Sunderlin (Eds.). *When children play: Proceedings of the international conference on play and play environments* (pp. 121–127). Wheaton, MD: Association for Childhood Education International.

Stern, D. (1977). *The first relationship: Infant and mother.* Cambridge, MA: Harvard University Press.

Storr, A. (1988). *Solitude: A return to self.* New York: Free Press.

Strickland, D. S., & Morrow, L. M. (Eds.). (1989). *Emerging literacy: Young children learn to read and write.* Newark, DE: International Reading Association.

Sullivan, M. (1982). *Feeling strong, feeling free: Movement exploration for young children.* Washington, DC: National Association for the Education of Young Children.

Tanner, J. (1990). *Fetus into man.* Cambridge, MA: Harvard University.

Thernstrom, S. (Ed.). (1980). *Harvard encyclopedia of American ethnic groups.* Cambridge, MA: Belknap Press.

Thomas, A., & Chess, S. (1977). *Temperament and development.* New York: Brunner/Mazel.

Thomas, A., & Chess, A. (1980). *The dynamics of psychological development.* New York: Brunner/Mazel.

Tompkins, G. E. (2001). *Literacy for the 21st century: A balanced approach.* Upper Saddle River, NJ: Merrill/Prentice Hall.

Trawick-Smith, J. (1994). *Interactions in the classroom: Facilitating play in the early years.* Upper Saddle River, NJ: Merrill/Prentice Hall.

Trawick-Smith, J. (2000). *Early childhood development: A multicultural perspective.* (2nd ed.). Upper Saddle River, NJ: Merrill/Prentice Hall.

Trelease, J. (1995). *The new read aloud handbook* (Rev. ed.). New York: Penguin.

U.S. Consumer Product Safety Commission. (1991). *A handbook for public playground safety.* Washington, DC: U.S. Government Printing Office.

Van Hoorn, J., Nourat, P., Scales, B., & Alward, K. (1993). *Play at the center of the curriculum.* Upper Saddle River, NJ: Merrill/Prentice Hall.

Van Hoorn, J., Nourot, P, M., Scales, B., & Alward, K. P. (1999). *Play at the center of the curriculum* (2nd ed.). Upper Saddle River, NJ: Merrill/Prentice Hall.

Vergeront, J. (1987). *Places and spaces for preschool and primary (indoors).* Washington, DC: National Association for the Education of Young Children.

Vergeront, J. (1988). *Places and spaces for preschool and primary (ourdoors).* Washington, DC: National Association for the Education of Young Children.

Vondra, J., & Belsky, J. (1993). Developmental origins of parenting: Personalty and relationship factors. In T. Luster & L. Okagaki (Eds.). *Parenting: An ecological perspective* (pp. 1–33). Hillsdale, NJ: Erlbaum.

Vygotsky, L. S. (1962). *Thought and language.* Cambridge, MA: MIT Press.

Vygotsky, L. S. (1978). *Mind in society: The development of higher psychological processes.* Cambridge, MA: Harvard University Press.

Waxman, S. R., & Hall, D. G. (1993). The development of a linkage between count nouns and object categories: Evidence from fifteen- to twenty-one-month-old infants. *Child Development, 64,* 1224–1241.

Weaver, C. (1994). *Reading process and practice: From socio-psycholinguistics to whole language* (2nd ed.). Portsmouth, NH: Heinemann.

Weiser, M. G. (1991). *Group care and education of infants and toddlers* (2nd ed.). Upper Saddle River, NJ: Merrill/Prentice Hall.

Wells, G. (1986). *The meaning makers: Children learning language and using language to learn.* Portsmouth, NH: Heinemann.

White, B. (1975). *The first three years of life.* Upper Saddle River, NJ: Merrill/Prentice Hall.

Winter, S. M. (1985). Toddler play behaviors and equipment choices in an outdoor playground. In J. L. Frost & S. Sunderlin (Eds.). *When children play: Proceedings of the international conference on play and play environments* (pp. 129–138). Wheaton, MD: Association for Childhood Education International.

Winter, S. M. (1995). *Bright ideas—outdoor play and learning for infants and toddlers.* Little Rock, AR: Southern Early Childhood Association.

Wood, D., Bruner, J. S., & Ross, G. (1976). The role of tutoring in problem solving. *Journal of Child Psychology and Psychiatry, 17,* 89–100.

Yendovitskaya, T. V. (1972). Development of attention. In A. V. Zaborozhets & D. B. Elkonin (Eds.). *The psychology of preschool children* (pp. 65–88). Cambridge, MA: MIT Press.

Yopp, H. K. (1992). Developing phonemic awareness in young children. *The Reading Teacher, 45,* 696–703.

Yopp, H. K. (1995). Read-aloud books for developing phonemic awareness: An annotated bibliography. *The Reading Teacher, 48,* 538–542.

Yopp, H. K. & Yopp, R. H. (1996). *Oo-pples and boo-noo-noos: Songs and activities for phonemic awareness.* Orlando, FL: Harcourt Brace.

Children's Literature

Ahlberg, J., & Ahlberg, A. (1983). *The baby's catalog.* Boston: Little, Brown.

Ashley, B. (1991). *Cleversticks.* New York: Crown.

Barton, B. (1986a). *Airplanes.* New York: Crowell.

Barton, B. (1986b). *Boats.* New York: Crowell.

Barton, B. (1986c). *Trains.* New York: Crowell.

Barton, B. (1986d). *Trucks.* New York: Crowell.

Bishop, C. (1989). *Five Chinese brothers.* New York: Putnam.

Bridwell, N. (1985). *Clifford the big red dog.* New York: Scholastic.

Brown, M. (1947). *Stone soup: An old tale.* New York: Scribner's.

Burton, V. L. (1939). *Mike Mulligan and his steam shovel.* Boston: Houghton Mifflin.

Cleary. B. (1955). *Beezus and Ramona.* New York: Dell.

Cleary. B. (1968). *Ramona the pest.* New York: Dell.

Cleary. B. (1975a). *Ramona and her father.* New York: Dell.

Cleary. B. (1975b). *Ramona the brave.* New York: Dell.

Cleary. B. (1979). *Ramona and her mother.* New York: Dell.

Cleary. B. (1981). *Ramona Quimby, age 8.* New York: Dell.

Cleary. B. (1984). *Ramona forever.* New York: Dell.

Dooley, N. (2000). *Everybody serves soup.* Minneapolis, MN: Carolrhoda Books, Inc.

Flournoy, V. (1985). *The patchwork quilt.* New York: Dutton.

Gilman, P. (1992). *Something from nothing.* New York: Scholastic.

Kimmel, E. (1990). *Gingerbread Man.* New York: Holiday House.

Lankford, M. (1992). *Hopscotch around the world.* New York: Morrow Junior Books.

Leonard, M. (1990). *Three little pigs.* Columbus, OH: Simon & Schuster.

Lobel, A. (1970). *Frog and toad are friends.* New York: Harper & Row.

Marshall, J. (1976). *George and Martha rise and shine.* Boston: Houghton Mifflin.

Pickney, A. D. (1993). *Seven candles for Kwanzaa.* New York: Dial.

Soto, F. (1993). *Too many tamales.* New York: Putnam.

Spier, P. (11971). *Gobble growl grunt.* New York: Scholastic.

Spier, P. (1980). *People.* Garden City, NY: Doubleday.

Taback, S. (1999). *Joseph had a little overcoat.* New York: Viking.

Waber, B. (1972). *Ira sleeps over.* Boston: Houghton Mifflin.

Warner, G. C. (1942). *The boxcar children.* Niles, IL: Whitman.

Williams, M. (1983). *The velveteen rabbit: Or how toys become real.* New York: Little Simon.

Young, E. (1992). *Seven blind mice.* New York: Scholastic.

Name Index

Subject Index